MW00994688

Humor in Contemporary Native North American Literature

European Studies in American Literature and Culture

Edited by Reingard M. Nischik
(University of Constance)

Humor in Contemporary Native North American Literature

Reimagining Nativeness

Eva Gruber

CAMDEN HOUSE

Rochester, New York

Copyright © 2008 Eva Gruber

All Rights Reserved. Except as permitted under current legislation,
no part of this work may be photocopied, stored in a retrieval system,
published, performed in public, adapted, broadcast, transmitted,
recorded, or reproduced in any form or by any means,
without the prior permission of the copyright owner.

First published 2008 by Camden House
Transferred to digital printing 2009

Camden House is an imprint of Boydell & Brewer Inc.
668 Mt. Hope Avenue, Rochester, NY 14620, USA
www.camden-house.com
and of Boydell & Brewer Limited
PO Box 9, Woodbridge, Suffolk IP12 3DF, UK
www.boydellandbrewer.com

ISBN-13: 978-1-57113-257-4
ISBN-10: 1-57113-257-0

Library of Congress Cataloging-in-Publication Data

Gruber, Eva.
    Humor in contemporary Native North American literature :
reimagining nativeness / Eva Gruber
        p. cm. — (European studies in American literature and culture)
Includes bibliographical references and index.
ISBN-13: 978–1–57113–257–4 (hardcover : alk. paper)
ISBN-10: 1–57113–257–0 (hardcover : alk. paper)
    1. American literature—Indian authors—21st century—History and
criticism. 2. Humor in literature. 3. American literature—Indian
authors—20th century—History and criticism. 4. Canadian literature—
Indian authors—21st century—History and criticism. 5. Canadian
literature—Indian authors—20th century—History and criticism.
6. Indians of North America—Intellectual life.   I. Title. II. Series.

PS153.I52G83 2008
810.9'17—dc22

                                                        2008010685

A catalogue record for this title is available from the British Library.

This publication is printed on acid-free paper.
Printed in the United States of America.

Contents

Preface and Acknowledgments   vii

Introduction   1

1: Humor in Native North American Literature and
Culture: Survey   7

2: Reimagining Nativeness through Humor:
Concepts and Terms   19

3: Expressing Humor in Contemporary Native
Writing: Forms   55

4: Humor at Work in Contemporary Native Writing:
Issues and Effects   116

Conclusion   224

Appendix: The State of Research on Humor in Native Writing   229

Works Cited   235

Index   257

Preface and Acknowledgments

E. B. WHITE ONCE CAUTIONED: "Humor can be dissected, as a frog can, but the thing dies in the process and the innards are discouraging to any but the pure scientific mind" (1989, 173). John Lowe further observes that humor "is absolutely central to our conception of the world. Despite this fact, we tend to become suddenly solemn when we begin to write, particularly for scholarly purposes. To be funny indicates a lack of seriousness" (1986, 439). With this book I attempt the seemingly impossible: to analyze, yet also convey, some of the comic spirit that fascinates me in contemporary Native writing. Like traditional trickster tales that teach by mirth, this study thus hopefully both offers academic insight and evokes laughter. Despite necessitating my very personal survival humor at times, to work on this project has been a wonderful chance for which I am very grateful. I thank Prof. Dr. Reingard M. Nischik for her unceasing support and encouragement in every respect. I am grateful to Prof. Dr. Helen Hoy (University of Guelph, Canada) and Prof. Dr. Luci Tapahonso (University of Arizona, Tucson) for helpful suggestions. I express my gratitude for generous financial assistance received from the State of Baden-Württemberg, the German Academic Exchange Service (DAAD), and the Equal Opportunity Council of the University of Constance in order to conduct my research; and for the publication subsidy granted by the Association for Canadian Studies. The Research Colloquium in American Studies at the University of Constance accompanied my project throughout with interest and constructive criticism. Thanks are also due to Christina Kannenberg for diligent proofreading, to Anja Ging for excellent work compiling the index, and to two dear friends and colleagues, Dr. Caroline Rosenthal and Julia Breitbach, for inspiring discussions, helpful suggestions, and encouragement. My deepest thanks go to my family and close friends for supporting me and being there for me at all possible (and impossible) times.

E. G.
Constance, October 2007

Introduction

COMMENTING ON REPRESENTATIONS OF NATIVE PEOPLE[1] in Western fiction, Margaret Atwood observes that diverse attributes were assigned to them. However, "lacking among them was funny. . . . On the whole Natives were treated by almost everyone with utmost gravity, as if they were either too awe-inspiring as blood-curdling savages or too sacrosanct in their status of holy victim to allow any comic reactions either to them or by them. Furthermore, nobody ever seems to have asked them what if anything *they* found funny" (1990, 243–44). Looking at a wide range of texts from genres as diverse as fiction, poetry, drama, and film by contemporary Native, mixedblood, or Métis writers,[2] this study not only abundantly illustrates the Native sense of humor. It also underlines humor's centrality in contemporary Native North American writing, reveals that there is plenty that "*they*" — that is, Native people, or Native writers in particular — find funny, and demonstrates how humor enters into the constant renegotiation of Nativeness.

The cover image, "Shuffle Off to Buffalo" by Nisenan Maidu/ Hawaiian artist Harry Fonseca, exemplifies several features of humor in contemporary Native writing. The image prominently features Coyote, who is not only the classic trickster figure in the oral traditions of many Native cultures, but in the continuation of these traditions lives on in texts by contemporary Native writers. Dancing onto the stage, this ultimate survivor, like Native humor itself, constitutes an assurance and celebration of Native survival and Native identity. Yet clearly this is a Coyote in contemporary American guise, and the painting's title (a song from the Broadway musical *42nd Street*) marks him as an amalgamation of both Native traditions and mainstream Western (popular) culture. Such hybridization characterizes most contemporary Native North American literature[3] — most fundamentally in its use of Western literary forms and the English language — and thus also its humor.

The painting's transcultural approach is most pronounced in Coyote's Stars and Stripes suit. While donning the colonizers' most symbolic attire, Coyote's tail still sticks out, implicitly mocking Uncle Sam and all that he stands for. Taking center stage and endowing himself with the apparel of the character understood as personification of America itself, Coyote tongue-in-cheek claims Native primacy in North America. Humor in contemporary Native texts also figuratively "dons Uncle Sam's suit" to some extent. Just as Coyote impersonates the ubiquitously present and highly familiar figure of

Uncle Sam with a twist, humor in contemporary Native literature frequently works *with* familiar, symbolically charged, stereotypical images and representations of Native people and Native-White history — in order to subversively reencode or reimagine them. By evoking laughter, it creates a liminal space where familiar interpretive patterns are rendered invalid and readers are free to reevaluate their own perspectives and epistemologies. This carnivalesque leveling of established hierarchies and annulment of habitual readings affords the opportunity to engage in dialog, renegotiation, and reassessment — not only of Nativeness as such (that is, of stereotypical ideas and images or essentialist positions), but also of the very dynamics and frames of reference that generate biased or one-dimensional readings of Nativeness, Native-White history, or present Native-White (power) relations.

Entering into the dynamics of representation and identification in a colonial context, Native humor both reflects and shapes aspects of Native as well as Euro-American life and cultures. Since by definition it hinges on the resolution of playful incongruities, humor provides the perfect instrument for exploring differences between the two. As a strategy of *re*-presentation, it reworks existing misrepresentations such as the imaginary "Indian," seducing both a Native and non-Native readership to reconsider their respective conceptualizations of self and other. While Uncle Sam typically serves as a figure of identification that stands for a reaffirmation of US American values, the reimaginative humor used by contemporary Native writers may trigger shifts in identification and allegiance with regard to both Native and Euro-American identity. When readers laugh *with* Native characters, narrators, or authors *at* stereotypical or restrictive images of "Indians" and notions of Euro-American superiority, for instance, they subconsciously subscribe to new conceptualizations of Nativeness and new perspectives on Native-White relations. Ojibway stand-up comedian Don Kelly's retort to the question of whether he, as a Native person, celebrates Thanksgiving may briefly illustrate this effect. The year before, Kelly explains, he actually "had a traditional Native Thanksgiving: The European guy who lives next door came over, claimed he 'discovered' my apartment and now he's living in the place! . . . Oh sure, my neighbour kept a little spot in 'reserve' for me. It's right next to the cat's litter box — thanks a lot!" (2005, 58–59). Enticing audiences to laugh about and concomitantly reassess American history from a Native point of view, humor here works as a mediational strategy to address controversial issues, as a "Trojan horse" for sneaking into the readers' minds and hearts. Similarly, mocking Uncle Sam as "the nation's conscience," Coyote in Fonseca's painting may serve as a reminder of those aspects of American history that Euro-America tends to forget in order to be able to uphold its positive self-assessment.

While humor and laughter in a colonial context are often subversive, this is not the whole story. Just as in postcolonial literary criticism the paradigm of "writing back" to the metropolis or center has been under attack for actually reaffirming the distinction into center and margin, to look at Native humor only in terms of its subversive potential in the context of Native-White relations risks not doing justice to the phenomenon of Native humor in its entirety. Native humor is more than "laughing back": Light-hearted laughter and gallows humor, teasing and acerbic satire, healing and self-deprecating humor, flat jokes, carnivalesque laughter, and intricate wit all appear in contemporary Native writing. Moreover, humor in Native texts is directed at both Native and non-Native characters, institutions, and history. The power imbalance that arises from colonization and that in its present constellation still characterizes Native-White relations does provide the matrix for much Native humor. Yet such humor is an instrument for negotiating Nativeness not only in an intercultural but also in an intracultural context, that is, within Native communities.

Rather than aiming at completeness with regard to humor in contemporary Native writing in general, the following discussion concentrates on works that show in an exemplary manner how humor serves to reimagine representations of Nativeness and Native-White relations, both past and present. And rather than aspiring to provide exhaustive analyses of the respective works, it highlights the specific aspect of humor and its link to Native identity in these texts. Still, this approach makes visible a larger pattern created by humor in contemporary Native writing: The analysis of the ways in which Native authors humorously and imaginatively transform degrading images, colonial paradigms, and essentialist ideas, shows humor to be an amusing and highly effective tool for reclaiming Native representational sovereignty, and an indispensable strategy for renegotiating Native identity. Humor thus clearly exceeds the possibilities of more factual or rational ways of countering restrictive representations.

In my position as a White European critic studying Native literature I am acutely aware of the restrictions I might be subject to when it comes to interpreting works originating from another culture. I share the concern expressed by Helen Hoy, who declares the position of the non-Native academic working on Native literature "a fraught and suspect one. The position is replete with opportunities for romanticizing, cultural ignorance, colonization — and, ironically, simultaneous professional advancement" (2001, 16). Yet essentialist claims for excluding all but Native critics from the study of texts by Native writers are both unfounded and counterproductive in getting Native literature the recognition it deserves. As Choctaw/Irish writer and critic Louis Owens points out: "Certainly, you have to have respect and be careful, but [to bar non-Native critics from analyzing Native writing] is absurd . . . because writing is about communication, and art is about dialog, and that's what we are trying to do" (in Purdy 1998, 16; see also Krupat 1996, 11–13). I therefore try to proceed along the lines of what Renate Eigenbrod calls "responsible" or

"'Indigenized' criticism" (1996, 97; 2002, 72), showing respectful consideration for the selected texts' unique cultural origin and trying to integrate the voices of Native critics and writers wherever possible. The new readings, interpretations, and findings on Native humor this book offers, therefore, hopefully do not constitute another imposition of Western interpretations on Native texts, but contribute to further intercultural dialog and interest in Native writing.

The discussion proceeds along the following lines: Chapter one provides a brief survey of humor in Native North American cultures in general, and in Native writing in particular. Chapter two situates humor in Native writing in the wider context of Native cultural identity and representation. It introduces models from literary criticism and cultural studies that conceptualize *re*-presentation, explores various aspects of humor in contemporary Native writing, and develops a framework for the subsequent readings of exemplary literary texts. In chapter three, readings focus on the forms humor takes in contemporary Native writing, mapping the literary, linguistic, and cultural means by which the texts actually convey humor. Arranged according to different modes of expression rather than along the lines of individual texts, each section provides a brief consideration of the respective form or means and its relevance in a Native cultural context, before illustrating these modes by specific textual examples. This formal discussion is complemented by a detailed look at the thematic foci, functions, and effects of humor in contemporary Native literature. To what ends do Native writers use humor, in order to address which topics? And how may this use of humor affect a Native and a Euro-American readership?

As Thomas King points out, "the appearance of Native stories in a written form has opened up new worlds of imagination for a non-Native audience" (1992, xi) — and, as I may add, to some extent, for Native readers as well. This study looks at the role of humor in such "stories" and the "worlds of imagination" they open up. Throughout the analyses, humor emerges as a powerful strategic device, consciously employed to trigger reconsideration, reevaluation, and shifts in allegiance. As a Hopi saying states: "Serious men make good *koshares*, or clowns," since in their language "the word for 'clowning' means 'to make a point'" (Lincoln 1993, 15). Native writers indeed use humor to "make a point," reimagining Nativeness anew.

Notes

[1] I use the terms Native, Indigenous, First Nations (for Canada only), and Indian interchangeably throughout this book. Wherever used in quotation marks, "Indian" refers to the generic stereotype. While some Native people consider the term Indian to be a racist European misnomer (especially in Canada), others appro-

priated and redefined the term in self-reference (more so in the US), rejecting the more politically correct Native or First Nations as token gestures rather than an actual change. Both "Native" and "Indian" homogenize the diverse cultures indigenous to North America. Of necessity, I nonetheless use these terms to describe general tendencies. But I introduce all writers with their cultures' specific denominations at first mention. (Where there is more than one possible term to refer to the same cultural designation — such as Chippewa/Ojibway/Anishinaabe or Navajo/Diné — I give preference to the name by which the authors refer to themselves.) For the sake of brevity, unless I specify otherwise, I use the term Euro-American for both US Americans and Canadians of European descent in general.

[2] These writers originate from vastly different backgrounds. They differ not only with respect to tribal affiliation, but also with respect to the degree to which they have been immersed in their respective culture. The latter point frequently gives rise to heated discussions. Many Native writers, in addition to being confronted with general stereotypes about "traditional Indian storytellers" by a larger non-Native public, also face allegations of not being "Indian enough" or not being "authentic" by other Native people. Frequently, Native writers are academics teaching and writing in English, using Western literary forms and representing a rather pan-tribal perspective. These writers' right to refer to themselves and their writing as Native — especially when they are mixedblood and/or did not grow up in a Native community — is often questioned by those holding a more essentialist outlook on Native identity and Native literature. Cf. for instance Cook-Lynn (1996) for such an essentialist view and Dumont (1993) for a perceptive scrutiny of the intricacies of being a mixedblood writer.

[3] The phrase "contemporary Native North American literature" entails ethnic, geographical, and temporal aspects. To subsume texts by contemporary Native writers under one category of Native literature is not uncontroversial. It risks thematic or racial pigeonholing, evoking preprogrammed responses, or facilitating the (further) marginalization of Native writing. Yet the emerging body of Native writing needs a unifying heading and appearance in order to get the recognition it deserves. Attempts to define Native literature — the most voluminous attempt to date is Robert Berner's *Defining American Indian Literature: One Nation Divisible* (1999) — often center on the writers' racial origins (blood quanta) and cultural background (upbringing and education according to Western or traditional Native terms; linguistic competence in their Native language, etc.) that is, basically, on the question of nature or nurture; and/or on the thematic foci, community relevance, and style of their works. Scholars use widely differing criteria to establish whether a text qualifies as Native literature, so that Cherokee/Greek/German writer Thomas King rightly observes that "when we talk about contemporary Native literature, we talk as though we already have a definition for this body of literature when, in fact, we do not. And, when we talk about Native writers, we talk as though we have a process for determining who is a Native writer and who is not, when, in fact, we don't. What we do have is a collection of literary works by individual authors who are Native by ancestry, and our hope, as writers and critics, is that if we wait long enough, the sheer bulk of this collection, when it reaches some sort of critical mass, will present us with a matrix within which a variety of patterns can be discerned" (King 1992, x–xi). With regard to the geographical delineation,

the writers dealt with originate from Native cultures throughout North America (excluding Inuit writers). Many Native people consider the border dividing Turtle Island into the United States and Canada an artificial imposition (see for instance King in Rooke 1990, 72 and Taylor 1998, 43). Therefore the authors' nationality in Western terms will be secondary to their respective Native tribal/national background here. As to the temporal aspect, finally, while the works selected for analysis date from 1972 to 2003, the vast majority of them were published after 1989, humor playing a far more prominent role in Native texts from the 1990s onwards than in those from the 1970s and early 1980s.

1: Humor in Native North American Literature and Culture: Survey

From first contact up to the present, Native people in North America have been represented and perceived in Euro-American accounts in terms that, even today, make the expression "Native humor" appear almost an oxymoron. Indians were either fierce, brutish savages or noble, tragic victims — but certainly not funny. This lack of general, and to a large extent also scholarly, recognition of Native humor constitutes a precarious falsification, especially when considering the prevalence of humor in virtually every aspect of Native life. As Vine Deloria observes:

> It has always been a great disappointment to Indian people that the humorous side of Indian life has not been mentioned by professed experts of Indian Affairs. Rather the image of the granite-faced grunting redskin has been perpetuated by American mythology. . . . The Indian people are exactly the opposite of the popular stereotype. I sometimes wonder how anything is accomplished by Indians because of the apparent overemphasis on humor within the Indian world. (1977, 146–47)

Of course these vastly discrepant assessments of the place of humor in Native cultures — the distinct stress on its centrality by Native people (see also P. Allen 2001, xii) versus the image of the stoic Indian perpetuated by non-Natives — raise the question of why "the picture of the humorless Indian [has] been so common in so much of the literature, in so many of the film and television depictions of Native Americans?" (Bruchac 1987b, 22). Possible answers include: that humor may not have been a prominent feature in early Native-White interactions; that many of those who depicted "Indians" never actually encountered any Native people themselves; or else that they failed to recognize Native humor, due to cultural differences or the intricacies of translation. Moreover, from an ideological perspective humor may have been absent from early representations of Native people because it is, at heart, a sign of shared humanity — and explorers and early settlers had little interest in "humanizing" the indigenous population. Yet even today Native people are not seen in humorous terms. Popular images of the stoic Indian may just have etched themselves too deeply into the collective imagination, while belated Euro-American guilt, which frames Native people as tragic victims, or a popular fascination with Native spirituality, which conceptualizes "the Indian" as a sternly pessimistic seer or sage, may also be contributing factors. In view of these blatant misconstruals, it seems helpful to first of all situate Native humor in a wider, diachronic approach to Native cultures before moving on to humor in contemporary Native writing.

Humor in Native Cultures

Early accounts describe Native humor through the eyes of White travelers, missionaries, ethnographers, and anthropologists. If not missed altogether, the presence of humor in Native communities is frequently registered with surprise in these texts. Even in the twentieth century, ethnographic descriptions of Native humor are characterized by their patronizing style, as when Burton writes: "To the casual observer Indian women are a silent unexpressive people who slink stealthily about and keep quietly in the background. To those who are privileged to work among them, they are a humorous and fun-loving people" (1935, 24). Nevertheless, it is interesting to note that records of Native humor date back as far as missionary Father Le Jeune's seventeenth-century report on Montagnais clowning (see Edmunds 1976, 150), Washington Irving's 1832 comments characterizing the Osage as highly humorous, or Lieutenant James Henry Carleton's descriptions of Pawnee buffoonery dating from the 1840s (Edmunds 1976, 150). Stripped of their colonial condescendence, texts such as the handbook/dictionary entries by Chamberlain (1907) and Voeglin (1949), or the more specific anthropological accounts by Hill (on Navajo humor, 1943), Wallace (on the Hupa, 1953), or Skeels (on Nez Perce humor, 1954), simply attest to the diversity and omnipresence of humor in Native cultures and intercultural relations. Some of the characteristics and functions of humor recorded then (for instance, that it frequently hinges on incongruities between Western and Native cultures; that it takes the form of mimicry or punning; and that it is often used in teasing) can still be found in written Native humor today. The importance of humor in Native cultures becomes especially apparent in descriptions of institutionalized humor such as rituals and joking relationships (see Edmunds 1976, 142–43; Hill 1943, 7–8), as well as in traditions such as the Diné (Navajo) First Laugh celebration, which honors a child's first laughter with a feast and give-away (see Beck and Walters 1977, 283–84). What stands out in particular is how humor pervades areas of Native life that in Western cultures are exempt from humor, such as religious ceremonies.[1] Ritual clowns and sacred fools have serious as well as hilarious dimensions in that they ridicule established customs but simultaneously function as the very guardians of tradition. Much like the trickster characters in both traditional tales and contemporary Native writing, they breach boundaries in permitted disrespect. They challenge accustomed patterns, subvert authority, hold up a mirror to the audience, and address issues that otherwise would not be discussed openly:

> In general, with Clowns, we, the audience, have to "read between the lines" to understand their dramatic message. By making us read between the lines, the Clowns make us think about things we do not usually think about in ways we do not usually think; or look at things in a way we do not usually look. . . . The Sacred Clowns . . . teach by not teaching; they make us see by stumbling around. (Beck and Walters 1977, 307)

As the texts under analysis reflect, this tradition of teaching through humor, of making readers stumble, laugh, and reconsider, very much continues in contemporary Native writing, where humor also forces the audience to "read between the lines" and to reexamine their frames of reference.

Much Native humor of the early colonial era arose from the culture clash experienced by both the Native population and White invaders alike, as they encountered each other's customs, ideas, and modes of life. Such humor is often discussed in terms of the initial superiority of Native people over the White "greenhorns," and their ensuing amusement at insufficient White attempts to cope with the new environment (see Edmunds 1976, 145; Perry 2000, 26; Thompson 1989, 29). But it also served as a communication strategy with substantial mediational potential (see van Keuren 1993, 88). Both aspects still characterize humor in contemporary Native writing: It may still evoke laughter at White expense, or serve as an intercultural mediator.

Even though Native cultures underwent massive changes as a consequence of colonization, humor and laughter continue to hold a special place in traditional ceremonies and in everyday life. Opinions diverge on the impact of prolonged contact and colonization on Native humor. In an interview, Leslie Silko (Laguna Pueblo/Euro-American/Mexican) indicates that her culture's humor has not changed at all at its core (in Coltelli 1990, 146–47). Paula Gunn Allen (Laguna Pueblo/Sioux), on the other hand, finds contemporary humor to be decidedly more bitter than its traditional form (in Coltelli 1990, 21–22), postulating: "Of necessity, Indian humor must reside alongside rage and grief" (Allen 2001, xii). Such different assessments may be accounted for by the fact that contemporary Native humor in itself is far from homogeneous. What Silko refers to is the omnipresent humor of everyday social interaction in Native communities, in extended families, and among friends and neighbors, who exchange funny stories and tease each other. Such intrinsic humor surfaces in Native *writing* only to a limited extent, with examples coming from Diné writer Luci Tapahonso, or from the Anishinaabe authors Jim Northrup and Donald E. Two Rivers. Allen, by contrast, emphasizes those aspects of

Native humor that arose in response to the devastating consequences of White presence, such as forced relocation or genocide.

Both Silko and Allen agree, however, that humor is indispensable to Native cultural survival and that it constitutes a principal means to cope with life. Lame Deer (Laguna Pueblo/Sioux) notes this coping or survival quality of Native humor in traditional ritual humor (in Erdoes 1972, 23), and it is generally accepted as an aspect of contemporary forms of Native humor. Garnet Raven, the young protagonist of Ojibway writer Richard Wagamese's novel *Keeper 'n Me* outlines how contemporary Native humor derives from traditional uses and remains as vital to Native (cultural) survival today as it used to be in the past:

> The first thing most people notice about us Indians is how we're laughing most of the time. It doesn't really matter whether we're all dressed up in the traditional finery or in bush jackets and gumboots, seems like a smile and big roaring guffaw is everywhere with us. Used to be that non-Indians thought we were just simple. . . . But the more they stick around the more they realize that Indians have a real good sense of humor and it's that humor more than anything that's allowed them to survive all the crap that history threw their way. Keeper says laughin's about as Indian as bannock and lard. Most of the teaching legends are filled with humor on accounta Keeper says when people are laughing they're really listening hard to what you're saying. Guess the old people figured that was the best way to pass on learning. Once you stop to remember what it was you were laughing at you remember the whole story, and that's how the teachings were passed on. (1994, 40)

When Giago claims that in its present form "Indian humor was developed as a coping tool for the sadness, fear, trepidation, anger that are present to the very roots of what we refer to as Indian country" (1990, 56), he thus unduly restricts contemporary Native humor to a reaction to Euro-American presence. Not only do Native writers time and again stress the dominance of humor among Native people — Allen attesting: "Wherever Native people gather, laughter reigns" (Allen and Anderson 2001, xii; see also Bruchac 1987b, 29) —; in contemporary Native writing, such humor is only partly characterized by bitterness and definitely exceeds a "gallows humor" response to colonization. Rather, it may be considered an intercultural instrument of mediation, as Ottawa comedian Wilf Pelletier jokingly points out:

> Laughter is a great teacher. You learn from it with your gut more than your head. And what you learn as you are laughing is that nothing should be taken seriously except, perhaps, food and drink. When the Western world learns the art of conquest by laughter, peace will descend upon us and bless us. (1972, 4)

Contemporary Native writers rely on this mediating and didactic capacity of humor, on its transcendence of the purely rational, to renegotiate images of Nativeness that are located in the readers' imaginations.

Nowadays, the omnipresence of Native humor in cultural expression and social interaction attracts attention beyond the initial ethnographic/anthropological focus. Its manifestations in Native art — as in the works of Gerald McMaster, Harry Fonseca, or the traveling exhibit on "Indian Humor" organized by "American Indian Contemporary Arts," which between 1996 and 1998 displayed works by numerous Native artists — elicited critical responses that may add to the understanding of humor in Native writing (see S. Harjo 1998; Sarkowsky 2003; Ryan 1999), especially since the increase of humor in recent Native visual art observed by Ryan shows analogies to the increase of humor in Native literature. "Over the last decade and a half," Ryan states,

> Native artists have become particularly skilled at re-presenting cultural stereotypes in humorous and ironic fashion to reveal not only their ideological underpinnings but also the way in which historical misconceptions have hindered cross-cultural understanding and interaction. Needless to say, there is also great satisfaction to be derived from merely portraying the ironies of everyday life and reveling in pure play. This is no less trickster's agenda. (1999, 14)

Among the analyses of the humor of social interaction, teasing, in particular, — also referred to as "ribbing" or "razzing" — is a well-researched phenomenon. Shutiva (1994) identifies it to be an intricate communication strategy that promotes group solidarity, relieves tension, and diplomatically sidesteps direct criticism. These functions are also found by F. Miller (1967) in his analysis of humor in Native tribal councils, in S. Pratt's (1998) study of ritualized "razzing" as a form of group-identification, and in Gelo's (1999) comments on the joking and teasing practiced by powwow emcees. Theisz (1989), in her study of Lakota Sioux humor, further argues that humor may comprise a form of delineation between Native in-group and non-Native out-group.

Finally, Native humor plays an important role in the media and in the performances of Native stand-up comedians.[2] Darby Li Po Price claims that the latter, apart from challenging the cliché of the humorless Indian directly, serve as "cross-cultural entertainers and educators" (1998, 255) who subvert and defy stereotypical expectations about "Indians." This is also testified to by Ojibway author/playwright Drew Hayden Taylor's documentary *Redskins, Tricksters, and Puppy Stew* (2000), which, in addition to portraying Native humorists and stand-up comedians all across Canada, introduces the crew of the "Dead Dog Café Comedy Hour," a highly popular show on CBC radio (1996–2001) written and performed by Thomas King. King is but one example of an increasing number of Native authors who extend their creative sphere beyond literary writing to script-writing for radio shows, TV series, or feature films, which gives them the opportunity to reach a wider audience (see Taylor 2002, 96). Ojibway playwright Ian Ross creates "Joe from Winnipeg" for CBC radio. Both Drew Hayden Taylor and Thomas King wrote episodes for the CBC series *North of Sixty*, and several of King's short stories and his novel *Medicine River* have been produced for radio and TV. Anishinaabe mixedblood author and scholar Gerald Vizenor wrote the award-winning screenplay for *Harold of Orange*. And Spokane/Coeur d'Alene author Sherman Alexie's hilarious film *Smoke Signals* (1999, an adaptation of his 1993 story collection *The Lone Ranger and Tonto Fistfight in Heaven*) even won the Sundance Film Festival audience award. Most Native humor, however, circulates in media of a much smaller scale in the form of jokes, caricatures, or humorous stories in small Native journals and newspapers.

Humor in Native Literature

Looking at humor in Native writing, one ought to keep in mind that what is referred to as Native literature — deriving from Latin *littera*, the letter — was in fact, initially, orature. Knowledge and narrative were and are passed on from generation to generation orally. (The oral tradition is still alive in Native cultures and must not be considered an antecedent for written literature.) Oral humor differs from humor in writing because of its dramatic and performative components, such as body language, gesturing, facial expression, modulations of voice, or the opportunity to don costumes. In addition, the audience in oral telling participates in the performance by responding to or even modifying what is presented to them. Consequently, Native oral humor loses important aspects in its written form. On top of cultural differences and the ensuing misunderstandings, this frequently makes early recorded oral stories appear not very humorous to contemporary readers. Moreover, as "folk tales" or "myths" such stories were not only documented but probably heavily edited and sanitized by White ethnographers and anthropologists, examples including the material Franz Boas collected at the beginning of the twentieth century and Paul Radin's *The Trickster* (1955). There are also Native collections, however, such as Salish author Mourning Dove's (Christine Quintasket, 1885–1936) *Coyote Stories by Mourning Dove (Humishuma)* (1933).

The beginnings of modern pan-tribal Native humor in written form lie mostly with Alexander Posey (Creek) and his contemporaries at the turn of the century (see Littlefield 1993, 1). Posey was the most successful among them, and his *Fus Fixico Letters* (written between 1902 and 1908), in which he comments on US Indian policy and Indian-White relations through the persona of Fus Fixico, a fictional Creek observer, constitute the "first major excursion into literary humor by an American Indian" (Littlefield 1993, 9). The humor in Posey's texts arises, on the one hand, from his use of intentionally naïve characters, who, as Littlefield points out, "are amazed, amused, and puzzled by the greed, materialism, political ambition, dishonesty and hypocrisy in the whites, especially in the federal bureaucrats, merchants, petty entrepreneurs, and would-be politicians" (1993, 37). On the other hand, Posey has recourse to Este Charte or Red English, an indigenized idiom that he employs to comic avail through mispronunciations and misunderstandings. In contrast, as pointed out above, Will Rogers, another satiric Native writer who emerged roughly two decades after Posey, in weekly columns for the *New York Times* commented on events from the standpoint of a "cowboy philosopher" (collected in five books between 1919 and 1929) without much reference to his Cherokee ancestry.

Later twentieth-century Native literary voices before 1968 (mainly Alexander Eastman, John Milton Oskinson, John Joseph Mathews, D'Arcy McNickle, and Luther Standing Bear), with the exception of E. Pauline Johnson, were scarcely noticed by the reading public, and none of them used humor to any considerable degree. The amount of public interest and recognition changed dramatically with the so-called Native American Renaissance, initiated by Kiowa writer N. Scott Momaday's Pulitzer-Prize winning novel *House Made of Dawn* in 1968. Yet humor and satire, while not totally absent, can hardly be considered outstanding characteristics of most Native literary works published in the 1970s and early 1980s. Rather, texts such as Blackfoot/Gros Ventre author Jim Welch's *Winter in the Blood* (1974) and *The Death of Jim Loney* (1979), N. Scott Momaday's *House Made of Dawn* (1968), Leslie Silko's *Ceremony* (1977), and to some extent also Métis writer Maria Campbell's *Halfbreed* (1973) focus on the dilemmas that alienation and lack of identification create for their protagonists, who often struggle with a hostile mainstream society (struggles that are sometimes resolved by their eventual return to their community on the reservation). Velie describes these protagonists of Welch's and Momaday's novels as "alienated, not only from white society, but even from their own tribe. They are incapable of attachments to lovers, friends, or relatives . . ., passive, drifting without job or goal, drinking heavily. When they snap out of their torpor they commit acts of violence" (1984, 315). Velie nevertheless goes on to argue that a more thorough reading of the texts will show the underlying positive or even comic currents (see also Vangen 1987). I agree that these texts certainly should not be read as tragic accounts, and that they do contain instances of humor, especially Welch's *Winter in the Blood*, which displays moments of biting sarcasm. Still, problematic aspects and controversy dominate the mood, and it is their resolution rather than the presence of humor that comprises their positive aspects. In contrast, more recent works by Native writers, although also centering on the problematic question of Native cultural identity and issues of colonization, are frequently marked by the presence of clearly detectable and far less bitter humor. Gerald Vizenor's *Darkness in Saint Louis Bearhart* (1978) and

Louise Erdrich's (Turtle Mountain Chippewa/German) *Love Medicine* (1984) and *The Beet Queen* (1987) are early examples. The majority of such writing, however, appeared from the late 1980s and early 1990s onwards.

Humor in contemporary Native writing figures in practically all genres:[3] In the field of the novel, Louise Erdrich's highly successful North Dakota quartet is among the first Native works since the beginning of the Native Renaissance to clearly exemplify humor in Native fiction. Together with her husband Michael Dorris, Erdrich also wrote *The Crown of Columbus* (1991), which, similar to Gerald Vizenor's *The Heirs of Columbus* of the same year, employs humor to unmask as Eurocentric and hypocritical the celebratory quincentennial hype around the discovery of America. Vizenor not only includes humor in his own fictional works, he makes it the determining principle of his theoretical and critical writing (explored in chapter three). His fellow critic and author Louis Owens (Choctaw/Irish) uses sophisticated irony and satire in his novels to comment on the difficulties and challenges of being mixedblood, especially when moving between worlds as vastly different as the Western academic world (*Bone Game* 1994), the war in Vietnam (*The Sharpest Sight* 1992 and *Dark River* 1999), and traditional Choctaw tribal life. Always influenced by aspects of Owens's own biography, these mysteries (as well as *Wolfsong* 1991) use a cast of characters that include traditional figures, such as the evil gambler or the trickster, alongside contemporary Native characters. They integrate mythic elements into realistic plots and challenge readers' imaginations to follow the narrative into unfamiliar spheres. Excursions into the fantastic and an extensive use of irony and sarcasm are also trademarks of writer and filmmaker Sherman Alexie. The sharp humor in his novel *Reservation Blues* (1995) spares neither the Catholic Church nor White "wannabes," Western capitalism, hypocritical historiography, nor the Indian protagonists themselves. (His subsequent novels, *Indian Killer* from 1996 and *Flight* from 2007, are by and large much darker and less funny than *Reservation Blues*). Similarly wide in scope is Thomas King's brilliant novel *Green Grass, Running Water* (1993), which is clearly more humorous than his two other novels, *Medicine River* from 1989 and *Truth and Bright Water* from 1999. It makes use of elements from Native mythology, oral narrative structure, allusion, and intertextuality to create a uniquely humorous panorama of contemporary Native life and Native and Western history and literature. In Richard Wagamese's previously mentioned novel *Keeper 'n Me* (1994), elder Keeper — somewhat in the tradition of Posey's Fixico — comically comments on the White world in Red English, mostly focusing on intercultural differences. In contrast, the biting humor in Haisla writer Eden Robinson's *Monkey Beach* (2000) and Robert Alexie's *Porcupines and China Dolls* (2002), which are more concerned with the characters' human abysses and the devastating consequences of colonization, respectively, is less readily apparent and darker.

The short story is arguably the most fertile ground for humor in Native writing and most strongly contributes to what may justifiably be labeled a "humorous turn" in Native literature — maybe because it is easier to sustain the humorous mode in the briefer scope of the short story than throughout the length of a novel. Among the writers of short fiction strongly relying on humor, some have published only the occasional story in journals or anthologies (although they may have published much more prolifically in other genres). Examples are Lorenzo Baca (Laguna), Gordon Henry (Anishinaabe), Lee-Ann Howe (Choctaw), Carter Revard (Osage), Patricia Riley (Cherokee/Irish), Gary Robinson (Creek), Suleiman Russell (Laguna/Cherokee), Paul Seesequasis (Cree), and Emma Lee Warrior (Peigan). Others have published story collections, though not all stories in these collections are humorous. Only some of Mohawk writer Beth Brant's stories (*Mohawk Trail* 1985, *Food and Spirits* 1991) are strongly humorous, while others are just the opposite, and the same can be said about Cherokee author Diane Glancy's short fiction (*Trigger Dance* 1990, *Firesticks* 1993, *Monkey Secret* 1995, *The Voice That Was in Travel* 1999). In contrast, Sherman Alexie's collections *The Lone Ranger and Tonto Fistfight in Heaven* (1993), *The Toughest Indian in the World* (2000), and *Ten Little Indians* (2003), and especially Thomas King's *One Good Story, That One* (1993) and *A Short History of Indians in Canada* (2005), contain hardly any stories that are not humorous. The bulk of collections by contemporary Native writers that use humor constitute a rather heterogeneous mix of humorous and less humorous stories: Powhatan/Delaware author Jack D. Forbes's *Only Approved Indians* (1995), Jim Northrup's *Walking the Rez Road* (1993), Acoma Pueblo writer Simon Ortiz's numerous stories and collections (best exemplified by his *Men On the Moon: Collected Short Stories* 1999), Eden Robinson's *Traplines* (1996), Drew Hayden Taylor's *Fearless Warriors* (1998), and Donald E. Two-Rivers's *Survivor's Medicine* (1998). Ojibway writer Basil H. Johnston's *Moose Meat and Wild Rice* (1993) and *Indian School Days* (1998), while basically also consisting of stories, are episodic and partly autobiographical. Likewise, other contemporary humorous Native texts defy genre classification, often due to their strong connection to the oral tradition or mythic stories. Examples are *Elderberry Flute Song* (1989), *The Other Side of Nowhere: Contemporary Coyote Tales* (1990), and *I Am Turtle* (1991) by Mohawk writer Peter Blue Cloud and most notably Okanagan storyteller Harry Robinson's oral narratives, which were documented in writing by Wendy Wickwire in *Write It On Your Heart: The Epic World of an Okanagan Storyteller* (1990) and *Nature Power: In the Spirit of an Okanagan Storyteller* (1992).

In the field of poetry the range of humor is just as wide as in the prose texts. There is the gentle humor of Diné writer Luci Tapahonso (in, for example, *Blue Horses Rush In* 1997). But there are also rather sarcastic poetic comments, such as those by Cherokee writer Carroll Arnett,

Chemehuevi/Anishinabequai author Diane Burns (*Riding the One-Eyed Ford* 1984), Chrystos (*Not Vanishing* 1988), or Métis writers Mickie Poirier and Jo-Ann Thom/Episkenew. And finally, there are the subversive ironies and celebratory survival humor of Muscogee poet Joy Harjo (in, for example, *She Had Some Horses* 1983, *The Woman Who Fell From the Sky* 1994) and Anishinaabe writer Lenore Keeshig-Tobias. Simon Ortiz's humor, with its strong link to the Acoma Pueblo tradition, stands next to Sherman Alexie's combinations of classical forms and contemporary Native content in his satiric revisions of Euro-American representations of "Indians" (for example, *First Indian on the Moon* 1993, *Old Shirts, New Skins* 1993, *The Summer of Black Widows* 1996). The humor in Cree/Métis poet Marilyn Dumont's (*A Really Good Brown Girl* 1996) and Plains Cree writer Louise Halfe's poetry (*Bear Bones and Feathers* 1994) seemingly hinges on personal experience, but, tricksterlike, also critically engages with issues that vastly surpass the personal sphere. Shoshone-Chippewa writer Nila Northsun's texts (for example, *diet pepsi & nacho cheese* 1977 and *A Snake in Her Mouth: Poems, 1974–96* 1997) are concerned with tribal traditions in a Western world, as is Marie Annharte Baker's poetry (Little Saskatchewan First Nations; *Being on the Moon* 1990, *Coyote Columbus Café* 1994), which is strongly linked to the trickster.

While Native theater generally is much more prominent and prolific in Canada than in the USA, it is Kiowa dramatist Hanay Geiogamah's *New Native American Drama: Three Plays* that, in as early as 1980, marks the first pronounced use of humor in published Native drama. Sometimes shockingly open, Geiogamah's *Body Indian* tragicomically portrays contemporary Native life without omitting problematic aspects such as alcoholism and violence — as does Ojibway playwright Ian Ross in his award-winning *fareWel* (1996). In *Foghorn*, Geiogamah satirically reviews Native-White history — a task also hilariously accomplished by Gerald Vizenor in his screenplay *Harold of Orange* (1984). In Canada, Cree playwright Tomson Highway's darkly funny plays *The Rez Sisters* (1988) and *Dry Lips Oughta Move to Kapuskasing* (1989), centering on life on the reserve, were hugely successful. The hilarious *Princess Pocahontas and the Blue Spots* (1990), by Kuna/Rappahannock writer and actress Monique Mojica, concentrates on the role of Native women throughout postcontact history, while Mojica's "Post-Colonial Traumatic Stress Disorder: A Theatrical Monologue" (2001) satirically deals with the consequences of colonization. Jim Northrup's play *Shinnob Jep* (2002) parodies the popular game show *Jeopardy!*, preposterously scrutinizing Native-White history and relations. Just like Anishinaabe writer Ruby Slipperjack's comical play *Snuff Chewing Charlie at University* (2001), it addresses intercultural differences and difficulties — the latter in the constellation of a Native student and his grandmother encountering Western academia. Finally, prolific playwright and journalist Drew Hayden Taylor's plays (eleven to date) all employ humor to some extent: some of the lighter slapstick and comedy variety, such as in *The Bootlegger Blues* (1991), some more bitingly, especially when focusing on intercultural encounters, as in *alterNatives* (2000), for which he was actually accused of instrumentalizing humor in an anti-White racist fashion (see Taylor 2002, 86–89).

Some of Taylor's sharpest humor, however, can be found in his non-fictional writing, his side-splitting *Observations From a Blue-Eyed Ojibway*, thus the subtitle of his four volumes of essays and columns entitled *Funny You Don't Look Like One* (1996, 1999, 2002, 2004). Commenting, as his predecessor Posey did at the beginning of the twentieth century, on cultural differences, the current situation of Native people, Canadian Indian policy, cultural production, and a myriad of other topics, Taylor frequently manages to hit readers where it hurts — all the while making them shake with laughter. The best known example of the witty use of humor within the earlier tradition of so-called "protest" or "activist" nonfiction of the 1970s is certainly Vine Deloria's *Custer Died For Your Sins* (1969), which not only contains a chapter about Indian humor, but uses humor and satire throughout as a strategy for attacking colonial oppression, exposing hypocrisy, and shattering misconceptions.

The only anthology of Native primary texts with a specifically humorous focus to date is an issue of *Gatherings: The En'owkin Journal of First North American Peoples*, published annually by the En'owkin School of Writing in Penticton, British Columbia. Entitled *Shaking the Belly, Releasing the Sacred Clown*, the 1997 volume concentrates entirely on humorous Native texts. It contains poetry, short fiction, and essays by both lesser-known and well-established writers, such as Kimberley Blaeser (Anishinaabe), Marie Annharte Baker, Jack D. Forbes, Jeannette C. Armstrong (Okanagan), and Drew Hayden Taylor. The texts are arranged in categories entitled "Trickster," "Feminist/Mother/Woman," "Song," "Dark Humor," "Identity," "Home," "Colonization," "Children," and "Celebration," showing the wide thematic scope covered by contemporary humorous Native writing. Paula Gunn Allen's anthology *Hozho: Walking in Beauty* (2001) also shows a strongly humorous inclination (as postulated in the introduction; see Allen 2001, xii), and Drew Hayden Taylor's anthology *Me Funny* (2005) assembles instances of Native humor in stories (by Louise Profeit-Leblanc), stand-up routines (by Don Kelly), and jokes, together with several scholarly assessments of and nonfictional comments on humor (for instance, by Ian Ferguson and Thomas King) in Native art, literature, and social interaction. Finally, works by two Native American authors, Sherman Alexie and Jim Northrup, are included in *Humor Me: An Anthology of Humor by Writers of Color*, edited by John McNally in 2002.

This overview demonstrates that humor figures prominently in contemporary Native literature, that indeed it may even be a defining characteristic of large parts of it. But whereas this fact in itself has been widely acknowledged (see Georgi-Findlay 1997, 398; Lowe 1994, 203), it has not yet led to a significant increase in research focused on this topic. This study subsequently addresses this situation by developing an approach for analyzing the abundant humor in Native writing in a more encompassing and productive manner than has been accomplished to date.[4]

Notes

[1] See Apte (1983, 189; 1985, chapter 5); Palmer (1994, 26–30); Sanner (1993); Voeglin (1949); for a more detailed discussion of the diverse ritual clowns, buffoons, and Heyokahs in American Indian cultures see Plant (1994), Beck and Walters (1977, chapter 13), and Steward (1929). Giago considers Native religion/spirituality one of the main sources of contemporary Native humor (see 1990, 54–55), and Lowe even traces humor in contemporary Native literature to sacred clowning (see 1994, 193).

[2] The most successful Indian comedians to date are probably Will Rogers and Charlie Hill. Rogers, who as a humorist, journalist, and actor was most productive in the 1920s and 30s, hardly drew on his Cherokee heritage, whereas Hill, an Oneida actor and stand-up comedian who appears in such widely seen shows as Jay Leno or Johnny Carson's *Tonight Show*, bases a large part of his routines on cultural differences and Native realities.

[3] Though in Native literature it is sometimes hard to categorize texts according to genre, for the sake of clarity the following overview proceeds along these lines.

[4] The appendix provides a survey on the state of research on humor in Native writing.

2: Reimagining Nativeness through Humor: Concepts and Terms

THE FOLLOWING CHAPTER FURTHER EXPLORES the connections between identity, representation, and humor in contemporary Native North American writing. The discussion proceeds in four consecutive steps: First, I take a brief look at the factors that influence Native identity; second, I analyze the interconnections between representation, identity, and (Native) literature; and third, I discuss concepts or models from literary criticism and cultural studies that may be productively applied to describe Native writers' strategies of engaging with representations of Nativeness. I conclude by looking at the role that humor plays in the sphere delineated by these parameters.

Constructed Images — Constructing Identities

The "overarching question of cultural identity" or even "the quest for identity: What does it mean to be Indian — or mixedblood — in contemporary America?" according to Choctaw/Irish writer Louis Owens (1992, 7, 20) is absolutely central to all Native American writing. Obviously there cannot be any definite answer to this question; identity, is, after all, never fixed, but continuously negotiated in varying contexts and discourses.[1] Still it is worthwhile to consider some of the factors and circumstances that have an impact on contemporary Native existence[2] in order to explore some of the intricacies of Native identity formation and to come to an understanding of what may necessitate a humorous reimagining of Nativeness in the first place.

Native people are faced with a long history of distorting misrepresentations and commodifications of Native identity. Not only is the term Indian a misnomer, going back to a geographical error on Columbus's part; the whole idea of a collective "Indianness" is, as Berkhofer points out, in itself "a white conception" (1978, 3). From first contact, depictions of "the Indian" served particular functions for European self-conceptualizations. The guise of the deficient "heathen devil" (who had to be either "civilized" or exterminated) proved vital in the creation of an Othering discourse on Native Americans, justifying and rationalizing the civilizing mission of manifest destiny. On the other hand, the image of the noble savage (who was tragically unfit to survive) was a welcome instrument to critique a decadent European society. Regardless of their respective orientation,[3] accounts of European explorers, settlers, missionaries, and philosophers all enlisted in the project of creating the simulacrum of "the Indian" — an image that persists today. Consequently, one of the most problematic aspects of Native identity is the imposition of definitions and characterizations of Nativeness from the outside, through the dominant Euro-American society. According to Michael Green, "a culture identity arises through the exercise of powers of self-determination by a group which defines itself" (1995, 4). Native people under Euro-American domination, however, were denied such a self-determined cultural identity. On the contrary, "the identity of the individual and collective Indian throughout postcontact history has been largely one of manipulation and schematic Other destruction . . . written into the public consciousness by non-Indians" (Vickers 1998, 43, 107).

I single out three major influences on both the perception and definition of Nativeness today for exemplary discussion: the popular imagination, historiographic accounts, and legislation.[4] Stereotypical representations of Native people in the popular media, especially in the Western romance format of dime novels and films, continue to determine ideas about Nativeness to a large extent. In a process analogous to what Said described in *Orientalism* (1991), the popular media have created a vast body of popular knowledge about "Indians." As Vine Deloria sardonically remarks, "there is no subject on earth so easily understood as that of the American Indian" (1977, 5); indeed, "it would be 'un-American' not to know about Indians" (Hobson 1979, 104). "Typical Indians" are either fierce horseback-riding warriors and buffalo hunters, replete with war bonnet and face paint, whooping and yelling war cries as they attack the wagon trains of innocent White settlers; or they are wise seers who lament the demise of their culture and advocate a life in harmony with mother earth. Such clichéd images not only block out the immense cultural diversity and vastly diverging lifestyles traditional Native cultures followed and continue to follow, they also confine Indians to a long gone past and most forcefully deny Native people *contemporary* identities, since clearly these do not comply with such antiquated images and ensuing stereotypical expectations. Paula Gunn Allen thus sarcastically comments: "If we live in the past, and by 1850 it's all over, you know what that tells a young Indian person? It tells a young Indian person you died in 1890, so what are you doing here?" (in Coltelli 1990, 19). Read in this context, Sheridan's saying, "The only good Indian is a dead Indian" (the actual words were "The only good Indians I ever saw were dead," see Mieder 1995) assumes a tragicomic new meaning: Since Native people today no longer match stereotypical notions of "the Indian," only the dead or vanished Indian of the nineteenth century — basically, the Indian that never was, created by Euro-American writers and Hollywood productions — qualifies as a good or "real" Indian.

Native people have neither vanished nor have they been preserved in the "stasis box of the nineteenth century" (Weaver 1997, 8), however. On the contrary, contemporary Native culture and identity are transculturally negotiated every day, as elder Keeper in Richard Wagamese's novel *Keeper 'n Me* explains:

> The truth is that most of us are movin' between Indyuns. Movin' between our jobs and the sweat lodge. Movin' between school and pow-wow. Movin' between English and Anishanabe. Movin' between both worlds. Movin' between 1990 and 1490. . . . Culture's what you find yourself doin' day in and day out, he said. Culture's the way of livin' and we gotta admit that these days our culture's made up of sweat lodge, TV, radio, huntin', school, fishin', sweetgrass, cedar, work and all sortsa things. Whatever we find ourselves doin' day in and day out. That's our culture now and that's why most of us are the movin'-between kinda Indyuns. (1994, 137–38)

The problem is that these contemporary Native realities are hardly ever depicted in Euro-American representations (not even in documentaries, which also tend to confine Native existence to the past). Consequently, Native people are offered little they can relate to, and instead end up defending themselves against allegations of being inauthentic — which may come from both White and (sometimes essentialist) Native sides.

Misconceptualizations about "Indians" also dominate the historical discourse on Native people. Knowing and having pride in one's own history are important factors in the cultural identity formation of a group, since a group's self-conceptualization strongly relies on the imagination of its own past (see Assmann 1997, 133). The victors, however, write history, and Euro-American colonial paradigms have long denied Native people a history of their own. Instead, in a manner that Fanon regards as typical for processes of colonization (see 1988, 170), Eurocentric and revisionist historiographic accounts reduced indigenous presence to an obstacle in the way of progress and civilization. This systematic devaluation of Native history has devastating consequences for Native identity today: "If Indian history since 1492 has been 'written' (authored) by white authority, then how can Indians attain or retain authentic identities in the present? The author of history also assumes the power of the author of identity and the arbiter of authenticity" (Vickers 1998, 9).

Analogous to the processes at work in historiography, finally, Euro-Americans within the framework of legislation have been in a position to define who is Indian and who is not[5] — a state of affairs that seems highly ironic to most Native people in the United States and Canada, as frequently such legislation appears to be motivated by the respective nation's desire to control indigenous access/treaty rights and land claims. Yet this colonial power over defining Native status influences the very identity formation of Native and mixedblood people, raising questions of geographic, cultural, and emotional belonging (see Gruber 2007). It induces Native people to "hold a yardstick to our lives and our families' lives by way of measuring to what extent we should be considered 'really' Native. How Native do we look? Do we have status or not? Do we speak our language? How much do we know about our culture? In essence, how much Native we can be said to be" (Lawrence 2000, 82).

Such severe self-questioning, along with processes of internalization and dissociation are among the most devastating consequences of the vast discrepancy between Euro-American conceptualizations of "the Indian" and contemporary Native realities. Powerful misrepresentations have led to close scrutiny and controversial discussions of the very concept of Nativeness itself within Native communities. Are there any reliable criteria for Nativeness? Arguments exchanged in a frequently emotionally charged discussion are based on "blood quanta" and appearance, one's cultural grounding, education, or whether one currently lives with one's community. In a complex maze of differing cultural expectations, Native people and especially mixedbloods trying to identify with their (part) Native origins are frequently faced with the dilemma that they are "still too Indian for some but 'never Indian enough' for others" (Bruyere 1997, 198). Especially when living outside Native communities, in an attempt to develop a distinctively Native identity, they may resort to the only markers of Indianness still available to them — those created by mainstream society. In order to identify as Indian at all, they internalize stereotypical ideas and "become the invented Indians of popular imagination, wearing long hair, beads, plastic ornaments, and imported leather" (Weaver 1997, 145). Paradoxically, as Vine Deloria describes it, "the more we try to be ourselves, the more we are forced to defend what we have never been" (1977, 2). To summarize the impact of externally imposed conceptualizations and definitions of Nativeness on Native identity with the words of Ojibway/mixedblood writer Kateri Damm: " 'Who we are' has been constructed and defined by Others to the extent that at times we too no longer know who we are. The resulting confusion, uncertainty, low self-esteem and/or need to assert control over identity are just some of the damaging effects of colonization" (1993, 11).

Cultural Identity Formation, Representation, and Native Literature

If "the Indian" looms so large in the collective imagination — especially in that of Euro-Americans, but certainly to a substantial extent also in that of Native people themselves — how does this influence Native identity formation? Marilyn Dumont raises several pointed questions in this context:

Why do popular images of us lag behind our reality? . . . I would argue that there is a connection between domination and representation. Which prompts me to ask the questions, "if the representation of me is inaccurate, how does this impact on my art?" But more importantly, "*How does this representation affect my self-image?*" I would argue that the misrepresentation of me makes me doubt my experience, devalue my reality and tempts me to collude in an image which in the end disempowers me. (1993, 48; emphasis added)

Dumont's considerations reveal how crucial images of Nativeness are to Native people in terms of identity formation. The underlying relation between power, representation, and identity that Dumont describes here has received increasing attention in recent decades, especially by postcolonial thinkers like Edward Said or Homi K. Bhabha. According to Bhabha, a "reading of colonial discourse suggests that the point of intervention should shift from the *identification* of images as positive or negative, to an understanding of the *processes of subjectification* made possible (and plausible) through stereotypical discourse" (1990, 71). In the field of Native studies, the former task has been widely taken on, with much energy being directed towards identifying distorting images of Native people in literature, film, commercials, and so on. The latter task, that is, looking at the processes of subjectification based on stereotypical representations, has yet to be recognized as just as or even more relevant, and so far has only received limited attention. In the following, such practices are briefly explored as part of the argument. The ultimate goal of this study, however, is to take Bhabha's proposition still one step further: Transcending an investigation of the discursive practices employed by the West in processes of subjectification, the analysis explores the ways in which Native writers can *interfere with* these stereotypical processes of representation through the use of humor. The following paragraphs therefore introduce the terms we need to discuss how practices of representation produce and articulate cultural identities, so we can understand the role humor plays when Native writers engage in these representational practices.

In common usage, the term identity describes something like the unalterable essence of a thing or person, just as its adjective identical refers to characteristics that remain constantly the same. Cultural or collective identity from this vantage point describes "the idea of one, shared culture, a sort of collective 'one true self'" that provides a people with "stable, unchanging and continuous frames of reference and meaning, beneath the shifting divisions and vicissitudes of our actual history" (Hall 1989, 69). Such a view of cultural identity as a fixed entity, an unalterable and time-transcending "inner core," however, largely ignores the possibilities of development, change, or interference — some of the very premises that the subsequent argument builds on. Rather than a stable essence, cultural identity should, as Stuart Hall therefore argues, be regarded as a *processural* concept, that is, something that is constantly negotiated in discourse. Cultural identities "undergo constant transformation. Far from being eternally fixed in some essentialised past, they are subject to the continuous 'play' of history, culture and power" (Hall 1989, 70). Consequently, one cannot really speak of cultural groups as *having* an identity, but should rather conceive of them as constantly *forming* and *re-forming* their cultural identity — the process determined by both their history and whatever they are confronted with in their present situation.

Representation, like identity, can be considered from various angles (see Hall 1995, 1997a, 1997b). In a *mimetic* approach, the process of representation is considered to be separate from what it represents. Things that exist in the world are determined by their material or natural characteristics, thus they have "a perfectly clear meaning, outside of how they are represented" (Hall 1997a, 5). A *constitutive* approach, in contrast, sees no such separation between the material or natural existence and its representation. While things, events, relations, and so on have an existence outside representation, it is only within representation that they acquire meaning:

> How things are represented and the "machineries" and regimes of representation in a culture do play a *constitutive*, and not merely a reflexive, after-the-event role. This gives questions of culture and ideology, and the scenarios of representation — subjectivity, identity, politics — a formative, not merely an expressive, place in the constitution of social and political life. (Hall 1995, 224)

Linking a processural concept of identity to a constitutive model of representation, Hall postulates that: "Identities are . . . constituted within, not outside representation" (1996, 4). They are not stable entities merely reflected in representation. On the contrary, how an individual or group is represented has a *retroactive* effect on the constitution of its identity. In the continuous process of identity formation, individuals or groups constantly select certain elements from the sum of representations they are faced with and integrate them into their conceptualizations of themselves. Cultural identities in that understanding are "the unstable points of identification or suture, which are made, within the discourses of history and culture. Not an essence, but a *positioning*" (Hall 1989, 72). It is through representations that new subject positions are offered to groups and individuals in processes of interpellation. They can fill these positions through acts of *identification*, that is, through (conscious or unconscious) decisions to take on a certain identity. As expressed by Woodward:

> Representations produce meanings through which we can make sense of our experience and of who we are. We could go further and suggest that these symbolic systems create the possibilities of what we are and what we can become. *Representation as a cultural process establishes individual and collective identities* and symbolic systems provide possible answers to the

questions: who am I?; what could I be?; who do I want to be? (1997, 14; emphasis added)

What are the implications of all this for the context of Native identity and Native writing as a form of cultural representation? With regard to Native identity, one-dimensional representations have limited "the possibilities of what we are and what we can become" severely for Native people. Possible answers to the question "what could I be?" have been restricted to the stereotypical image of "the Indian" or conceptualizations that suggest a rigid/fundamentalist adherence to tradition. Considering that identity is both determined by and exists in representation, the way that Native people have been *mis*represented by others clearly poses problems for Native identity formation. As Paula Gunn Allen writes: "The colonizers' revisions of our lives, values and histories have devastated us at the most critical level of all — that of our minds, our sense of who we are" (1992, 193).

If one follows through with the assumption that identity is constituted within representation, however, this also implies that altered (literary) representations of Native people, by offering different positionalities, may exert influence and effect change in the ongoing constitution of Native cultural identity. This may be a daring undertaking, considering the still small emerging Native literary scene in comparison to the impact of Hollywood's mass media portrayals; yet to create new representations of Nativeness in order to contribute to such change constitutes a strong impetus for many Native writers. "Image casting and image control," according to Allen, "constitute the central process that American Indian [people] must come to terms with, for on that control rests our sense of self, our claim to a past and to a future that we define and we build" (1992, 192). Native writers — albeit to varying degrees and some more explicitly than others — participate in this struggle over the contested image of "the Indian" in order to reclaim representational sovereignty for themselves. That this contested identity is continually renegotiated and is basically an imaginative concept does not mean that it is without effects in the world: Identities "arise from the narrativization of the self, but the necessarily fictional nature of this process in no way undermines its discursive, material or political effectivity," as Hall (1996, 4) points out. The mass of distorting images of Native Americans in the past did have tangible effects in "cumulatively [building] a separate reality about Native cultures" (J. Price 1978, 201). Previous distorting representations of "Indians" continue to shape Native realities and identities. Consequently, it is precisely the realm of imagination that Native writers choose as their arena for revising the narrative of Native identity. How does the negotiation of identity in representation take place, after all? It is language (in the widest sense, also including nonverbal forms of cultural expression and communication) that conveys representations, language that "provides the terms by which reality may be constituted . . ., the names by which the world may be 'known'" (Ashcroft, Griffiths, and Tiffin 1995, 283). Basically, therefore, identity can be known, generated, and communicated only through its formulation in language.[6]

Contemporary Native literature as a form of cultural representation acknowledges this inherent power of language and puts it to use in an effort to reformulate Nativeness — a process that Anishinaabe writer and critic Gerald Vizenor calls "narrative recreation" (1994b, 6). As "postindian warriors" (6) Native writers contribute to the "recovering or rearticulation of an identity" (Owens 1992, 5), a task that Owens sees "at the center of American Indian fiction" (5). Not only do they write about contemporary Native realities and thus inherently defy the confinement of Native existence to the past, they also counter stereotypes or shatter essentialist ideas.

While such contemporary texts thus help Native people overcome the (counterfeit) identities assigned to them by the colonizer and reclaim their right to define themselves, they refrain from doing so in any prescriptive way (there simply is no definite characterization of "Indianness"). Instead, they offer a wide variety of playfully imaginative "alterNatives" (Taylor 2000a). Addressing questions such as, Who is an Indian? How do we develop this idea of Indianness?, contemporary authors like Thomas King try to "show Indians in different positions . . . so that there are Indian people out there who see that and say, 'Oh, OK, I don't feel so bad now that I'm not a fullblood Indian on the back of a pinto pony, living in the 19th century'" (King in Weaver 1997, 149). Contemporary Native writers thus overcome the narrow restrictions that both mainstream representations and essentialist Native thinking place on the range of subject positions for Native people. By writing against the inhuman simulacrum of "the Indian," by exposing it as such, and by (often humorously) presenting diverse Native characters instead, they both confront the non-Native audience with new representations and provide new points of identification for a Native audience. Contemporary Native literature therefore empowers Native people to reinvent themselves, or, as Jace Weaver puts it: "Native writers . . . help Indians imagine themselves as Indians" (1997, 45).

To subscribe to this idea, one has to acknowledge the (socioculturally) *formative* dimension of (Native) literature. Earlier Western schools of literary criticism frequently regarded aesthetic expression as independent of (and thus also inconsequential for) historical, political, and social realities. Starting at the latest with New Historicism, traditions and models of purely text-centered formalist criticism and interpretation have been renounced, and texts were situated in their historical, material, and ideological contexts. The movement emphasized the mutual influence of world and (literary) work, claiming that texts exert a retroactive effect on society by altering its modes of interpreting the extratextual reality. "For great works of art are not," as Stephen Greenblatt explains, "neutral relay stations in the circulation of cultural materials" (1990, 227); rather, they shape and produce their subjects in representation. From this vantage point, it appears not only legitimate but also essential to look at contemporary Native literature not from an "art for art's sake" perspective, but with a view to its involvement in the social, psychological, and political processes relevant to the cultural identity formation of Native people. In the words of Craig Womak: "Native artistry is not pure aesthetics, or art for art's sake: as often as not Indian writers are trying to *invoke* as much as *evoke*" (1999, 16).

Interestingly, a belief in the generative function of language — often in a very literal sense, for instance in creation stories — is deeply rooted in many Native cultures. In many traditional Native contexts, there was or is no sharp dividing line between story and reality. Stories both reflect and shape reality, and "the word carried the power to create, to make things happen. . . . Words did not merely represent meaning. They possessed the power to change reality itself" (Petrone 1990, 9).[7] This belief in "the coercive power of language to 'bring into being' " (Owens 1992, 14) surfaces in contemporary Native writing, be it in Leslie Silko's novel *Ceremony*: "I will tell you something about stories, / [he said] / They aren't just entertainment. / Don't be fooled" (1977, 2; brackets in original), or in Kiowa writer N. Scott Momaday's *The Way to Rainy Mountain:* "A word has power in and of itself. It comes from nothing into sound and meaning; it gives origin to all things" (1976, 33). When Native authors write to bring about change, as, for instance, Adrian C. Louis (Paiute/mixed-blood) claims the texts of Sherman Alexie do (in Alexie 1993b, viii–ix), they thus align themselves with a long-standing tradition.

For the context of Native identity, Momaday spells out the generative potential of narrative in his seminal essay "The Man Made of Words": "It seems to me that in a certain sense we are all made of words; that our most essential being exists in language" (1979, 162). Consequently, the idea of Nativeness, of being Indian, "in order to be realized completely, has to be expressed" (162). Although originating in vastly differing cultural backgrounds, the ideas of Momaday, the first Native Pulitzer Prize winner, and Hall, the Caribbean-British sociologist, thus complement each other in astonishing ways when Momaday locates "our most essential being . . . in language" and Hall refers to identities as "narratives, . . . stories we tell ourselves" (1995, 66). Especially for colonized and still traumatized cultures, literature in a healing way relies on the notion of identities as "stories we tell ourselves" to tell *different* stories and thus constitute new kinds of subjects. These new stories/new representations invade the Euro-American as well as the Native imagination, as becomes apparent below, in order to transform the empty myths about Native people and Native-White history, which all too often comprise the image of Indians.

Emphasizing the ensuing responsibilities, Ruppert has called contemporary Native writing "literature with a purpose" (1995, xii). Accordingly, the argument presented here builds on the assumption of an undeniably revisionist aspect of contemporary Native writing. Through changed representations of Nativeness, Native readers are offered new possibilities for identification, whereas non-Native audiences are required to rethink their preconceptions.[8] Since, as outlined above, identity is not only constituted by how a group sees itself but by how it is seen by others, any contribution of Native writing to Native cultural identity has to address an audience comprised of both Native and Euro-American readers in order to take hold — a process that is not without intricacies.[9] Still, the hopes placed in this ability of Native literature to reformulate Nativeness are very substantial. Convinced of its attitude- and world-changing potential, Paula Gunn Allen commented in 1990:

> The fact that Native American people have writers of their own is so new that it's taken awhile, but we're beginning to have a real effect. We're beginning to take control of the image-making again. And that's what most happens, because whoever controls your definition controls your sense of self. And so the more writers we have and the more readers we have, the more Native American people are going to be able to claim themselves, and take it back from Hollywood, take it back from the anthropologists. Isn't that exciting? (in Coltelli 1990, 18)

Since then, Native writing, especially in Canada, has experienced an even greater upsurge. Texts by Native writers today reach a far greater audience, also owing to the immense popularity of Native theater in Canada and the way in which some of the most popular Native writers, such as Sherman Alexie, Thomas King, Ian Ross, Drew Hayden Taylor, and Gerald Vizenor have added radio, film, or both to their range of artistic expression (see Taylor 2002, 96). While the idea of Native writers contributing to changes in Native cultural identity may still be idealistic, it is far from illusory.

Conceptualizing Re-Presentation

Having looked at representations of Nativeness and their impact on Native cultural identity, the discussion now turns to strategies of *re*-presentation. How do Native writers shatter existing patterns of representation and offer "alterNatives"? The following pages attempt to conceptualize and describe the processes at work in contemporary Native texts. In light of the clichés and pseudo-facts about Native people discussed above, two very simple options for "setting the record straight" may initially present themselves: merely reverse the stereotypes or counter the clichés with detailed, faithful information about Native people. Neither of these, however, would go very far in deconstructing the one-dimensional images of Nativeness that prevail in the collective imagination. The first, that is, a blunt reversal of images or roles, would still pigeon-hole both Native people and Euro-Americans, cementing dichotomies that are little helpful in representing the complexities of contemporary Nativeness. "When frozen models are only inverted, stereotypicality still triumphs," as Amossy (1984, 697) writes. The second, countering widespread misconceptions about Indians by providing ethnographically correct information on Native cultures, is also bound to fail. Detailed documentation of, for instance, the dress, foods, modes of transportation, or housing of traditional woodland Indians would hardly dislodge the image of the fierce painted buffalo-hunting Plains warrior so deeply etched into the collective imagination by Hollywood films and dime novels. The two kinds of information first of all work on different epistemological levels, and, if a documentary approach to contemporary Native existence is chosen, additionally, they address different temporal and historical spheres.

Rather than replacing previous depictions, much contemporary Native writing takes the approach of working *with* the extant representations and transforming them. Countering clichéd misrepresentations, many of these texts employ a strategy that "locates itself *within* the complexities and ambivalences of representation itself, and tries *to contest it from within*" (Hall 1997b, 274). That is, the writers engage directly with the one-dimensional forms of representation used by the colonizer and attempt "to make the stereotypes work against themselves" (274). Such a reshaping may leave the original form of representation visible, but it exposes the original as stereotypical, ethnocentric, or derogatory. The following introduces three models or sets of terms that can all be productively enlisted in discussing how contemporary Native texts contest representations of Nativeness from within. There is some overlap between these concepts, but they are not identical in their approach. Rather, they complement each other, each highlighting different aspects of such re-presentation.

The first is Mary Louise Pratt's concept of autoethnography and transculturation, by which she describes communication (and cultural production) in the "contact zones," that is, "the social spaces where cultures meet, clash, and grapple with each other, often in contexts of highly asymmetrical relations of power, such as colonialism" (1991, 34). Rather than conceptualize the relationship between colonizer and colonized as a one-sided imposition, Pratt's model stresses the relationship's actively dialogic characteristics. The model examines the processes by which the subaltern engages with and makes use of the colonizers' culture to create new forms of self-representation. As introduced into literary criticism by Pratt, autoethnography describes a form of writing that has at its center the very challenge of representation from within, which is necessary for countering

externally imposed images. Within the asymmetrical power relations resulting from conquest and colonization, by means of autoethnographic texts

> people undertake to describe themselves in ways that *engage with repre-*
> *sentations others have made of them.* Thus if ethnographic texts are those
> in which European metropolitan subjects represent to themselves their
> other (usually their subjugated others), autoethnographic texts are repre-
> sentations that the so-defined others construct *in response to or in dialogue*
> with those texts. (M. L. Pratt 1994, 28; emphasis added)

This very much describes what happens in the contemporary Native texts
under discussion: The selected Native writers take extant representations
of Indians, enter into dialog with them, and incorporate them into their
new "alterNative" representations of Nativeness in order to alert the
reader to their stereotypical qualities, racism, or irrationality. The process
is not so much one of replacing previous representations with new ones,
then, but one of reshaping or even constructing palimpsests, where the
original representations remain visible but are ridiculed and recontextual-
ized in order to achieve defamiliarization and, consequently, reorientation.
"Autoethnographic texts are not, then, what is usually thought of as
autochthonous or 'authentic' forms of self-representation" (M. L. Pratt
1994, 28), in that they do not ignore but purposely address the misrepresentations created by the dominant culture. The Native works discussed
here certainly do not attempt to retain or regain precontact, "unspoiled"
(by Western influence) Native modes of representation. "Rather," as Pratt
explains, autoethnographic texts "involve a selective collaboration with
and appropriation of idioms of the metropolis or conqueror. These are
merged or infiltrated to varying degrees with indigenous idioms to create
self-representation intended to *intervene* in metropolitan ways of understanding" (28). These — in the context at hand, Euro-American — ways
of understanding, as we have seen, in turn substantially influence Native
people's self-understanding.

Contemporary Native writers do indeed, to a certain extent, collabo-
rate with and appropriate the colonizers' idiom by writing in Western literary forms and by using the English language. Many Native writers are
just as immersed in Western literary and cultural traditions as in their
Native background, so that their texts are characterized by a transcultural
integration of Western traditions and Native elements, be they terms from
indigenous languages, narrative structures originating from the oral tradition, or fragments from indigenous texts such as creation myths.
Transculturation, as established by Pratt,[10] describes how, in situations
characterized by hierarchical power relations, subordinate groups selec-
tively incorporate elements from the dominant culture: "While subordinate peoples do not usually control what emanates from the dominant
culture, they do determine to varying extents what gets absorbed into their

own and what it gets used for" (M. L. Pratt 1991, 36). While Native people are inevitably faced with an overpowering Euro-American cultural output — in education, the media, literature, and so on — it is still up to Native writers (or Native people in general) which elements of that "avalanche" they incorporate into their work (or their culture). Further, a selective adoption of Western elements and their playful recombination with Native material does not leave either unchanged. The incorporated elements are modified and transvalued in a process that often involves humor. Transculturation, therefore, on the one hand, bears obvious subversive qualities. On the other hand, it fulfils a mediating, dialogic role of rereading the colonial confrontation between White settlers and Native inhabitants as a " 'cultural encounter' that leads to reciprocal communication, exchange, and cooperation" (Fitz 2001, 11). The notions of autoethnography and transculturation are therefore compatible with a highly flexible conceptualization of identity that defies both fixed Euro-American clichés and rigidly essentialist qualms about a loss of Native authenticity through the integration of Western elements.

Closely linked to the strategies of transculturation and autoethnography, but already taking one more step towards a concept of reimagining identity through humor, are Dee Horne's ideas on "creative hybridity" and "subversive mimicry" (1999). In postcolonial and cultural studies, the notion of hybridity[11] is used to expound the complexities inherent in the relations between periphery and center, colonizer and colonized, subordinate and dominant groups. It is based on the assumption that the processes at work in situations of cultural contact are better described in terms of mutual penetration or interweaving than as a dualistic clash between two distinct and unchangeable cultural groups. Hybridity therefore tends to emphasize interconnections rather than rigid dichotomies and unbridgeable differences. Horne's model of creative hybridity is based on Homi K. Bhabha's notion of hybridity as a strategy of authorization. Bhabha argues that "the hybrid strategy or discourse opens up a space of negotiation where power is unequal but its articulation may be equivocal. Such negotiation is neither assimilation nor collaboration. It makes possible the emergence of an 'interstitial' agency that refuses the binary representation of social antagonism" (1996, 58). It is hybridity's potential to reformulate rather than replicate that, according to Horne, best characterizes contemporary Native American writing: "Creative hybrid texts . . . partially represent or repeat the colonial discourse to contest and re-present it" (1999, xix–xx). Hybridity's ability to partially deploy colonial discourse while contesting it from within opens up a space for productive dialog, especially with non-Native readers. As Horne argues, such dialog enables non-Native readers to identify (with) Native characters as complex personalities rather than flat, empty images. Paralleling my own argument, Horne's concept claims that contemporary Native writing can trigger a reconsideration of the image of Nativeness ingrained in public consciousness: "Creative hybrid texts are productive of meaning (reforming society by re-formulating it within the text); they are not simply reflective or expressive of existing reality" (1999, xix).

Horne argues that such texts clearly distinguish themselves from texts that merely mimic the dominant colonial discourse in order to partake in its authority and power. Colonial mimicry, according to Bhabha, on the one hand, constitutes a powerful instrument of oppression, in that it entices the colonial subject to imitate the colonizer, but simultaneously denies its sameness and thus a share in the colonizers' power. On the other hand, it is the very arena for subversion and mockery because mimicry, rather than mere imitation, may be "repetition with a difference" (see Bhabha 1994). Horne contrasts colonial mimicry with the concept of "subversive mimicry," which writers from subordinate groups can employ to make use of the dominant group's discourse for their own purposes without actually ever conforming to that dominant group's demand for assimilation.[12] Arguing that the writers she looks at use "subversive modes of mimicry [that] allow [them] to partially represent the colonial discourse without perpetuating it" (1999, 3–4), Horne's approach offers a useful first conceptualization of the strategies Native writers choose to actually reconfigure colonial modes of representation.[13]

Finally, the model of reimagining to be developed here partly builds on John Purdy's use of "remagining," a term he uses in his article "Tricksters of the Trade: 'Remagining' the Filmic Images of Native Americans" (2001).[14] Purdy briefly examines a novel (by Thomas King) and two films (by Gerald Vizenor and Arthur Masayesva) in their "attempt to 'remagine' the images, for their texts evoke both memory and imagination with the hope of reinscribing the metaimages of Hollywood" (2001, 108). These metaimages created by Hollywood still dominate most people's ideas about Indians. Attempts by Native writers and filmmakers to counter such depictions of Native people are, in Purdy's opinion, therefore destined to fail if they do not show, as a precondition, "an intimate understanding of both the attraction the images possess and, more importantly, the psychology of their initial inscription. It is this primal dynamic, this act of enculturation, that must be engaged, and the texts that do so must also reach a wide audience" (2001, 100–101). Accordingly, critical academic studies about the misrepresentation of Native people or ethnographic accounts about Native cultures cannot dislodge the popular images of Indians from people's imagination to any substantial degree. In order to achieve a reconsideration of common preconceptions, new texts and films must become similarly popular as the texts or films that initially created the distorting images. They have to deploy the fascination inherent in these stereotypical images in order to engage readers in imaginative . . . activity. It is on this level that a few contemporary Native artists have attempted to engage the popular power of Hollywood's conventions of reinventing the American Indian. . . . These artists appropriate the conventional images and employ the tricks of the trade to recontextualize them in situations that dislocate their audience's earlier, imaginative experiences with these images. (Purdy 2001, 108)

Similar to Pratt's concept of autoethnography, Purdy's "remagining" describes a mode of representation that neither ignores nor tries to exclude the earlier representations. Instead of pointing to the shortcomings of previous depictions of "the Indian" or trying to deconstruct them, the texts described by Purdy move on to literally re-form them, working with previous representations and familiar frames of reference in a transformative process. It is in this way, as Purdy argues, that the Native writers and filmmakers he looks at in his brief discussion "manipulate the apparatus itself — the evocative power of film and novel . . . — to turn the stage upon which images of Indians have been imprinted into an imaginative quagmire, a humorous destabilizing that ultimately has as its goal a 'remagining' of images" (2001, 116).

In *Harold of Orange* (1983), a screenplay by Gerald Vizenor, protagonist Harold "insists that he is a trickster . . . He believes that he can stop time and change the world through imagination" (1993a, 75–76). In analogy, the approach to be developed here postulates that imagination is crucial in changing if not the world then at least its representations. As discussed at the beginning of this chapter, some of the most problematic aspects of Native identity arise from stereotypical ideas about Indians that are lodged firmly in the (Euro-American and to some extent also the Native) collective imagination. Consequently, building on the interconnections between identity, representation, and literature established previously, as well as on the considerations by Pratt, Horne, and Purdy, what emerges is a model that conceptualizes the imagination as the site of resistance and struggle over new representations — and thus ultimately new realities, since these are constituted within representation. It has become clear that only an engagement with existing representations eventually leads to a transformation of stereotypical images and clichés. The contemporary Native texts discussed here do indeed present familiar images and patterns in order to engage their readers' imagination. Through (humorous) processes of recontextualization or defamiliarization, they subsequently twist these familiar depictions, and the frames of reference within which they are usually perceived, tricking readers into a reconsideration of their initial assumptions. Accustomed patterns of interpretation and identification are comically disrupted, seemingly self-evident representations of colonial power turned on their heads — and against themselves, as especially Euro-American readers realize the breaks and biases in the colonial agenda. In reading such texts, a non-Native audience cannot comfortably remain in their privileged position at the center. Euro-American readers are humorously displaced from the dominant roles of frontiersmen or pioneers, who in countless colonial representations heroically battled the savages in the glorious opening of the American West. Instead, they are inadvertently (and laughingly) brought to identify and empathize with witty Native characters. "The ability to be empathetic is rooted in our capacity to imagine," writes Bell Hooks, and adds: "Imagination can enable us to understand fictive realities that in no way resemble where we are coming from" (1991, 57–58). By reimagining Nativeness, Native writers manage to lure (especially Euro-American) readers from their familiar terrain of stereotypical conceptualizations of "the Indian" into the realm of a new, different understanding of Native people.

Within a context of asymmetrical power relations, the imagination, moreover, constitutes a space in which the oppressed groups themselves can formulate alternatives to their present situation. In the context at hand, the imagination is a way for Native people to conceive of themselves in terms different from the cut-out frames they had been restricted to in the past. This is not to be mistaken for escapist fantasizing. Rather, as Hooks points out, it ought to be considered as the very beginning of change: "For the colonized mind to think of the imagination as the instrument that does not estrange us from reality, but returns us to the real more fully, in ways that help us to confront and cope, is a liberatory gesture" (1991, 55). Tellingly, it was books, Hooks explains, that let her "know firsthand that if the mind was to be the site of resistance, only the imagination could make it so. *To imagine, then, was a way to begin the process of transforming reality*" (1991, 54–55; emphasis added). As the subsequent text analyses make apparent, the Native texts under discussion do indeed humorously reimagine Nativeness in order to "return [it] to the real more fully," helping Native people both to confront and to cope with colonial realities. They use the imagination as a site of contestation, liberation, and regeneration, and thus strongly contribute to the continuance and constant flexible renewal of Native cultural identity. How crucially the imagination figures in this process becomes apparent when one thinks of Native (pan-Indian or culturally specific) collective identity in analogy to what Benedict Anderson calls an "imagined community" in the context of nation states and national identities (1983). That is, the collective is given meaning and enables identification mainly through a "narrative of Nativeness," through a set of representations comprised of stories, images, memories, and so on. This accentuates once again the fact that distorting representations and externally imposed definitions have left Native people largely bereft of options for positive identification, making the task of imagining themselves as a community an especially complex one: To ensure their cultural survival as communities, Native people not only have to constantly imagine themselves, they have to literally *re*imagine themselves.

While the present need to *re*imagine Nativeness is thus to a substantial extent the consequence of colonization, the concept of the imagination as a generative source of identity is strongly rooted in Native cultures, in ways similar to the generative power of language discussed above. In their oral traditions, Native cultures imagined and conceptualized themselves in narrative, making sense of the world around them and their place in it. Momaday's core statement in "The Man Made of Words" consequently is: "We are what we imagine. Our very existence consists in our imagination of ourselves. Our best destiny is to imagine, at least, completely, who and what, and that we are. The greatest tragedy that can befall us is to go unimagined" (1979, 167). Native writers now reimagine Native people in order to fill the vacuum that the simulacrum "Indian" left, reworking both external perceptions and the self-conceptualization of Native people by offering identity-bestowing narratives of Nativeness.

The Role of Humor in Contemporary Native Writing

For too long, as Louis Owens points out, there has existed a "predetermined and well-worn path between signifier and signified" for "the sign 'Indian'" (1992, 231). This path has been trodden not only by Euro-Americans but also, sadly, as pointed out above, by Native people themselves. Owens therefore considers it imperative for contemporary Native writers to "free the play between these two elements, to liberate 'Indianness,' and in doing so to free Indian identity from the epic, absolute past that insists upon stasis and tragedy for Native Americans" (231). One of the most important activities in the process of liberating Nativeness is the use of humor. Humor interferes with one-dimensional representations of "the Indian" and Native-White history on various levels: Most basically, it directly defies the stereotype of the stoic, humorless Indian through Native texts and/or characters that are deeply humorous (and consequently complex and multidimensionally human rather than one-dimensionally "Indian"). In addition to directly flouting the image of the stoic Indian, however, humor also serves as a more encompassing facilitator of reimagining by defamiliarizing and twisting stereotypical patterns of expectation. In this vein, humor figures as the agent of imaginative subversion and is instrumental in a regeneration of Nativeness. To get people laughing can create spaces in which previous assumptions lose their validity, so that new perspectives can be playfully introduced and readers are prompted to reconsider their assumptions and preconceptions. To gain a better understanding of these processes first of all requires a basic comprehension of the phenomenon of humor.

Defining Humor in Contemporary
Native North American Writing

The Irish satirist Jonathan Swift (1667–1745) observed: "What Humor is, not all the Tribe/Of Logick-mongers can describe" (quoted in Levin 1972, 2); and Henri Bergson in 1900 demanded: "we shall not aim at imprisoning the comic spirit within a definition. We regard it, above all as a living thing" (1991, 2). Today, scholars still have a hard time defining humor, and it is not the focus of this book to contribute to this discussion or to fathom humor as such. Yet I do consider it indispensable to establish a working definition of Native humor and to elucidate some of its complexities (which in my opinion need not foreclose its status as "a living thing," which indeed it very much is, as the text analyses will show). Various academic fields conduct research on humor, mainly sociology, psychology, anthropology, and ethnology, but also literary and cultural studies as well as linguistics. From the beginnings of interest in humor, as we use the term today,[15] there were differing theories — some of them rather adventurous — about how humor works, what its effects are, and why it is employed. Today, humor theories can roughly be grouped into four different approaches. These are not mutually exclusive but overlap and complement each other; none of them can provide a conclusive and exhaustive explanation for all instances of humor, as all concern themselves with different aspects (see Lewis 1989, 4). In the following, the most common conceptualizations of humor are sketched and examined with regard to their possible relevance in contemporary Native writing.

Superiority theories go back to Plato and Aristotle, with prominent later advocates being Thomas Hobbes and Henri Bergson. Their basic common tenet is that laughter can be seen as expressing a feeling of superiority — as exemplified in laughing at or making fun of another person's misfortune or clumsiness. This, to some extent, comes to bear on Native literature in that such humor may also serve to integrate a group (see Fine 1983, 173) and bolster its self-esteem: To ridicule an out-group, and especially a dominant out-group (as in Native jokes on White people or satiric accounts of Euro-Americans and their behavior) may allow the oppressed community to feel morally superior as a group to the satiric objects of their humor. The limitations of a conceptualization of humor and laughter in terms of superiority are obvious, though: It restricts laughter to self-aggrandizement and cannot account for any kind of empathetic, gentle, or merely joyous laughter, let alone the mediational aspects of humor.

These aspects figure prominently, however, in the conflict/control views of humor held by sociologists (see Stephenson 1951; Martineau 1972). Within situations of conflict, such conceptualizations maintain, humor can serve as an instrument for indirectly articulating otherwise strongly provocative propositions, mellowing the blow of criticism and thus avoiding the consequences of overt aggression. The means by which such conflict-humor can be expressed in literature, according to Fine, are "irony, satire, sarcasm, burlesque, caricature, and parody" (1983, 174). As we see below, the conflict function of humor, and consequently the forms of expression just mentioned, figure prominently in the subversive strategies employed in the texts under analysis, both for the discussion of problematic issues in Native-White relations (ethnocentric historiography, stereotyping, discrimination, and so on) and for the renegotiation of Nativeness within Native communities. Especially the latter also enlists humor as a device for social control, expressing approval or disapproval of certain characteristics and actions in order to mark them as appropriate or inappropriate within a particular conceptualization of Nativeness. In effect, such humor serves to foster or prohibit a particular behavior: When someone is laughed at disapprovingly for doing or saying something, the embarrassment created by that situation will most likely keep them from repeating it in the future.

Release and relief theories, proposed by, among others, Herbert Spencer and Sigmund Freud, describe the way in which humor and laughter, as a kind of safety valve to avoid further escalation, serve to release tensions and anxieties arising from social inhibitions, taboos, or conflicts (but also constitute a reaction to positive outcomes of dangerous situations). This often occurs in the form of jokes that bring up issues in a way that is otherwise prohibited by social restrictions. Racist, vulgar, or misogynist statements that would be unacceptable if uttered seriously can thus be expressed and laughed at. To some extent, such a notion may apply to the way in which Native writers use humor as a Trojan horse to express issues that, outside such a humorous frame, would be deemed offensive by a Euro-American readership.

Incongruity theories, finally, go back to early proponents Immanuel Kant and Arthur Schopenhauer, and were further developed by Henri Bergson, Arthur Koestler, and John Morreall in the twentieth century. Today, incongruity theories probably constitute the most common and least disputed approach to humor.[16] Their basic proposition is that humor is created from the combination of elements, images, and ideas from vastly disparate fields not usually thought of together. Laughter, according to this view, comprises a surprised intellectual reaction to incongruity, more specifically to "something that is unexpected, illogical, or inappropriate in some way" (Eckardt 1992, 63). Incongruity theories in themselves can be divided into two major strands: "Some theorists argue that we only need incongruity for humor to be present; others argue that one needs both incongruity and resolution of that incongruity" (Rishel 2002, 279). The latter, called configurational theory, considers the presence of incompatible concepts, images, and so on a necessary but not sufficient precondition for humor; in order to make sense of the incompatibility, the receiver of humor has to find the connecting element between the two inconsistent fields: "To get a joke we must resolve its incongruity by retrieving or discovering an image or idea that can connect its oddly associated ideas or images" (Lewis 1989, 34). In configurational theory, humor is thus seen to result from the delight we gain from our successful resolution of the riddle that inconsistent concepts pose.

Such a view explains some of the problematic aspects of the reception of humor in Native writing: The incongruities inherent in these texts may not be recognized as such or may not be resolved by readers from a different cultural background, the result being that the humor is lost on them. Still, incongruity theories seem best suited for the analysis of humor in contemporary Native literature. Not only does the humor in the selected Native texts frequently hinge on the discrepancies between Euro-American and Native cultures; as already outlined above, it frequently works with defamiliarization and recontextualization to deprive readers of the option to see things, ideas, or actions within their accustomed (clichéd) frames of reference. "Incongruity occurs when we expect something coherent and it veers off the track. . . . Incongruity theorists believe we laugh because our line of thought has been surprisingly switched from one context to another," writes Rishel (2002, 34, 279). Translated into the context at hand, this may be described the following way: Native writers, by engaging with previously conventionalized representations of Nativeness within largely familiar literary forms, lure readers into believing they are on familiar terrain — just to playfully confront them with ideas and materials vastly incongruous to these familiar patterns, consequently eliciting humor. Readers initially call up their conventional images and interpretations, but end up regarding the subjects of representation (and possibly their own interpretive practices and reading paradigms) from a different vantage point. While it is obviously hard to conceive of any definition that is applicable to all instances of humor, a first notion of humor for the task at hand could thus be:[17] Humor is what results from the sudden (imaginative, intellectual, and emotional) resolution of playful incongruity, causing a surprising and amusing shift of perspective.

Before even approaching the subject of Native humor in an analytic fashion, and in view of the many parentheses qualifying the general term Native as "pan-Indian" or "culturally specific" throughout the text, the first question to be answered is to what extent one can really speak of Native humor in light of the fact that the indigenous population of North America in itself consists of diverse cultures. There is an increasing number of Euro-American as well as Native critics and voices from within Native communities that suggest that humor today has a pan-tribally unifying and integrating capacity. It serves as a kind of "ethnic glue" (Lincoln 1993, 23) holding Native cultures together.[18] For the field of contemporary Native literature, Lowe thus explains:

> Critics of Indian literature have quite properly warned themselves and others to avoid the assumption that any one description or literature represents all American Indians; we may, however, find somewhat of a common ground in many aspects of the humor employed, especially in the contemporary era. (1994, 198)

Such assessments, in addition to the fact that humor has been strongly rooted in the traditions of most Native cultures, sufficiently justify the use of a general term Native humor: "As current Native writers demonstrate, Native American humor now seems to speak for all citizens of this land" (Lowe 1994, 203). Today, a shared humor enables Native people to deal with such pan-Indian problems as being confined to the past, confined to reservations, confined to stereotypical images. Native writers employ it as a kind of road sign, pointing to possible ways for Native people to step out of some of these confinements, but also towards an enhanced cross-cultural understanding.

Yet how could a characteristically *Native* form of humor be defined? Faced with the same task, Thomas King, in his inimitable tricksterlike way, tries to sidestep the question by stating:

> Maybe . . . we don't need a definition of something we can see and hear, if we simply pay attention. Besides, what would we do with a definition of Native humour anyway? We'd just waste time trying to apply the definition, and we might miss the performance. Worse, we might try to insist that Native humour measure up to the definition, even though we know that humour will change while definitions, once stuck, will not. . . . Besides, trying to define Native humour, in any formal way, would require close readings, footnotes, and several panel discussions. In the end, it's probable wiser and more judicious to put nothing in writing and pretend we know what we're talking about, so that, when the need arises, we can change our minds and never have to worry about being wrong. Or right. (2005, 183)

As much as I am tempted by King's line of argument — which would after all, spare me some footnotes and close readings — in a study of this scope I cannot avoid to at least attempt to define Native humor, however imperfect the result may turn out to be.

There are, of course, universal traits to humor, and some topics — for instance, the most universally human issues of eating, sex, and body functions — provide subjects for humor in most cultures. Quite surprisingly, Native scholars and writers, despite recognizing cultural differences, rather tend to stress the commonalities (see Taylor 2005, 1–2; King 2005, 181). Nonetheless, what people consider funny, which situations they experience as humorous, obviously strongly depends on their cultural background, and within a given culture, on further factors such as their race, class, age, gender, and so on. In a conceptual framework of humor as playful incongruity this makes sense: The notion of incongruity, of course, depends on what is seen as congruous within a given culture. Circumstances, situations, things, or utterances are "not incongruous *simpliciter*, but only relative to someone's conceptual scheme" (Morreall 1983, 60).[19] Many of the values, ways of knowledge, and worldviews of a specific culture can thus be detected by looking at their humor, what they laugh at, and at which situations and what times laughter arises. Some scholars even suggest that Euro-Americans can reach a better understanding of Native people when they take a look at what makes them laugh (see V. Deloria 1977, 146; Spielman 1998, 107, 112). Based on the premise that humor is, at least to some extent, culture-specific, any definition of Native humor has to acknowledge that it originates from and reflects the particularities of Native history and culture (or, in a more differentiating formulation, even histor*ies* and cultur*es*). Since Native cultures comprise fourth world nations that have been surrounded by a dominant Euro-American society for half a millennium, this also includes Euro-American customs and views (particularly Euro-American views of Native people) as targets of Native humor. Moreover, not only does humor reflect how a group sees itself and how it is seen by others, it also partakes in shaping both the image and the self-image — and thus ultimately the identity — of the group.

In light of these considerations and the preceding discussion of humor, Native humor can be defined as: humor *created by Native people that reflects and shapes* aspects of *Native as well as Euro-American* life and culture. It arises from the resolution of playful incongruities, which often hinge on the differences between Euro-American and Native cultures and their respective representations of self and other. In the Native texts under discussion, the surprising and delightful shift of the readers' perspectives is basically triggered by an amusing violation of fixed patterns of expectation and interpretation (Morreall's "conceptual frames") that the audience brings with them to their reading of the text.[20]

Admittedly, such a sparse definition provides but an abstract idea of the phenomenon, merely determining the parameters involved. It therefore has to be augmented by a more descriptive approach. This can be accomplished either in comparative fashion, that is, by contrasting Native humor with the humor produced by other groups, or in the manner of "social biography" (Eckardt 1992, 131), which focuses on the cultural and historical conditions Native humor originates from and takes stock of its present manifestations. The extensive text analyses of this study largely explore the idiosyncrasies of Native humor through the latter strategy, by looking at the various shapes Native humor takes and by contextualizing the instances of humor in Native literature in a Native cultural and historical background. And because a contrastive strategy can also provide some useful insights — despite the obvious drawbacks, namely that comparisons of this kind must inherently rely on generalizations and can only be conducted in the most rudimentary fashion — the following paragraphs offer some brief considerations along those lines as well.

Obvious differences between Native and Euro-American humor[21] lie in the background and the subject matter chosen by each, that is, on the level of *motivation* and *content.* Hoffmann argues that American humor typically centers on "the myth or idea of the American dream, comprising the idea of newness, and the ideals of infinite possibility, of happiness and progress" (1985, 145). He stresses that in American humor incongruity arises from the contrast between ideal and fact, between high beliefs and realistic assessments. In contrast, as we will see, the thematic focus of Native humor is entirely different. While Native humor certainly should not be considered a result of colonization but, rather, precedes the colonial presence (see Geiogamah in Lincoln 1993, 335), as with all fourth world nations, the sociohistorical condition of subalternity shapes Native humor to a substantial degree:[22] "Native humour comes from five hundred years of colonization, of oppression, of being kept prisoners in our own country. With legalized attacks on our culture, our languages, our identities and even our religion, often the only way left for Native people to respond to the cruel realities of Fourth World existence was in humour" (Taylor 2005, 69). Therefore, in addition to continuing a long tradition of intracommunity humor — here there is a strong consensus on teasing and self-deprecatory humor as the most prevalent forms (see Hirch 2005, 107; Kelly 2005, 62; Taylor 2005, 75) —humor in contemporary Native writing to a substantial degree centers on the way in which Native identity and existence are in constant jeopardy as a consequence of colonization. It subversively ridicules features of the dominant society and, arising from the situation of seeing oneself as Other, stereotypes that members of the dominant society hold about the subaltern ("the Indians"). Such features can hardly be said to exist in American or Canadian humor, in spite of their own past as British colonies.

On the *formal* level, however, the humor employed by contemporary Native writers is more often than not comparable to that used in a Euro-American tradition. There are, of course, idiosyncratic Native forms of expression, such as the use of trickster characters or Red English. Nonetheless, as the subsequent chapter on techniques and forms of expressing humor makes apparent, contemporary Native literature to a great degree uses the same means employed for creating humor in Western writing — irony, sarcasm, satire, parody, "frequent teasing, outrageous punning, constant wordplay, surprising association, extreme subtlety, layered and serious reference" (Ryan 1999, xiii). Moreover, there are astonishing parallels between some forms of (humorous) writing as it emerges from Native narrative traditions and mainstream postmodern literature, especially with regard to the use of multivalent narrative and intertextuality (for example, by Thomas King and Louis Owens), metafiction (Carter

Revard), and playfulness and disruption in Gerald Vizenor's notion of trickster discourse.

These admittedly very basic observations are borne out by Paula Gunn Allen's encompassing description of Native humor:

> In Indian country the sense of play, of humor, satire, irony, and wit plays as central a role in ceremony as it does in day-to-day life. Wherever Native people gather, laughter reigns. Nor is the humor confined to jokes — though there are plenty of them. Mostly it rests on pun, on irony and ambiguity that several centuries of occupation and genocide occasion. It's a matter of laugh or die. So we laugh. At ourselves, at our situation, at the ludicrous circumstances in which we live and move and have our being. Our laughter is sometimes unabashed hilarity, sometimes bitter cynicism, sometimes embedded in a complexity of observation and tradition. Of necessity, Indian humor must reside alongside rage and grief. Perhaps there is something profoundly funny about spitting in the eye of death. After all, the Native nations of the Americas have looked extinction in the eye, and survived to tell the tales. In Indian Country it's been nuclear winter for centuries. We know all about survival, including the fact that without a wry view of history, survival is impossible. And that is a history that goes back thousands of years, long before the most recent challenges to our endurance and our sense of humor began. (2001, xii)

Allen's description necessitates a concluding look at an only apparently straightforward issue, namely, what is to be considered *funny* in Native writing. Approaching this question, one has to keep in mind — however frustrating it may be for academic analyses — that responses to humor are "subjective and contextual" and that "one reader's joke is another's sad irony" (Lewis 1989, x). Nevertheless, in determining the "humorousness" of the texts under discussion it may be helpful to look at the ends that the humor serves and the target it is directed towards. Eckardt establishes a useful distinction between teleological-ideological humor and integral or nonutilitarian humor. Nonutilitarian "integral humor . . ., which, like foals gamboling in the fields, is directed to no special end beyond itself but only to itself in spontaneity and joy" (1992, 146). Such humor, which is essentially a form of clowning, certainly exists in Native literature and culture, continuing a long tradition of Native (ritual) clowning and humorous performance. Clearly, however, in the context of colonial domination, much of the humor in contemporary Native writing falls under the category of "teleological-ideological 'humor' [which] is, in conception, totally humor-*less*, totally serious, for it is aimed at a moral goal wholly beyond itself. It is strictly an incarnation of politics, of the unending power-political struggle against injustice" (1992, 145–46). Naturally, the "funniness" in some teleological-ideological humor may be harder to detect, especially where it addresses basically tragic issues; yet this kind of humor clearly also serves most effectively to reimagine — and thus deal with and possible alter — depressing realities, a function that is at the center of the subsequent paragraphs.

Gallows Humor or Survival Strategy?

The phenomenon under scrutiny here is characteristic not just of Native people but can be observed in many oppressed groups: Under the most threatening conditions oppressed groups, be they African-Americans during slavery, Jews during the Holocaust, or Native Americans during and after Euro-American conquest, decimation, and colonization, retain or even develop an especially robust kind of humor. At first glance, such humor may appear paradoxical under the circumstances. Father Arnold, a reservation missionary in Sherman Alexie's novel *Reservation Blues*, asks himself: "What did [Indians] have to laugh about? Poverty, suicide, alcoholism?" (1996a, 36). From a different vantage point, however, humor emerges as an indispensable means that helps people confront and cope with the tragedies life holds in store. This is what Vine Deloria comments on when he explains that in Native cultures "the more desperate the problem is, the more humor is directed to describe it" (1977, 147). Humor in this view is an instrument that subordinate groups employ to liberate if not their entire existence then at least their minds, by laughing at what keeps them down. Should this be considered gallows humor or survival strategy, then? I would argue that in Native literature this is not a question of "either . . . or" but rather a case of "as well as." Allen writes that for Native people "reconciling the opposites of life and death, of celebration and grief, of laughter and rage is no simple task, yet it is one worthy of our best understanding and our best effort" (1992, 158). Accordingly, we should take a closer look at the motivations behind such humor in Native writing.

One employs gallows humor, on the one hand, to make unalterable, harsh realities bearable by distancing or detaching oneself from them. Psychologically, it may be conceptualized as an escape into laughter to avoid more suffering or insanity. Taken literally, gallows humor even points to an impending and inevitable death, its purpose being to downplay the absolute force and finality of such an ending. This gives gallows humor a decidedly fatalistic and passive slant: It constitutes a means of preserving dignity and sanity in the face of inevitable peril by ignoring its impact, but it no longer fosters any hopes of *altering* the situation as such. Even though it is intended to alleviate pain, its inherent bitterness ultimately points to passive resignation. Such resignation, the very fatigue resulting from centuries of struggle against oppression, undoubtedly characterizes some of the humor in contemporary Native writing, as Paula Gunn Allen points out:

It's almost gallows humor. . . . When you've gone through five hundred years of genocidal experiences, when you know that the other world that surrounds you wants your death and that's all it wants, you get bitter. And you don't get over it. It starts getting passed on almost genetically. It makes for wit, for incredible wit, but under the wit there is a bite. It's not defensive so much as it's bitter. It also makes for utterly brilliant, tragic writing as well. Because it's so close to the bone. It's not some middle class person sitting around imagining what it would be like to be in trouble. It's about your own life. . . . And so when you laugh you know perfectly well that you're laughing at death. Real death. (in Coltelli 1990, 21–22)

On the other hand, humor in contemporary Native writing can also be considered a strategy for survival. Humor then points in the direction of continuity rather than termination, hope for change rather than resignation: "As expressed by survivors of tragedy, nonvanishing Native Americans, this humor transcends the void, questions fatalism, and outlasts suffering. . . . At cultural ground zero, it means that Indians are still here, laughing to survive" (Lincoln 1993, 45–46) — and surviving laughingly. Called "the one universal thing about Native Americans from tribe to tribe" by Louise Erdrich (quoted in Lincoln 1993, 209), survival humor connotes activity and resistance. It is a subversive weapon for defending one's identity against an overpowering colonizer, and it may actively strengthen group solidarity by drawing a group together against a common threat — a capacity that may literally be vital since unity can enhance a group's chances to overcome adversity. Allen thus balances her preceding (rather bleak) assessment by observing that

the interesting thing about the use of humor in American Indian poetry is its integrating effect: it makes tolerable what is otherwise unthinkable; it allows a sort of breathing space in which an entire race can take stock of itself and its future. Humor is a primary means of reconciling the tradition of continuance, bonding and celebration with the stark facts of racial destruction. (1992, 158)

Survival humor thus defies resigned self-relinquishing; in contrast, it strengthens collective identity and enables Native people to take their situation with a grain of (trickster) salt, as Native Canadian playwright Mary Annharte Baker stresses in an article with the telling title "An Old Indian Trick is to Laugh": "In spite of efforts to declaw, detooth, detail the Coyote or trickster within us, we continue to find some thing about our oppression as Aboriginal people funny" (1991, 48).

As this assessment shows and the subsequent text analyses make apparent, contemporary Native writing contains both gallows humor and survival humor. Since the humor mostly *addresses* rather than distances adverse circumstances and tragic issues (in order to transform them), however, there is a clear tendency towards the latter. Gleason writes, with regard to

Louise Erdrich's *Love Medicine:* "Laughter is not merely a by-product of survival, it is a critical force behind it. Northrop Frye, pointing out humor's regenerative effect, notes that 'something gets born at the end of comedy'" (1987, 66). What "gets born at the end" in the texts by Native writers discussed below are altered representations of Native people, impacting both Euro-American and Native understandings of Nativeness.

Bridging or Widening the Chasm between Cultures?

"Laughter," writes Pfister, "is always a *fait social*. . . . Each instance of laughter is inextricably tied up with social and power relations and framed within a social situation" (2002, vi) — in the case of Native humor, most visibly the fourth world status of North America's indigenous population. Pfister's observation that in societies characterized by a distinction into center and margin "the most significant form of laughter can arise from the margins, challenging and subverting the established orthodoxies, authorities and hierarchies" (vi) calls for a closer scrutiny of humor in Native-White relations. While the question of the effects of humor in Native writing can hardly be determined to conclusiveness (empirical testing being out of the question), an understanding of humor in the texts analyzed below may benefit from some prior theoretical explorations in this direction. Considering the hierarchical situation, can Native humor be a humor of inclusion, a laughing *with*, or must it not by definition be a humor of exclusion, a laughing *at* (see Pfister 2002, ix)? And as a consequence (to polarize, for the sake of the argument), does Native humor bridge or widen the chasm between cultures?

Humor constitutes a form of interaction between self and other — with regard to the subject at hand, either among characters in a given text or between text and reader — that may communicate aggression (against colonial domination) or intercultural cooperation. Two contrasting hypotheses on "Joking and Ethnic Stereotyping" (Zenner 1970) might be helpful for elucidating this question: on the one hand the assumption that "inter-ethnic joking involves depreciation of the out-group and enhances the self-image of the in-group"; or on the other hand that "inter-ethnic joking sidesteps issues of superiority and inferiority and is used as a bond between the in-group and the out-group" (Zenner 1970, 97). To simplify, this would conceptualize humor as a form of separatism or as a mediation strategy, respectively.

Langston Hughes, Black writer and activist, writes about White racists: "Since we have not been able to moralize them out of existence with indignant editorials, maybe we could laugh them to death with well-aimed ridicule" (1957, 12). Indeed, humor can be instrumental in drawing drastic lines between cultural groups. Whenever Native humor has as its target

Euro-American history, values, and characteristics, both in direct interaction[23] and in contemporary Native literature, it can use ridicule as a form of indirect aggression. This puts Euro-American readers in a situation of occupying two of the three standardized positions in humorous interactions (teller, audience, and butt of a joke; see Pfister 2002, vi): They are simultaneously audience and butt of the humor and are thus essentially forced to laugh at themselves. Whereas, by triggering recognition, this can serve as a form of mediation, with strongly offensive humor, it achieves just the opposite. If Euro-American readers deem the subject of laughter inappropriate the effect is not dialog but distancing; "just as one man's meat is another man's poison, one man's joke is another man's offensiveness" (Palmer 1994, 177). Euro-American readers might thus be taken aback by humor at White expense, while Native readers may react quite differently. Humor that disparages the dominant out-group does, after all, according to Zenner's first hypothesis, enhance group solidarity and the image the in-group holds of itself. Native people cannot ignore the power that the dominant Euro-American society holds in North America, because they are constantly confronted with it; but they can try to downplay it through the use of aggressive humor. Purdie writes about the ambivalence inherent in a subordinate group's laughter at the dominant society: " 'laughing at' . . . 'puts people down' in signaling that they are down-put, but that could not happen unless they were originally perceived as 'up' — as in some way holding power over and thus (by definition) potentially threatening the laugher" (1993, 60–61). While being conscious of Euro-American dominance, Native laughter at White expense can thus basically be interpreted as a defiant "declaration that 'You thought you had power over me — but you haven't' " (61).

A more subtle form of drawing boundaries that relies on the cultural relativity of humor may arise from privileging Native readers. Humor may deliberately rely on Native cultural knowledge to such an extent that Euro-American readers are effectively excluded and cannot "get" what is funny. This can, of course, happen unintentionally (see Bruchac 1987b, 23; Taylor 2002, 89–97); but Native writers can also make a conscious decision to make the humor in their texts inaccessible to a non-Native audience. Sherman Alexie calls such insider jokes, which hold a specific subtext for Native people that non-Natives cannot decipher, " 'Indian trapdoors.' You know, Indians fall in, white people just walk right over them" (in Purdy 1997, 15). As humorous "resistance writing" in more than one sense, such texts resist not only Euro-American dominance and oppression but also Euro-American decoding.

The underlying motivations for "separatist" — that is, offensively anti-Euro-American or inaccessible — humor in Native cultures and Native writing are quite obvious: An emphasis on Native-White boundaries and a derision of White power may be considered a necessary defense of Native cultural identity against such forces as cultural appropriation or compulsory assimilation. Yet despite a short-term bonding effect or feeling of moral superiority over the oppressor, such humor contributes little to enhancing Native-White understanding in the long run, since it forecloses productive interaction and dialog. This is exactly the challenge that Native literature needs to rise to, according to Okanagan writer Jeannette C. Armstrong: "Lies need clarification, truth needs to be stated, and resistance to oppression needs to be stated, *without furthering division* and participation in the same racist measures" (1998, 241; emphasis added). Humor in contemporary Native writing is an important means in this process. Exemplifying characteristics described by Zenner's second hypothesis, it forges a link between in-group and out-group. As a mediational strategy, it makes criticism less offensive and emphasizes commonalities without brushing aside extant differences. Dreadful and contested issues can be addressed in ways that avoid the tragic victim pose often ascribed to Native people and that inoffensively trick White readers into trying on (and possibly acknowledging the validity of) Native perspectives. Lincoln's observations with regard to Native cartoons on Indian-White relations may be equally applied to the texts under scrutiny here: They "tone insults toward cultural negotiation. We can laugh at ourselves, . . . laughing with natives laughing at us. This generates an intercultural sense of humor. . . . Both sides double back reflexively to work toward bicultural acceptances of differences" (1993, 101).

The use of humor in the texts under discussion does not serve to gloss over conflicts or to downplay the impact of conquest and colonization; rather, it offers a possibility (sometimes the only possibility) to *confront* these concerns in a nondisruptive manner, as the pleasure gained from humor makes up for the transgressions of established rules and paradigms. As Thomas King puts it in an interview with Drew Hayden Taylor: "You can get in the front door with humor, and you can get into their kitchen with humor. If you're *pounding* on the front door, they won't let you in" (King in Taylor 2000c).[24] Thus, through humor Eurocentric norms and viewpoints can be playfully mocked — or (essentialist) ideas of Nativeness discouraged — without offending Euro-American or Native traditionalist readers. Margaret Atwood describes this effect in King's short stories: "They get the knife in, not by whacking you over the head with their own moral righteousness, but by being funny" (1990, 244). Rather than frivolous entertainment, humor is seen as playing a decisive role in establishing and maintaining a vital dialog about Nativeness and Native-White relations. Thomas King explains about his own, mediational use of humor:

> I think of myself as a dead serious writer. Comedy is simply my strategy. I don't want to whack somebody over the head, because I don't think it accomplishes much at all. There's a fine line to comedy. You have to be funny enough to get them laughing so they really don't feel how hard

you hit them. And the best kind of comedy is where you start off laughing and end up crying, because you realize just what is happening halfway
through the emotion. If I can accomplish that, then I succeed as a storyteller. (in Canton 1998, 96–97)

Reimagining through Humor

Based on an exploration of the intricacies of Native identity and the concepts of representation and identity in general, the discussion has thus far
addressed the need for a revision of representations of Nativeness and subsequently conceptualized the possibilities for such rewriting in Native literature. Through the close interlink between identity and representation,
Native cultural identity has in the past been adversely affected by stereotypes. This same interconnection, however, has been identified as an
opportunity for initiating change. Clichéd and one-dimensional images of
Nativeness and popular notions of "Indians" are deeply engrained in the
(Euro-American and partly also Native) collective imagination. It is only
by engaging *with* these previous discourses and representations that they
can be effectively rendered invalid. Therefore, the imagination was mapped
as *the* terrain for renegotiating Nativeness. As the final part of the discussion showed, humor, because of its entertaining and persuasive characteristics, comprises a perfect instrument for both dispute and mediation in
this context. So how can these findings be synthesized in an approach for
analyzing humor in contemporary Native texts?

"For most Whites, throughout the past five centuries, the Indian of
imagination and ideology has been as real, perhaps more real, than the
Native American of actual existence and contact," writes Berkhofer (1978,
71). The omnipresence of this invented Indian, but, contrastingly, also the
way in which the imagination allows readers to conceive of possible alternatives, make the imagination the most promising site for challenging
degrading images. Humor is closely tied to fantasy and imagination in that
one of humor's pleasures is the way in which it permits transgression of
otherwise rigid frames and conventions. The authors under discussion creatively exploit the border-crossing, mediating, and entertaining potential
of humor and imagination for transforming the audience's previous conceptualizations of Nativeness and Native-White relations and history.
Neither the line between imagination and reality, nor that between Native
and Euro-American modes of representation, let alone that between
humor and tragedy, is as firm as usually believed: Invented images influence real people's identities, and Native writers make use of both Native
and Western narrative traditions to intervene in this very process. In the
tradition of Native tricksters, they transgress established categories and
open up a liminal space[25] in which readers shed their cultural baggage and

leave behind fixed identifications and hierarchical assumptions. It is through liberating laughter that readers are transported to such a transitional space or state of liminality "betwixt and between the positions assigned and arrayed by law, custom, convention, and ceremonial" (Turner 1969, 95). At the interface between imagination and reality, images and identities, Native and Euro-American signifying codes and frames of reference, and humor and tragedy, established values and habituated patterns of interpretation are annulled. Outside their familiar interpretive patterns, readers are free to reevaluate their own perspectives and epistemologies and to imaginatively assume alternative viewpoints. This is facilitated by the fact that humor also brings unfamiliar issues closer by ignoring any accustomed and respectful distance. Bakhtin writes that

> all comical creativity works in a zone of maximal proximity. Laughter has the remarkable power of making an object come up close, of drawing it into a zone of crude contact where one can finger it familiarly on all sides, turn it upside down, inside out, peer at it from above and below, break open its external shell, look into its center, doubt it, take it apart, dismember it, lay it bare and expose it, examine it freely and experiment with it. Laughter . . . [clears] the ground for an absolutely free investigation of it. (1981, 23)

It is from this peculiarly detached and yet very immediate position that the opportunity of dialog arises. This unfamiliar perspective allows for a renegotiation and reassessment not only of stereotypical ideas or essentialist positions as such, but also of the very frames of reference that generated these conceptualizations of Nativeness, Native-White history, or present Native-White relations. Humor may therefore induce readers to question the validity of Western epistemologies and master narratives or of an essentialist outlook on Native identity on a scope that vastly exceeds the level of the single text. Purdie maintains that "it is possible . . . to produce comedy which challenges the basis of social codings and explores living with different ones as a real possibility. Just as repressive ideologies often operate by tiny 'snowflakes' of effects that build to huge drifts of constraints, so many small inroads will shift them" (1993, 148). Instances of humor in contemporary Native writing are such small inroads, slowly shifting representations of Nativeness away from the stereotypical "Indian" as the only possibility of identification and towards more complex and diverse images.

The considerable transformative force ascribed to humor within this approach obviously largely derives from its capacity to make us see things in a new way. But it is also based on humor's potential for making us all the same in a Bakhtinian sense, that is, to level hierarchies and create mutual solidarity (resembling what Turner described as *communitas;* 1969, 96). Laughing not only triggers a "shock of recognition of common humanity" (see Eckardt 1992, 23), showing the readers Native characters that in no way resemble the usual Hollywood stage props; it also in a trick-sterlike fashion mobilizes identification, since shared laughter indicates the shared assessment of the subject of laughter. When readers are tricked into laughing *with* Native characters, narrators, or authors *at* stereotypical or restrictive conceptualizations of Nativeness (regardless of whether these are of Euro-American or Native origin) and notions of Euro-American superiority, they thus subscribe to and identify with more differentiated Native viewpoints, more timely, multilayered, and critical representations of Nativeness.

The following text analyses explore how Native writers, through their use of humor and imagination, thus "liberate Nativeness" and Native-White history towards more complexity for both Native and Euro-American readers. "Once the Indian is free to imagine his own destiny or plot — and, incredibly, to empower himself through laughter at others as well as himself — he escapes from the gothic dialectic that demands nothing less than his doom (and gloom)," writes Louis Owens (1998, 92). The humorous and reimaginative revisions offered by the contemporary Native texts discussed in the following indeed help Native readers to escape restrictive definitions and depictions. Ultimately, these texts thus contribute to Native cultural survival.

Notes

[1] As Owens's comment already indicates, I explore the connection between representation and *cultural* or *collective identity* rather than individual or personal identity — though, of course, the two forms are directly interrelated through processes of identification. In the following, "cultural" or "collective" identity is used according to Jan Assmann's definition of the term, which also takes into consideration that identity is a flexible concept, an ongoing process rather than a fixed essence: "As a *collective* or *we-identity* we understand the image which a group builds of itself and with which the members identify. Collective identity is a question of *identification* on the part of the individuals involved. It does not exist *per se*, but only to the extent to which particular individuals confess to it. It is as strong or weak as it is alive in and manages to motivate the thoughts and actions of its members" (Assmann 1997, 132; my translation).

[2] While I am aware that there is no single form of "contemporary Native existence" and the Native cultural identities and processes of identity formation are as diverse as the groups of Native people in North America, I work with this generalization to explore some of the factors and tendencies pertaining to the majority of Native people.

[3] For a comprehensive list of "good" and "bad" Indian stereotypes see Vickers (1998, 4–5, 36); see also Berkhofer (1978, 28) and Lutz (2002, 49), who both point to the basic duality of the "Indian" stereotype.

[4] There are, of course, many further factors from the fields of popular literature, the media, education, politics, anthropology, and historiography, as discussed in greater detail in Bataille and Silet (1980), Bataille (2001), Berkhofer (1978), Churchill (1992), P. Deloria (1998), Kilpatrick (1999), Lutz (1985), and Stedman (1982).

[5] For a concise account of the legal definitions by which Canada and the USA determine who is Indian see McMaster (1995). For the legal and historical/anthropological aspects of this question see Bordewich (1996, 65–68, 72–74) for the USA and Lawrence (2000) for Canada.

[6] See Assmann: "The consciousness of social belonging which we call 'collective identity' is based on the participation in a shared knowledge and memory which is created through the use of a shared language or, more generally, a shared system of symbols" (1997, 139; my translation).

[7] From the Navajo or Diné, as they call themselves, for example, Witherspoon reports that "reality was created or transformed as a manifestation of symbolic form. In the Navajo view of the world, language is not a mirror of reality; reality is a mirror of language" (1977, 34).

[8] For such processes to be effective, however, it takes time and a growing readership. A critical look at audiences of Native writing reveals difficulties yet to be overcome. Due to economic reasons, a lower-than-average literacy rate, geographical isolation, or diverging interests, the indigenous readership of Native texts has so far remained limited (see Forbes 1987, 21). Thus while many Native authors claim to write predominantly or even exclusively for a Native audience, they realistically have to admit that it is hard to reach this group in substantial numbers. Then again, many of the White readers of Native literature are interested in and relatively informed about Native issues anyway, and thus may not constitute the primary target audience for overcoming stereotypes. Isernhagen nonetheless argues that Native literature contributes to contemporary cultural identity formation, claiming that "there is only an apparent paradox in native literature with a still comparatively small and diversified audience aspiring to contribute decisively to the formation of a group consciousness. Firstly, the aspiration of any kind of literature 'to write the consciousness of its race' — a perfectly classic aspiration, of course — almost always appears ludicrous if one compares the numerical relation between its real (reading) audience and the entire population of the group: literature, *as literature*, has a small audience. And secondly, . . . the creation of newly emergent literatures (with their aspirations and with their real effects) cannot go forward except in parallel with the creation of audiences for them" (1991, 193). Contemporary Native literature will therefore have to co-create its audience.

[9] Writers aiming at a broad Native and non-Native audience have to find a balance between retaining a text's (culturally specific) Native characteristics and making it accessible to a non-Native readership. While it is desirable that especially a non-Native audience take unfamiliar perspectives, to alienate Euro-American readers with material that is too foreign to them will obviously not accomplish much either. Due to the heterogeneity of Native cultures, the level of understanding of Native readers will also vary according to their respective background. Depending on the Native author's own experiences, finally, the writing may be as much determined

by the author's immersion into a Western cultural (and often academic) system as by his or her respective Native background.

[10] Pratt points out that the term was coined in the 1940s by the Cuban sociologist Fernando Ortiz to replace the simplifying concepts of acculturation and assimilation commonly applied to situations of conquest or colonization. It was used in an ethnographic framework to "describe processes whereby members of the subordinated or marginal groups select and invent from materials transmitted by a dominant or metropolitan culture" (M. L. Pratt 1991, 36).

[11] Hybridity generally describes a state that results from the mixture of elements from (most often two) disparate systems, entities, or groups that were originally incompatible. The term originates from biological usage where it describes the reproduction of organisms from two different species to form a hybrid descendent. Vivan (like Bhabha) suggests that through processes of hybridization elements are combined "to compound a new and creolized organism or product" (Vivan 2000, 3). Goetsch, on the other hand, points out that hybridity does not imply a merger in which two formerly disparate entities fully blend into each other to form a new one, but a mixture or patchwork in which fragments of the original entities remain detectable: "If [the term hybridity] suggests mixture, then not in such a way that the parts blend into a new entity, but rather as combinations of still recognizable fragments" (Goetsch 1997, 137, my translation).

[12] Horne thus ignores the fact that the potential to disrupt colonial authority, according to Bhabha, is inherent in *all* forms of mimicry; instead, she reduces colonial mimicry to mere imitation of and identification with colonial paradigms, claiming that "the colonial mimic often loses sight of his/her differences in efforts to become like the colonizer" (1999, 13).

[13] At the same time, the application of paradigms from postcolonial theory to Native North American issues is not unproblematic for various reasons: First of all, North America's Native cultures are fourth world nations. The annexation of their original land base is irreversible rather than temporary, and despite efforts towards self-government Native people are still to a large extent under colonial rule — circumstances that foreclose the interpretation of "post" in a temporal sense (see Krupat 1996, 30–31; Owens 2001, 15). Further, as Thomas King implies in "Godzilla vs. Post-Colonial" (1990), to view Native literatures in a postcolonial framework neglects the existence of precontact Native cultural expressions and Eurocentrically reduces Native literature to a response to/result of White presence. Finally, while postcolonial literary theory takes into consideration the complexities of colonial power and hierarchies, it is at risk to remain caught within Western epistemologies itself and most often fails to integrate Native paradigms for the analysis of Native writing. The present approach tries to integrate both Western and Native voices and paradigms into the analysis of humor in contemporary Native writing.

[14] Purdy apparently uses this neologism to blend the prefix "re-" with the beginning of "image." In the following, I use "remagine" when referring specifically to Purdy's text, but "reimagine" for the concept developed here.

[15] The term humor in its current usage is relatively recent (for the origins and development of the term see Hoffmann 1985, 142–43; Rishel 2002, 33–34; and Levin 1972, 7–8, 13). Stemming from the Latin word for moisture or fluid,

"humor" was used to designate the four body fluids — choler (bile), melancholy, phlegm, and blood — and subsequently also the psychological dispositions or temperaments resulting for persons in which one of the fluids was in excess, disturbing the normal balance or "good humor." In the seventeenth century Ben Johnson composed plays or comedies on the various humor types, introducing "humorous" characters into comedy. In this function humor also started to be used for temporary moods a person displayed and thus gradually came to be largely synonymous with "mood" during the eighteenth century. Whereas a "humorist" thus initially designated a moody, whimsical eccentric, it gradually "shifted from the objective to the subjective mood, and from the passive to the active sense" (Levin 1972, 13), that is, from the humorous characters whose eccentricities where described to the person who described these eccentricities to the amusement of others.

[16] See Eckardt (1992, 63, 67, 71); Edmunds (1976, 143–44); Fine (1983, 160); Lewis (1989, 34); Morreall (1983, 15–19); Palmer (1994, 93–102); and Rishel (2002, 279–81).

[17] This definition draws on Morreall (1983) and to some extent Rishel (2002). While laughter is what results from (and thus is not synonymous with) humor, terms such as humor, comedy, wit, quip, and joke are less easy to distinguish. Theorists tend to either use them synonymously or distinguish them according to vastly differing criteria (see Hoffmann 1985, 142, 145, 147; Lincoln 1993, 32–33; Lewis 1989, 8–14; or Rishel 2002, 82, 87–88). Humor in the following is used as the generic term, while other terms describe particular occurrences of humor. Comedy refers exclusively to the genre, while the adjective comic/comical is used interchangeably with humorous. Wit, though not clearly discriminate from humor, mostly refers to a character trait; jokes or quips, finally, are considered specific, strongly condensed realizations of humor.

[18] See Bruchac (1987b, 29); V. Deloria (1977, 146–67); Lincoln (1993, 5, 23, 29–30); Lowe (1994); Theisz (1989); and Ryan (1999, xiii).

[19] This also implies, however, that if the "conceptual schemes" of people from different cultures diverge too vastly, they cannot understand each other's humor (which leads some theorists to the notion that jokes are "untranslateable"; see Purdie 1993, 171). Or, as Drew Hayden Taylor describes it: "Venturing outside [your] sphere of knowledge can reveal your ignorance and affect the nature of your humour" (2005, 74). The analysis of Native humor by a cultural outsider such as myself thus by definition, to some extent, constitutes a precarious undertaking.

[20] I therefore disagree with Thomas King's definition of Native humor, which is based on the criterion of audience rather than producer of the humor: "I'm not sure that a valid definition of Native humour exists. If I were threatened with bodily harm, I would probably find myself saying that Native humour is humour that makes Native people laugh, and hope that you didn't ask me to define a Native" (2005, 170). Such a definition would not only declare anything that makes Native people laugh (be it Charlie Brown or Jay Leno) Native humor, it would also entirely exclude a non-Native audience. It is here, however, that humor most prominently figures as an intercultural mediator, as is discussed in more detail below.

[21] Both "Native" and "Euro-American" humor, the categories that suggest themselves for such a comparison, are, of course, rather heterogeneous in themselves.

What is referred to as "Euro-American humor" here is also influenced by non-European cultures and traditions, since immigrants of African and Asian descent have also contributed to and shaped what today is conflated as "American humor." In the only monograph on Native American humor to date, Lincoln sets out to analyze Native humor in much the same vein as American humor in general. He claims that just as the American Renaissance preceded the Native American Renaissance, providing a kind of template (a rather hazardous claim in itself), "so Constance Rourke's 'study of the national character' in *American Humor* (1931) provides an analogue for our analysis of Indian humor. The obvious differences of history and culture do not obviate the useful 'American' parallels, as Western theory and tribal context intersect" (Lincoln 1993, 52–53). It goes without saying that the current analysis attempts to avoid a mainstreaming of Native cultures.

[22] I disagree with Kelly's first assessment that the two views that Native humor has either always been part of the oral tradition or arose as a response to the trauma of colonization "cancel each other out. . . . Either we've always had humour and laughter pumping through the veins of our culture (witness the legends and stories), or we developed humour as a reaction to a history of being dispossessed" (2005, 63). Rather, I subscribe to his later specification that Native humor did not originate in, but has obviously been strongly affected by, the experience of colonization: "Perhaps the last couple of centuries have sharpened and honed our wit, but laughter has echoed across Turtle Island for centuries" (2005, 63–64).

[23] V. Deloria (1977, 146–67) provides numerous examples of jokes and puns at White expense. Basso, in his analysis of "the Whiteman" as a social category and cultural symbol among the Western Apache, observes that the Apache impersonate White people in mocking ridicule, "portray[ing] them as gross incompetents in the conduct of social relations" (1979, 48).

[24] See also Hanay Geiogamah's production notes to his play *Foghorn* (1980, 49); and Drew Hayden Taylor's comment: "I've always thought the best way to reach somebody wasn't through preaching or instructing, but through humour" (2002, 95).

[25] Based on van Gennep's (1909) work on liminal ("threshold") phases in rituals of initiation, in the 1960s cultural anthropologist Victor Turner developed the concept of liminality as an explanatory model for complex social processes, arguing that in processes of social transition the individual undergoes a phase of liminality that is outside of established hierarchies, space, or time concepts (see Stierstorfer 2001; Turner 1969, 1977).

3: Expressing Humor in Contemporary Native Writing: Forms

AFTER THESE THEORETICAL CONSIDERATIONS, it is high time we look at some texts. While a formal analysis of humor in contemporary Native literature cannot (and should not) be conducted in disregard of thematic issues, in the following I focus predominantly on the means and strategies that authors employ to achieve comic effects — the question of *how* humor is conveyed. The topics, functions, and effects of such humor, that is, the question of *what* such humor deals with and *why* it is used in a specific context, is explored in chapter four. As pointed out above, most of the writers discussed here draw on both Western and Native traditions and work with, rather than outside of, previous discourses. Consequently, the forms of humor they use originate from both Western literary and Native oral traditions and are explored according to criteria deriving from either set of cultural paradigms. Each form or variety is briefly introduced before its use in contemporary Native texts is illustrated by brief examples or close readings.[1] The "categories" into which the wide range of literary, linguistic, and cultural means of humorous expression have been divided are not to be understood as mutually exclusive, however. Quite in contrast, it is often impossible to assign a particular textual example to just one category. Parody, for instance, builds on intertextuality, just as wordplay may be used to allude to something, or dramatic irony may be anchored in oral storytelling techniques; yet for the sake of clarity, these are discussed under separate headings.

Irony and Sarcasm

Irony is one of the most frequently used forms of humorous expression in contemporary Native writing. It can occur in the characters' and/or narrator's direct ironical utterances; but it can also be expressed in the author's design of the text — for example, through plot, register, or perspective.[2] While to define irony seems an almost impossible undertaking (see Barbe 1995, 71; Booth 1974, 2), a most general description is that in irony the implied or intended meaning differs from or even opposes the ostensibly expressed meaning. More specifically, the implied meaning subverts the straightforward or surface meaning, which makes irony "the intentional transmission of both information and evaluative attitude other than what is explicitly presented" (Hutcheon 1995b, 11).[3] Irony is not always easy to detect, because it depends, on the one hand, on the obliqueness or directness of the clues provided by the author, such as, for instance, meiosis, hyperbole, litotes, antiphrasis, *reductio ad absurdum*, metonymy, or innuendo (see Barbe 1995, 71), and, on the other hand, on a shared situational and sociocultural background, that is, shared experience and knowledge. Irony can thus be described as an unstable joint venture of the ironist (that is, speaker/character or author), who intends an utterance or situation to be ironic, and the interpreter, who has to attribute an ironic meaning to it (see Hutcheon 1995b, 11). Rather than invariably producing one fixed interpretation, it is a negotiation of meaning that "happens in the space *between* (and including) the said and the unsaid; it needs both to happen" (Hutcheon 1995b, 12–13). The ironic meaning arises from a true interaction of the explicitly stated and the implied, incorporating both.

This makes irony especially well suited for negotiating Nativeness in a way that integrates preexisting representations (as a surface meaning) but simultaneously undercuts them (in the implied assessment). There is, of course, always the risk that some readers might not notice particular ironies or might be offended by them; if irony succeeds, however, it is highly integrative and among the most effective means to trigger a shift in perspective and identification. "Recourse to irony by an author tends to convey an implicit compliment to the intelligence of readers, who are invited to associate themselves with the author, and the knowing minority who are not taken in by the ostensible meaning" (Abrams 1999, 135). On the one hand, readers can therefore feel flattered by their successful decoding of the irony. On the other hand, by acknowledging the irony, they laughingly recognize the author/ironist as a kindred spirit whose assessment of who- or whatever is mocked (even if it is themselves) they implicitly share — even if they come from a vastly different cultural background.

Jack Forbes's "An Incident on a Tour Among the Natives" demonstrates this effect. In this short story, William, a Native writer on a reading tour through Britain (which makes the title itself ironic), is faced with the stereotypical expectations of a British woman in the audience. In their conversation, the woman admits that before encountering William she had conceptualized Indians as "well . . . I don't like the word 'primitive' but, well, I mean, rather unsophisticated and not at all Westernised. But you seem educated and, if I may say so, quite refined" (1995, 18). William first tries to correct her misconceptions quite factually. Eventually, however, he resorts to irony: He not only claims to be "very primitive and not nearly so sophisticated as I might seem" (18); when admiringly asked how he keeps in shape he declares: " 'I like to chase antelopes.' 'Really?' 'Yes, and buffalo, too. I catch them bare-handed and eat them raw' " (20). By overconfirming the woman's clichéd expectations with hyperbole, exaggerating the stereotype of the buffalo-hunting Plains warrior, irony works to make the readers laugh at and consequently rethink and reimagine the woman's (and possibly their own) ideas about "Indians." By laughing at the woman's ignorance and with William's retorts, they effortlessly identify with the Native character in this story and are effectively shown the reductive and degrading nature of "Indian" clichés. As becomes clear, it is only the woman's uninformed and stereotypical ideas about Native people that deserve the label "primitive" here.

Irony may be used to camouflage disapproval where open protest or criticism is not an option. Sherman Alexie's short story "The Approximate Size of My Favorite Tumor" exemplifies such a use of irony in a situation of (colonial) oppression and racism. In an act of police arbitrariness, the Native couple Jimmy and Norma are stopped by a (White) police officer who charges them with having "failed to make a proper signal for a turn a few blocks down" (1994, 164) — even though they had been driving straight on the highway for several miles. Since Jimmy knows that directly offending the officer would only lead to further random charges, he uses irony to protest the officer's racism and to vent his own frustration. When the officer illegally fines them for ninety-nine dollars — knowing that they have exactly one hundred dollars on them — Jimmy tells him:

> "Take it all. That extra dollar is a tip, you know? Your service has been excellent."
> Norma wanted to laugh, then. She covered her mouth and pretended to cough. His face turned red, I mean redder that it already was.
> "In fact," I said as I looked at the trooper's badge, "I might just send a letter to your commanding officer. I'll just write that Washington State Patrolman D. Nolan, badge number 13746, was polite, courteous, and above all, legal as an eagle." (166)

Since he cannot frankly express his opinion without facing penalty, Jimmy makes use of irony's characteristic double coding to obviously compliment yet implicitly condemn the patrolman's despotic behavior. This strategy becomes even more apparent when the enraged policeman threatens arrest and Norma flatters/threatens him back with promoting/ruining his reputation: "If you do , . . . I'll just tell everyone how respectful you were of our Native traditions, how much you understood about the social conditions that lead to the criminal acts of so many Indians. I'll say you were sympathetic, concerned, and intelligent" (166). Most amusingly, irony in this context substitutes for more direct criticism. Called "a kind of intellectual tear-gas that breaks the nerves and paralyses the muscles of everyone in its vicinity" by Northrop Frye (1975, 115), rather than a strategy of politeness, as it is sometimes characterized, irony is a powerful weapon against oppression in situations were no other defense is available.

With regard to the representation and self-conceptualization of colonized/oppressed groups, irony moreover may subvert colonial modes of representation from within, mimicking the dominant discourse on the surface, yet sabotaging it through the implied meaning or subtext — what Hutcheon called "double-voiced" or split discourse (see 1992, 13; 1995b, 133). "Saying one thing and meaning another is," as Hutcheon points out, "by definition, a dialogic or doubled mode of address. And any attempt to juggle simultaneously both literal and ironic meanings cannot help but disrupt our notions of meaning as single, decidable, or stable" (1992, 13). Irony therefore constitutes a powerful strategy for undermining hegemonic ideologies, authoritative Western claims to Truth and the power ensuing from them, as postulated in Foucault's power/knowledge paradigm. It enables Native writers to expose how particular discourses and epistemologies inherently construct and substantiate colonial superiority. While this is especially apparent in the thematic explorations of chapter four, the examples just discussed already illustrate how irony, because of its inherent doubleness, both amuses and subverts. "Operating almost as a form of guerrilla warfare, irony is said to work to change how people interpret," writes Hutcheon (1995b, 32), and this is exactly how Native writers use it: By offering both familiar situations or images *and* their re-presentations, irony in effect changes readers' perspectives and allegiances, humorously dislocating the image of "the Indian" and accustomed interpretations of Native-White interaction.

Whereas there are varying opinions on how to distinguish sarcasm from irony, it is mostly agreed upon that sarcasm is less subtle than irony (see Barbe 1995, 27; Feinberg 1967, 180; Muecke 1970, 51). With sarcasm, the underlying meaning is more easily recognizable and can hardly be ignored — which is why it may be less entertaining, less funny, and thus ultimately less diplomatic (see Barbe 1995, 28). Much of irony's delight, after all, derives from the audience's deciphering of the implied meaning that the ironist wants to convey. When Jeannette C. Armstrong starts her poem "Indian Woman" with "I am a squaw / a heathen / a savage / basically a mammal" (1998, 229), readers straight away know better than to take these words at face value. Furthermore, while irony may also comprise gentle, almost benevolent mockery, sarcasm, deriving from the Greek *sarkazein* ("to tear flesh") is always a form of crude assault, which is why it is sometimes not classified as humor at all. Admittedly, sarcasm may be dark and bitter, coming closest to the previous conceptualization of humor as separatism. Nevertheless, it ought to be considered in the framework of a humorous renegotiation of Nativeness, since it is frequently used as a coping tool and weapon against misrepresentation and oppression. It is not surprising, then, to find that in the context of Native writing the choice of sarcasm strongly correlates with specific thematic fields: It most often targets the darkest sides of colonization, be they genocide, cultural destruction, structural racism and discrimination, or poor living conditions for Native people. The opening scene of Hanay Geiogamah's play *Foghorn* makes use of such biting sarcasm when a United States senator explains: "The Indian problem is a matter for the courts and the Congress to deal with. We've been victorious over them on the battlefield, now they must settle on the reservations we have generously set aside for them. They have stood in the way of our great American Manifest Destiny long enough" (1980, 53). Brutal conquest and colonization in this announcement are highlighted rather than disguised by nostalgic regret or alleged charity in the face of the supposedly inevitable. As Geiogamah's use of sarcasm implies, while Euro-America laments the Vanishing Indian, it mobilizes considerable energies to ensure that Native people will vanish for good. Drew Hayden Taylor exposes a similarly patronizing and revisionist Euro-Canadian attitude in a Canadian MP's allegation that the status of Canada's Native people resembled that of "children living on a South Sea island, financially supported by an over anxious rich uncle." Taylor uses acerbic humor to comment on the alleged Native "privileges": "To put it bluntly, our secret is out. The last five hundred years of oppression, geno-cide, brainwashing, disease and other assorted afflictions were all a vast and incredibly well managed smoke screen. The truth is, it was all an ingenious master plan to achieve this wonderfully luxurious and envied position we now relish" (1998, 40). Taylor's sarcastic mock-admission expresses a combination of incredulity (at such ignorance and arrogance), bitterness (at how clearly history is written by the victors), and humor (to be able to continue). Such humor is obviously pungent, but it nevertheless more effectively aligns readers with a critical Native perspective than would assailing the MP's irrational and presumptuous statement with rationality and statistics.

Sherman Alexie is probably the Native author who most frequently uses sarcasm today. His imaginative revisions of history and bleak depic-tions of reservation reality mercilessly illuminate the darkest corners of past and present Native existence. The full force of Alexie's sarcasm is exempli-fied in the "Ten Commandments as Given by the United States of America to the Spokane Indians," which Thomas Builds-the-Fire, the protagonist of Alexie's novel *Reservation Blues*, notes down in his journal. Using the form and structure of the biblical ten commandments (which also marks it as parody), Alexie's cynical adaptation attacks the still devastating conse-quences of colonization for Native people: racism in legal matters — "You shall not give false testimony against any white men, but they will tell lies about you and I will believe them and convict you"; the forced Native dependence on government support due to the destruction of traditional ways of sustenance — "Remember the first of each month by keeping it holy. The rest of the month you shall go hungry, but the first day of the month is a tribute to me, and you shall receive welfare checks and com-modity food in exchange for your continued dependence"; the social injus-tice and poverty on the reservation — "You shall not covet the white man's

house. You shall not covet the white man's wife, or his hopes and opportunities, his cars or VCRs, or anything else that belongs to the white man";
and the disregard of Native land claims — "You shall not steal back what
I have already stolen from you" (1996a, 154–55). Through its very
brusqueness Alexie's sarcasm achieves several things at once. It first of all
points to Euro-American injustice and hypocrisy in the dominant society's
dealings with Native people, and to the consequences arising from such
policies. And it lets readers glimpse some of the bitterness that arises from
these circumstances. Yet it still avoids the "Indian lament" stance that characterized much Native writing in the 1970s. In rewriting the Bible, of all
texts, Alexie both subverts the authority of this Western master narrative
and highlights the complicity of the church in the project of colonization,
which was, after all, frequently justified in terms of the Christian civilizing
mission. And finally, by equating the US government with the vengeful
and volatile God of the Old Testament, he implicitly accuses it of arbitrary
cruelty and exposes America's self-conceptualization as a chosen people as
a self-serving myth. Like irony, sarcasm thus inherently combines humor
and subversion. By expressing protest in a less concealed way, however, it
allows Native writers to vent some of the bitterness that arises from ongoing injustice, oppression, and misrepresentation. It might therefore help
Native readers exorcise pain in liberating laughter in the most direct way.

Satire, Parody, Burlesque, and Caricature

Satire, with its explicit mockery, most openly relies on humor as an instrument of criticism, be it of individuals, social conditions, images, or patterns
of interpretation.[4] In tone, it can range from mild ridicule to biting scorn,
evoking amusement or contempt, deriding its target in order to expose a
perceived incongruity or fault. It is thus comprised of two components:
"One is wit or humour, the other an object of attack. Attack without
humour, or pure denunciation, thus forms one of the boundaries of satire;
humour without attack, the humour of pure gaiety or exuberance, is the
other" (Frye 1975, 109). Within these boundaries, theorists disagree about
the main emphasis. Some argue that satire is chiefly a means of reforming
society by critically exposing its stupidity or evil (see Rishel 2002, 141;
Hellenthal 1989, 60). Others place a stronger emphasis on its amusing
aspects: "Satire may criticize evil but the didactic elements are incidental,
not primary. The essential quality is entertainment" (Feinberg 1967, 7). In
my opinion, it is in the mélange of both aspects that satire's secret lies: By
being entertaining, it holds the readers' attention despite addressing controversial issues; it allows for criticism by making it more palatable.

Northrop Frye argues that "in order to attack anything, satirist and
audience must agree on its undesirability" (1975, 110). Yet this describes

an outcome rather than initial agreement, since it is the merit of the writer to *present* an object in such a way as to *make* the audience consider what is satirized as undesirable through the process of satiric representation. Much like irony,[5] therefore, satire characteristically unites readers in an agreement on the satirist's viewpoint. For Native writers, it constitutes a means of deriding commonly held clichés of Nativeness or hypocritical representations of Native-White history. Satire is often characterized as concerning itself with the extratextual reality. Yet, "unlike other arts, which emphasize what *is* real, satire emphasizes what *seems* to be real but is not. It ridicules men's naïve acceptance of individuals and institutions at face value" (Feinberg 1967, 3). Satire thus operates on the metalevel of representations, which makes it well suited for exposing the simulacrum of "the Indian" for what it is — a cliché that lacks an authentic basis. Diane Burns's "Sure You Can Ask Me a Personal Question," for instance, by its sheer hyperbolic accumulation of familiar clichés satirically deconstructs representations of "the Indian" held in the Euro-American collective imagination. Providing a Native woman's side of a conversation with an implied interlocutor, the poem candidly exposes the latter's stereotypical perceptual frames:

No, not Apache.
No, not Navajo.
  No, not Sioux.
No, we are not extinct.
  Yes, Indin . . . .
Yeah, it was awful what you guys did to us.
  It's real decent of you to apologize.
No, I don't know where you can get peyote.
  No, I don't know where you can get Navajo rugs real cheap.
No, I didn't make this. I bought it at Bloomingdales.
  Thank you. I like your hair, too.
I don't know if anyone knows whether or not Cher is really Indian.
  No, I didn't make it rain tonight.
Yeah. Uh-huh. Spirituality.
  Uh-huh. Yeah, Spirituality. Uh-huh. Mother
Earth. Yeah. Uh-huh. Uh-huh. Spirituality.
  No, I didn't major in archery.
Yeah, a lot of us drink too much.
  Some of us can't drink enough.
This ain't no stoic look.
  This is my face.   (1983, 40)

As the example demonstrates, the immediate effects of satire are deconstructive rather than transformative. It mostly leaves the imaginative work of reconstructing alternative images up to the reader (in contrast to, for instance, irony, which in itself may present both deconstruction and

alternative). Yet in humorously showing the familiar in a new light, it offers
fresh perspectives and dislodges readers from accustomed patterns of interpretation. "Satirists . . . look at familiar conditions from a perspective
which makes these conditions seem foolish, harmful, or affected. Satire jars
us out of complacence into a pleasantly shocked realization that many of
the values we unquestioningly accept are false" (Feinberg 1967, 16). It is
this potential of satire that Native authors draw on for dissecting stereotypical images and ideas. Satire not only exposes the images or ideas themselves to liberating and literally "unsettling" laughter, however; it also
discloses their underlying (hypocritical and biased) assumptions.

Hanay Geiogamah's play *Foghorn* makes extensive use of satire in this
vein. In an exemplary scene, the First Lady of the United States — clearly
modeled on Lady Bird Johnson and her conservationist endeavors —
delivers a speech on the occasion of dedicating a national park. To be more
specific, she declares an Indian reservation a national park, because the
"Indians get very little use of them anyway" (1980, 69) — a comment that
echoes the earlier settlers' rationalizations for taking Native land. Against
the background of cheap recorded applause and "America the Beautiful,"
she addresses the assembled (partly Native) audience:

> Thank you. Thank yoooou. I want to say right away that I have never seen
> such lovely, stoic faces as those of our Indian friends here with us
> today. Just look at those beautiful facial lines, those high cheekbones,
> those wonderfully well-rounded lips, those big dark eyes. And their cos-
> tumes. Aren't they simply too beautiful? Let's-give-them-a-big-hand-
> ladies-and-gentlemen, let's-give-them-a-big-hand . . . . I know, I just
> know they are going to be wonderful assets to the new national recre-
> ational park which I am here with you today to dedicate. In the next few
> years, there will be hundreds-of-pretty-pictures-of-these-colorful, uh,
> Indian natives, taken-here-in-this-neeyew park of ours, adding the
> excitement of a great outdoors vacation in the great American West to
> family photo albums in homes all across our land. Isn't-that-wonderful?
> (68–69)

Geiogamah combines *reductio ad absurdum* in his treatment of Native
people (who are only perceived in terms of their physiognomy and pic-
turesqueness) with hyperbole in the character's exaggerated pronunciation
and register (taken from official representations, popular entertainment,
and tourism) to satirize the stereotype of the stoic Indian and noble savage. The audience, in laughing at the speaker's ignorance and shallowness,
is induced to reconsider their own preconceptions about Native people
and to examine whether they themselves may (unwittingly) participate in
the commodification of Native cultures or hold similarly Disneyesque conceptualizations of Native people. Geiogamah's play "help[s] audiences
exorcise [stereotypes] with knowledgeable laughter" (Huntsman 1980,
xviii). Together with sarcasm, satire thus falls among the most openly

manipulative or political means of expressing humor. While it does not transform or replace previous misrepresentations, it works towards reassessment, humorously provoking a reevaluation of previously held opinions and ideas. With regard to representations of Nativeness, it offers readers a glimpse behind the stoic face of the cigar-store Indian and exposes fabrications like the "White Man's Indian" (Berkhofer) or Euro-American "superiority" to blatant ridicule.

Parody is sometimes subsumed under the wider category of satire because it also mockingly targets a preexisting condition. It differs from satire, however, first in that it concentrates on preformed literary or historical *textual* material;[6] secondly, in that it does not necessarily concern itself with the extratextual reality; and finally, in that it proceeds by transforming rather than just exposing its subject matter. As a specific form of intertextual allusion that involves imitation plus humor or mockery (see Dentith 2000, 6, 193), parody may be characterized as a "critical refunctioning of preformed literary material with comic effect [, which] makes the object of attack part of its own structure, and thus also depends in part on the reader's conditioned reaction to this object of attack for the response to itself" (M. Rose 1979, 35). That is, as outlined for the reimaginative use of humor in general, parody in contemporary Native writing depends on and works with the readers' familiarity with preexisting representations of Nativeness in order to transform these. Rather than just ridiculing the hypotext's contents, parody extends to the very mode of representation, the literary and/or historical conventions and paradigms characterizing the hypotext. Parody is thus especially attuned to exposing how discourses in fact determine or constitute their subjects (rather than merely presenting them). It is a potent means of undercutting the authority claims of realistic representation, and — like satire — attacks not only degrading images or ideas as such but also the ontology and epistemologies they are based on.

Osage writer Carter Revard's "Report to the Nation: Claiming Europe" serves to illustrate how parodic Native texts raise preexisting reader expectations (through mimicry of the hypotext), but then proceed to defy these expectations. Through incongruities between hypo- and hypertext, they trigger a humorous, reimaginative shift of the readers' frames of reference. For this purpose, Revard appropriates the discourse of exploration accounts and travelogues, and parodically infuses it with a literally reversed orientation.[7] The text imitates the narrative mode of Columbus's diary and later reports from the New World, but applies this style, structure, and line of argument to the description of a Native journey to Europe. Consequently, readers are, for once, presented with an ethnocentrically *Native* point of view when the text's narrator, an Osage explorer introduced as "Special Agent Wazhazhe" (which is how the Osage refer to themselves), reports back to his nation:

When I claimed England for the Osage Nation last month, some of the English chiefs objected. They said the Thames is not the Thames until it's past Oxford; above Oxford, it is two streams, the Isis and the Cherwell. So even though I'd taken a Thames excursion boat and on the way formally proclaimed from the deck, with several Germans and some Japanese tourists for witnesses, that all the land this river drained was ours, these Oxford chiefs maintained our title was not good, except below their Folly Bridge at most . . . So I said the hell with England for this trip and went to France and rented a little Renault in Paris and drove down past the Chateaux to Biarritz, stopping only to proclaim that everything the Loire and the Seine flowed past was ours . . . . Whether they understood that France now belongs to us was not clear, but they were friendly and they fed me well, accepting in return some pretty paper and some metal discs with which they seemed very pleased; if they are this credulous we shouldn't have much trouble bargaining with them when we come to take the rest of France. (Revard 1983, 166–67)[8]

Revard, through his comic inversion, not only mocks and exposes the way in which European explorers took for granted that their claims were justified, and that glass beads and other worthless trinkets constituted an appropriate compensation (offering Western readers an unfamiliar perspective on their own currencies). He also subverts the modes of representation employed in exploration accounts to describe America's indigenous population to European readers. When the agent cautions that it "may be impossible to civilize the Europeans" (166) and announces: "If our elders decide it's worth the bother and expense, possibly we could teach the poor souls our Osage language, although if our faith and goodness can't be pounded into them we may just have to kill them all" (169), he mimics the discourse of the postulated Euro-American/Christian civilizing mission while exposing its hypocrisy and indifference towards Native suffering.

Basically, Revard's scenario makes readers explore the question raised by Blaeser, namely, would a reversal of history's course "affect the moral interpretations of events? What if history's heroes were not what textbooks make them out to be? What if white society were envisioned as the demonic 'other'? How would their actual cultural practices measure up to their professed standards of evaluation?" (1998, 164).[9] Revard's text defamiliarizes the familiar by reimagining Europeans in the stereotypical terms usually reserved for Native cultures: Europeans "do not know how to use the land; for one thing — they insist on spreading oil and tar all over it" (169); they "kill each other pretty casually, as if by natural instinct, not caring whether they blow up women, kids or horses, and next day display the mutilated corpses on front pages or television screens" (167); they can be pacified by "a few drinks of firewater" (169–70); and they use "shrines" in their sacred ceremonies that "have a lot of torture scenes in them. That may explain the bombings that keep happening among them" (169). Showing Euro-American readers their own society through the Native explorer's eyes, Revard enables them to take on a new perspective of themselves and of the way in which they conceptualized the settlement of the American continent and the subjugation of its Native population. The text exposes the hypocrisy inherent in sentimental Euro-American laments for the Vanishing Indian while simultaneously advocating settlement by taking a similar stance towards Europe:

> It would at first be a hard and semi-savage life, and there would be much danger from the Europeans who in many cases would not understand our motives; as a chosen people, setting up standards, we would probably have to oppress some opposition, and at times it might be best to temporize. We will, however, as the superior race, prevail in the end. (170)

Through parody, notions of Euro-American superiority and the American self-conceptualization based on the Puritan concept of manifest destiny are thoroughly deconstructed. The agent even more directly mocks this particular hypotext when he concludes: "And it is probably our destiny anyway, if our elders don't mind our sounding so Ameropean, to get the whole thing anyhow" (178). Revard engages the well-known historical discourse on discovery (in itself a revisionist term) and conquest to fundamentally throw into doubt the ability of this very discourse to neutrally present historical "facts." The story on the one hand directly attacks conquest and colonization; on the other hand, playing on Michel de Certeau's claim that "historiography is writing that conquers" (1988, xxv), it exposes the rhetoric of exploration and of manifest destiny as self-serving and inherently biased fictions. This blatantly shows in the story's final twist, in which the special agent suddenly renounces material conquest in favor of "cram[ming] most of Europe into a word-processor and bring[ing] it back to deal with in our own terms" (170): Revard's story clearly is as much concerned with stolen (and distorting) representations as with stolen land. The agent's suggestion thus articulates the story's basic parodic principle of turning the power inherent in representations back on itself. The text sugarcoats potent criticism with humor, and while some readers may nonetheless be offended at seeing their master narratives debunked, most will be laughingly tricked into an experimentally imaginative alternative to accepted historical paradigms. Parody in contemporary Native writing therefore doesn't just deconstruct (as satire does) or integrate a "textualized past into the text of the present" (Hutcheon 1995a, 86). Rather, it both shows how this textualized past still impacts the present through particular discourses and epistemologies, and provides a humorous way to imagine "alterNatives."

Burlesque, "a kind of parody that ridicules some serious literary work either by treating its solemn subject in an undignified style, or by applying its elevated style to a trivial subject" (Baldick 1996, 27),[10] in this strict form to my knowledge does not appear in contemporary Native literature. If opened up to refer to the use of one particular register for addressing an incongruent subject, however, there are several examples. Drew Hayden Taylor, for instance, phrases his mock-definition of "White people" in the register of political correctness, revealing the futility of striving for termi-nological correctness while actual politics does not follow suit: "Politically incorrect term for those of European descent. More currently acceptable terms are People of Pallor, Colour-Challenged, or the Pigment-denied" (1998, 124). And Sherman Alexie, in *Reservation Blues*, hilariously reimagines Christ's feeding of the five thousand (Luke 9) in burlesque fashion. The scene, modeled on the biblical story of Christ turning five loaves of bread into enough to feed the crowd, describes a Native feast with too little fry bread (which in view of the meager provisions is the only thing that turns the gathering into a feast in the first place). In the charac-ter of Big Mom, the spiritual leader of the Spokanes in the novel, it imi-tates biblical discourse and simultaneously evokes common clichés about "Indian spirituality":

> "There are only one hundred pieces of fry bread," Big Mom said, "and there are two hundred of us . . . . But there is a way," Big Mom said. "I can feed all of you."
> "How?" asked somebody . . . .
> "By ancient Indian secrets," Big Mom said . . . .
> "Watch this," Big Mom said as she grabbed a piece of fry bread and held it above her head. "Creator, help me. I have only a hundred pieces of fry bread to feed two hundred people."
> Big Mom held that fry bread tightly in her huge hands and then tore it into halves.
> "There," Big Mom said. "That is how I will feed you all."
> The crowd cheered, surging forward to grab their fry bread. There was a complete feast after all.
> "Big Mom," Thomas asked later as they were eating, "how did you do that? What is your secret?"
> Big Mom smiled deeply.
> "Mathematics," Big Mom said. (1996a, 301–302)

The register in which Alexie describes this "mirage" mocks biblical claims to authority, on the one hand, and stereotypical ideas about Native mysti-cism, on the other. Big Mom's anticlimactic common-sense answer "Mathematics" deflates the readers' built-up expectations for a more spir-itual explanation, fed by Big Mom's allusion to "ancient Indian secrets," the "Creator," and of course by the knowledge of the miraculous biblical hypotext. As amusing as effective, it liberates this Native character from formulaic conceptualizations. Like parody in general, therefore, burlesque provides a means to engage with previous representations in a way that most wittily makes transparent how particular discourses both produce their subjects and endow themselves with authority.

Basically, caricature concentrates on particular objectionable qualities and describes or portrays an individual or group exclusively in those terms, exaggerating them out of proportion. In contemporary Native texts this technique is sometimes used in direct response to stereotypes in White fictions that reduce Native people to a few clichéd characteristics, turning the tables on this degrading practice. In Thomas King's novel *Green Grass, Running Water*, for instance, caricature is employed for various patriarchal Judeo-Christian figures (God, Noah, A. A. Gabriel, Young Man Walking On Water), who are all defined in terms of egotism, hypocrisy, and obsession with (authoritative) rules (see chapter four); and it is also the novel's main technique for portraying Americans and Canadians as national groups. Latisha and George, a mixed Native Canadian/White American couple, argue throughout the novel about what characterizes the members of each nation. Latisha usually vehemently defends Canadians against George's allegations of their being weak and indecisive; yet her description of a group of Canadian tourists visiting her restaurant nonetheless constitutes a hilarious example of caricature. When the busload of tourists arrives at the "Dead Dog Café," the cook inquires: "What flavor?" (1994, 155), that is, Canadian or American. Latisha, instead of a direct response, simply lists stereotypical qualities usually attributed to Canadians:

> As the people got off the bus, Latisha could see that they all had name tags neatly pasted to their chests. They filed off the bus in an orderly line and stood in front of the restaurant and waited until they were all together. Then, in unison, they walked two abreast to the front door, each couple keeping pace with the couple in front of them.
> "Canadian," Latisha shouted. (155)

This caricature of the polite, orderly Canadian is rounded off by George's comment: "When a cop pulls a Canadian over for speeding on an open road with no other car in sight, the Canadian is happy. I've even seen them thank the cop for being so alert" (158–59). Conscious of the fact that his audience consists largely of Euro-American and Canadian readers, King uses caricature to hold up a mirror to his non-Native readership, offering them a comical but also slightly discomforting glimpse of what it feels like to be reduced to clichés, be they war bonnets and tomahawks or name tags and traits of orderliness. Because it exposes particular traits and ideas to laughter, caricature directly influences readers' assessments of these issues. In contemporary Native texts, as chapter four demonstrates, caricature is put to use in renegotiating Native and Euro-American characteristics and paradigms while simultaneously, as King's example shows, making transparent the reductive and denigrating aspects of stereotyping in general.

Wordplay and Punning

Wordplay and punning have always been among the most prominent forms of expressing humor in Native cultures, and are still very much alive today, surfacing frequently in contemporary Native literature.[11] "Wordplay," as Redfern (2000, 209) argues, "suits those unconvinced that rational argument suffices" — a characterization well in line with the concept of reimagining, which is also based on the notion of transcending rational argumentation. The transgressive potential of puns and wordplay lies in their characteristic renunciation of the binary nature of the linguistic sign, disrupting the linear process of interpretation. One signifier — or at least similarly sounding signifiers, depending on whether the pun is based on homophony or polysemy — may relate to more than one signified. In Louise Erdrich's novel *Love Medicine*, Lipsha's comically misguided considerations on the term "malpractice suit," for instance, hinge on the polysemy of "suit": "I heard of those suits. I used to think it was a color clothing quack doctors had to wear so you could tell them from the good ones" (2001, 245). In puns and wordplay, instead of one prescriptive meaning, readers are offered the possibility for secondary meanings, an ambiguity requiring them to creatively imagine various interpretations. In some instances, pure delight in humor appears to be the main motivation behind puns and wordplay, such as in the title of Jim Northrup's "Holiday Inndians" (1993, 63–66) or Mickie Poirier's reference to a "Wet Dream Catcher Drive-In" (1997). In most cases, however, the authors engage in wordplay to critically comment on particular situations or circumstances. The narrator in King's novel *Green Grass, Running Water* puns on the initial lines of the Canadian national anthem, "O Canada! Our home and native land!" and turns them into "Hosanna da, our home on Natives' land" (1994, 270), in effect protesting colonization. Sherman Alexie, in a story about a Native student applying for college, reinterprets the acronym CAT (for Comprehensive Assessment Test) as "Colonial Aptitude Test" (2001, 165–66), drawing attention to racist biases in the educational system. And in Alexie's novel *Reservation Blues*, protagonist Thomas Builds-the-Fire refers to himself as a "recovering Catholic" (1996a, 146), highlighting the complicity of the church in the colonization of Native people: Because of the similar sound of the idiomatic expression, this groups Catholicism with alcoholism, a serious illness that destroys the addicts' personalities and reduces them to helpless dependents.

As these brief examples demonstrate, Native writers employ puns and wordplay as humorous "stumbling blocks" that trigger surprised laughter, defy habitual and unreflected interpretations, and force readers to establish new connections. They manage to convey several messages within one expression, confirming Redfern's proposition that "pun appeals to those who want to say several things at once, and for whom unambiguous utterance is too linear and restricting" (2000, 209). By definition, puns and wordplay thus defy restrictive one-dimensional representations and liberate Nativeness towards more complexity.

In Native writing, wordplay frequently targets issues and terms connected to conquest and colonization. Highlighting incompatible usages of "reservation" (something set aside for someone versus restricting a people's space to a defined area of land), Pueblo artist Popovi Da, when asked why the Indians were the first ones on this continent, quipped, "we had reservations" (quoted in V. Deloria 1977, 166). And in *Green Grass, Running Water*, Lionel's excuse for not joining an AIM protest evokes a similar quip: " 'I'm not sure I'll be able to make it. I have to fly back. I've got a reservation.' The man took Lionel by the shoulders, looked at him hard, and said, 'Some of us don't' " (King 1994, 58). "White" as ethnicity/skin color versus regular color is played with by Sherman Alexie in his short story "Saint Junior," when the narrator observes: "First snow was a good time for most Indians . . . who possessed a good sense of rhythm and irony. After all, it took a special kind of courage for an Indian to look out a window into the deep snow and see anything special in that vast whiteness" (2001, 153–54). Readers here are required to make the transition from the image of a snow-covered field on the reservation to the North American continent in general which today is predominantly populated by White Euro-Americans. Non-Native readers are thus literally compelled to see America through Native eyes, induced to put themselves in the position of the subaltern, and enticed to reconsider their own "specialness," that is, their claim to superiority. Lenore Keeshig-Tobias's poem "The White Man's Burden" (which is part of the cycle "Trickster Beyond 1992: Our Relationship"), finally, plays both with the eponymous phrase as a whole and with white as a word, suggesting various possibilities to alleviate "the white man's burden / (as he sees it)/ to spread culture/ among the primitive/ (indigenous)/ peoples of the world" (1998, 258). All "solutions" to the "problem" hinge on wordplay. There are imaginatively reworked dictionary definitions of "White Wash," playing on the homophone dye/die; comparative forms — "Clorox bleach gets whites whiter"; and an allusion to the white paper in which the Trudeau government in 1969 proposed a radical termination of Native status. Eventually, Keeshig-Tobias's trickster humor defies all biased and racist solutions with a single authoritative: "PUT DOWN THE LOAD, STUPID" (1998, 263). Yet throughout, the poem sensitizes readers to the implications "white" can carry and playfully lures them into assuming new viewpoints.

Wordplay focusing on Nativeness instead of colonization is usually affirming rather than bitingly critical, but nonetheless it deconstructs "the Indian." Sherman Alexie's short story "Whatever Happened to Frank Snake Church?" for example, plays on "vision" as ability to see, on the one hand, and spiritual revelation (as expected in the context of the "wise Indian"), on the other. Protagonist Frank speeds home from a hike in the mountains, picturing his father dead, just to find him sitting at the kitchen table:

> "You're alive," said Frank, completely surprised by the fact.
> "Yes I am," Harrison said as he studied his bloody, panicked son.
> "But you look half dead."
> "I had a vision," Frank said.
> Harrison sipped his coffee.
> "I saw you in my head," Frank said. "You're supposed to be dead. I saw you dead."
> "You have blurry vision," said Harrison.   (2003, 201)

Similar to Big Mom's deflation of mysticism in the rewriting of the feeding of the five thousand, the built-up tension based on Frank's presumed vision collapses when Harrison employs the term in its basic meaning, stripping it of any spiritual connotations associated with Indianness. He defies his son's but also the readers' expectations when the image of the Indian sage is deftly replaced with a down-to-earth old man, confirming Kant's definition that laughter is "the affection arising from the sudden transformation of a strained expectation into nothing" (1982, 223).

Thomas King's novel *Green Grass, Running Water* abounds with puns and wordplay, such as Adam's renaming as "Ahdamn" (1994, 38); having three cars float on a lake that sound conspicuously like Columbus's three ships, the Niña, Pinta, and Santa Maria — "A Nissan, a Pinto, and a Karmann-Ghia" (407); or Alberta trying to pick up a man to anonymously father her child in a bar named the "Shagganappi Lounge" (66), Shagganappi not only being the Algonquian word for rawhide cord (see Flick 1999, 149), but also combining the slang word "shag" (to pick up a person and have sex with them), with nappy (as in napkin/diaper). Discussing all of the novel's instances of wordplay is neither feasible nor useful for the purpose at hand, so the following reading focuses on the novel's beginning. Right at the outset, the novel establishes one of its main themes through the use of wordplay, namely, the relation between Native cultures and the Judeo-Christian traditions that have influenced colonial policies right from their Puritan beginnings. The novel's first sentences are reminiscent of Genesis. But the familiar creation account is immediately contrasted with a typically Native trickster character, Coyote, as the first being:

> So.
> In the beginning, there was nothing. Just the water.
> Coyote was there, but Coyote was asleep. That Coyote was asleep, and that Coyote was dreaming. When that Coyote dreams, anything can happen. (1)

One of Coyote's dreams "gets loose and runs around. Makes a lot of noise. Hooray, says that silly dream, Coyote dream. I'm in charge of the world," and when Coyote wakes up and asks the narrator about the source of all the noise, he is told: "It's that noisy dream of yours . . . . It thinks it is in charge of the world" (1). Coyote gives the dream an identity by telling it: "You can't be Coyote. But you can be a dog. . . . Dogs are good. They are almost as good as Coyote" (2). While this already humorously subverts the authority of the Judeo-Christian account, placing a Native trickster at the center of creation, the story gains momentum through King's subsequent use of palindrome: "when that Coyote Dream thinks about being a dog, it gets everything mixed up, it gets everything backward," which eventually results in the dream's claim: "I am god" (2).

This wordplay bears several implications. First, read within a Native cultural background it alludes to the existence of so-called contraries in many Native cultures, as Coyote emphasizes by commenting: "Isn't that cute. . . . That Dog Dream is a contrary" (2). Such contraries choose to do everything backwards (for instance riding horses backwards or wearing summer clothes in winter) and behave contrary to normal and appropriate social behavior and expectations, either only during ceremonies, as ritual clowns and buffoons, or as a general mode of life. Part of their mission is to shake up the moral values and traditional codes of conduct of a culture, demonstrating to people what may result from a reversal of conventions. This role, however, is not unlike that of the trickster Coyote him or herself (tricksters are frequently able to transgress sex/gender lines and take both male and female shape), which implies that the similarities between this dog and Coyote exceed purely biological features. Rather, King's use of wordplay both alludes to Coyote's divine characteristics and ascribes certain chaotic and imperfect aspects to the allegedly infallible Judeo-Christian god. The second implication is that not god but Coyote is the origin of the world, and it is only because of Coyote's inattentiveness that god comes into being and is ascribed authority:

> I am god, says that Dog Dream. . . .
> But why am I a little god, shouts that god.
> "Not so loud," says Coyote. "You're hurting my ears."
> I don't want to be a little god. I want to be a big god!
> "What a noise," says Coyote. "This dog has no manners."
> *Big one!*
> "Okay, okay," says Coyote. "Just stop shouting."
> There, says that GOD. That's better." (2)

When King first creates a Coyote dream that wants to be like Coyote and thus becomes a dog, then identifies it as a contrary and turns it into a (small) god, and finally characterizes it as an aggressive, selfish, uppercased GOD (the uppercasing being a sideswipe at the customary capitalization of the word God in Western writing conventions), in a *mise-en-abymic* move he brackets the Judeo-Christian ontology and reduces it to a "silly Coyote dream" within a Native creation story. Readers who had hitherto relied on the Judeo-Christian master narrative for their conceptualization of the beginnings of the world and on the unquestioned dominance of a Judeo-Christian God are thoroughly decentered as the biblical narrative is transculturally infiltrated with Native elements. Swept up in a creative-hybrid reimagination of Judeo-Christian Genesis and Native creation tale, as readers laugh at Coyote's lapse and the cranky dog/god/GOD, they also laugh at their own accustomed perspective. Through his use of wordplay, King most amusingly destabilizes and unhinges customary worldviews and induces readers to reimagine other options — which makes King the ultimate trickster himself.

"Double-talk is not necessarily mendacious," claims Redfern, but rather, in some cases, "the only way to communicate" in order to "convince the doubting" (2000, 209). As demonstrated by the examples discussed here, punning and wordplay, through their transgression of linguistic linearity, are means by which Native authors may express several meanings at once. This allows for criticism without lecturing and dislocation without offense, by engaging readers in an imaginative activity of decoding that amuses as much as it destabilizes. By making readers stumble, laugh, and rethink, in that order, humorous wordplay thus proves most effective in reimagining habitual representations of Nativeness.

Contesting Colonial Language and Writing

The "Indianlect," or garble, attributed to Indian characters in Hollywood movies and TV series (often played by non-Native actors) usually consists of "grunted monosyllables and grammatically and idiomatically flawed rudimentary English which characterized the speaker as silly and of substandard intelligence and linguistic competence" (Lutz 2002, 53). In most cases, "Indians were mute and silent, uttering nothing but screaming war cries when charging to attack" (53). Regardless of whether it is the stereotypical "Indian" utterances ("How," "ugh," or "Kemo sabe") or the pseudopoetic diction that Johnston calls "the 'many moons' phenomenon" (1987, 55),[12] both varieties deny Native people communicative abilities and additionally ignore the linguistic diversity of Native cultures. Often, the snippets of "Indian" language employed in film were simply invented on the set (see O'Connor 1998, 33), or in some cases created "by running their normal English dialogue backwards. By keeping [the actors] relatively motionless when they spoke, the picture could be printed in reverse and a perfect lip-sync maintained" (J. Price 1978, 206). Small wonder Emma LaRoque sarcastically comments on Hollywood Westerns that

> these "dusters" carry the distinction of at least recognizing that the Indian had a viable language of his own. The Indian could say "How" and "Ugh." And in his more verbose moments, he could also comment,

"Heap Big Chief," or "Me pow wow." Why, the Native was almost talk-
ative — thanks to Hollywood. (1975, 59)

Contemporary Native writers meet these misconstructions with plenty
of humor. Keeper, the character of an Ojibway elder in Richard
Wagamese's novel *Keeper 'n Me*, explains that he fulfills the expectations
towards flowery "Indian language" willingly — when paid for:

> Me, I'm just an old man that's been down many trails. How they say in
> them movies? The ones that got lotsa Mexicans bein' Indyuns? I lived
> many winters? Heh, heh, heh. Guess that's true, only me, I don't talk so
> romantic anymore 'less some of them rich Americans are ready to dish
> out cash to hear a *real* Indyun talk 'bout the *old days*. (1994, 1–2)

Keeper literally performs for a White audience to give them what they
expect: not a real Native person, but their image of "the Indian." Yet by
presenting Keeper's thoughts, Wagamese lets readers take a look behind the
scenes of this staged Indianness. Readers thus see the witty, complex character behind the mask of "the Indian" that Keeper puts on for the tourists,
and are brought to share his humorous denunciation of White stereotypes.

An even more likely target of Native humor than this quaint paraphrasing language, however, is the debilitating clichéd "Indian" inarticu-
lateness. Stedman explains how "Indian" words like "how" or "squaw"
found their way into English: Based on the White settlers' inability to cor-
rectly pronounce the sounds of the Native language (which is also the
source of the stereotype that Indians "grunt"), an approximate imitation
was adopted and then generalized — "based upon the misconception that
all the nations spoke something called 'Indian.' Thus 'How!' (an approxi-
mation of Sioux or Osage words of greeting) was put into the mouth of
every Indian from Canada to Mexico, and beyond" (1982, 71–72).
Sherman Alexie mocks such ignorance in his poem "Translated from the
American," which is fittingly set in a drive-in movie theater. The speaker
mimics yet undermines the general "Indian language" that Native characters speak in Hollywood films:

> after all the drive-in theaters have closed
> for winter   I'll make camp alone
> at THE NORTH CEDAR   replay westerns
>
> the Seventh Cavalry riding double formation
> endlessly . . .
>
> . . .   I'll wrap myself
> in old blankets   wait   for white boys
> climbing fences   to watch this Indian speak
>
> in subtitles   they'll surround me
> and when they ask   "how"
> I'll give them exact directions   (1993a, 35)

Playing on the polysemy of what is presumably an Indian greeting but also an English interrogative, the speaker ironically turns the stereotype of the linguistically deficient and thus apparently ignorant "Indian" right back on the White boys. As a result, he presents *them* and their willingness to accept the simplistic notion of an "Indian" language as ignorant.

In other instances, mocking the cliché of the verbally deficient "Indian" may — like Keeper's pretend verbosity — intentionally confirm stereotypical (Hollywood) ideas for profit. In *Green Grass, Running Water*, Native actor Portland provides his son Charlie with the following advice for his job of parking cars at a bar in Los Angeles (that is, right where the dream factory produces the degrading depictions): "Remember to grunt . . . The idiots love it, and you get better tips" (King 1994, 209). Likewise, when in King's novel *Truth & Bright Water* protagonist Tecumseh and his father cross the border into Canada (smuggling biohazardous waste), the father fulfills the border guards' expectations in order to fool them. He "shakes his head and smiles and talks like the Indians you see in the westerns on television," commenting afterwards: "They love that dumb Indian routine. You see how friendly those assholes were" (1999a, 86). Again, by being initiated into the strategy readers identify and chuckle with the Native characters at the tricked White border guards, who fall prey to their own stereotypical expectations; readers who may have held similar ideas (and basically everyone is at least aware of the stereotype created by Hollywood) in effect laugh at themselves.

The most prominent example of the inarticulate Indian is probably Tonto, the Lone Ranger's loyal Indian sidekick from the popular Western show, which started out on radio in the 1930s, developed into a TV series in the 1940s and 50s, and subsequently even produced some feature films (see Chadwick 1996). Tonto — whose name means "fool" or "stupid one" in Spanish, whereas his term for the Lone Ranger, "Kemo Sabe," allegedly translates as "the one who knows" (see Ridington 1999, 28) — "was everything that the white man had always wanted the Indian to be. He was a little slower, a little dumber, had much less vocabulary, and rode a darker horse. Somehow Tonto was always *there*. . ., a silent subservient subspecies of the Anglo-Saxon whose duty was to do the bidding of the all-wise white hero" (V. Deloria 1977, 200; see also Stedman 1982, 50–51). As *the* stereotypical Indian sidekick, Tonto became the target of defiant Native humor, as Native people imagined him to break his restrictive frame:

> The standard joke, developed as group consciousness arose, had the Lone Ranger and Tonto surrounded by a tribe of hostile Indians, with Tonto inquiring of the Lone Ranger, "Well, White Man?" The humor came from Tonto's complete departure from his stereotype. The real Tonto would have cut down his relatives with a Gatling gun rather than have a hair on said Ranger's head mussed. (V. Deloria 1977, 200)

Such a sudden imaginative shift of Tonto's allegiances figures in Marie Annharte Baker's poem "Squaw Guide" (1997) and is at the center of a scene from Hanay Geiogamah's play *Foghorn,* in which the Lone Ranger and Tonto appear as characters. In a hilariously reflexive lengthy monologue, the Lone Ranger explains to Tonto his qualms about having to "rely on an illiterate Injun like you to do all the clever thinking, and even outsmarting the white man" (1980, 65) in order to bail him out in crisis situations. Trying to find a solution to this problem, the Lone Ranger rumbles on and on and imagines a scenario in which he, for a change, can come to the aid of Tonto:

> I got it! I got it! (piano interlude suggesting wickedness, villainy). Tonto, you get shot, real badly, right smack in the chest by a no-good Injun varmit who says you stole his squaw. You're about to die, and I find you. I get you to a friendly rancher's house, one where they'll let me bring my Injun friend inside, and do an operation on you to remove the bullet. How's that, Tonto? (66)

The Lone Ranger's verbosity and relentless babbling are comically contrasted with Tonto's silence as he shines the Lone Ranger's boots. Only when the Lone Ranger vies for approval and applause with brief (rhetorical) questions — "How's that, Tonto?" — does Tonto offer an occasional "Kemo Sabay." The impression that Tonto does not really possess language is reinforced when he does not object to the scenario the Lone Ranger paints: While he would try to save the injured Tonto, Tonto would eventually have to die, so that the Lone Ranger could finally become an entirely self-reliant White hero. Part of the humor here derives from the fact that Geiogamah blurs the boundaries between movie characters and actors. The characters he presents on stage *are* the (fictional) movie characters; at the same time, however, they appear as actors who are self-reflexively aware of their own fictional status, endowed with character traits and motivations that clearly exceed those of their movie personalities. This implicitly demonstrates to the audience how viewers (including themselves) tend to take the movie image of "the Indian" for the real thing, conflating the Native people they encounter with movie-kind "Tontos"; and it makes the scene's surprise ending all the more effective. After two pages of self-enamored Lone Ranger monologue, shoe-shining, and five interjected "Kemo Sabays," Tonto suddenly rises and cuts the Lone Ranger's throat. With his typical combination of humor and brutality (also characteristic of his play *Body Indian*), Geiogamah doesn't merely shock the audience into questioning the popular culture icon Tonto. Rather, he destabilizes the stereotype of "the Indian" as such, and the whole idea of White (language-based) superiority, as Tonto turns from subservient, near-mute, passive fool to cunning avenger. Together with the Lone Ranger, the audience, relying on their familiarity with the original, mistake Tonto's silence for (dim-witted) agreement, loyalty, or even admiration — just to be amusingly jolted from their habituated patterns of interpretation. Mocking and defying "Indianlect" thus emerges as a subversive strategy to directly confront degrading representations that portray Native people as verbally deficient and stupid. It partially fulfills colonial clichés in order to expose them as racist simulations.

Red English is another strategy Native writers employ to "write back" to colonial representations of "the Indian" and reinscribe Native presence. Characterized by "its concise diction, distinctive inflections, loping rhythms, iconic imagery, irregular, reverse twists on standard English, and countless turns of coiling humor" (Lincoln 1993, 15), this idiom constitutes a pan-tribal, truly indigenized version of English that pervades all forms of Native cultural expression (see Lincoln 1993, 124; Mattina 1985, 9). To appropriate but modify the colonizer's language, that is, to deliberately deviate from its standard use, is in itself subversive, as John Lowe observes: "Since dialect, at least to the oppressor, is part and parcel of the negative stereotype, pride in dialect constitutes inversion, transforming an oppressive signifier of otherness into a pride inspiring prism, one which may be used for the critical inspection of 'the other'" (1986, 448). Red English, on the one hand, provides contemporary Native writers with an opportunity to represent certain Native characters credibly, in the process also furthering identification (see Campbell in Lutz 1991, 48). On the other hand, it denies the dominant society, which forced this very language upon them by sometimes brutal means (in boarding schools, children were often punished for speaking their Native language), any further power to regulate its use. Like many of the "englishes" employed by colonized or oppressed cultures all over the world, Red English thus constitutes a form of resistance.

Red English deviates from standard English in various ways. It may use colloquial/"rez slang" markers such as contractions or slurs, as exemplified in Garnet's language in Wagamese's *Keeper 'n Me:* "Most people never hearda the Ojibway. Probably because we never raided wagon trains or got shot offa horses by John Wayne" (1994, 6). But it may also show profound changes in syntax and grammar, as in the writing of Thomas King discussed below, or in pronunciation, as in poetry by Marie Annharte Baker ("Coyote Columbus Café," 1998) and Louise Halfe ("Valentine Dialogue" or "Stones," 1994). In several of Halfe's poems a Native woman addresses letters to the pope, expressing her thoughts on Catholicism and Native cultures in Red English ("In Da Name of Da Fadder," "Der Poop," and "My Ledders," 1994). The humor in Halfe's texts arises, on the one hand, from subversive phonetic transcriptions or mischievously misspelled words. This is the case in expressions such as "Der Poop" (102) instead of "Dear Pope," the scatological humor disrespectfully undermining the pope's sacrosanct authority, or "drainin from doze schools" (103) instead of "training from those schools," which implies a mind-numbing educational system "draining" Native children of their cultural knowledge and putting them to sleep so that they will not notice the power imbalances of the colonial system. On the other hand, humor in these texts is based on the comic contrast between the speaker's "flawed" demotic language — by which she presents herself as naïve and ignorant by colonial standards — and the complex criticism of forced conversion, patriarchal oppression, and cultural and spiritual appropriation that is expressed between the lines. For instance, the speaker bitingly unmasks White Christian hypocrisy in such sentences as: "I don't understand why geezuz say I be / poor, stay on welfare cuz *moniyas* [white people] say/ I good for nuddin' cuz I don't have/ wisdom. Forgive me poop I is/ big sinner" (100–101). Using Red English as a vehicle, Halfe presents readers with the cliché of the illiterate Indian, yet undercuts it through puns resulting from phonetic spelling and through witty lines of argument, severing the alleged correlations between standard forms of expression and the speaker's presumed intelligence. Red English therefore enables Native writers both to express pan-Indian unity and continuity and to undermine colonial practices in which language serves to cement hierarchies and exert power by imposing ethnocentric standards.

Code-switching, also exemplified in Halfe's writing through interspersed Cree words (see Eigenbrod 2003, 45), is a strategy that contemporary Native writers may use to invoke a distinctly Native presence in the text, to overcome English's limitations in expressing certain concepts originating from Native cultures, or to draw a boundary that for once denies English-speaking readers access and makes them aware of the limits of their world language. The humor expressed by such code-switching is not always readily apparent. Yet it is a way to reach even those readers who consider themselves liberal towards Native causes, but at the same time pride themselves on their sophisticated "superior" use of English. When the otherwise oppressed, exploited, and objectified Métis women in Monique Mojica's play *Princess Pocahontas and the Blue Spots* (1991) effortlessly switch from English to French to Cree, for instance, they challenge notions of White superiority with subtle irony. After all, their White Euro-Canadian husbands have to rely on their Métis wives to translate, as one of them explains: "I speak for them when they have no words" (44). A similarly decentering strategy is at work in King's *Green Grass, Running Water*. The four old Indians who act as narrators of part of the novel try out several authoritative formulaic English story beginnings: "Once upon a time . . ." (11), "A long time ago in a faraway land . . ." (12), and "In the beginning, God created the heaven and the earth" (14). It is not until they remember the ceremonial opening of storytelling in a Cherokee divining ceremony, "Higayv:ligé:I" (15), however, that the story can actually "begin well" (15). King's use of Cherokee not only makes readers aware of cultural difference and the respect such difference necessitates, it also humorously implies that English by itself can never suffice for telling the whole story truthfully, since the (English) medium is inseparably intertwined with the (colonial Eurocentric) message, story, and history.[13] This implication — that story and history recorded exclusively in English and from a WASP perspective can only be "partial" in either sense of the word — is confirmed throughout the novel, as King deconstructs various canonical narratives by countering them with Native mythology and rewriting them to include the Native perspective. While not inherently humorous, code-switching may hence serve to express humor by playfully contrasting Native expressions with English in order to comment on or defy anglocentric notions of superiority and centrality.

Elements or characteristics of traditional oral storytelling may also work to comic avail in contemporary Native texts, to the extent that Western readers are confronted with a narrative tradition blatantly different from their own written mode. To introduce elements from oral narrative into a text creates an informal, immediate mood as readers find themselves transformed into listeners. The narrator of Simon Ortiz's story "What Indians Do" explains: "The storyteller participates in the story with those who are listening. In the same way, the listeners are taking part in the story. The story includes them in. You see, storytelling is more like an event. The story is not just a story then. It's occurring, it's happening; it's coming into being" (1999, 130). Part of Thomas King's writing — which, as King acknowledges, owes much to traditional Okanagan storyteller Harry Robinson's influence — exemplifies this, as can be demonstrated by the beginning of King's short story "One Good Story, That One":[14]

> Alright.
> You know, I hear this story up north. Maybe Yellowknife, that one, somewhere. I hear it maybe a long time. Old story this one. One hundred years, maybe more. Maybe not so long either, this story.
> So.
> You know, they come to my place. Summer place, pretty good place, that one. Those ones, they come with Napiao, my friend. Cool. On the river. Indians call him Ka-sin-ta, that river, like if you did nothing but stand in one place all day and maybe longer. Ka-sin-ta also called Na-po. Napiao knows that one, my friend. Whiteman call him Saint Merry, but I don't know what that mean. Maybe like Ka-sin-ta. Maybe not. (1993, 1)

The entire passage establishes a conversational mode, not just by addressing the readers directly, but also through the old narrator's interjections "Alright," "So," and "Anyway," as well as through the slow pacing and rhythm of the story. In addition, the unfamiliar elliptical syntax, the truncated sentences, and repetition serve to signal the oral telling situation. The storyteller gets sidetracked from his story, veers off into other stories, but eventually remembers what he was about to tell his audience and takes up that thread again. Most amusingly, he offers alternatives — "Maybe . . . Maybe not," which leaves readers/listeners with the impression that they are purposely denied one "fixed" version. Meaning, quite obviously, is not fixed but created in the telling, and so this trickster-narrator cannot be trusted, and, indeed, the entire tale actually turns out to be a huge trickster snare (more closely discussed in chapter four).

In *Green Grass, Running Water,* King uses oral features to comic effect both on a microlevel (single words, expressions, or scenes) and a macrolevel (narrative structure). On the microlevel, King works with puns that are based on the sound effects of oral performance, as well other markers that signal the immediate and interactional nature of the narrative. Even more than the above-mentioned puns on Columbus's ships, for instance, King's play on the Métis revolutionary Louis Riel relies on being spoken aloud. Only then do the fishing buddies "Louie, Ray, Al" from Manitoba who plan to "hang around Scott Lake" (335), reveal themselves as Louis Riel, whose provisional government hanged Thomas Scott for bearing arms against the state. King thus comically manipulates readers into recreating the oral storytelling situation, a move that is reinforced by the way in which the narrator addresses not only Coyote, his immediate interlocutor, but also the extratextual audience. The readers actually become part of the unfolding story, as they are drawn into a storytelling performance: Story in this novel is a dialogic joint venture of various "tellers" — Coyote, the narrator "I," the four old Indians, *and* the readers. When the Lone Ranger (one of the four old Indians who tell the four parts of the story), starts "his" version of the story, he is immediately interrupted by the others:

"Wait a minute," said Robinson Crusoe.
"Yes?"
"That's the wrong story," said Ishmael. "That story comes later."
"But it's my turn," said the Lone Ranger.
"But you have to get it right," said Hawkeye.
"And," said Robinson Crusoe, "you can't tell it all by yourself." (14)

Readers who expect to be told a stable story by a reliable narrator find themselves, in King's novel, in a maze of multiple narratives with "tellers" who offer different versions of the same story. Monolithic accounts of Native-White history are thoroughly deconstructed in the storytellers' comic squabbles over whose turn it is to tell the story. The constant renewal that characterizes oral storytelling inherently defies the stability and permanence ascribed to written accounts. Its playful use in contemporary Native texts is therefore intrinsically subversive: It undermines the hierarchy by which the written is ranked above the oral in Western paradigms, and it deconstructs any postulations of one authorial/authoritative Truth. Instead, elements from oral narration signal continuance of Native traditions in written texts.

Intertextuality, Metafiction, and Comic Reversal

Intertextuality, like parody, works with preexisting texts. For intertextuality to generate humor readers must have a basic knowledge of or at least acquaintance with the intertext; only then can the incongruity on which humor by definition hinges be perceived.[15] Because Native writers frequently possess hybrid cultural backgrounds and typically address mixed audiences, intertextual references in contemporary Native texts are often linked to canonical American literary texts, master narratives of Western civilization, and elements of American popular culture,[16] but also to narratives from the Native oral tradition. Regardless of origin, these intertexts can be used reverentially or critically. The playful references to modernist poetry in Louis Owens's novel *Bone Game* — to Robert Frost's "Stopping By Woods on a Snowy Evening" (1994, 43) or William Carlos Williams's "The Red Wheelbarrow" (170), to name but two — apart from signaling both Owens's and his protagonist Cole's profession as literature professors, express a sheer delight in language. Cole's students quoting T. S. Eliot's "The Love Song of J. Alfred Prufrock" — "I do not think that they will sing to me" (23, 219) — thus rather constitutes a form of reverence. In contrast, Marilyn Dumont's reference to Eliot — "I have since reconsidered Eliot/ and the Great White way of writing English/ standard that is" (1996, 54) — stresses how canonical Western writing restricts Native writers and discriminates against Native texts. Sherman Alexie's poem "Song of Ourself," finally, links Walt Whitman's exceptional poetic accomplishments during the American Renaissance to the ethnocide and genocide of Native Americans in the same time period. It brings to attention that while White America experienced its first cultural heyday it simultaneously eradicated other whole cultures: "While Walt Whitman sang about his body, the still body/ of one Indian grew into two, then ten, then multitudes" (1996c, 20).

While literary intertexts may be integrated as a form of homage or derision, historiographic intertexts most often exemplify the latter. Euro-American historiography has, after all, systematically misrepresented Native people or even deleted them from the record completely in order to retroactively validate conquest and settlement. Contemporary Native texts rely on intertextuality to reverse such revisionism. As Linda Hutcheon points out, postmodern intertextuality that makes use of literary and historic texts is

> a formal manifestation of both a desire to close the gap between past and present of the reader and a desire to *rewrite the past in a new context*. . . . It is not an attempt to void or avoid history. Instead it directly confronts the past of literature — and of historiography, for it too derives from other texts (documents). It uses and abuses those intertextual echoes,

inscribing their powerful allusions and then subverting that power through irony. (1995a, 86; emphasis added)

Intertextuality therefore comprises an opportunity for contemporary Native writers to incorporate former representations of Nativeness into an altered context, ridiculing them in their original form or transforming, reencoding, reimagining them. In the simplest form, such ironical references are mere quotations. This is the case with Alex, a trickster character from Owens's *Bone Game*, citing an "anthropological" account, "a book on the missions published in the forties by a guy named Berger" (1994, 177). By reading several especially absurd passages aloud to Cole, Alex openly exposes Berger's hypocrisy and racism to derision, thereby throwing the alleged Euro-American civilizing mission as such into severe doubt. In a more complex strategy, the intertextual fragments are integrated into the plot. This is realized in Gerald Vizenor's novel *The Heirs of Columbus* (1991), which starts with excerpts from Columbus's diary and continues to incorporate historical documents and the accounts of Columbus's biographers throughout, as it tells the story of Columbus's descendant Stone. The most interesting and most humorous form of intertextual play, finally, results when the text at hand and the intertexts are truly amalgamated and thus transformed into something new. In these cases, "texts do not just utilize previous textual units but . . . transform them" (G. Allen 2000, 53), reimagining their original content. The result influences the readers' understanding and interpretation of both the source text and the text at hand. Intertextual reimagining thus opens up the possibility of rewriting the past, building on the very premise that meaning is contextual and constituted in representation.

King's *Green Grass, Running Water*, again, illustrates this point, making use of comic intertextuality on various levels and relating to a vast number of intertexts, their scope ranging from the Bible to canonical American literary texts, texts from literary criticism, Canadian art, Western films, and Shakespeare's works. King merges Native and Western textual elements, narrative strategies, settings, characters, and imagery. All pretexts are transformed in the process; yet the changes appear more dramatic with regard to the Western texts. The oral stories are more flexible to begin with, and King mostly retains their tenor. The Western texts, in contrast, are rigidly fixed in writing, and their quintessence is transformed substantially in the novel. On the level of character configuration, for example, King merges mythical characters from various Native oral traditions with canonical Western literary and filmic characters. The four old Indian storytellers, on whom part of the novel centers, are named the Lone Ranger (relating to the TV series), Ishmael (from Herman Melville's *Moby Dick*), Robinson Crusoe (as in Daniel Defoe's *Robinson Crusoe*), and Hawkeye (from James Fenimore Cooper's *Leatherstocking Tales*). In addition to these familiar White male individualist heroes, however, the four old Indians also embody community-oriented female characters from Native creation myths: First Woman (Diné/Abenaki), Changing Woman (Diné), Thought Woman (Laguna Pueblo), and Old Woman (Blackfoot/Dunne-za), respectively. This amalgamation of Western literary and Native oral traditions in the form of (shape-shifting) Native tricksters transforms both sources. The resulting contrast between the caring women and the ruthless men, however, most obviously discloses the hypocrisy inherent in the Western texts: Western individualism is humorously exposed as egotism and the alleged Western superiority shown to be mere conceitedness. Moreover, the trickster characters' ability to change their outer appearance implies that the defining characteristics (civilized, refined, superior) of the White male heroes they embody lack any real basis, but are highly situational and constructed. Whenever endangered in any way, the tricksters take on their White male personae in order to partake in colonial authority — and colonial society is deceived by these impersonations. When Ahdamn and First Woman are confronted by hostile rangers searching for the Indians who killed their colleagues, for instance, First Woman escapes by transforming herself into the masked figure of the Lone Ranger:

> Definitely Indians, says one of the rangers, and the live rangers point their guns at First Woman and Ahdamn.
> Just a minute, says First Woman, and that one takes some black cloth out of her purse. She cuts some holes in that black cloth. She puts that black cloth around her head.
> Look, Look, all the live rangers says, and they point their fingers at First Woman. It's the Lone Ranger. Yes, they says, it is the Lone Ranger.
> That's me, says First Woman. (71)

Through the rangers' eager acceptance of this transparent transformation, the scene first of all evokes laughter, as do similar transformations of Changing Woman (into Ishmael, 225), Thought Woman (into Robinson Crusoe, 324), and Old Woman (into Hawkeye, 396; see King in Gzowski 1999, 67). But it also teaches a lesson about the deceptive powers of popular cultural icons and implicitly cautions readers not to be fooled so easily.

Throughout, King's novel turns selected canonical texts into an imaginative quagmire, so that readers who deem themselves on stable ground find out differently.[17] In a maze of interconnections, it is not only the four old Indians/mythical women who make appearances as canonical heroes; the very heroes themselves appear in humorously distorted fragments of their own stories. As Rainwater points out, by selecting Ishmael, Hawkeye, the Lone Ranger, and Robinson Crusoe, King implicitly comments on the relationship between Euro-American cultures and their indigenous subjects, because in each of these stories the colonial Euro-American hero has an indigenous sidekick (see 1999, 143). King rewrites these representations of colonial relations with comic disrespect. When the canonical heroes encounter the tricksters/mythical women, they automatically perceive them in exclusively colonial frames of reference and accordingly try to name them Queequeg, Chingachgook, Tonto, and Friday. The text thus humorously reveals the colonizers' desperate need to create an inferior Other to set their own civilized selves off against, a need that starkly contradicts the high ideals postulated in their European/Christian civilizing mission. Upon encountering Thought Woman, for instance, Robinson Crusoe exclaims, "Thank God! . . . It's Friday!" and explains his joy with the fact that "as a civilized white man, it has been difficult not having someone of color around whom I could educate and protect" (294). He refuses to see Thought Woman as anything but his sidekick Friday and thus remains caught in the rigid frame of the archetypical Robinsonade. The reader, however, is comically liberated from the colonial tale by being encouraged to identify with Thought Woman's stubborn resistance and self-determination rather than with Crusoe's patronizing arrogance. In contrast to the original passive subject of White description, in King's reimagined version Thought Woman talks back to colonial subjectification ("No, says Thought Woman. It's Wednesday," 294) and would rather be Robinson Crusoe herself. This reimagined version of *Robinson Crusoe* defies the allegedly natural and god-given hierarchy of the original. The encounters between the other mythical women and canonical colonial heroes lead to similar outcomes: All mythic characters eventually opt out of participating in colonial tales and float off into other stories, exemplifying Native people's need to free themselves of colonial representations.

King's textual amalgamations are characterized by satire and defamiliarization, retaining enough of the original material to trigger recognition yet comically distorting details to ascribe underlying motivations other than those postulated in the source texts. On the level of narrative, King deliberately transgresses conventional categories of (realist, historiographic, or ethnographic) representation and integrates texts and contexts from history, fiction, and myth. In all four parts of the novel, the mythical women are introduced in the framework of Native creation stories and subsequently encounter biblical figures and canonical literary characters or popular culture icons. Eventually, however, they all get captured and taken to Fort Marion in Florida. King thus links oral stories to various reimagined Western written texts but always ends up in historical reality: In 1875, seventy-two Indian leaders of the Plains Tribes' resistance against forced relocation and confinement to reservations were indeed taken to Florida and incarcerated at Fort Marion (see Goldman 1999, 21–23). By intertwining and putting into dialog Native oral, biblical, literary, and historical "stories," King uses intertextuality to defy the existence of one authoritative mode of representation. As Graham Allen points out, the concept of intertextuality is meant to designate a kind of language which, because of its embodiment of otherness, is against, beyond and resistant to (mono)logic. . . . Intertextuality encompasses that aspect of literary and other kinds of texts which struggles against and subverts reason, the belief in unity of meaning or of the human subject, and which is therefore subversive to all ideas of the logical and the unquestionable. (2000, 45)

Subverting (Western) reason, (mono)logic, hierarchy, and above all fixed interpretations, the novel comically challenges its readers to creatively reimagine familiar and new as well as Native and Western stories in a web-like discourse. As a result, it "shows us that difference is a question of perspective [, that o]therness is always relational" (Schorcht 2003, 68). It offers new perspectives on texts that have so far allowed for only one authoritative reading or been interpreted exclusively within a particular (Eurocentric) frame of reference. These canonical literary and historiographic texts can no longer be read as manifestos of a heroic civilizing mission, and the Native creation stories can no longer be viewed from an anthropological/ethnographic vantage point only. Instead, their juxtaposition stresses their common nature as textual representations and comically defies their alleged hierarchies. (If anything, King's use of humor grants primacy to a Native viewpoint.) Consequently, Ridington observes: "Sharing stories with Thomas King is not always unproblematic, but it is guaranteed to increase one's knowledge by connecting what you do know to something you ought to know. If you are lucky, you may even deconstruct something you thought you knew" (1999, 27).

Last but not least, the title of King's novel *Green Grass, Running Water* in itself constitutes an instance of comic intertextuality (which within Genette's classification would qualify as a paratextual element, see 1997, 3). "As long as the grass is green and the water runs" is an expression frequently employed in treaties between Euro-Americans and Natives to signal the Euro-American settlers' willingness to honor the agreement infinitely (see chapter four for a closer discussion).

The humorous use of intertextuality in contemporary Native writing, as King's text demonstrates, builds on its capacity to recontextualize, re-present, and reimagine Euro-American *and* Native cultural texts from a new vantage point, in the process destabilizing and deconstructing established hierarchies and habitual patterns of reading and interpretation. It not only transforms preexisting representation, but also inherently undercuts the possibility of definite readings in general. Through the humor arising from the incongruity between a text's original presentation and its altered re-presentation within a contemporary Native text, earlier readings are thrown into doubt and new perspectives can be freely adopted.

Like intertextuality, metafiction, that is, fiction that comments on or makes transparent its own fictional status, inherently highlights how narrative in general constitutes its subjects and therefore destabilizes the readers' credulity towards master narratives and historiography (see Hutcheon 1995a). The emphasis on a text's fictionality may, on the one hand, remove it from a given reality, that is, serve as a distancing device. On the other hand, it can also be a means to make readers confront this very reality more immediately by imagining it on a different level, enabling scrutiny. Hutcheon therefore disagrees with postulations

> that in metafiction the life-art connection has been either severed completely or resolutely denied. Instead, I would say that this "vital" link is reforged, on a new level — on that of the imaginative process (of storytelling), instead of on that of the product (the story told). And it is the new role of the reader that is the vehicle of that change. (1984, 3)

As outlined in chapter two, the connection between life and art/imagination in Native cultures was and is often perceived as stronger than in Western cultures. Moreover, it is considered reciprocally influential rather than reflective or mimetic. When Native writers make use of metafictionality, in addition to postmodernly utilizing its ability to highlight the fictional quality of *all* kinds of representation, they thus situate themselves within a Native narrative tradition that has always believed in an inseparable connection between word and world, between story and reality.

Consequently, the use of metafictional elements in contemporary Native texts is often related to characteristics of traditional oral narrative. In recreations of oral storytelling situations, the story may first introduce a storyteller in a framing plot, who subsequently — most often from a first-person perspective — relates the story itself. This creates at least two levels of narrative — embedded story and framing plot — which often mirror each other in *mise-en-abymic* fashion, as for instance in Suleiman Russell's "How Old Man Coyote Lost His Manhood" (2001) and in Thomas King's stories "The One About Coyote Going West" (1993; see Ruffo 1995 for a detailed narratological analysis) and "One Good Story, That One" (1993). In all of these stories, trickster narrators set up a framing plot in which they tell further stories, but eventually they blur the boundaries between these story levels and thus expose the "linguisticality of our constructed world and the illusoriness of that construction" (Doueihi 1993, 198). As far as these stories are concerned, the ultimate tricksters are therefore the authors themselves, who through their metafictional schemes lure readers into their stories.

Metafiction also offers the possibility of presenting more than one version of a story. The humor within such patterns also frequently arises from the storyteller him or herself either having trickster qualities or relating a trickster tale or both. In King's *Green Grass, Running Water* the four old Indian tricksters who relate four different versions of the same story contribute substantially to the novel's humor. In combination with the novel's structure, instances of metafiction comically highlight that the story is never fixed but continuously reshaped in a cyclical process of telling. Readers are, for instance, sent back to check on a previously told version:

> "Gha! Higayv:ligé:i," said Robinson Crusoe.
> "We've done that already," said Ishmael.
> "Have we?" said Robinson Crusoe.
> "Yes," said the Lone Ranger. "Page fifteen."
> "See. Top of page fifteen."
> "How embarrassing." (231)

Similarly, when the four old Indians joke about one of them "being omniscient again" (49), King intrigues readers by implicitly raising questions about narrative authority and the ability of textual representations to convey ultimate "facts" or Truths —questions the narrator seems to answer later in the novel by declaring: "There are no Truths, Coyote . . . Only stories" (391).

The four storytellers' humorous squabbles among themselves about whose turn it is to tell the story and the importance of getting the story right therefore add to the message already conveyed in the reimagined intertextual passages discussed above, namely that narrative, as all discourse, is both flexible and inherently interpretive. Coyote, the classical Native trickster figure, in King's novel can transcend the boundaries between various narrative strands, which leads to hilarious scenes, such as when he complains, "Boy . . ., this is a lot of running back and forth" (327); when he observes, "I was safer in that other story" (394); or when, after a longer absence from one narrative strand, he is chastised by the narrator for having left it unattended, "That's what happens when you don't pay attention" (293). This directive to pay attention is quite obviously also aimed at the readers, challenging them to closely scrutinize and question the information they are confronted with. They are, after all, caught in King's story web themselves, as becomes most amusingly apparent in a conversation that takes place between the narrator "I" and Coyote, but turns out to include the readers as well. Resuming one of the narrative strands after a longer intermission, the narrator asks:

> "You remember Old Woman? You remember that big hole and Young Man Walking On Water? You remember any of this at all?"
> "Sure," says Coyote. "I remember all of it."
> "I wasn't talking to you," I says.
> "Who else is there?"   (391)

The audience is, of course, which readers find out in comic self-recognition. With metafictional commentary, King not only mocks his own novel's complicated narrative structure and shifting perspectives (which sometimes ensue in interruptions of close to a hundred pages), he draws his audience into a text that may come closer to a storytelling performance than a written novel, and makes them part of the telling itself. Hutcheon, in view of the "emphasis on its enunciative situation — text, producer, receiver, historical context," calls historiographic metafiction a "communal project" (1995a, 82) that readers cannot detach themselves from. King's reliance on metafiction and elements from oral telling similarly engages readers in reimagining a narrative that for once gives equal attention to Euro-American and Native perspectives and epistemologies.

Carter Revard's "Never Quite a Hollywood Star" is probably the contemporary Native text that most fully relies on metafiction. Satirically conceptualized as an "Indian attack" on its readers, the text from the outset conveys complete awareness of its own fictionality:

> If your scalp itches, it may be because I'm temporarily controlling your mind. So don't try dandruff shampoo unless you have already looked out the window for the Indian attack; we are hiding behind the trees and shrubs on your lawn . . . . These words popping out on the page as you read are pouring out of the constellation you call the Big Dipper. Like neutrinos they pass through everything until they just happen to get the right brain to interface: then they break into the word-hoards, put on English, and come marching out altogether, clause left, clause right, wherever England was pink on the globe, and while you watch them take cover behind a yew hedge you can uncover the plot we are involved in. (2001, 53)

Rather than offering a continuous plot, the story consists of partly related fragments from different temporal and geographical settings. These fragments are interrupted by the narrator addressing the readers — "You feeling more at ease, reader, now the story has taken us this far?" (57) — or even the characters. After introducing the character of "William F. Buckley," or rather putting him "on [the] Firing Line in the back of this reader's mind," for instance, the narrator continues: "Of course he will get very frustrated if I keep talking over his head to you, so please, sweet William, keep quiet for a moment and let my story begin" (54). Revard's transgression of the boundaries between narrator, readers, and characters all within one sentence is funny enough in itself through its destabilizing of narrative conventions. The narrator's admonition gains momentum, however, when readers are aware that Revard also blurs the line that separates reality and fiction: "sweet William Buckley" is modeled on the conservative founder and chief editor of the *National Review* (that is, on a real person who indeed would not have it that others "keep talking over his head"). Moreover, the text conveys the impression that the story is cocreated by reader and narrator in a dialogic, almost conspiratorial process. It is entirely told in the present tense; the narrator soon replaces the initial "my story" with "our story" (55), and eventually he describes the plot as directed by narrator and readers alike. The death of one of the characters, for instance, is not referred to as "he died" but rather as "We kill him" (55).

Like King's intricate allusions, Revard's metafictional technique draws readers into the story and turns them into listeners and even accomplices. Together with the narrator — who in this particular case is identical with the author, as becomes apparent at the end of the story — the readers imaginatively revisit the AIM protests at Wounded Knee, witness one of the many car wrecks on Indian reservations, and are eventually taken to a powwow. Throughout, Revard makes (Euro-American) readers look through Native eyes — quite literally, since all sensory details appear unmediated — and by means of mocking commentary shifts their allegiances to Native viewpoints. In the final step of this progressive integration, he even turns the (Euro-American) readers into the story's Indian protagonists, blurring yet another boundary, that of ethnicity: "You see, reader? I have made you for the occasion one of us" (59). Revard's text starts out with the Indian attack, deliberately invoking stereotypical images from Western movies. Subsequently, however, through its use of metafiction, it makes Euro-American readers experience a contemporary Native reality that turns out to be vastly different from clichéd expectations. Eventually, Revard comically deflates the initial "Indian attack" to a trip into his own study: "Now, you can scratch your scalp, if it itches; you see it's safe . . ., this Indian just professor" (62). On the whole, Revard's story turns the intricacies of (linguistic/literary) representation into a subversive weapon against debilitating stereotypes. With imagination being "the only weapon on the reservation" (Alexie 1994, 150), Revard's tale about the invasion of the readers' mind, despite all its martial metaphors, can thus be read as a most literal example of a mediating humorous reimagining of Nativeness. As illustrated by this and the previous examples, the use of metafiction in contemporary Native writing on the one hand ties in with an oral mode of telling, in that it highlights the enunciative situation as such. On the other hand, it constitutes a means of blurring boundaries between text and reader and of undercutting binary oppositions such as reality versus fiction, White versus Native, mimetic versus constitutive concepts of representation. By drawing readers into the text, it wields substantial power to revise previous representations.

In contrast with the highly dialogic and integrative use of metafiction, comic reversal may appear less compatible with the idea of reimagining Nativeness through humor, since by simply reversing existing stereotypes, binary oppositions might be reconfirmed rather than deconstructed. Yet, where it comically shatters conventional patterns of interpretation by "holding up a mirror to reality (and sometimes giving it a slight twist)" (Goodman 1983, 15), comic reversal may cause an imaginative revision nonetheless. The surprised laughter that an upside down perspective may elicit can liberate readers from underlying clichés and conventional vantage points. Carter Revard's "Report to the Nation: Claiming Europe," discussed above, which reverses the European conquest of America, is a case in point. A comparable effect is achieved in Gerald Vizenor's story "Trickster Photography," which reverses nineteenth-century photographer Edward Curtis's practice of photographing Indians in stoic poses, adorned with (generic) "Indian" paraphernalia. The story features Tune Browne, a "tribal photographer who [not only] pictured stoical whites and focused on their noses, necks, ears" (1994a, 142) but also sends a picture of his Native grandmother in a boy scout uniform to a hypocritical curator, thereby reversing the popular game of "playing Indian" (see P. Deloria 1998). This and similar reversals in contemporary Native texts — such as Vizenor's reversal of the Bering Strait theory or Thomas King's reversal of the outcome of a John Wayne and Richard Widmark Western, discussed below — do not cement dualisms by merely providing a view from the other side; they playfully expose the arbitrariness and bias inherent in binary oppositions in general, and thus overthrow rather than reinforce fixed categories.

Naming and (Historical) Allusion

Naming as a strategy within contemporary Native texts figures on various levels: First of all, Native authors can name characters, settings, or other elements in their writings in (ironical) allusion to historical persons, places, or circumstances; secondly, they may use stereotypically "Indian" names with a comic twist in order to parody clichéd expectations; and thirdly, the process of naming itself and its role in the process of colonization may, on a metalevel, be targets of satiric revision. Subsequently, these possibilities are discussed in reverse order.

"One of the most subtle demonstrations of the power of language is the means by which it provides, through the functions of naming, a technique for knowing a colonised place or people. To name the world is to 'understand' it, to know it and to have control over it" (Ashcroft, Griffiths, and Tiffin 1995, 283). Naming, clearly a prerogative of power, is a privilege held by Euro-American explorers and settlers, who simultaneously named and claimed new territories while ignoring existing Native inhabitants and names. This practice, with its inherent disrespect for other cultures, is mocked in *Green Grass, Running Water* when Ahdamn (in a parody of Genesis) names the animals and plants in the garden:

> You are a microwave oven, Ahdamn tells the Elk.
> Nope, says that Elk. Try again.
> You are a garage sale, Ahdamn tells the Bear.
> We got to get you some glasses, says the Bear.
> You are a telephone book, Ahdamn tells the Cedar Tree.
> You're getting closer, says the Cedar Tree.
> You are a cheeseburger, Ahdamn tells Old Coyote.
> It must be time for lunch, says Old Coyote. (King 1994, 41)

By providing both the already existing names and Ahdamn's new names, King stresses that the inhabitants of the garden already *have* names and that only Ahdamn's need to refer to them in terms familiar to *him* necessitates renaming. This, of course, derides similar practices by European explorers, who brought their Old World expectations and ideas to the new continent, and renamed and classified everything accordingly. It is no coincidence that Ahdamn renames everything along the lines of consumer products: The explorers also showed little interest in how Native cultures referred to themselves or their land, but conceived of the newly discovered continent mostly in terms of its resources. The absurdity of Ahdamn's suggestions, finally, mirrors the absurdity of colonial naming practices, while the renamed subjects' sardonic retorts subvert colonial dominance.[18]

Colonial naming practices also characterize the behavior of the above-mentioned canonical heroes in *Green Grass, Running Water*. As a rule, they ignore the names of the mythical female characters they encounter and try to name them according to their preestablished ideas of the indigenous Other/colonial sidekick. *Moby Dick's* Ishmael, for instance, tries to turn Changing Woman into Queequeg, as the story he originates from calls for one: "This book has Queequeg in it, and this story is supposed to have a Queequeg in it, but I've looked all over the ship and there aren't any Queequegs" (95). Similarly, a list-obsessed Robinson Crusoe, upon encountering Thought Woman, exclaims in a hilarious send-up of the wish for the working week to end: "Thank God! . . . It's Friday! No, says Thought Woman. It's Wednesday" (294). And lastly, "Nasty" Bumppo — King's ironical version of Natty Bumppo, Cooper's hero from the *Leatherstocking Tales* — names Thought Woman Chingachgook on the basis of a generic Indianness: "I'm not Chingachgook, says Old Woman. Nasty runs to the next tree and hides behind it. Nonsense, he says. I can tell an Indian when I see one. Chingachgook is an Indian. You're an Indian. Case closed" (392). The text therefore ridicules the combination of ignorance, disinterest, and Eurocentrism that led to the colonial renaming of North America's cultures and landscapes and the conflating misnomer of all Native people as Indians. In laughing at the text's re-presentations, readers are freed from the colonially determined patterns of interpretation that so clearly govern the male canonical heroes' behavior and are enticed to question colonial naming practices.

In addition to such mockery of the procedure of naming, Native writers may use the names themselves, in a strategy of subversive mimicry, to partially comply with accustomed patterns of expectation, just to destabilize from within. Mocking formulaic "Indian" names in the vein of *Dances With Wolves*, for instance, elder Keeper suggests names such as "Wind in His Pants, Plenty Bingos, Busts Up Laughing or Sneaks Off Necking. Somethin' really Indyun. Heh, heh, heh" (Wagamese 1994, 36). Other examples are characters named Luke Warm Water (Northrup 1993) and

"Eddie Tap Water. Used to be Spring Water. But I'm Urban Indian now" (Alexie 1996a, 150). Speaking names may comically characterize their bearers, as in Jim Northrup's story "Looking with Ben" (1993). The story's trickster protagonist Ben Looking Back steps inside of an empty diorama space at the Smithsonian Museum in Washington, holds up a sign that says "Contemporary Chippewa," and literally "looks back" at the White visitors. The readers, as implied in the title, are "looking with Ben," that is, taking on the outlook of the reified Indian as object of the colonial gaze.

Humor also arises when such names are intended satirically, but are mistaken for "real Indian names" by a society more familiar with the simulacrum of "the Indian" than with real Native people named Smith or Jones. Will, the protagonist of Thomas King's novel *Medicine River*, answers the nurse's question of how to name his partner's newborn with the first words his eyes fall on — a sign in the hospital directing visitors to the " 'South Wing.' I guess I expected the nurse to laugh, but she didn't. 'Is that a traditional Indian name?' 'I was just joking.' 'No, I think it's a beautiful name' " (1995, 40). Yet telling names may also satirize White people who, in an attempt to "go Indian," adopt "Indian" names for themselves. In Emma Lee Warrior's short story "Compatriots" (1992), for instance, a self-appointed (originally German) expert of Native culture, who tries to be more Indian than the Blood Indians around him, is named "Helmut Walking Eagle," an allusion to the real "German Blood Indian" Adolph Hungry Wolf.[19] This name is doubly ironic, as Lutz points out: "On the physical level you simply have to picture an eagle walking — on the ground he is little more than a lame duck. On the historical and political level, the author reflects changes in German political leadership: No longer an 'Adolph,' but there were two consecutive chancellors called 'Helmut' " (2002, 93). By naming this wannabe character Helmut Walking Eagle, the story therefore on the one hand ridicules his narrow-minded seriousness in trying to be Blackfoot, and on the other hand wittily cautions against Euro-American appropriative tendencies in general.

Finally, contemporary Native writers may reverse colonial naming strategies by assigning telling/allusive names to Euro-American characters. Allusion by definition does not explain but makes reference to shared knowledge. That is, preexisting representations are activated, but the ensuing incongruous recontextualizations of these representations leave it to the readers to imaginatively establish the right connections. As with intertextuality or parody, the reliance on shared knowledge as a precondition for humor may become problematic. If, for instance, readers lack the knowledge that Cotton Mather was a Puritan preacher and scholar who considered Natives to be the devil's children, the fact that an ignorant and patronizing White professor of Native literature in Sherman Alexie's novel *Indian Killer* is named C. Mather loses all significance. If allusion succeeds, however, it is highly effective. Decontextualizing historical specifics or characteristics of historical persons from their original background and recontextualizing them in contemporary Native texts then triggers recognition while simultaneously effecting defamiliarization and reimagining.[20]

In *Reservation Blues*, which focuses on the members of "Coyote Springs," an all-Indian rock band on the Spokane Reservation in Washington, Sherman Alexie uses both naming and historical allusion. With dark humor, he allusively reimagines history in order to elicit a reinterpretation of both historical and contemporary (Native) America within as well as beyond the text. Alexie flouts linear notions of time: The contemporary plot (set in 1992) is interspersed with scenes from the 1858 slaughter of the Spokanes' horses at the hands of two US Army generals, Phil Sheridan and George Wright. This hybridization of past and present is signaled by the reappearance of Sheridan and Wright in the contemporary plot, as well as by the character of Big Mom, a musical genius and spiritual leader who lives outside linear time. She both witnessed the original massacre (which Alexie repeatedly alludes to through the "screaming horses") and lives on the Spokane reservation at the time the novel's contemporary plot takes place:

> One hundred and thirty-four years before Robert Johnson walked onto the Spokane Reservation, the Indian horses screamed. . . . The song sounded so pained and tortured that Big Mom could never have imagined it before the white men came, and never understood it later, even at the edge of the twenty-first century. . . . Finally, the horses stopped screaming their song, and Big Mom listened to the silence that followed. Then she went back to her work, to her buckskin and beads, to CNN. . . . As she stepped out the front door, Big Mom heard the first gunshot which reverberated in her DNA . . ., she saw the future and the past, the white soldiers in blue uniforms with black rifles and pistols. She saw the Indian horses shot and fallen like tattered sheets. (1996a, 9–10)

In addition to thus blurring past and present and hybridizing Native and Western cultures (buckskin and beads and CNN), Alexie progressively erases the distinction between the killed horses and Spokane Indian people. This alludes to the genocidal practices by which the US Army in the nineteenth century decimated America's indigenous population (see especially 142–44, 306); yet Alexie also extends the allusion to the poor living conditions and still shorter than average life expectancy of Native people in the twentieth century when he writes: "That colt fell to the grass of the clearing, to the sidewalk outside a reservation tavern, to the cold, hard coroner's table in a Veterans Hospital" (10). In either case, the past refuses to remain within its tidy historiographic boundaries. (In an interview Alexie asserts: "The past is still here for us. We carry all of that with us"; in Bellante and Bellante 1994, 14). Instead, it spills over into imagination, where it influences the readers' understanding of history. Throughout the novel, history is reimagined to demonstrate how revisionist readings of the past continue to influence the contemporary Native characters' (and contemporary Native people's) self-conceptualization.

Most of the humor in Alexie's allusive scheme originates from the transferal of the initial encounter between the Spokanes and Sheridan and Wright in 1858 to the twentieth-century music business. Not only do the slaughtered "horses" now return to Big Mom "in different forms and with different songs, call[ing] themselves Janis Joplin, Jimi Hendrix, Marvin Gaye, and so many other names" (10); her latest protégés, Coyote Springs, are contacted by two short, mustached music agents who introduce themselves as "Phil Sheridan and George Wright from Cavalry Records in New York City. We've come to talk to you about a recording contract" (189). To support the link between the contemporary characters and the historical figures of Sheridan and Wright, Alexie intersperses the contemporary plot with historical allusions. The music agents wave their cigarettes "like a saber" (236); they drink from an antique flask that they "had been drinking from . . . for a century, give or take a few decades" (193); and they address each other as "soldier" and "officer" (193) and are referred to as "Cavalry officers" (226). Their company is called "Cavalry Records," ironically headed by a "Mr. Armstrong" (named after General George Armstrong Custer[21]), which reframes their contemporary exploitation of "Coyote Springs" in terms of the so-called "Indian Wars" of the nineteenth century. Instead of taking the Indians' land and horses, Alexie implies, today Euro-Americans help themselves to Indian culture and talent.

Readers, introduced to the historical Sheridan and Wright at the beginning of the novel, are encouraged to enjoy decoding these little hints and incongruities, in the process recontextualizing the historical events in light of the contemporary plot and vice versa. The full force of the text's reimaginative humor unfolds in the blatant parallels between the behavior and attitudes of the army generals and the record company executives. The novel comically challenges the glorifying representations of the honored Indian fighters' achievements by exposing their contemporary counterparts' (selfish) motivations. Just as the contemporary music agents are only out for their own financial gain (at all cost for Coyote Springs), the US government and army, the text insinuates, had cared little about Native people in their alleged civilizing mission, but had craved Native lands and resources. After hearing Coyote Springs play, for instance, Sheridan and Wright report their first impressions back to the company's president in a fax message that clearly reveals their exploitative impetus: "We can really dress this group up, give them war paint, feathers, etc., and really play up the Indian angle. I think this band could prove very lucrative for Cavalry Records" (190). Most ironically, they sign this message with "Peace, Phil Sheridan, George Wright" (190), belying their historical counterparts' reputation as merciless Indian fighters, as exemplified in Sheridan's well known aphorism, "The only good Indian is a dead Indian."

Alexie's novel thus most amusingly mocks America's historical self-conceptualization. American history tends to represent the indigenous population as poor heathen savages whose introduction to the "benefits" of progress and Christianity was a task the new nation took upon itself with the best intentions, almost sacrificially. This distorted self-image is bitingly epitomized in music agent Sheridan's reaction to Coyote Springs not being as cooperative as expected during a recording: " 'That's it,' Sheridan said to Wright. 'I'm out of here. I tried to help these goddamn Indians. But they don't want help. They don't want anything' " (229). In a dream one of the band members has after the ill-fated audition, Sheridan even undergoes a complete metamorphosis to become his historical self. He relates the band's contemporary failure to the historical "failure" of Indians to "cooperate": "*You blew it up by acting like a bunch of goddamn Indians. I might have been able to talk Mr. Armstrong into listening to you again. . . . We gave you every chance. All you had to do was move to a reservation. We would've protected you. The U.S. Army was the best friend the Indians ever had*" (236–37). The connections these allusions establish constitute a piercing reassessment of US history, while the contemporary Sheridan's continued racism sadly insinuates that America's relations with its Native people are still tainted by distrust and oppression. Yet Alexie's reimaginative puzzle also points towards change and possibly a better future. In contrast to Sheridan's ever deepening hatred for Indians, the character of Wright slowly takes on more positive features in the course of the novel. Recognizing his own historical wrongs in the faces of Coyote Springs, and driven by guilt, he offers penance and retribution. The text "rights" Wright's perspective on the past, and it partly tones down Sheridan's full-fledged loathing to mere annoyance with Indian resistance: "We keep winning the war. But you won't surrender" (237). History in *Reservation Blues*, while bitingly pointing to ongoing colonial oppression and misrepresentation, consequently is eventually transformed into a celebratory tale of Native survival — which, to Sheridan's comic frustration, constantly repeats itself, with Native people refusing to vanish. At the end of the novel Big Mom teaches the band "a new song, the shadow horses' song, the slaughtered horses' song, a song of mourning that would become a song of celebration: we have survived, we have survived" (306).

As these examples show, the practice of naming, both as theme and strategy, holds an immense subversive potential for contemporary Native texts. It undermines stereotypical ideas of "the Indian" and defies colonial subjectification and appropriation of "Indian" names by Euro-Americans. Most importantly, in conjunction with allusion it serves as an instrument for recontextualizing history. With humor and imagination, Native writing opens up new vistas and consequently calls forth reconsiderations of both America's historical self-conceptualization and its contemporary relations with Native people. Through allusion, Native writers may point to particular "facts" and interpretations but playfully present them in an entirely different light. In some instances, they may even transcode the original reading of particular Western cultural values or icons — transcoding here describing the practice of "taking an existing meaning and re-appropriating it for new meanings (for example, 'Black is Beautiful')" (Hall 1997b, 270).

Trickster Characters

"The trickster arises in imagination and the trickster lives nowhere but in imagination. We all have a trickster in the mind if we have any sense of play and imagination about literature. The trickster is a brilliant tribal figure of imagination that has found a new world in written languages," writes Gerald Vizenor (1993b, 68). What better means for Native writers to negotiate Nativeness? A "key player in Indian humor, from the early narratives up to today" (Lowe 1994, 194), the trickster is part of the oral tradition of nearly every tribe, taking on various human and animal embodiments. To try to analyze the trickster is in itself a tricky business, though. Essentially, this figure defies categorization and analysis, shape-shifts to eclipse her/himself from academic view, and disrupts all attempts at (academic) definition.[22] Most often, tricksters appear as Coyote, but in the Northwest he/she is Raven, in the East Hare, in some cultures Mink, Wolverine, Napi, Old Man, Bluejay, or Badger, in others Ishimiki, Manabozo, Nanabush, Wee-sak-a-chak, Iktomi, or Spider. Trickster's transformational possibilities include cross-dressing, sex- and gender-switching,[23] and even complete shape-shifting when the situation requires it. Tricksters often literally "embody" the grotesque or paradox in that they "possess anatomical and physiological incongruities such as grotesque form, intestines outside the body, a long penis wrapped around the body, eyes that are uneven and both inside and outside the sockets, and so forth. Tricksters also lack a sense of unity and coordination of their body parts" (Apte 1983, 193). In traditional mythologies, trickster figures are characterized by a seemingly contradictory set of traits: They are amoral and irresponsible, cunning and sly. Although they are basically preoccupied with the satisfaction of their own basal desires — and for that may steal and cheat, seduce and break rules — they are not intentionally malicious, but in their impulsiveness display an infantile innocence (see Baker 1991, 49). Restless wanderers and bricoleurs, insatiable gluttons and lechers, they give in to all their appetites, and ultimately are both spoilers and clowns, losers and survivors (see Bright 1987, 340, 356). Their survival skills are especially important since many of the schemes they hatch for others backfire on them because they overestimate their abilities. In trickster cycles, the protagonist often dies at the end of one tale, but is resurrected at the beginning of the next. Tricksters are both culture heroes and fools. Their chaotic exploits are, on the one hand, socially and morally disruptive because they commit sacrileges; yet on the other hand, tricksters' pranks also have beneficial results for humankind (for example, introducing fire or salmon into the world or slaying monsters, see Bright 1987). A trickster thus is "between God and man, and as such is both a link to God and a comic butt who mirrors man's own failings and glories" (Lowe 1994, 194; see also Radin 1972, xxiii).

Of the various functions of traditional trickster tales, the most important in the context of this study is their use in the "reexamination of existing conditions," that is, the way they provide "an opportunity for realizing that an accepted pattern has no necessity . . ., that any particular ordering of experience may be arbitrary and subjective" (Babcock-Abrahams 1974, 183–84).[24] In this capacity, trickster tales, as Babcock points out (and as chapter two, in its discussion of reimagining through humor, argues), can liberate the audience from all norms and habitual categories, in effect, creating a *communitas* in Victor Turner's sense, where "hierarchies are leveled, distinctions dissolved, and roles reversed" (Babcock-Abrahams 1974, 185). Within classical trickster tales the audience is free to imagine (along with the trickster) a transgression and flouting of constraints or rules. Leading to a "startl[ing] into fresh views," trickster stories thus create a space of liminality, "a realm of pure possibility whence novel configurations of ideas and relations may arise" (185).

While trickster characters in contemporary Native writing rarely display the graphically transgressive sexual or scatological behavior of their traditional predecessors,[25] they retain their disconcerting qualities. Accordingly, they may open up an imaginative liminal space where the monolithic "Indian" chiseled by Hollywood and nineteenth-century literature can be shattered and where one-dimensional readings of Native-White history can be transgressed. In the clash between Native narrative traditions and Western cultural contexts, trickster characters introduce a healthy amount of liberating chaos, answering Gerald Vizenor's demand that "some upsetting is necessary" (in Bowers and Silet 1981, 47). Simultaneously, as ultimate survivors, they metaphorically stand for the survival, continuity, and reaffirmation of Native cultural values (see Allen 1992, 158; Blaeser 1993, 60). Thomas King, for instance, claims the trickster is "an important figure for Native writers for it allows us to create a particular kind of world in which the Judeo-Christian concern with good and evil and order and disorder is replaced with the more Native concern for balance and harmony" (1992, xiii).[26] Finally, in the same way that traditional tricksters mediate between gods and humans, men and women, inanimate and animate beings (see Horne 1999, 129; Babcock and Cox 1994, 100–101), contemporary trickster characters may serve as humorous mediators between Euro-American and Native, traditionalist and progressive views and conceptualizations. In summary, contemporary trickster tales disrupt pretensions of White superiority and stereotypical representations of Nativeness, directly strengthen Native cultural identity, and mediate the (re-)negotiation of cultural values and representations.

The tricksters who appear in contemporary Native writing are a wide variety. Some are "classical" tricksters, for instance, in coyote tales such as Beth Brant's "Coyote Learns a New Trick" (1985), Thomas King's "The One About Coyote Going West" and "A Coyote Columbus Story" (1993), and Suleiman Russell's "How Old Man Coyote Lost His Manhood" (2001). Others are complex characters endowed with

> several of the key attributes of the trickster figure. Rather than create characters who are inferior and dying, Native writers have consciously created characters who are resourceful, vibrant, and tenacious. . . . Whatever the damage, contemporary characters, like their traditional trickster relations, rise from their own wreckage to begin again. (King 1987, 8)

Gerald Vizenor's screenplay *Harold of Orange* presents such characters. Written in 1983 and shot in 1984, the film tells the story of Harold and his Warriors of Orange, out to fool liberal White foundations into funding (nonexisting) tribal projects. Tricksterism underlies the entire film. The theme is introduced in the opening music, Buffy Sainte-Marie's "Trickster Song." The song explains the underlying rationale for Harold and his Warriors' behavior throughout the film. That rationale is made explicit in framing voice-overs at the beginning and end of the film, in which Harold and the Warriors are introduced as "descendants of the great trickster who created the new earth after the flood . . ., determined to reclaim their estate from the white man" (Vizenor 1993a, 53). And finally, on a metalevel, tricksterism is also the determinative principle of Vizenor's writing itself, inherent in his playful use of language, structure, and ideas. The Native/mixedblood protagonists' very names indicate their trickster nature: Harold's telling last name is Sinseer, as he explains to a police officer:

POLICE OFFICER:	Sincere?
HAROLD	Sinseer, yes, my name is on this letter . . .
POLICE OFFICER:	Sincerely, is that it there?
HAROLD:	Sinseer on the top, sincerely on the bottom. (73–74)

Far from being sincere (he is a trickster, after all), he rather "sees sins" — both his own and society's — and makes them visible for the audience as well. His "Warriors of Orange," likewise, playfully allude both to previous pranks of the group and to the Irish Orange Order — which is especially ironic since this organization arose in defense of Protestant beliefs, whereas Native people in America suffered tremendously from the aggressive conversion and civilizing mission at the hands of the Puritans and later settlers. In their previous hoax, the Warriors had tricked the Bily Foundation into supporting an imaginative project of growing "miniature oranges . . . in a

secret place to avoid pests and competition" (64). These only exist, however, in one token pot in the "Harold of Orange Coffee House," the
Warriors' headquarters, and in crates ordered from an organic farmer to
take along to the foundation meeting as evidence of the project's success.
Moreover, Harold's very appearance defies clichéd ideas of the stoic, mus-
cular Hollywood Indian "warrior": He is deeply humorous, and like his
Coyote predecessor in his motley coat, Harold arrives on the scene in a
"damaged car, assembled from multicolored parts . . . [with] bald tire[s]"
and *"has a round brown face and black hair. His cheeks are full and his
relaxed stomach behind the wheel folds over his wide beaded belt about two
inches"* (55).

Together, Harold and his Warriors constitute "the new school of
socioacupuncture where a little pressure fills the purse" (55).
Socioacupuncture is one of Vizenor's typical neologisms, which he considers "a mixed blood tribal effort at 'deconstruction.' I want to break the
language down, I want to re-imagine the language" (in Bruchac 1987a,
293). The term describes "the right pressure at the right place at the right
time and tricksters are marvelous at that, especially tribal tricksters. You
apply just the right humor and the right pressure at the right moment to
convince or persuade or to achieve something" (293). Harold and the
Warriors apply this principle, on one level, in their latest scheme of per-
suading the foundation to fund yet another project, the growing of tribal
pinch bean coffee. They employ their Nativeness to push the right buttons
of the all-White and anxiously liberal foundation board members. They
thus fulfill the classical double trickster role of schemer and culture hero by
tricking the foundation for a beneficial purpose, namely, to raise money for
the community (ironically, the shooting of *Harold of Orange* itself was
financed by foundation money, see Silberman 1985, 6). And, on a metalevel between text and reader/viewer, it describes Vizenor's own tricksterlike strategy of "applying just the right humor . . . to convince or
persuade" his audience (Vizenor in Bruchac 1987a, 293).

The screenplay serves as a showground for scrutinizing and reinter-
preting historical and contemporary Native-White relations from a trickster's vantage point. In subversive mimicry, the Warriors dress up as
civilized entrepreneurs, counting on the fact that "no one can resist a skin
in a necktie" (58) — just as Harold assures the audience that he and the
Warriors "run a clean coffee house, tend to our miniature oranges" (55),
and consequently constitute splendid specimens of the fully assimilated
Indian. But for these tricksters the capitalist system is one huge game:
"You know the old foundation game, we get the money and the foundation gets the good name" (63), Harold explains. Accordingly, the idea of
gambling (which appears in many traditional trickster tales) plays a substantial role in Vizenor's text. Much of the humor, as Blaeser demonstrates, arises from Vizenor's juxtaposition of two incompatible frames of

reference, "the serious, conventional ideas about foundations, their methods, and their intentions" on the one hand, and elements that "stem from the subplots of comic intrigue and game playing" on the other (1996, 152), with the latter comically undermining the first.

Harold and the Warriors try to charm/trick the foundation with three schemes: first, a fake naming ceremony, second, a staged "ghost dance," and third, a softball game. In all of these scenes, Vizenor uses trickster humor to expose "the Indian" as a simulacrum, but also to reimagine how contemporary Native people may put this cliché to their own use. In the highly comic naming ceremony, for instance, Harold in pseudoritualistic manner ascribes urban dream names drawn from "a cigar box with a cigar store Indian on the label" (69) to the foundation board members. He comically fulfills their desires to partake in "authentic" Indian culture in order to ensure the project's funding.

The second scene, set in front of the artifact cases of an anthropology department, stages a contemporary reenactment of the ghost dance, a movement that in the nineteenth century united many Native nations under the leadership of the Indian visionary Wovoka, who foretold the return of the buffalo and the disappearance of White settlers from America. Thereby, Harold not only denounces anthropologists for misconstruing the image of Native people and appropriating Native cultural material and remains — "those anthropologists over there will be buried upside down with their toes exposed like mushrooms"; himself a mixedblood, he also sarcastically derides orthodox and essentializing ideas of racial purity held by Native people themselves: "Mixedbloods will be buried as deep as their white blood . . . The more the deeper . . . Fullbloods will levitate in a sacred dance at the treelines" (72–73). In classical trickster manner, he disrupts one-dimensional representations of Nativeness in an apparently paradoxical statement by explaining: "The cultures anthropologists invent never complain about anything" (75). Harold thus exposes "authentic Indianness" as a popular, as well as an academic fabrication, but simultaneously points to the deplorable fact that this invention has partly been internalized by Native people. As Vizenor explains in an interview: "The hardest part of it is I believe we're all invented as Indians. . . . We're invented from traditional static standards and we are stuck in coins and words like artifacts. So we take up a belief and settle with it, stuck, static. Some upsetting is necessary" (in Bowers and Silet 1981, 47).

The third and last part of the Warrior's playful promotion tour, the softball game, does, as a prototypical instance of trickster inversion, offer "some upsetting." Here, the Warriors wear shirts that read "Anglos," and the foundation board members are clad in "Indians" shirts. Harold coaches both teams, and like the traditional shape-shifting trickster, transforms himself by changing shirts depending on who he is talking to. In a biting satire, he advises the Warriors (as "Anglos"):

> Listen gang, we are the "Anglos" and we're here to win and win big . . .
> Play by the rules if you must, but rape and plunder to win the game . . .
> When the "Indians" talk about the earth and their sacred ceremonies,
> steal a base, win the game like we stole their land, with a smile . . . Score,
> score, score, in the name of god, win, and send those "Indians" back to
> the reservation as victims, where the slow grass grows . . . We'll mine the
> resources later. (76–77)

With the "Indians" team (that is, the foundation board members), in contrast, Harold uses romanticizing ideas of Indian spiritualism and peacefulness to talk them into a hopelessly unconfrontational strategy. In the liminal space created by satire and an imaginative transferal of history to the setting of a softball game, Vizenor here dislocates the audience from accustomed readings and interpretations. The Puritan ideology of manifest destiny is decontextualized and re-presented from a Native perspective. Euro-American policies are caricatured and the hypocrisy inherent in both the alleged civilizing mission itself and its revisionist historiographic accounts made blatantly transparent.

Throughout, Vizenor engages tricksterlike with clichéd notions of Nativeness, essentialist ideas, and the appropriative tendencies displayed by White "wannabes" or academics. He expounds these issues in conversations between the Warriors and the White foundation board members that reveal the latter's stereotypes and patronizing attitude. One of them, for instance, lauds the Warriors' intention to "*better yourselves* in a miniature orchard of your own reservation" (65; emphasis added). And another inquires about alcoholism on the reservation: "My question is, ahh, how did all of you overcome the need and temptation to use alcohol? You are so sober, *a credit to your race*" (81; emphasis added). A typical trickster character, Harold does not answer this question straightforwardly. Instead, he takes up the inversion from the softball game and comments: "The 'Indians' seemed sober to me during the ball game . . .," to which one of the Warriors adds: "Even the 'Anglos' . . ." (80). This intentional mix-up results in a carnivalesque leveling of Natives and Whites, as it implies that alcoholism is a problem shared by *both* groups. It is these trickster strategies of undercutting hierarchies by comically disrupting the very categories and assumptions they are built on that make characters like Harold and his Warriors such wonderful (and ubiquitous) instruments of humorous reimagining in contemporary Native writing.

Two scenes from Vizenor's screenplay that are especially exemplary of trickster subversion conclude this discussion, the first dealing with Eurocentric Western scientific reasoning, the second aimed at historiographic paradigms. In the first, New Crows, one of the Warriors, in conversation with (White) foundation board member Andrew shakes the latter's unquestioning belief in Western science. He opposes it with an equally strong conviction in tribal origin mythologies, and casually inverts the Bering Strait theory (which, held by Europeans as early as the sixteenth century, maintains that Native Americans must have traveled from Asia via Alaska into America over a then-existing land bridge):

ANDREW:	I have considered the origin theories of the American Indians . . . Some are *quite* interesting. I find the Bering Strait migration theory to be the most credible . . . How about you then, what are your thoughts on the subject?
New Crows:	Which way, east or west?
ANDREW :	Which *way*? What do you mean?
New Crows:	Which way across the Bering Strait, *then*?
ANDREW :	Yes, I see . . . Well, I hadn't really thought about it that way. Which way do *you* think?
New Crows:	From here to there, we emerged from the flood here, the first people, unless you think we are related to the panda bear.
ANDREW :	Oh, not at all, not at all . . . Actually, What you say makes a great deal of sense, but the problem I seem to have, you see, is that there is so little evidence to support your idea . . .
New Crows:	Jesus Christ was an American Indian . . . (66)

Through New Crows's inversion, the text in effect establishes Indians as the first people (just as King's *Green Grass, Running Water* does by reducing the Judeo-Christian God to a Coyote Dream). Especially the last sentence of the quote reveals that statements are relational and that authority and truth are never fixed but always constructed in discourse. New Crows's "unfounded" claims turn presumably stable epistemological ground into a minefield for Andrew (who thinks himself liberal and sympathetic to "the Indian cause"), and implicitly expose the way that science ethnocentrically substantiates notions of White superiority. Humor in this case arises from the surprising clash between the views held by Andrew and New Crows. Yet readers basically laugh at themselves in realizing that they, along with Andrew, "hadn't really thought about it that way," either, and had accepted the Eurocentric reasoning simply because of its mode of representations as scientific fact. Tricksterlike and unwittingly, Vizenor thus shifts the readers' perspective. As Blaeser points out: "The moment of humor and imbalance such a scene creates for the audience is Vizenor's wedge in, his ploy to soften their resistance to other 'betrayals' of historical dogma, and move to incite the audiences own re-reading of history" (1998, 164).

Another such "betrayal" occurs in a scene in which foundation board member Ted, referring to an article in *National Geographic*, speculates about the number of indigenous people at the time of Columbus's arrival:

TED:	Christopher Columbus, when he discovered the New World . . . Well, actually an island . . . How many Indians were there then, here I mean, on this continent?
SON BEAR:	None.
TED:	None? What do you mean *none*?

SON BEAR: None, not one. Columbus never discovered anything, and when he never did he invented us as Indians because we never heard the word before he dropped by by accident . . .

TED: Of course, I see what you mean . . . Well, let me phrase the question in a different way then. How many tribal people were there here then, ahh, before Columbus invented Indians? . . .

SON BEAR: Forty-nine million, seven hundred twenty-three thousand, one hundred and ninety-six on this continent, including what is now Mexico . . . (68)

Son Bear here subverts Ted's "scientific neutrality" in a two-step process. By forcing Ted to rephrase his question through his pretend ignorance, he first of all draws attention to the way particular forms of discourse construe biased representations of history: America was neither "discovered" by Columbus — as it was already inhabited — nor could the diverse cultures living there be subsumed under a common denominator "Indians." In a second step, however, Son Bear suddenly mimics Ted's pseudoscientific discourse and beats Ted with his own weapons by providing ridiculously exact data, that is, the *exact* number of Native people living on the continent at Columbus's arrival.

Both New Crows and Son Bear startle the audience into laughter through their highly incongruous claims: They liberate them from accustomed perspectives and interpretations and induce them to reimagine "alterNative" (Taylor 2000a) versions and viewpoints. In an interview, Vizenor explains that "writers in general are tricksters in the broadest sense of disruption. I don't think it's worth writing, for myself, unless you can break up a little bit. I don't think it's worth the energy unless the formulas can be broken down, unless the expectations of the reader are disrupted" (in Bruchac 1987a, 294). This is exactly what he does in *Harold of Orange*. Closely engaging with existing representations of Nativeness and Native-White history, the text, as Blaeser claims, "take[s] for granted, and force[s] recognition of, the already embattled visions all readers bring to the text. Is America virgin land or widowed land? Did Native peoples migrate to this continent or emerge here? Are the stories of Native peoples to be classified as myth or history? Was America discovered or invaded?" (1996, 86). The text does not answer these questions. Rather, it relies on the subversive and "mind-bungling" powers of humor to "challenge" the audience's "very foundations" (53), as Harold puns at the beginning of the screenplay in reference to the foundation grant. Buffy Sainte-Marie's "Trickster Song" claims: "Trickster change how everything seem" (54), and Harold "believes that he can stop time and *change the world through imagination*" (76; emphasis added). Vizenor himself may just share his character's belief, using humor and imagination to bewilder and inspire, to tease and teach, to ultimately effect change in his audience by inciting an imaginative revaluation of restrictive and ethnocentric paradigms.

The classical trickster "wanders through the dark field of liminal imagination until he arrives to summon into play the forces at work in some dimly lit social scene. There for a few moments he exercises his trickery, displays his foolishness, sparks some sure flash of imagination and insight" (Wiget 1990, 86). Trickster characters in contemporary Native writing still follow that classical vocation of "sparking flashes of imagination and insight," as exemplified in Vizenor's text. Like the trickster figures from traditional oral tales, they are transformers, using the powers of humor and narrative to overthrow conventional images of Nativeness and to disrupt the categories people think in. Originating from deep within Native narrative traditions, today they trick readers into negotiating, into reimagining the narratives of both Native cultural identity and Native-White history.

Trickster Discourse, Grotesque Humor, and Dramatic Irony

Whereas the discussion of forms and techniques of humor has so far mostly focused on single textual elements, this last section looks briefly at the way linguistic representation in general and narrative structure on the whole may contribute to a humorous reimagining of Nativeness. Trickster, according to Gerald Vizenor, exceeds the level of the single character within a text. Rather, trickster discourse is a rhetorical principle in Native narrative, a multivocal presence in narrative form and structure that disrupts conventional patterns of representation and expectations as they relate to how (linear) narrative ought to proceed. In this sense, the trickster is "a *holotrope*, a comic holotrope, and a *sign* in a language game . . ., a consonance of sentences in various voices, ironies, variations in cultural myths and social metaphors" (Vizenor 1989, 187, 190). In Vizenor's understanding the trickster becomes "a semiotic sign . . . [that] *wanders between narrative voices* and comic chance in oral presentations" (Vizenor 1989, 189; emphasis added). Characterized by this creative instability, trickster discourse on the level of narrative inherently defies the existence of one (ethnocentric or "monologic") authorial voice or one fixed meaning. Instead, storytelling becomes a communal venture of multiple voices and perspectives, intertwining in a multilayered, heteroglossic narrative. It even exceeds the confines of the text itself, in that trickster narrative "situates the participant audience, the listeners and readers, in agonistic imagination: there, in comic discourse, the trickster is being, nothingness and liberation; a loose seam in consciousness; that wild space over and between sounds, words, sentences and narratives" (Vizenor 1989, 196). So just as trickster characters in their complexity transgress categories and classifications, the trickster as narrative principle transgresses (Western) narrative conventions, and in the process liberates the readers' imagination from restrictive distinctions and predetermined expectations. Native writers use metafiction, intertextuality (including elements from mythical narrative), Native concepts of time and space, trickster characters, and multiple narrative perspectives to break down distinctions between world and story and to lure readers in. Jeanne Rosier Smith explains:

> Storytelling makes the reader one of the community of listeners, and trickster authors implicitly or explicitly invite and even demand reader involvement. The dialogue is not resolved in a trickster narrative, and the reader must negotiate a place within it. Leaving things open ended or contradictory forces the reader to play a more active role in the construction of meaning, filling in the "gaps." (1997, 23)

Especially for Western readers, then, Native writers' use of trickster discourse is for both amusement and challenge: "By becoming involved in the interpretive work, the reader becomes more sensitive to cultural boundaries and better equipped to cross them. A multiplicity of voices and perspectives . . . can effect change in the reader; by engaging in dialogue with the text, readers open their own thoughts to change" (Smith 1997, 24). As this statement illustrates, trickster discourse is instrumental in Native authors' attempts to effect change in their readers by humorously reimagining Nativeness. The multilayered "stories" told in contemporary Native texts sneak tricksterlike into the readers' imagination in order to rework the restrictive images of "Indians." In this challenge to immerse themselves in a Native perspective, readers themselves become the target of the trickster authors' pranks: "What is the story but a trick played by the discourse of the trickster? The illusion of a clear, unique, referential meaning given by the rhetorical body of the discourse is precisely what the trickster, as discourse, is able to conjure forth" (Doueihi 1993, 197). Or, to say it with the Coyote form of Beth Brant's "Coyote Learns a New Trick": "What good is a joke if you can't trick creatures into believing one thing is true when Coyote knows truth is only what she makes it?" (1985, 31). Native writers as tricksters conjure up imaginary worlds that are as real or unreal as the imaginary "White Man's Indian" identified by Berkhofer (1978). Introducing new, imaginative truths of their own that oppose a Eurocentric Truth, they create seemingly stable deceptive narrative surfaces that eventually, however, reveal rather than conceal the fact that reality is but a construction.

Trickster discourse is especially prominent in works by Gerald Vizenor and Louise Erdrich and, to some extent, in Thomas King's and Louis Owens's novels. A thorough discussion of trickster discourse using any of the novels included here would exceed the limited scope of this chapter;

instead, Thomas King's *Green Grass, Running Water* can serve as a brief illustration. Linking trickster to Bakhtin's concept of dialogism, Vizenor writes: "The comic holotrope is a 'dialogism' in these 'translinguistic' theories of discourse. The trickster is a comic discourse, a collection of 'utterances' in oral traditions; the opposite of a comic discourse is a monologue, an utterance in isolation, which comes closer to the tragic mode in literature and not a comic tribal world view" (1989, 191). King's trickster narrative is truly dialogic in relating oral to written, fictional to factual, and previous representations to new ones in a process of interaction between text and reader. Through its use of oral storytelling techniques, intertextuality, and transcendent characters and metafiction, as well as multiple narrative voices, it draws readers into a narrative that turns out to have neither a true beginning nor an end. Rather, through its cyclical structure the novel forgoes closure by offering boundless possibilities of revision, and through its various tellers demonstrates that "story" is a communal undertaking. In a frame narration, the omniscient narrator "I" and Coyote are engaged in a conversation, mostly about the occurrences in the other strands of the novel. These include a linear Western plot told in a realistic mode (which in itself is divided into various substrands featuring different characters), as well as four Native creation stories (with their protagonists subsequently entering various literary and biblical intertexts), related by the four old Indian trickster-storytellers. Especially this latter part of King's narrative puzzle, in combination with the conversation between the narrator and Coyote, provides much of the humor regarding both content and structure. Each of the four old Indians tells his/her version of what at heart turns out to be the same story, introduced (in parody of the biblical gospels) by: "This is according to" (the Lone Ranger/Ishmael/Robinson Crusoe/Hawkeye; 9, 103, 231, 327). Moreover, the four chapter headings, given in Cherokee syllabary, are the designations for East/Red, South/White, West/Black, and North/Blue, underlining the cyclical structure.

Part of the humor inherent in this design arises from the readers realizing the parallels, gradually recognizing that they are dealing with one and the same story in different guises, "uncover[ing] the distinctions and ironies between narrative voices" (Vizenor 1989, 192). This process culminates at the end of the novel when the narrative comes full circle on basically all levels: The four old Indian tricksters, who had escaped from a mental institution at the beginning of the novel, have returned there; the head of this institution, Dr. Hovaugh, who chased after them, has settled again behind his desk, contemplating his garden (which King relates in exactly the same phrases he used at the beginning of the novel; see 16, 425); and the narrator "I" and Coyote are back for yet another attempt to tell the story, this time with Coyote as the teller. *Green Grass, Running Water*'s intricate structure therefore constitutes a story-web made up of several narratives that initially appear to proceed in parallel and linear fashion, but eventually turn out to be closely intertwined and cyclical.

In addition, King plays with the novel's episodic composition by linking the various strands of narrative together. He starts passages belonging to one narrative strand on the same note that the preceding passage of another narrative strand ended, either in identical words or at least thematically. The Lone Ranger ends a passage of his telling with "What else would you like to know?" (49), for instance, and this is immediately followed by the question "What else would you like to know?" from Babo Jones in an entirely different story-strand (50). Also, after Hawkeye ends one episode with the question "Why is he standing in a puddle of water?" (106), the next begins at the Dead Dog Café with Billy shouting "Toilet's backed up again" (107, a joke taken up repeatedly). Initially, this link between apparently unrelated parts of the novel is simply amusing. Yet, as the novel progresses, it also signals to the reader that there may be a deeper connection, that the seemingly unconnected events are all part of the same story, as trickster indeed wanders through the text. The novel abounds with trickster signals that flash up in various narrative voices and plots, building a comic loom that holds the novel's various strands together: There is the water imagery appearing in all narrative strands (see Andrews 2002, 99–100); the "list-mania" of Robinson Crusoe (King, 293–95, 323–24, 346); the idea that Lionel needs "help with his life" (64, 167, 179, 183, 216, 387); the manner in which Coyote jumps from subplot to subplot, transgressing the boundaries between the various strands and intruding on the conversations between the other characters (296–303, 317, 383–87); and the intermedial ploy by which King has characters in various subplots watch or read versions of the same Western, *The Mysterious Warrior* (Eli reads the book; Alberta, Charlie, Latisha, Bill Bursum, and Babo all separately watch the movie; Lionel gets John Wayne's jacket from the movie as a birthday present; Charlie's father Portland plays the Indian lead; and the four old Indians "fix" the movie by ironically changing its outcome).

Through these various connecting strategies King not only ties the plots together, he also flaunts the distinction between "mythical" and more recognizably "realistic" parts of the novel. Readers who initially trust the realism and linearity of (parts of) the narrative, who rely on linguistic signification to be clearly referential, are eventually taken in as the (hierarchical) distinctions between various forms of narrative (oral and written, fictional and factual, authoritative Western and "quaint" indigenous, literal and metaphoric) are overthrown altogether. King himself is thus a notorious trickster/boundary-breaker, embodying Babcock and Cox's observation that "trickster today holds a pen, or sits at a typewriter or computer, 'processing' words which heal, fool, incite, inspire, anger, and empower all who read in/between the lines" (Babcock and Cox 1994, 103). He transcends the fictional frame of the novel and challenges readers to reimagine reality according to story. Through its oral, trickster-cycle-like structure, the text subversively undermines any trust in the written as fixed or in language to convey a univocal meaning; instead, it stresses the openness, playfulness, constant renewal, and change inherent in Native storytelling. Characteristically, the book's last sentence returns to the last sentence of the prologue: "And here's how it happened" (3, 431). The telling, and with it constant change and reinterpretation, will continue. *Green Grass, Running Water* demonstrates how trickster discourse in contemporary Native writing, through its dialogic interaction between author, text, and audience, defies absolute perspectives on Nativeness, one-sided interpretations of history, and unequivocal readings in general. "In trickster narratives the listeners and readers imagine their liberation; the trickster is a sign and the world is 'deconstructed' in a discourse," writes Vizenor (1989, 194). Yet trickster discourse may (as became apparent here) even exceed deconstruction as such, as readers are tricked into imaginatively reconstructing their own perspectives, to comically establish new connections and viewpoints in transgression of accustomed boundaries and interpretations.

Like trickster discourse, Native writers' use of the grotesque produces texts that inherently defy the validity of conventional logic and accustomed frames of reference. The notion of the grotesque is based on surprise and incompatibility, that is, on the linking of elements from different areas and the sudden departure from reality to reveal a surreal, illogical, and unpredictable world (see Hellenthal 1989, 65). Even more than for many of the means discussed so far, its humor therefore results from defamiliarization. It may range from the slightly bizarre, as in Sherman Alexie's story "South by Southwest" (2001), which depicts a weird robbery for love instead of money, to the overtly grotesque, as in Thomas King's "How Corporal Colin Sterling Saved Blossom, Alberta, and Most of the Rest of the World as Well" (1993), in which Aboriginal people are abducted by blue alien coyotes in space ships. Such humor flouts the rules of realism and logic and thus shakes the readers' trust in narrative coherence, causality, and mimetic capacity.

Thomas King's "A Short History of Indians in Canada" juxtaposes concepts and terminologies from vastly disparate fields — ornithology and Native cultures — in a contemporary urban setting. In realistic mode, the story introduces Bob, a businessman who is in Toronto for the first time. Unable to sleep, he leaves his hotel and is heading for Bay Street when he sees "a flock of Indians fly into the side of a building. Smack! Smack!" (1999b, 62) and runs into two birdwatchers/rangers, Bill and Rudy:

> Got a Mohawk, says Bill.
> Whup! Whup!
> Couple of Cree over here, says Rudy.

> Amazing, says Bob. How can you tell?
> By the feathers, says Bill. We got a book. . . .
> Bob looks around. What's this one? He says
> Holy! Says Bill. Holy! Says Rudy.
> Check the book. Just to be sure.
> Flip, flip, flip.
> Navajo!
> Bill and Rudy put their arms around Bob. A Navajo! Don't normally
> see Navajos this far north. (63)

Through the combination of ornithological determination and Indians, King first of all evokes laughter — the idea of "telling Indians by their feathers" is simply hilarious. Yet he also lures readers into pondering this connection, especially through the discourse in which the rangers frame their observations of the "Indians." They tell Bob, for instance, that he is lucky to witness the spectacle: "A family from Buffalo came through last week and didn't even see an Ojibway" (64). "Indians," they explain, are "nomadic" and "migratory," and fly into sky scrapers because "Toronto's in the middle of the flyway . . . . The lights attract them" (64). Their policy is to "bag" the dead ones and "tag" the live ones — "Take them to the shelter. Nurse them back to health. Release them in the wild" (64). Quite obviously, haunting parallels emerge between "wild" birds and "savage" Indians (who are, as the text implies, unfit for the city and best off "in the wild"). Moreover, to tell Indians by the book insinuates a similarly detached and reifying academic approach by White anthropologists, reducing Native people to fascinating and slightly exotic objects of study.

As Eckardt points out: "Humor parades before us its own brand of seeming illogic, yet unless it nurtures some kind of deeper logic it fails to realize itself" (1992, 47). King's brief sketch seems, on the surface, grotesque and illogical. It develops logic, however, once the reader realizes the implicit satiric criticism of popular and academic conceptualizations of "the Indian" as belonging to the world of "natural phenomena," still but an interesting "feathered species," a nostalgically tinted spectacle to be enjoyed as a remnant of a long-gone past. The story closes by thoroughly mocking the cliché of the Vanishing Indian as an endangered species, when Bob, upon his return to the hotel, is told: "Not like the old days. The doorman sighs and looks up into the night. In the old days, when they came through, they would black out the entire sky" (64). Especially in light of the title, King's "A Short History of Indians in Canada" thus bitingly derides the way in which Canadians pride themselves on their liberal attitude towards "their" Native people, but tend to hypocritically neglect that, like their Southern neighbors, they in fact decimated their Native population, just to sentimentally miss it afterwards. As this example shows, more than other forms, grotesque humor challenges readers to decode its seeming illogic. Because its sense-making takes place on a deeper level, however, it also allows for highly imaginative texts and enlarges the writers' range of creative expression by opening up the possibility to comment on the real from the vantage point of the apparently surreal.

In addition to verbal irony, a text can also be ironic on the level of plot or structure, a characteristic Feinberg designates dramatic irony: "The term 'dramatic' is used here not in reference to the theater but to differentiate ironic events and situations from verbal irony. [It designates] a state of affairs or events which is the reverse of what was expected; a result opposite to and as if in mockery of the appropriate result" (1967, 157–58). Such dramatic irony is most pronounced when the outcome of a particular situation or text directly opposes reader expectations, or establishes totally unexpected (causal) connections, as in various instances in Thomas King's *Green Grass, Running Water*. From the novel's very beginning (Coyote dreaming up GOD) readers are conditioned not to take anything for granted. Yet some of the comic connections King establishes still take readers by surprise. The regular disappearance of the four old Indian tricksters from the mental hospital they are confined to, for instance, in each case is followed by a major catastrophe. Allusions hint at the Black Friday of the Great Depression, the volcanic eruption of Mount Saint Helens, and the forest fire that devastated Yellow Stone National Park, and after a while, readers start to identify these disasters as the four tricksters' attempts to "fix the world," characteristically backfiring on them. Further such ironic twists arise from Coyote's blunders, which not only cause the dam to break ("'Earthquake, Earthquake!' yells Coyote. 'Hee-hee-hee-hee-hee-hee-hee-hee,'" 411), but also bring on the biblical flood ("The last time you fooled around like this . . . the world got very wet," 416). Moreover, Coyote not only brings GOD into existence, but is shown to have unwittingly laid the foundations for Christianity, being responsible not just for Alberta Frank's miraculous pregnancy but also for Jesus Christ's immaculate conception:

> "But I was helpful, too," says Coyote. "That woman who wanted a baby. Now, that was helpful."
> "Helpful!" said Robinson Crusoe. "Your remember the last time you did that?"
> "I'm quite sure I was in Kamloops," says Coyote.
> "We haven't straightened out that mess yet," said Hawkeye.
> "Hee-hee," says Coyote. "Hee-hee." (416)

King, with uproarious humor, stands habitual worldviews on their head and most amusingly reimagines world history and world religions. Christianity becomes a trickster prank to be straightened out, which on the one hand reduces its importance and dislocates it from its centrality, and on the other hand allows for liberating laughter at the partly devastating consequences of forced conversion on Native cultures. Instead of lecturing about ethnocentrism and the way it affects Native people, through trickster characters and dramatic irony the text imaginatively overthrows steadfast convictions, ideas of cause and effect, and ultimately also the hierarchies built on these assumptions.

A specific instance of dramatic irony is the use of anticlimax, that is, when previously built-up anticipations and tensions suddenly collapse or deflate into triviality. Illustrating Kant's theory of laughter as frustrated expectation, anticlimax is especially well suited for humorously confronting readers with their own clichéd expectations. A hilarious case in point is the ending of a scene in Hanay Geiogamah's play *Foghorn*, in which Pocahontas relates the story of her encounter with "the Captain," that is, John Smith. Relying on anticlimax and body humor (a field I decided not to expound here in greater detail, but which is of course also part of Native humor, especially in Geiogamah's plays, such as *Body Indian*), the text satirically exaggerates the romanticizing and sexual/sexist undertones popularly attributed to the Pocahontas legend in order to comically undercut them. Pocahontas initially tells her handmaidens that "'the captain' (*gesturing with her hands*) . . . was so . . . big. Ooooooh, uuuh" (1980, 63), and subsequently launches into longwinded explanations of *what* about the Captain was "so big," from his chest to his ears to his hat, and so on, alluding, of course, to the size of his penis. Through this sexual allusion and subsequent wealth of details, the text comically builds up tension, exacerbated through Pocahontas's description of Smith's courting: "He looked at me deeply with his big blue eyes and told me that he was . . . in . . . in *luff* with me and he wanted me to . . . to . . . know his body and that he wanted to know, know my body, too" (64). The handmaidens' (and audience's) curiosity piques when Pocahontas and the Captain have undressed:

POCAHONTAS: And the big captain was standing above me, looking down at me, breathing like a boy after a footrace, and I saw that his . . .

The handmaidens huddle closely with Pocahontas for the intimate details. One of them pops up, exclaiming "Pink?" Then Pocahontas rises above them, lifts her arms in a manner to suggest an erect phallus. The handmaidens gasp. Then a kazoo whistle indicates that the erection falls quickly, and the handmaidens explode with laughter.

POCAHONTAS: (*fighting for their attention*) He said to me, I love you, dear Pocahontas. I promise you it won't happen the next time, I promise, I promise, I promise. (64–65)

Together with the captain's erection, the text in this literally anticlimactic ending collapses a whole set of audience expectations: the West's fascination with the erotic/exotic Other, Euro-American pretensions of potency on both a political and a sexual level, and the idea that Native women are somehow naturally enchanted by White men. Dramatic irony, especially because of its elements of comic deceit and surprise, therefore effectively dislodges preset ideas and familiarized patterns of expectation and interpretation. By establishing unusual connections or building tension just to explode it in laughter, it unwittingly stuns readers into imagining new options and different readings of familiar images, stories, or paradigms.

As this chapter makes apparent, contemporary Native North American authors employ a broad array of linguistic, literary, and cultural techniques to articulate humor in their writing. They amalgamate strategies originating from Western and Native cultural traditions in order to turn previous representations and interpretations into a humorous quagmire, thoroughly destabilizing fixed meanings and restrictively linear readings. Instead, readers are brought to engage in an imaginative activity that changes not only their interpretation of the texts at hand, but possibly also their subsequent encounters with (distorting) representations of Nativeness. Wittily seducing readers into both laughter and reassessment, Native writers here emerge as shrewd tricksters: They play with, yet ultimately defy, audience expectations; they level hierarchies between Native and Euro-American forms of narrative and epistemologies; and they open up a liminal sphere of laughter that allows for renegotiation.

Notes

[1] Many of the examples in this chapter are taken from Thomas King's novel *Green Grass, Running Water*, which is a rich source for almost all of the forms of humor to be discussed here. Various other texts are introduced wherever they are considered more representative for the particular forms under discussion. King's novel is divided into four chapters and consists of various narrative strands: a mythical narrative strand, in which four old Indian tricksters on the run from a mental institution in Florida relate Native creation stories, whose female protagonists (First Woman, Changing Woman, Thought Woman, and Old Woman) subsequently encounter heroes from canonical literary and biblical intertexts; a realistic strand involving contemporary Blackfoot characters (mainly Lionel, a television salesman, his partner Alberta, his aunt Norma, uncle Eli, and sister Latisha, who runs a restaurant, as well as his cousin Charlie and uncle Portland) and the White people they interact with (Lionel's boss Bill Bursum, Latisha's and Eli's spouses, and the engineer Clifford Sifton); and finally the story of Dr. J. Houvaugh, the head of the mental institution, who together with his black janitor Babo Jones chases after the escaped old Indians. All these strands are bound together in a frame narrative, a conversation between a narrator "I" and "Coyote," a trickster character who transcends the boundaries between the various subplots. The major plot lines are the Native creation stories and resulting contestation of the canonical and biblical narratives, former university professor Eli's blockage of a dam project on the reserve, and Lionel's search for an identity. Eventually, all subplots converge and turn out to be another of the four old Indian tricksters' repeated attempts to "fix the world."

[2] Muecke distinguishes between intentional and unintentional/unconscious irony and basically restricts the former to verbal irony, "an ironist being ironical," and the

latter to situational irony, "a state of affairs or an event seen as ironic" (1970, 49–50). I consider it impossible to uphold this distinction in every case; yet Muecke's considerations may deepen an understanding of the various levels on which irony may work. Whereas the author creates irony intentionally, within the text it may be realized as both intentional and unintentional irony. Two examples from Thomas King's *Green Grass, Running Water* briefly illustrate this distinction: When Native university professor Alberta Frank is treated with (racist) condescendence by a hotel desk clerk who doubts her professional identity, she herself reacts with intentional/verbal irony, that is, she is *being ironical:* "Alberta pulled out her university identification card and her driver's license. The desk clerk smiled and handed her cards back to her. 'You can't always tell by looking,' he said. 'How true it is,' said Alberta. 'I could have been a corporate executive' " (1994, 174). In contrast, what happens to her partner Lionel qualifies as situational irony: Portrayed as placid/phlegmatic throughout the novel, Lionel at one point is mistaken for a radical activist leader of the American Indian Movement (57–63), a misunderstanding that will, in a deeply *ironic* outcome, block his career chances for the rest of his life.

[3] Like Hutcheon herself, I hesitate to use terms such as "meaning" and "intention" — as if there was one "fixed" meaning or as if "intention" could be clearly ascribed. Yet they are indispensable in this discussion: "After all, the touchy political issues that arise around irony's usage and interpretation invariably focus on the use of intention (of either ironist or interpreter)" (Hutcheon 1995b: 11).

[4] Originally, satire referred to a specific form or genre rather than style (see Frye 1975, 108; Abrams 1999, 276–78). This strict reference has given way to a much wider usage of the term, so that now one has to distinguish between the *genre*, in which satire acts as an organizing principle, and a particular style of mockery referred to as satirical, which may appear in or characterize texts that on the whole would not be considered satires in the generic sense. It is in the latter sense that I use the term in the framework of this analysis. The contemporary Native literary work most fully relying on satire as its organizing principle, to my knowledge, is Hanay Geiogamah's play *Foghorn.*

[5] Even though it is hard to distinguish between these terms, satire may be set off against irony and sarcasm, in that it does not necessarily hinge on divergence between what is meant and what is said (see Purdie 1993, 115), and against parody in that the latter, in contrast to satire, concentrates on a preexisting literary text, making it "a constituent part of its own structure" (M. Rose 1993, 81).

[6] A clear distinction between satire and parody thus depends on the definition of "text." Hutcheon, for instance, maintains that literary parody need not have as its target a literary text, but might also refer to nonliterary discourse in what she calls "cross-genre" parody (see 1985, 18). In the following, parody designates a humorous rewriting of preexisting literary/historiographic material (specific texts, but also genres and literary conventions); "hypotext" refers to the original text, and "hypertext" to the result of parodic transformation.

[7] Revard's text is a general parody in that it targets an entire genre (that of the exploration account), as is Sherman Alexie's "How to Write the Great American Indian Novel," which parodies the popular Western romance; examples of specific parody — that is, parody focusing on a particular hypotext — are, for instance,

Thomas King's short story "A Seat in the Garden" (in King 1993), which parodies W. P. Kinsella's novel *Shoeless Joe* and its filmic adaptation *A Field of Dreams;* and King's reworking of the Leatherstocking Tales in *Green Grass, Running Water.*

[8] Similar parodic inversions appear in Geiogamah's *Foghorn*, when the AIM activists who occupy Alcatraz deliver a speech that parodies the explorers' claiming of land for the Spanish and British crown (see 1980, 56); and in Drew Hayden Taylor's account of his trip to Germany, which he also wants to "discover," claim, and rename Drewland (see 1998, 39).

[9] See also Bruyere, asking Euro-Americans to "imagine a world where your values, customs, beliefs and language are not recognized or respected. Imagine living in such a society where few people look like you do or treat each other in a way that you are used to" (1997, 196). She reimagines the boarding/residential school system; the practice of adopting out; the forced imposition of Native religion, cultural traditions, customs, language, and education; and discriminating legal practices and appropriation. In conclusion, she outlines how Native normative discourses will affect Euro-American identity when "we will be civilized and you, quaint yet barbaric" (196).

[10] For various (contradicting) ways of differentiating parody and burlesque see Abrams (1999, 26); Baldick (1996, 27); and Rishel (2002, 215).

[11] This is acknowledged from an anthropological/cultural perspective by Beck and Walters (1977, 307); Chamberlain (1907, 578); Hill (1943, 7–8); Ryan (1999, xiii); and Wallace (1953, 135). It is also postulated by Native authors Paula Gunn Allen (2001, xii); Leslie Silko (in Coltelli 1990, 146–47); and James Welch (in Coltelli 1990, 191–92). Previous to the spread of English, punning and joking were based on features of the respective Native language, posing problems of translation and consequently interpretation for anthropologists (see Bruchac 1987b, 23). Today, puns and wordplay make use of Native languages and English (see Silko about the Laguna Pueblo, in Coltelli, 1990, 146–47; and Sanner for the Hopi, 1993, 153).

[12] For an overview of "Indian" language in the movies see Stedman's chapter on "Indian Talk" (1982, 58–73).

[13] See also Flick (1999, 144). For a more detailed discussion of code-switching in *Green Grass, Running Water* see Andrews (2002, 94–95).

[14] Further examples of humorous texts told partly or entirely in an oral style include Richard Wagamese's novel *Keeper 'n Me*, Lorenzo Baca's "San Lorenzo Day in Laguna," and Suleiman Russell's "How Old Man Coyote Lost His Manhood" (both in Allen and Anderson 2001).

[15] The concept of intertextuality as it is used here owes more to the concrete and clearly delineated forms of intertextuality and hypertextuality established by Genette in his classification of transtextual relationships than to Barthes's or Kristeva's poststructuralist views of text as unbounded and meaning as infinitely instable. Genette describes intertextuality as "a relationship of copresence between two texts or among several texts: that is to say, eidetically and typically as the actual presence of one text within another. In its most explicit and literal form, it is the traditional practice of *quoting* (with quotation marks, with or without specific references). In another less explicit and canonical form, it is the practice of *plagiarism* . . . which is an undeclared but still literal borrowing. Again, in still less explicit and less literal guise, it is the practice

of allusion: that is, an enunciation whose full meaning presupposes the perception of a relationship between it and another text, to which it necessarily refers by some inflections that would otherwise remain unintelligible" (1997, 1–2). Hypertextuality, which encompasses such practices as parody or travesty, describes "a text derived from another preexistent text" either through transformation, which "evokes [a hypotext] more or less perceptibly without necessarily speaking of it or citing it" (5), or through imitation. The difference between transformation and imitation is most basically that between "saying the same thing differently" (transformation) and "saying another thing similarly" (imitation) (6). Intertextuality, as the term is used in this section, encompasses both kinds of transtextual relationships.

[16] References to popular culture often have to do with film, as, for example, in Geiogamah's use of the Lone Ranger series; Thomas King's and Sherman Alexie's use of John Wayne and Richard Widmark Westerns in *Green Grass, Running Water* and "Dear John Wayne," respectively; and Alexie's references to George Lucas's *Star Wars* saga in *Reservation Blues* (1996a, 203–4). It is also interesting to note that contemporary Native authors have started cross-referencing each other's works. Monique Mojica's play *Princess Pocahontas and the Blue Spots* quotes Native writers Diane Burns and Chrystos; Gerald Vizenor's novel *The Heirs of Columbus* mentions Louise Erdrich, Thomas King, N. Scott Momaday, and Leslie Silko, as well as (hilariously) non-Native critic Arnold Krupat (see 1991, 110–11); and Sherman Alexie's novel *Indian Killer* playfully alludes to the protagonists of three of the most canonized Native American novels (Jim Loney from James Welch's *The Death of Jim Loney*, Tayo from Leslie Silko's *Ceremony*, and Abel from N. Scott Momaday's *House Made of Dawn*, see 1996b, 220).

[17] Other intertexts that enter into King's character conceptualizations and surface throughout the novel are Melville's novella *Benito Cereno* (in the characters of the black janitor Babo and police officers Cereno and Delano; see Fast 2001), which is used to hilariously mock notions of innate White superiority and colonial dominance, and Northrop Frye's work on literary criticism (in the character of Dr. J. Hovaugh; see Schorcht 2003, 62–68), deriding a Western compulsive need for categorization and classification. The novel's biblical intertexts and its use of the *Leatherstocking Tales* are discussed more closely in chapter four.

[18] See also Fitz (2001, 143, 146) and Horne (1995, 261–62). Interestingly, Witherspoon explains about the Diné (Navajo) creation story: "Unlike Adam, First Man did not go about naming things (creating symbols); he went about learning the names of things" (1977, 43).

[19] Adolph Hungry Wolf was adopted into the tribe by marriage (see Berner 1999, 2). Lutz relates a "funny little story from the contemporary pan-Indian oral tradition about an aged hippie from California who returned to 'his' medicine man, many months or years after the name-giving ceremony, to ask him somewhat belatedly, 'What is the symbolic significance and the spiritual meaning of the name 'Walking Eagle,' which you gave me a long time ago?' to which the medicine person replied: 'Too stupid to fly!'" (Lutz 2002, 94).

[20] While King's *Green Grass, Running Water*, again, would offer more than fertile ground for this discussion — "Many, perhaps all, of King's characters are named after figures from literature or history, this being one of the many delights of this

hilarious but deadly serious novel: discovering who the characters are named for" (Stratton 1999, 94) — I decided not to discuss this aspect of the novel in detail. Many of the references are discussed elsewhere (see Flick 1999), and a comprehensive discussion would exceed the limited scope of this section.

[21] Custer and his defeat at Little Big Horn are a favorite subject of humor in contemporary Native writing and oral tradition. Deloria even claims: "There are probably more jokes about Custer and the Indians than there were participants in the battle" (V. Deloria 1977, 148). References to Crazy Horse's battle against Custer appear, e.g., in Alexie's poem "Giving Blood," where a nurse, after running Crazy Horse's data through the computer at the blood bank, tells him: "I'm sorry Mr. Crazy Horse / But we've already taken too much of your blood / And you won't be eligible / To donate for another generation or two" (1992, 78); and in Louis Owens' novel *Bone Game*, which sports a drugged apathetic dog named Custer who is described as "a killer when he's awake" (1994, 150) and "incorrigible, just like his namesake" (190).

[22] For accounts of classical trickster figures from oral traditions see Blaeser (1993); Bright (1987); and Lincoln (1993, 22–23). On tricksters' typical characteristics see Apte (1983, 193–94, 206); Babcock and Cox (1994); Hynes (1993); and Velie (1989, 122).

[23] In most stories, trickster is represented as male (a fact sometimes attributed to male ethnographers' bias, see Wiget 1990, 89; Cox 1989, 18), but there are also female trickster figures (see Babcock and Cox 1994, 100; Ballinger 2000, 25; Doty 2001). Examples of contemporary texts that feature female Coyotes are Beth Brant's "Coyote Learns a New Trick" (1985) and Thomas King's "The One About Coyote Going West" and "A Coyote Columbus Story" (both 1993).

[24] The most differentiated analysis of the functions of trickster tales to date has been provided by Babcock-Abrahams (1974). For other classifications see Blaeser (1993, 55–57); Toelken (1987, 389–91); and Wiget (1990, 91).

[25] Yet scatological humor still surfaces in contemporary Native writing. Doty points out that "many trickster narratives do indeed incarnate, enflesh, *ennarrate* the grossly human/base/revelatory *body*" (2001, 3); and Baker points out: "All parts of [a trickster's] body are animated and are not gross anatomy as in today's deodorant-defined dominant society" (1991, 49). Examples in contemporary Native writing are a "singing butt hole" in Thomas King's "The One About Coyote Going West" (see 1993, 71) and overflowing toilets and sewer systems in *Green Grass, Running Water* (1994) and *Truth and Bright Water* (1999) (see Andrews 1999, 2002, 100, 106). In Louise Halfe's "Body Politics" (1994, 32) and Paul Seesequasis's "The Republic of Tricksterism" (1998), finally, defiant Native women fart at White women and tribal bureaucrats, subversively sabotaging ideas of "civilized" behavior.

[26] Lincoln considers Coyote, the archetypical trickster, "distinctly postmodern" (1993, 135). Tricksters indeed share many characteristics with postmodern techniques (deconstruction, fragmentation, and deferral of meaning); yet to interpret them predominantly in postmodern terms constitutes an imposition of Western paradigms, denying trickster's primacy and origin in Native cultures.

4: Humor at Work in Contemporary Native Writing: Issues and Effects

BASED ON THE THEORETICAL CONSIDERATIONS of identity and humor in chapter two, this analysis focuses on the major thematic and functional foci of humor in contemporary Native writing. While the unifying idea of reimagining Nativeness through humor runs through the entire chapter, the thematic range covered by humor in contemporary Native texts is far from homogeneous. Accordingly, rather than following a strict analytical pattern, the discussion has to accommodate the respective context. Humor is, after all, both a reaction to and a form of interaction in specific situations. Parameters for the analyses may include: the raw material or occasion that triggers the humor; the historical and cultural background the humor originates from and situates itself against; the motivation for the use of humor instead of other responses in that particular situation; the ends humor is put to; the participants in the humorous interaction; and the envisioned audience. The degree to which these parameters play a role in the various sections differs. Therefore, it may be useful to take an initial encompassing look at the chapter as a whole before starting in on the specifics of each of the functions by themselves. Mapping the thematic and functional terrain covered below, one can detect a gradual development: At the beginning stand issues mainly arising from and directed at Native-White interaction, that is, humor targeting externally imposed definitions of Nativeness in a deconstructive/critical way and addressing mainly Euro-American readers; towards the end of the chapter, humor is more concerned with intracultural Native issues, engaging in a renegotiation of Nativeness in a reconstructive/reconfirming or healing way and addressing mainly Native readers. These are not mutually exclusive poles; the deconstruction and dismantling of a particular set of images is, as reimagining implies, often inseparably tied to a reconstructive act, just as processes of internalization make it impossible to clearly distinguish between externally assigned and internally developed aspects of Nativeness. Rather, they should be taken as orientation markers in a maze of interlocking forces, motivations, modes, and audiences. Humor is basically directed at all areas of Native existence. While — as with the formal analysis conducted in chapter three — the categories established for the sake of clarity therefore show some overlap, the discussion concentrates on humor engaging with the following issues: colonization and its consequences, stereotyping, repressive historiographic accounts and epistemologies, the imposition of Christianity and patriarchy, cultural imperialism and appropriation, and the renegotiation of Nativeness within Native communities.

Joking/Choking Truths about Colonization, Oppression, and Discrimination

Many Indians, of course, believe it would have been better if Plymouth Rock had landed on the Pilgrims than the Pilgrims on Plymouth Rock.
— Vine Deloria, *Custer Died For Your Sins*, 177

More than 500 years after Columbus's "discovery," the continuing impact of conquest and colonization is impossible for Native people throughout North America to ignore. It is not only the historical decimation as such — whether resulting from military force or diseases — that Native people have to come to terms with; the shockwaves caused by land theft and forced relocation, the social and cultural disruptions caused by practices such as forced conversion, sterilization, child adoption, and recruitment for boarding or residential schools are felt up to the present. While both simplistic idealizations of the pre-Columbian era and essentializing notions of Nativeness are to be avoided, to expect Native people to forgivingly embrace a history of extermination, discrimination, and forced assimilation at the hands of White governments is asking a lot — especially when the physical and psychological consequences continue to determine their lives. Commodity food-induced diabetes, alcoholism, child abuse by Native parents who cannot but pass on what they experienced in their own childhood at the hands of White educators, and the effects of destructive prodevelopment schemes such as uranium mining or toxic waste sites on Native lands (see Jaimes 1995, 284) — these are just some of the problems that, in their final consequence, can be said to originate from the colonial condition.

Native humor has inevitably been influenced by this legacy of decimation and cultural disruption: "Indians were forced to take their culture and spirituality underground, and they sharpened their humor to make the horrible things happening around them more bearable" (Giago 1990, 54). The humor contemporary Native writers direct at the distressing aspects of Native-White copresence in America can essentially be analyzed from two angles. From a Native perspective, humor works as a successful strategy for coping with a traumatic past and handling oppression and tragedy, as Native actor Gary Farmer points out: "Because Native communities have gone through probably the worst situations in North America that any peoples have gone through they had to have the ability to laugh. If they didn't, they wouldn't be existing today" (in Ryan 1999, 72). This is spelled out by Garnet Raven, the young Ojibway protagonist of Richard Wagamese's novel *Keeper 'n Me*. Upon his return to his family on the reserve (after having grown up in White foster care against his family's will) he observes:

> See, one of the things I caught onto real quick was the humor. Reason no one minds the welfare so much, or the government's empty promises, or the lack of lots of things, is on accounta they always find some funny way of looking at it. They find a way to laugh about it. Keeper says that it's the way they survived everything and still remained a culture. Lotsa Indian ways changed when the whiteman got here, lotsa people suffered, but they stayed alive on accounta they learned to deal with things by not taking them so damn serious all the time. Go anywhere where there's Indians and chances are you'll find them cracking up laughing over something. (1994, 87)

Next to its use as a direly needed coping strategy, however, humor in this context can also be looked at from a different vantage point. Especially with regard to a non-Native audience, it may figure as a kind of "Trojan horse": Sneaking up on readers through shared laughter, humor can align their empathy with Native viewpoints, obscuring conflicts and hierarchies and triggering consensus and solidarity instead (see English 1994, 14, 16). Thus such humor may bring to attention aspects of Native-White history that a Euro-American viewpoint tends to cancel out, allowing sensitive issues to be addressed in a way that retains a basis for communication. Leslie Silko claims that "especially [for] areas in justice, loss of land, discrimination, racism, and so on, that there's a way of saying it so people can laugh or smile . . . so you can keep their interest, so you can keep talking to them. Oftentimes these things are told in a humorous way" (in Coltelli 1990, 146–47). With regard, therefore, to confronting contested and distressing issues such as the skeletons in the Native-White history closet, the mediational potential of humor is just as important as its coping aspect. In a discussion of the work of Native performance artist James Luna, Tama offers an interesting interpretation of humor as a subversive weapon-cum-snare:

> To entertain is to seduce, and to successfully seduce, trust has to be forged. What better way to create trust than through humor? Stand-up comics know this well, and they can get away with saying almost anything if they are funny because comedy disarms us. As such, the performance artist who strategically uses humor can more easily win over audiences and lure them into listening to more challenging material. Furthermore, laughter can help us confront painful truths that create guilt, and what greater scarlet letter on the American chest is there than the near genocide of the vanquished indigenous people whose voices are almost unheard of as a minority within minorities? (2001, 17)

Humor within this context gives license to criticism and is brought into play to address upsetting topics in a playfully castigating light.

Such humorous trickery can be realized most effectively with regard to Euro-American master narratives, that is, widely known and glorified events such as the "discovery," early "purchases," or the "heroic struggles" of the settlers on the frontier. Columbus's discovery of the New World, depending on the point of view, is Euro-America's glorious beginning or Native America's nemesis. These apparently irreconcilable views are the subject of countless jokes and texts. As the model of reimagining suggests, humor enables a mental shift of perspective, contesting and decentering accustomed viewpoints through various strategies of humorous defamiliarization, hybridization, and caricature. The process of discovery and conquest is, for instance, caricatured as an alien invasion from outer space (Carter Revard, "Discovery of the New World" from *Ponca War Dancers,* 1980), parodied by reversing its direction (Carter Revard, "Report to the Nation: Claiming Europe," 1983), and reduced to just another of Coyote's blunders that went out of control (Thomas King, "A Coyote Columbus Story," 1993). Moreover, Columbus's incompetence as a navigator and the destructive consequences thereof are exposed to biting ridicule in Sherman Alexie's "Postcards to Columbus": "we'll honor the 500th anniversary / of your invasion, Columbus, by driving blindfolded cross-country / naming the first tree we destroy America" (1993b, 41). The most interesting literary engagements with the history of discovery, however, are those that iconoclastically transcode the figure of Columbus himself, which reimagine both the explorer and his story in a different light. This is what happens in the Columbus novels by Louise Erdrich and Michael Dorris (*The Crown of Columbus,* 1991) and Gerald Vizenor (*The Heirs of Columbus,* 1991).

The Columbus that the academics Vivian Twostar and Roger Williams, the protagonists of Erdrich and Dorris's *The Crown of Columbus,* unearth from the hodgepodge of history and popular beliefs is neither ruthless colonizer nor daring explorer. Rather, he is shown to be a self-conscious outsider whose main motivation for his expedition turns out to be the escape from petty European conventions that deny him acceptance. This creates ironic parallels between Columbus and Vivian Twostar herself, a mixedblood Native professor of anthropology at Dartmouth College. Assigned an article about Columbus for the quincentennial, Vivian's initial boredom with the topic gives way to increasing fascination. Eventually, she can even

> relate to Columbus, stranger to stranger. There he was, no matter what version of his life you believe, pushing and pulling at the city limits of wherever he found himself. An Italian in Iberia. A Jew in Christendom. A *Converso* among the baptized-at birth. A layman among Franciscans. He spoke all languages with a foreign accent, and his sight was always fixed away from the heartland. He didn't completely fit in anywhere, and that was his engine. He was propelled by alienation, by trying to forge

links, to *be* the link, from one human cluster to the next. It's no wonder he positioned himself in the Atlantic, on the western horizon. He *had* to think global because the whole world was the only context in which he was unambiguously a full member. (1991, 167–68)

This assessment of Columbus as a pitiable "marginal man" bears highly comic features, especially when read against Vivian's directly preceding self-characterization. She is a mixedblood ("Irish and Coeur d'Alene and French and Navajo and God knows what else") who does *not* consider herself "marginal," does *not* feel "caught between two worlds" but rather "the *catch*" (167), and who unabashedly exploits her mixed ethnic origin to advance her professional career. In an ironic reversal of fortunes, Vivian defies a Native self-conceptualization as tragic victim and transfers this role to the explorer. In her cheeky insubordination against being relegated to the margin, against seeing herself in the colonial gaze, the text exposes the fictitious nature of Euro-American binary notions of power, superiority, and centrality. Eventually, Vivian's reflections on Columbus depict him as a marginalized trickster whose strategy as a player in the intricate game of representation and power she can decipher all too well:

> Columbus's paradoxes, his impossibilities, attracted me. He couldn't be all he said he was, yet I recognized the fiction that he had constructed and presented, never twice the same. He was a certain kind of man in court, another in the Caribbean; a mercenary, a saint, a scholar, a fanatic, and, of course, a slave trader. . . . His lies added up to a truth, but only if viewed at an angle, only if weighed by a fellow liar. He was a nexus of imaginary lives, of stories, with but a single foot in fact, and when by accident he was at last truly a part of the greatest, most farfetched tale of all, he didn't know what to make of it. Could he believe himself after so much deceit? He had stumbled into the unthinkable: A world in which there was no other was a world without bounds. By touching the rock of America, Columbus made Europe forever smaller. (168–69)

A Native academic sympathetically considering the adverse effects of discovery on *Europe*? In light of the fact that the consequences of Columbus's "discovery" for North America's Native population are often conveniently ignored altogether (as the quincentennial celebrations showed), this must strike the reader as just as grotesquely incongruous as the trickster version of Columbus. Erdrich and Dorris's humorous reimagining of Columbus as a hesitant conman defies both glorification *and* condemnation, and thus destabilizes such fixed positions altogether.

The novel is rather unusual for both these writers' oeuvres, with its decidedly popular orientation and "adventure meets romance" plot, which sends the discordant WASP-Native couple Roger and Vivian off on a Bahamian treasure hunt after the eponymous crown of Columbus. Indeed, some critics alleged that the novel was the product of commercial rather than literary ambitions and a sell-out of Native interests, pointing to the fact that it was commissioned to appear at the quincentennial in 1992 (see Beidler 1991 and Farrell 1999, 122–23 for such criticism). Yet a closer look reveals that the novel is characterized by a "playful self-reflexivity with which [the authors] have chosen to respond to the parallel importunities and inducements proffered them, as prominent Native writers, in the advent of the Columbus quincentennial" (Hoy 1991, 51). While designed to reach a large audience, the novel nonetheless postmodernly plays with both stereotypical expectations towards Native literature (see Farrell 1999, 123) and elements from popular culture that blatantly defy such expectations (see Breinig 1994; Hoy 1991). All this leads Hoy to conclude that the novel is "not a sell-out but a send-up" (53). It intentionally resorts to flat Native jokes on Columbus: Asked to write her article on Columbus's discovery "from the Indian, uh, Native American perspective," Vivian considers as an opening sentence "There goes the neighborhood" (15). Upon reading that, at the age of twenty-five, Columbus survived a shipwreck off the coast of Portugal and "was forced to grab a floating spar and kick his way back to the European mainland," she thinks to herself: "If only he had pointed himself in the other direction that time around" (28), and she jokes about Columbus taking "the scenic route" (29) on his quest for India. And the answer one of Vivian's Native colleagues gives to the National Endowment's query about what Native activities to sponsor for the upcoming quincentennial is "to advertise on reservations for a series of 'Discover Spain' tours. Twenty-eight days, flamenco included. I said the government should erect a huge sign near Samana Cay that flashed morning, noon, and night: 'Wrong Way to Calcutta'" (30). But the novel also alludes to mystery writing and provides comments that seem to anticipate and indeed mock criticism that the plot is too obviously contrived. Vivian writes that she "could feel the logic of it, almost touch it, so I invented a story to fit the existence, to make sense — Grandma's favorite pull-the-rabbit-out-of-the-hat device, the trusty oral tradition. Create a bridge between facts that somehow must be related" (287). Accordingly, her partner Roger sarcastically remarks about Vivian's version of the historic Columbus:

> Why did Columbus cross the sea? To get to the other side. How *neat* for him to have buried a treasure: film at eleven. How *perfect* for him to leave provocative clues, how *right* for me to be wrong. How well this emerging version reenforced Vivian's politics! And how beautifully the dates elided: five hundred years practically to the day. (317)

Yet not only the rather simple plot itself is comically deconstructed; exemplary of the postmodern endless deferral of meaning, even the destabilizing indeterminacy that Vivian ascribes to Columbus is subject to further deconstructive metacommentary, creating a *myse-en-abymic* effect.

Enraged by Vivian's (and treasure hunter Henry Cobb's) rather creative reading of history, Roger tells his colleagues:

> You should see the two of them together, quite prepared to negotiate away established history to suit their own purposes. Anything goes. Let's make Columbus this, let's make him that. Abandon context, oh yes. "The first modern man," full of self-contradiction and existentialism. Why not turn him black? Or gay? Perhaps he was actually a she? (355)

Fictionality, as Breinig points out, "is here shown to result virtually inevitably from any kind of narrative and to become more prominent the better-knit the story appears to be." He argues, however, that "this artificial side of emplotment will not diminish our sense of participatory illusion but rather enhance it" (1994, 339–40). It is the combination of humorous destabilization and imaginative re-creation, then, that draws the reader into the story and sparks the realization that, as Vivian's grandmother holds: "Truth was all in the story, in the way it was told and in who was doing the telling. It could change in a minute or remain the same forever. A truth lasted only until a better one came along and replaced it" (1991, 482–83). Contesting the monolithic Euro-American Truth about Columbus with an amusing "better" one, the novel seems to exemplify just that. The grandmother's words can thus be read as a poetological comment, just as Vivian's remarks on her research are a metalevel description of the process of demystification that drives the novel: "I might be able to nail *Christopher Columbus* . . . Without the myth, he's just another man. Not the father of manifest destiny. Not the hand of fate. Not the inevitable force. Not some agent of God. Just a man whose good luck was our bad" (221). Erdrich and Dorris humorously deflate both the cultural icon and his accomplishments. Upsetting one-sided readings, they imaginatively inscribe a Native perspective into history — ironically, the very perspective Vivian, in a token gesture, is asked to provide for the article on Columbus for the Dartmouth alumni magazine. But just as Vivian refuses to deliver the expected "vitriolic lament, an excoriation blaming Columbus for all the Indians' troubles" (71), Erdrich and Dorris make their novel an amusing puzzle rather than a righteous accusation, a playfully chaotic rather than finger-pointing encounter with history. Their humorous revision makes it impossible for readers to hold onto their accustomed viewpoints. Instead, in this "comic *jeu d'esprit*" (Hoy 1991, 51) they open up a liminal space for renegotiation in which tragic aspects of Native-White contact are neither neglected nor accusingly dwelt upon. Here, "both a heroic story of tragic suffering and what might be called a politically correct revisionist polemic" (Farrell 1999, 133) are rejected.

While Erdrich and Dorris's plot, in all its contrivedness, is still tentatively rooted in realistic Western narrative conventions (and is thus quite accessible), Gerald Vizenor's rejection of fixed readings of the historical encounter in *The Heirs of Columbus* more radically enlists and challenges the readers' imagination. In a large reimaginative trickster swipe, Vizenor overthrows the conventional history of colonization as a whole. In *Heirs*, Columbus is portrayed as the "crossblood" (Vizenor's term for mixed-blood) descendant of Mayan Indians who had "brought civilization to the savages of the Old World" (1991, 9). Thus from the very beginning Vizenor not only subversively challenges the primacy and exclusivity of Old World knowledge; by reversing the process of knowledge transfer — which is customarily presented as unilateral — he destabilizes the very representational structures that establish dichotomies such as savagism versus civilization. Shaking the foundations of American history with trickster humor, Vizenor's novel insinuates that the real reason for Columbus's voyage was his subconscious wish to return to his homeland — "the mariner heard stories in his blood and would return to the New World" (35). There he meets Samana, "a hand talker [who] eased his pain with lust and wild rapture; she released the stories in his blood" (37) and mothered his mixedblood offspring. These, then, are the title's "tribal heirs," led by the ingenious crossblood protagonist Stone Columbus. With subversive humor and the genetic "signature of survivance" (132) that they inherited from Columbus, these heirs try both literally and figuratively to heal the New World: from the wounds inflicted on tribal cultures, but also from the materialistic disease exemplified by the obscure "Brotherhood of American Explorers" (46). These "new fur traders" (47) are the "robber barons of sacred tribal sites" (50), stealing from tribal cultures in the name of museal conservation but ultimately for financial gain.

Vizenor's mode of presentation is as hybrid as the characters he writes about and thus contributes substantially to this imaginative decentering. The narrative is interspersed with excerpts from Columbus's journal and other sources (Vizenor used several Columbus biographies) and is presented in the form of court hearings, late night "talk radio" sessions, investigators' reports, and visionary tribal dreams. Vizenor intentionally blurs the boundaries between what is considered historical reality, the realistic level of the text, and the realm of the imaginary. He thus illustrates that, as expressed in the novel, "the real world exists and is remembered nowhere else but in stories" (75). Part of the novel, relating historical details, could almost be read as direct reversal, albeit with an ironic twist. In a parody of Columbus's journal account of discovery quoted earlier in the novel (3–4, 36), for instance, the heirs establish a sovereign nation "dedicated to protean humor and the genes that would heal" at Point Roberts on the US-Canadian border (renamed Point Assinika) 500 years after Columbus's arrival:

> Point Assinika was declared a sovereign nation on October 12, 1992, by the Heirs of Christopher Columbus. "At dawn we saw pale naked people, and we went ashore in the ship's boat," said the adventurer on an exclusive

talk show radio broadcast. "Miigis unfurled the royal banner, and the heirs brought the flags which displayed a large blue bear paw."

"The Heirs of Columbus bear faith and witness that we have taken possession of this point in the name of our genes and the wild tricksters of liberties, and we made all the necessary declarations and had these testimonies recorded by a blond anthropologist."

"No sooner had we concluded the formalities of taking possession of the point than people began to come to the beach, all as pale as their mothers bore them, and the women also, although we did not see more than one very young girl," said Stone Columbus. (119)

In addition, the new nation is overlooked by a statue of the "Trickster of Liberty [which] faced west on the point and would be higher than the Statue of Liberty. . . . The inscription on the statue promised to 'heal the tribes and huddled masses yearning to breathe free'" (122), mocking Emma Lazarus's poem "The New Colossus" inscribed on the Statue of Liberty (which faces east). Yet claiming Columbus as part Indian defies any simplistic interpretations of history — regardless of orientation. In Vizenor's novel, the explorer is the initiator of both destruction *and* survival (through his healing genes, which he passes on to the heirs). As Hardin points out, through the character of a part-Indian Columbus Vizenor deliberately breaks down restrictive categorizations such as Euro-American/Indian, conqueror/conquered, aggressor/victim:

> Since both of these stances merely serve to reinforce the established hegemony, either by capitulation or definition through opposition, another history/space must be created in which the individual can construct an identity free of the victimizing burden of the past without forgetting the events which have happened and have been instrumental in the construction of the culture's consciousness. (1998)

Vizenor creates such a space through humor and imagination. He liberates history (and its grasp on the present) from the binary oppositions by which its representation is habitually determined, and thus explodes the colonial regime of domination that it sustains. In both Vizenor's and Erdrich and Dorris's novels, the amusing alternative versions of Columbus and discovery are employed to substantiate Native claims: in the first case, through Columbus's lost diary, which clearly spells out his recognition of Native cultures as sovereign nations from the start (Erdrich and Dorris, 275–76, 500); and in the second case, through Columbus's genetic signature, which proves that the heirs are his offspring and entitles them to collect the tithe bestowed on him by Isabella and Ferdinand (one tenth of his discoveries, Vizenor, 160, 163, 176). Although in both cases, "humor has political significance" (Vizenor, 166), as one of the investigators in Vizenor's novel cautions the court, the main issue is not resistance or retribution within established frameworks; this would leave the norms as such intact. Rather, the trickster Vizenor aims at disruption. I don't think it's worth writing, for myself, unless you can break up a little bit. I don't think it's worth the energy unless the formulas can be broken down, unless the expectations of the reader are disrupted, because I think writing is revolutionary, radical in behavior. (in Bruchac 1987a, 294)

In *Heirs*, Vizenor makes Columbus himself the "Admiral of the Ocean Sea . . . a trickster overturned in his own stories five centuries later" (185). Just as the trickster embodies the contradictory forces of culture hero and fool, "Columbus arises in tribal stories that heal with humor the world he wounded; he is loathed, but he is not a separation in tribal consciousness" (185). And just as the trickster in Vizenor's work is a ubiquitous presence, a fluid textual principle rather than a clearly defined character, in *Heirs* "Columbus is ever on the move in our stories" (11), as Stone tells an interviewer when confronted with inconsistencies of the heirs' account of Columbus's story. Vizenor's Columbus thus becomes the disruptive force that imaginatively renders previously fixed categories and models futile, compelling both Native and Euro-American readers to rethink their respective positions and their ensuing relations. Rather than subscribing to what he himself refers to as the tragic mode, he has "turned around the Columbus story to serve healing rather than victimization; there is much to be gained politically from victimization, but there is more to be gained from the power of a good story that heals, and I think my story heals the victims in a poetic and imaginative way" (Vizenor 1990–91, 103).

Despite its futuristic references to laser shows and state of the art genetic engineering — which mocks the stereotypical confinement of Indians to a sentimentalized past — Vizenor's novel is much closer to the repeatedly invoked traditional tribal "stories in the blood" than Erdrich and Dorris's *Crown*, both in subject matter, with its references to Anishinaabe mythology, and in its poetic, imaginative style. The ending of *Heirs* reveals that the entire plot — and by inference Native-White history — is to be seen as but a further incarnation of the perpetual mythic game between the Wiindigoo, the evil gambler spirit, and Naanabozho, the Anishinaabe trickster, who is indirectly established as Stone Columbus's brother at the beginning of the novel (5). The comic revelation that discovery and colonization are part of the Anishinaabe mythic contest about the fate of the world and the humans in it does not play down or excuse the tragic dimensions of the colonial encounter, however. Rather, it denies Euro-America the sole power over history by leveling the hierarchies within which the West, in a self-licensing process, has accredited sole authority to fixed written accounts, while Native imaginative "stories in the blood" are dismissed. Like Erdrich's Vivian Twostar, Vizenor's heirs are not tragic mixedblood victims of circumstance. Appropriating Columbus, the cultural icon of colonial domination, they are the heroes of survivance, tricksters who outwit both the evil wiindigoo and the North American governments. "Trickster stories liberate the mind in language games" (82), testifies an investigator at the court hearing about stolen medicine pouches and remains. In analogy, Vizenor's boldly reimaginative story liberates the readers' imagination in a hilarious journey that leaves historical "realities" far behind and is destined for more healing humorous "truths."

As this study makes apparent, humor in Native writing serves in part to expose the processes by which, within colonial regimes, particular representations of the past serve to sustain hegemonic conditions in the present. With many land claims still unsettled and many Native groups struggling for sovereignty, the fraudulent practices of Euro-Americans in their legal dealings with Native people, as well as the intricacies of US and Canadian Indian policies, are frequent subjects for subversive humor. Whether it is jokes like "How is Halloween celebrated at the Bureau of Indian Affairs? . . . Trick or Treaty" (Vee Salabiye in Lincoln 1993, 40; see also V. Deloria 1977, 148, and Edmunds 1976, 148); brief sarcastic allusions such as those made to the historical 1626 "purchase" of Manhattan for twenty-four dollars worth of beads and trinkets in *The Crown of Columbus* or in LeAnne Howe's short story "An American in New York" (2000); or whole plays, like Hanay Geiogamah's *Foghorn*, which satirically denounces US Indian policy, broken treaties, and degrading mythmaking processes from 1492 until its production in the late 1970s; such humor defies a palliative glossing over of the injustices North America's indigenous population suffered at the hands of Euro-American colonizers, while simultaneously avoiding a direct affront to a White audience.

A case in point are Sherman Alexie's playfully incongruous declarations of love, which tragicomically allude to the many broken treaties that eventually left Native people with but a minute fraction of their original land base: "*After 500 years of continuous lies/ I would still sign treaties for you*" (1993a, 65) and "Baby, come make me promises, tell me/ you'll love me as long as/ *the winds blow/ the grasses grow/ the rivers flow*" (87). "As long as the grass is green and the waters run," an expression employed in Native-White treaties to signal the Euro-American settlers' willingness to honor the agreement infinitely, not only provides the title for Thomas King's *Green Grass, Running Water;* playing on this phrase, part of the novel's plot focuses on the blockage and eventual destruction of a dam that keeps the waters from running and accordingly the grass from growing. In the end, as a result of one of Coyote's schemes, the dam breaks, releasing the water and thus reestablishing the conditions under which the treaties were to be honored. Moreover, throughout the novel King intersperses references to the title that — through the very volatility of the promises made in the respective situations — sarcastically allude to the underlying insincerity of the historical treaties: "As long as the grass is green and the waters run" is the answer a Hollywood Western's Indian chief gives in response to his White captive's plea, "My darling, . . . I don't ever want to leave your side" (208) — both knowing perfectly well that they will be separated. It is Native university professor Eli's ironic retort to a remark by White engineer Clifford Sifton[1] that Eli cannot block the dam with his cabin forever (267). And intriguingly, it is also what a talking White Paper "in a nice, deep voice" (271) says to Thought Woman — alluding to the termination policy suggested by the Trudeau government in 1969, which planned to abolish the special status of Native people in Canada (basically the ultimate forfeiting of all treaties; see Flick 1999, 160). As Linton points out: "The title phrase resonates throughout the narrative as a code for betrayal, but betrayal compounded so many times that it has become predictable. In the mouths of Native characters, the phrase expresses bitter humor" (1999, 218).

It is this derisive humor, however, that makes non-Native readers sympathize with the Native position, for instance, when Eli answers Sifton's comment that "those treaties aren't worth a damn. Government only made them for convenience. Who'd of guessed that there would still be Indians kicking around in the twentieth century?" with a sardonic "One of life's little embarrassments" (141). The novel thus flashes numerous allusions to the historic ploys by which Euro-American settlers counted on the indigenous population to vanish. But it also establishes humorous connections to more recent and more specific events, connections that will not go unnoticed by Euro-Canadian readers: Eli Stands Alone, Sifton's opponent in the novel, alludes to Elijah Harper, who single-handedly blocked the Meech Lake Constitutional Accord in 1990 and thus ensured full consultation with First Nations for future decision-making processes (see Flick 1999, 150). Moreover, the novel's "Grand Baleen [Great Whale] Dam" project is "an obvious parody of the James Bay Great Whale Project, which threatened to destroy not only a vital living ecosystem but also the resident Crees' way of life" (Weaver 1997, 152) in Quebec. Taken together, when Eli answers Harley's question of whether the tribe could be making any money out of the dam with "Maybe we should give the Cree in Quebec a call" (376), the text transparently refers to the Crees' success in receiving millions of dollars in compensation and in securing control over some of their traditional lands (see Flick 1999, 152). Celebrating the first agreement that the Euro-Canadian side actually had to make good on, King hits Canadians close to home. Because he conducts his lessons on historical and contemporary Indian policy through humorous allusion and playfulness rather than preaching and accusation, however, Euro-Canadian readers may laughingly grant him this moment of malicious joy. Evoking laughter thus emerges as a diplomatic strategy: It makes non-Native readers reconsider contested issues and problematic statements without provoking defensive dogmatic indignation. Within the context of Native-White relations, it displays parallels to what Morreall observes about humorous criticism among friends: "By using the jocular gripe we don't set up a confrontation; rather we invite the person to step back and laugh with us" (1983, 116).

Such disarming laughter may also result from estrangement and defamiliarization caused by the use of discursive frames totally incongruous to the subject matter dealt with. Monique Mojica's "Post-Colonial-Stress-Disorder: A Theatrical Monologue" (first performed in 1997) satirically frames its full-blown critique of colonial regimes entirely in the discourse of clinical psychology. Her description of "Post-Colonial Traumatic Stress Disorder," a disease first manifesting itself in America "500 and 5 years ago [(1492), which] has now reached epidemic proportions" (2001, 88), lists the consequences of colonization as "symptoms." Establishing communication by direct address, the performer comically inveigles the audience to put themselves in Native people's shoes as they follow the diagnostic checklist:

> If you are profoundly disoriented by flesh-coloured band-aids,
>   you may be suffering from Post-Colonial Traumatic
> Stress   Disorder.
> If you are allergic to milk, WHITE flour, WHITE sugar and alcohol,
>   you may be suffering from Post-Colonial Traumatic
> Stress   Disorder.
> If you find yourself talking back to Walt Disney movies,
>   you may be suffering from Post-Colonial Traumatic
> Stress   Disorder — or —
>   ETHNOSTRESS!!!!!!!!!   (88)

Mojica's look at Euro-America from a Native perspective dismantles Eurocentric notions of Whiteness and Western culture as the norm — and the ensuing relegation of Native people to the position of the Other. It dislodges a Euro-American audience from its complacent position at the center, and engages in the colonizers' (medical) discourse to cause humorous self-recognition and reassessment. For instance, with increasing linguistic playfulness, the text draws attention to the degrading practices Native people are subjected to at the hands of Euro-American and Euro-Canadian bureaucracies:

> If you lose your identity and your nationality every time you put
> your   foot across a border,
>
>   "You must produce a tribal band card stating
> your   blood quantum"
>
>   Mmmongrel -g-r-r- ped-i-gree- gree g-r-r-r
>
>   "In addition you must produce a letter, on
> tribal   letterhead,
> stating your lineage at least as far

back as your grandparents proving that you are at
        least 51% or better Native American. " . . .

        Mmmongrel...bloodquantu...gree, gree, ped-i-
gree

        G-R-R-R-ROWL   (88–89)

In blurring the sounds of the colonizers' language to resemble the snarl of
an aggressive dog, Mojica's text makes visible, or rather audible, the racist
aggressiveness underlying colonial policies. The combination of matter-of-
factly quoted statements with the register of breeding and increasingly irrational wordplay acoustically epitomizes the very grotesqueness inherent in
these racist criteria themselves (which call up parallels to the proofs of
Aryan descent that people had to produce in Nazi Germany). The allusive
muttering incites laughter, but possibly also a reevaluation of standards,
definitions, and policies otherwise accepted as "normal."

The text continues to employ medical jargon in its sarcastically playful
scrutiny of the factors instrumental in the historical decimation of Native
people and the destruction of Native cultures. Naming the literally fatal
consequences of Euro-American presence, it quips that colonization has
been "known to kill on contact" (pun intended) through various infec-
tious diseases or

        . . . to lead to a long, lingering death from:
        Drug addiction, Diabetes, Tuberculosis, Suicide, Family
Violence,   In-grown
Toenails and —
        "...for Thine is the Kingdom and the Power, and the Glory,
        forev..., forev..., forev"
        Post-Col-mat...traum stress olonial alone colon- eth-eth
no...no
        Disor-Disor   (89)

Not only do the "In-grown Toenails" comically disrupt the nightmarish
catalog of the previously listed afflictions, their highly incompatible juxtaposition with the Lord's Prayer also constitutes a tragicomic reminder of
the church's complicity in the process of colonization, the immense cultural disruption caused through forced conversion, epitomized in the text
by the final disruption of linguistic coherence. Culminating in a perplexed
"Disor-Disor," evocative of both error and disorientation, the jumbled
language fragments must be hilarious when performed. Yet, by implication
they demonstrate how Native people, sentenced to mind-numbing repetitions of prayers they could initially not even understand, were forcefully
deprived of their own cultural systems, their own language, their own epistemologies — especially in the residential or boarding and mission schools,
in which Native children were forbidden to speak their Native language

and forcefully assimilated into a Western, Judeo-Christian mainstream. Consequently, loss dominates the remainder of the text: "Loss of belief or Anomie / Loss of joyful belief. / The belief that the earth is round, / The belief that the sun rises in the East and sets in the West . . . The belief that every being has the right to breathe air, drink water and take up space" (89). Nonetheless, the tragic dimensions of cultural loss are brightened up by mocking sideswipes at the erroneous European belief that the earth was a disk rather than a globe (which was still held by church authorities at the time of discovery, despite Columbus's or Galileo's argumentation to the contrary) or at the firm Euro-American belief in private ownership.

Mojica's "Post-Colonial Traumatic Stress Disorder" is exemplary of the Native "laughter and jokes . . . directed at the horrors of history, at the continuing impact of colonization, and at the biting knowledge that living as an exile in one's own land necessitates" (P. Allen 1992, 158). Its humor offers a pathway for coming to terms with incredibly sad episodes in Native-White history, while concurrently holding up Euro-American rationalizations for reinspection. Illustrating humor's mediating potential, it allows for criticism without foreclosing dialog through overt provocation. Consequently, the monologue's final repeated beckoning to "De-Colonize your mind" (90), like the entire text, should be read as addressing the audience regardless of racial or ethnic affiliation: It calls upon Native people to see themselves as independent of the colonizer's gaze (especially when read as an allusion to Ngugi wa Thiong'o's groundbreaking *Decolonizing the Mind,* which argues for African authors to write in their own tongue rather than the colonizer's language — shedding further light on the "loss of language" demonstrated by Mojica's text). But it also calls upon both Native people and Euro-Americans to transcend for good such binary categories of self and other, center and margin, past and present — from which they have been liberated temporarily by laughing at Mojica's performance. What Sarkowsky observed for the field of Native art, namely, that humor constitutes "a central device . . . in order to not only resist or reconcile, but also transcend this very paradigm" (2003, 91) consequently holds equally true for Native literature: Even for strongly contested issues, laughter opens up a liminal space that surpasses the binary choices of resistance and reconciliation, a space that can accommodate various alternative versions without privileging any of them, leaving room for renegotiation. Without ever downplaying the tragic consequences of colonization, humor imaginatively encourages intercultural communication in a minefield of mutual historical and contemporary infringements. It is disruptive, shaking loose fixed meanings and interpretations. Still: "Through humor, human contacts, always problematical, become less fragile" (F. Miller 1967, 271), so that humor's destabilizing effects may, in the end, contribute to a more stable intercultural understanding by sustaining dialog.

Deconstructing Stereotypes

I know this because an eagle came to me in my dreams, along with a coyote and a raven. They landed on the tree of peace, smoked a peace pipe, ate a baloney sandwich, played some bingo, then told me so.
— Drew Hayden Taylor,
"How Native is Native if You're Native?" 59

As outlined in chapter two, the simulacrum of "the Indian," created mostly by Euro-American writers and Hollywood productions looms too large in the imagination of both non-Native and Native people not to have any tangible effect on contemporary self-conceptualizations of Nativeness. Stereotypes not only simplify, reduce, and exaggerate a group's characteristics,[2] because they "essentialize, naturalize and fix 'difference,'" they draw boundaries that become insurmountable, especially where inequalities of power are involved: "Stereotyping is what Foucault called a 'power/knowledge' sort of game. It classifies people according to a norm and constructs the excluded as 'other'" (Hall 1997b, 258–59). Given these ideological implications, stereotypes in literature exceed the realm of the aesthetic and have to be considered in terms of their moral and political repercussions as well. Connecting the processes of stereotyping to "the mechanisms producing and manipulating public opinion, questions of ethnic identity, the role of art for the cultural and political self-esteem of a group, and the link between defamatory images and political discrimination," Franke postulates: "Situated at the interface between individual texts and the collective imagination, stereotypes provide a key to understanding the ways in which contemporary controversies enter literature and the ways in which literature participates in cultural negotiations" (1999, 25, 283). One look at contemporary Native writing reveals that by humorously reimagining stereotypical representations the texts indeed play a crucial role in the cultural renegotiation of Nativeness. They reach beyond a literary level to tap into that place in the collective imagination where ideas about "Indians" are located. They call up or even mimic familiar stereotypes — in order to expose clichéd notions for what they are, that is, to highlight their very nature as stereotypes, simulations that lack actual referents. Humor, as becomes apparent in the following discussion, may thus turn the power and force that stereotypes exert against themselves.

Historical/Literary Stereotypes

Richard Wagamese's second novel *A Quality of Light* (1997) describes the friendship between Johnny Gebhardt, a young Canadian of German descent, and Joshua Kane, the novel's young Ojibway narrator, who had been adopted into a White family at birth. Johnny grows up in an abusive surrounding that offers him little cultural orientation, and consequently tries to escape into an alternate reality: that of books, preferably about Indians. The first encounter between Johnny and Joshua exemplifies how (literary and historic) stereotypes influence the way non-Natives perceive Native people. When Joshua's (adoptive) father asks Johnny what he likes to read about, Johnny replies:

> "Indians, mostly, sir."
> "Indians?"
> "Yessir, I like 'em."
> "You know that Joshua's an Indian, don't you, John?" my mother asked.
> "Yes, ma'am. But I mean *real* Indians. You know, warriors and stuff."
> "I think there's more to Indians than just being warriors, isn't there, John?" my dad asked.
> "No, sir. I read about it. They were warriors."
> "Joshua is not a warrior," my mother said.
> "Yes, ma'am. That's what I mean. *Real* Indians." (56)

Shaped by the one-dimensional depictions encountered in his reading, Johnny's stereotypical expectations about *real* Indians effectively block his recognition of Joshua's (contemporary) Nativeness, as the latter does not comply with Johnny's ideas. Written texts and the authority they are endowed with — as exemplified by Johnny's insistence "I read about it" — have been instrumental in shaping the simulacrum of "the Indian" at every stage of North American history.[3] Yet the image of "the Indian" in American writing has adapted over time. It ranges from the noble savage created by Enlightenment philosophers such as Rousseau, over Puritan condemnations of the devilish Indian heathens in early explorer and settler accounts (such as those by Increase and Cotton Mather and John Smith) and captivity narratives (the most well-known being Mary Rowlandson's account, dating from 1682), to both bloodthirsty savage and noble sidekick varieties in James Fenimore Cooper's and Charles W. Webber's nineteenth-century frontier romances and today's popular pulp Westerns.[4] Fully developed Native characters or close resemblance to actual referents were never an issue. Rather, Euro-American writers "had metaphorically stripped the native of his/her present through creation of a surrogate literary reality, defined to the convenience of the colonizer" (Churchill 1992, 33). The image of the noble savage (and its contemporary version, the spiritual eco-saint) served to critique a presumably corrupt Western society, while the dehumanizing stereotype of the uncivilized animalistic brute (and the no-good drunk) allegedly justified conquest and imperial expansion.

To expose this close link between colonial expansion and domination and stereotypical literary depiction, or "literary Manifest Destiny," as Churchill calls it, is but one of the objectives in contemporary Native writers' attempts to cast off the yoke of stereotypical representations. Faced with "what is surely a literary wasteland for the Indian," as Louis Owens writes in allusion to modernist paradigms, Native writers "see inexhaustible opportunity and need to 'make it new'" (1992, 24). Consequently, prominent portrayals of "the Indian" in American literary history frequently surface and are comically deconstructed in contemporary Native literature. In reference to the very beginnings of American literature, Sherman Alexie's novel *Indian Killer* features a (White American) university professor named "C. Mather," whose ideas of Indians are just as one-dimensional as those proposed by his namesake, the Puritan Cotton Mather, in his *Magnalia Christi Americana* (1702) — though reversed in orientation. Several Native writers satirize the image of the Indian in John Smith's *Generall Historie of Virginia, New-England, and the Summer Isles* (1624), most hilariously, Hanay Geiogamah in *Foghorn* and Monique Mojica in *Princess Pocahontas and the Blue Spots*. Mary Rowlandson appears as a bored and inattentive student in an art history class in King's *Green Grass, Running Water* — which also mocks another favorite of literary Indian stereotyping, James Fenimore Cooper's *Leatherstocking Tales*. And Gerald Vizenor's texts, true to his predilection for simulations, single out two authors who more than likely never encountered an indigenous person at all. His screenplay *Harold of Orange* has the protagonists Harold and Fannie pose as Hiawatha and Minnehaha from H. W. Longfellow's *The Song of Hiawatha* (1855) (1993a, 55); and his short story "Reservation Café" slyly mocks European consumers' enthusiasm for a coffee variety named "Karl May Red Roast" (1983, 36). While this list could be expanded at will, the subsequent discussion focuses on selected examples: Mojica's subversion of the Pocahontas myth, King's undoing of the *Leatherstocking Tales*, and Alexie's and King's engagement with pulp Westerns.

John Smith's original account of his encounter with Pocahontas in *Generall Historie of Virginia, New-England, and the Summer Isles* (1624) is of questionable validity: Most likely, he was aware of the widely spread motif of the rescue tale — in which a young hero travels to a foreign land, is captured by the king, and rescued by the king's daughter, the Scottish Ballad of "Young Beichan" being but one popular example — and may have fashioned his narrative to fit this established pattern (see R. Green 1990, 15–16). This connection notwithstanding, the account has been engaging the American imagination ever since its publication. Starting with James Nelson Barker's play *The Indian Princess; Or, La Belle Sauvage* (1808), there have been almost countless adaptations of the myth for the stage, movies, commercials, ballads and novels, paintings, and toys (see Stedman 1982, 25–27; Bell 1994), Disney's animated *Pocahontas* (1995) being but the present endpoint of this steady stream. Accordingly, Beth Brant sardonically comments on Smith's story of Pocahontas throwing herself between himself and her father Powhatan (Wahunsonacock), who is about to execute the White intruder: "Quite a story. Even Hollywood couldn't improve this tale" (1998, 163). While Hollywood might not be able to improve on it, Monique Mojica sure can: Her play *Princess Pocahontas and the Blue Spots* (1991), in several of its thirteen scenes — or "transformations," as Mojica calls them, both because a cast of two actresses impersonate seventeen different characters who partly transform into each other and because previous material is transformed — playfully rewrites the tale of the noble princess. In a twofold approach, it satirically ridicules distinctly US American values and customs, and thus mocks the way in which the tale of Pocahontas was appropriated for American national mythology; and it exposes clichéd Pocahontas depictions as simulacra. Despite their constant reiteration, these images have very little to do with the historical person of Matoaka/Pocahontas/Rebecca (her official Powhatan name/nickname/later Christian name), who was an estimated twelve years old when she first encountered Smith. The play not only gives voice to Pocahontas's various historical "personas," including the stereotypical "storybook princess" of the collective imagination, it also juxtaposes these utterances with original quotes from John Smith's and William Strachey's (the first governor of Virginia) accounts of the myth, resulting in comic discrepancies between these versions. Even while laughing at the play, the audience is made aware that Smith's culturally ignorant interpretations — from Matoaka's point of view Smith is just as "uncivilized" with regard to her culture as she is to his — and all subsequent stereotypical depictions are, in fact, "valorizations of conquest . . . located in the genre of the romance, a patriarchal narrative which is, itself, dedicated to surrender and conquest" (Bell 1994, 64).

The play begins with a White host's announcement of the "498th annual . . . Miss North American Indian Beauty Pageant" (18), a device that simultaneously lampoons the superficial American emphases on appearances, competition, and (alleged) tradition; constitutes a sideswipe at the 1992 quincentennial of Columbus's "discovery" (the play premiered in 1990); and critiques the exoticized image of Native women in popular culture. Striving for authenticity, the host's introduction and the contestant's first appearance accumulate all conceivable characteristics of the "Indian Princess." These only reveal the full extent of the fabrication, however, as the setting, her paraphernalia, and her behavior speak volumes as to the artificiality of the scene: "Princess Buttered-on-Both-Sides" (a clearly materialistic American pop culture impersonation of Pocahontas) is said to have come "from her home in the deep green forest on the other side of the mountain, by the shores of the silver sea" (18). The music accompanying her appearance is *"a mixture of Hollywood 'tom-toms,' the 'Indian Love Call,' 'The Good, the Bad and the Ugly' and the 'Mazola' commercial"* (18). Clad in buckskin, the princess offers corn nuts from a plastic bag, but has to ask the audience, "Excuse me, which way is east?" (18) before she can toss them to the four directions. And to complete the

cliché, she "*rises, arms and face lifted to the heavens in a classic 'spiritual'*
Hollywood Indian pose" and eventually "in savage splendour" performs a
"*Hollywood 'Injun dance'* . . . the 'Dance of the Sacrificial Corn Maiden'"
(18–19). Taking Hollywood conventions of the "Indian princess" to the
extreme, Mojica's play not only ridicules the reductive manner in which
Native cultures in general and Native women in particular are represented
in America's popular culture, it implicitly critiques the shallowness and lack
of consideration with which an American audience accepts and even
encourages such fabricated images. Fittingly, the scene's ending quotes
another popular cliché, that of Native women being somehow inherently
fascinated with White men. Mocking what Rayna Green describes as the
"Pocahontas Perplex," the princess announces to the audience: "I shall . . .
proceed to hurl myself over the precipice, all for the loss of my one true
love, CAPTAIN JOHN WHITEMAN . . . OH, that's Niagara Falls down
there, but I just can't live without him" (19). While decontextualizing it
within the satirical framework of a beauty pageant, the play thus mimics an
established pattern:

> If unable to make the grand gesture of saving her captive lover or if
> thwarted from marrying him by her cruel father, the Chieftain, the
> Princess is allowed the even grander gesture of committing suicide when
> her lover is slain or fails to return to her after she rescues him. In the hun-
> dreds of "Lover's Leap" legends which abound throughout the country,
> and in traditional songs like "The Indian Bride's Lament," our heroine
> leaps over a precipice, unable to live without her loved one. (R. Green
> 1990, 17–18)

This strategy of subversive mimicry prepares the audience for the final
undoing of the motif later in the play: After repeated summonses from off-
stage to "JUMP! . . . JUMP NOW!" the "Virgin" hastily leaves the stage,
comically excusing herself: "I think I left something on the stove" (25).
Mojica's play therefore most amusingly discloses the spuriousness of the
countless portrayals of Native women's fascination with White men.

A love song the princess performs (accompanied by the eponymous
"Blue Spots" as doo-whooping background singers) further undercuts the
cliché and reveals the idea's full grotesqueness:

> Captain Whiteman, I would pledge my life to you
> Captain Whiteman, I would defy my father, too.
> I pledge to aid and to save
> I'll protect you to my grave.
> Oh, Captain Whiteman, you're the cheese in my fondue.
> Captain Whiteman for you, I will convert,
> Captain Whiteman, all my pagan gods are dirt.
> If I'm savage don't despise me,
> 'cause I'll let you civilize me.
> Oh, Captain Whiteman, I'm your buckskin clad dessert. . . .

> Captain Whiteman, I'm a little Indian maid,
> Captain Whiteman, with a long ebony braid.
> Please don't let my dark complexion
> Inhibit your affection.
> Be my muffin, I'll be your marmalade.   (26–27)

The princess's part frivolous, part ridiculous expressions of affection, of course, appear all the more amusing when contrasted with the image of the hardened frontier hero Smith. Yet the song includes references to serious issues such as the postulated civilizing mission, forced conversion and assimilation, or racism based on skin color, as well as facetious allusion to the sexual and romantic undertones frequently present in Pocahontas narratives. Laughter once more reveals the practice of stereotyping in the context of imperial domination as thinly veiled racism — an effect that builds on the audiences' previous realization that within such a framework signs no longer have any connection to the referents they supposedly stand for. This is demonstrated, for instance, when after her performance the Princess addresses the audience, "Many, many thanks, you have made my heart soar like the *noble rabbit*" (27; emphasis added) or when a Troubadour delivers a Pocahontas/Rebecca ballad with the nonsensical "Indian babble" chorus: "Heigh-ho wiggle-waggle / wigwam wampum, / roly-poly papoose tom-tom, / tomahawk squaw" (29): Both scenes string together formulaic "Indian" expressions devoid of sense or meaning and thus constitute a comic demonstration of the workings of simulacra.

To conclude the discussion, I want to quote the following passage from Mojica's play, which traces the "Indian Princess" cliché throughout the history of colonization:

> Princess, Princess Amazon Queen.
> Show me your royal blood, . . .
> Princess, priestess, Caribe Queen,
> What are you selling today,
> Is it corn, tobacco, beans?
> Princess, Princess, calendar girl.
> Redskin temptress, Indian pearl.
> Waiting by the water
> for a white man to save.
> She's a savage now remember —
> Can't behave! . . .
> Are you a real Indian Princess?   (20–21)

Behind its humorous façade, the song, like the entire play, targets the practice of routinely depicting Native women in a reductive and degrading fashion. While evoking laughter, it nonetheless shows that Native women in Euro-American thinking and writing have been stereotyped as either good, innocent, helper-type "princesses" or bad, lusting, and lazy "squaws" — depending on the colonizers' underlying intention. Pocahontas and other

Native women were stylized as princesses when their "royalty" was a pre-condition for the approval of their relationship with White men — though the notion of chiefs as kings was quickly abandoned when it became less opportune due to land claims to those kings' former empires (see Stedman 1982, 24). In contrast, Native women were conceptualized as easy "squaws" wherever the colonizers projected their own illegitimate desires on them. In this case, they were "redskin temptresses" who supposedly lusted after White men (see Acoose 1995, 45) and "couldn't behave."[5]

While the play does comprise serious aspects and scenes, indicating that stereotypes actually "foster cultural attitudes that encourage sexual, physical, verbal, or psychological violence against Indigenous women" (Acoose 1995, 55), it is humorous elements such as the ones discussed here that largely determine its character. It combines the instructive potential of humor with a widespread familiarity with elements from pop culture, such as the institution of the beauty pageant and the Pocahontas myth. After all, Henry Adams wrote as early as 1860: "No American . . . needs to learn that Pocahontas is the most romantic character in the history of his country. Her name and story are familiar to every schoolboy" (Draxlbauer 2003, 19). This combination creates a wonderful "play-ground" for satirically making transparent the very strategies by which a fabricated authenticity is attributed to degrading portrayals of Native women in mainstream American culture. It is no coincidence that Princess Buttered-on-Both-Sides finally wins the beauty contest for her appearance as a cigar store squaw, of all guises, the epitome of the degrading Indian stereotype. True to satire's basic intention to expose "what *seems* to be real but is not" (Feinberg 1967, 3), Mojica's play comically highlights the Pocahontas legend's simulated character, which is spelled out when the troubadour recommends to his audience, after his rendering of the Pocahontas ballad: "If you want any more, make it up yourself" (31).

Coming back to the aforementioned entanglement of stereotyping and imperial expansion, it is interesting to consider Bell's following observation: "Both Pocahontas and America carry the burden of female sexual stereotypes. They are represented as virgin and whore, innocent of history and identity but also a wild and corrupt challenge to the male colonial enterprise" (1994, 68). Reimagining the Pocahontas tale within a more complex, humorous frame, Mojica's play, in its final consequence, under-cuts stereotypes in their capacity as simplifying rationalizations of both the colonial enterprise and racial and sexual oppression.

As the section on intertextuality in chapter three showed, James Fenimore Cooper's *Leatherstocking Tales* are only one of many intertexts in Thomas King's *Green Grass, Running Water*. All four of the intertexts from which the names of the novel's trickster characters are taken (*Moby Dick*, *Robinson Crusoe*, the *Leatherstocking Tales*, and *The Lone Ranger*) are illustrative of colonial domination and its inherent depiction of indigenous people as deficient. It is in engaging with Cooper's texts, however, that King most obviously tackles the literary cliché of "the Indian." This is no coincidence, since it was Cooper's five-part *Leatherstocking* cycle that most firmly established "the Indian" within the popular consciousness, far beyond the time of its original publication, from 1823 to 1841 (see Churchill 1992, 25; Lee 2003, 101). Cooper's knowledge about Native people was very limited, to say the least — which shows in his mix-up of tribal attributes like customs, names, and languages (see Berkhofer 1978, 93; Stedman 1982, 48). Instead, he projected onto his characters whatever he considered useful in the construction of his romanticized adventures — which did not keep the audience from taking Cooper's detailed descriptions at face value, with obvious consequences for ideas about Nativeness. In view of this outcome, King creates his own version of Cooper's frontier romances. At the shores of Glimmerglass, the legendary lake from Cooper's *Deerslayer*, the mythic character Old Woman encounters "Nasty" Bumppo, an egocentric ignoramus version of Cooper's hero Nathaniel "Natty" Bumppo. King's Nasty holds a wide range of common stereotypes, first and foremost that of a generic Indianness. He mistakes Old Woman for Chingachgook and brushes her objections aside by arguing: "I can tell an Indian when I see one. Chingachgook is an Indian. You're an Indian. Case closed" (392). Testifying to Louis Owens's sardonic observation, "Not just America but most of the world knows precisely what a 'real' Indian is supposed to be" (1998, 128), Nasty is an authority on Indian and White "gifts":

> Indians have a keen sense of smell . . . That's an Indian gift. . . .
>   Whites are compassionate. That's a white gift. . . .
>   Indians can run fast. Indians can endure pain. Indians have quick reflexes. Indians don't talk much. Indians have good eyesight. Indians have agile bodies. These are all Indian gifts . . .
>   Whites are patient. Whites are spiritual. Whites are cognitive. Whites are philosophical. Whites are sophisticated. Whites are sensitive. These are all white gifts, says Nasty Bumppo.
>   So, says Old Woman. Whites are superior and Indians are inferior.
>   Exactly right, says Nasty Bumppo. Any Questions? (392–93)

Nasty here echoes an image of Indians as "cultureless savages" in a highly condensed mode. As Michael Green explains in his analysis of Indian portrayals: "Physically, since they were like wild animals, savages were well-developed" (1995, 6) — an observation also born out in Jack Forbes's darkly humorous short story "The Caged," which creates a scenario in which American Indians are kept in a zoo as an endangered species, "distantly related to the primitive ancestors of other humanoid groups" (1995, 10). The relegation of Indians to the natural — in contrast to the cultural and civilized — world basically follows the principle of "*naturalizing* 'difference,'" which Stuart Hall describes in the context of black slavery:

The logic behind naturalization is simple. If the differences between black and white people are "cultural," then they are open to modification and change. But if they are "natural" — as the slave-holders believed — then they are beyond history, permanent and fixed. "Naturalization" is therefore a representational strategy designed to *fix* "difference," and thus *secure it forever.* (1997b, 245)

Green Grass, Running Water thus comically exposes how texts like Cooper's saga — in which Natty Bumppo indeed repeatedly talks of "gifts" — help to set up artificially constructed boundaries between colonial Self and indigenous Other. King dealt extensively with non-Native literary representations of "the Indian," among them those in Cooper's *Leatherstocking Tales*, in his PhD Dissertation on "Inventing the Indian: White Images, Native Oral Literature, and Contemporary Native Writers" (University of Utah, 1986). He puts his knowledge to use in his fictional texts, bringing to light that such literally dehumanizing representations (the "Indian gifts" Nasty names all have a decidedly animalistic slant) actually reveal more about the colonial writers who devised them than about the Native people supposedly portrayed. Their underlying motivations and rationalizations for the reductive depiction of Native people shine through the image that King's incompetent, gun-toting Indian expert conveys. Simplified "Indians" are shown to have served as a benchmark to measure Euro-American civilizational progress, to justify an alleged White superiority and ensuing domination (see also Horne 1999, 38; Dvorak 1997, 68).

With the help of Coyote, the text discloses the binary oppositions for what they are and playfully deconstructs them: Following Nasty's lecture on "gifts," Coyote first concludes that he must be an Indian ("I have a keen sense of smell," 392), but subsequently finds that he must be a White person ("Wait a minute, . . . I'm compassionate, too . . . this is confusing," 393), revealing the nonsensical nature of Nasty's categorizations. Upon hearing about White superiority and Indian inferiority, Coyote finally comments "Ooops . . . We have a problem" — to which the narrator retorts: "Only if you're an Indian" (393), situating King's criticism of stereotyping within a framework of colonial domination. It is no accident, then, that King's Nasty introduces himself as "Post-Colonial Wilderness Guide and Outfitter" (392): King's post-colonial version of *Leatherstocking* conveys an acute awareness of the processes of subjectification in Cooper's colonial fiction.

Sherman Alexie's poem "How to Write the Great American Indian Novel" (an allusion to Philip Roth's *The Great American Novel*), finally, mocks the romanticized representations of Native cultures prevailing in popular Western romances. Alexie, who describes himself as coming "from a long line of exaggerators" (in Purdy 1997, 6), like King, uses extensive hyperbole and blatant generalization, accumulating as many stereotypical popular markers of Indianness as possible in order to ridicule the image of "the Indian":

All of the Indians must have tragic features: tragic noses, eyes, and arms.
Their hands and fingers must be tragic when they reach out for tragic
   food.

The hero must be a half-breed, half white and half Indian, preferably
from a horse culture. He should often weep alone. That is mandatory.

If the hero is an Indian woman, she is beautiful. She must be slender
and in love with a white man. But if she loves an Indian man
then he must be a half-breed, preferably from a horse culture.
If the Indian woman loves a white man, then he has to be so white

that we can see the blue veins running through his skin like rivers.
                                                    (1996c, 94)

Alexie's filmic descriptions call up Hollywood imagery and the cover "art"
of countless cheap Western novels, which by Alexie's own account strongly
influenced him as a child:

> I can still see the cover art. The handsome, blue-eyed warrior (the Indians
> in romance novels are always blue-eyed because half-breeds are somehow
> sexier than full-blooded Indians) would be nuzzling (the Indians in
> romance novels are always performing acts that are described in animalis-
> tic terms) the impossibly pale neck of a white woman as she reared her
> back in primitive ecstasy (the Indians in romance novels always inspire
> white women to commit acts of primitive ecstasy). (1998)

Accordingly, he demands that an Indian female protagonist of the great
American Indian novel "should be compared to nature: brown hills,
mountains, fertile valleys, dewy grass, wind, and clear water" (94). Even
while remaining within the register of such scenarios, though, he ridicules
the genre's pseudoerotic undertones, countering the alleged "wildness"
of Indian lovers with the incongruous world of well-groomed suburban
gardens: "Indian men are horses, smelling wild and gamey. / When the
Indian man unbuttons his pants, the white woman should think of topsoil" (95). The poem mocks the cliché of the spiritual Indian and the
commodification of Native cultures, pointing out that "Indians must see
visions. White people can have the same visions / if they are in love with
Indians" (95). Setting the pattern up like a cookbook recipe, outlining
which ingredients will yield the desired result — "There must be one
murder, one suicide, one attempted rape. Alcohol should be consumed.
Cars must be driven at high speed" — Alexie ridicules the highly stereotypical and redundant content, simplistic style, and predetermined plot
lines of typical Western dime-store novels. The poem sets up such formulaic patterns just to undercut them within the text itself, contrasting
the wild exaggerations with the meiotically subdued admission that, even
if one follows the instructions closely, "sometimes there are complica-
tions" (95).

The same subversive effect, though even more pronounced, is achieved in an episode of King's *Green Grass, Running Water* when Eli, a Native professor of English literature, gives in to his weakness for pulp Westerns. As Berkhofer reminds us: "If the elite artist is expected to create new visions and aesthetics, the popular artist generally reverts to formulas that have been successful before: For the Indians in popular literature and art, that formula was the 'Western'" (1978, 96). Pulp Westerns, with their formulaic reproduction, therefore inherently perpetuate stereotypes, and consequently offer a fertile ground for defying these through humor. In King's novel, after a few pages and a look at the cover of *The Mysterious Warrior* Eli can predict the rest of the book (199). Nonetheless, initially, his reading remains faithful to the stereotypical register of the Western romance:

> Chapter fourteen.
>   Iron Eyes and Annabelle were standing on the bank of a beautiful river. It was evening, and in the morning, Iron Eyes was going out with his men to fight the soldiers.
>   "It's such a beautiful evening," said Annabelle, brushing a wisp of hair from her glistening cheeks. "I don't want to leave," she said, trembling. "I don't want to leave this land. I don't want to leave you." (200)

This is soon interspersed, however, with observations on Eli's physical condition, resulting from boredom, while the elliptical constructions indicate the novel's lack of imaginative potential, and the quotation marks highlight the ridiculousness of the language:

> Eli shifted his body on the sofa. His left leg was going to sleep.
>   "Tomorrow is a good day to die," said Iron Eyes, his arms folded across his chest, etc., etc., etc.
>   Eli flipped ahead, trying to outdistance the "glistenings" and the "tremblings" and the "good-day-to-dyings."
>   Flip, flip, flip. (200)

> Chapter twenty-six.
>   Iron Eyes attacked the soldiers.
>   The cavalry came riding over the hill.
>   Etc., etc., etc.
>   Flip, flip, flip.
>   Eli tossed the book on the table, rolled up on his side against the cushions, and went to sleep. (218)

Like Alexie's poem, this paragraph not only points to the genre's degrading portrayal of Indians, in King's typical tongue-in-cheek manner, it implies that the main potential of such repetitively mind-numbing texts is soporific rather than culturally representative. As the preceding exemplifies, humor therefore meets literary/historic stereotypes on their own ground, exposes them to liberating laughter, and reworks them from within.

Hollywood Stereotypes

Motion pictures, with their visual dimension, deepened the imprint of the cliché even further, as they "preserved old clichés and developed new ones in the Western formula. . . . Vicious and noble savages peopled the movie and television screens just as they had the cheap and elite literature of the past" (Berkhofer 1978, 102–3). Probably more so than literature, Hollywood movies fixed the image of "the Indian" as nineteenth-century Plains warrior on horseback, clad in leather, feathers, and beads, without tribally distinctive features, linguistic abilities — apart from "how" and "ugh" — or humor (see Stedman 1982, 210–11).[6] Little did it matter that this hodgepodge "Holly-wooden" Indian never existed anywhere but in the producers' and directors' minds; since the fabrication was proven to generate box-office revenue, it was perpetuated countless times. Over time, "the illusory Indians were so authentic to most Americans that no alternate images were acceptable" (Stedman 1982; xv), that is, "the Indian" *became* what the media made him to be. (Unfortunately, neither the turn towards positive depictions from the 1970s onwards nor producers' and directors' attempts at more faithful depictions have changed that to any substantial degree, see O'Connor 1998, 29, 38; Stedman 1982, xv). In addition to naturalizing Euro-American presence in North America (if Indians do not exist beyond the nineteenth century, why not live on the land that used to belong to them?), these stereotypes severely affect the self-conceptualization of Native people through processes of internalization. Therefore, Native writers direct humor at these simulations to amend the effects of stereotyping on Native cultural identity. Three exemplary texts that demonstrate such humorous deconstruction of the "Hollywood Indian" and the winning of the West are Basil Johnston's "Cowboys and Indians," a scene from King's *Green Grass, Running Water*, and Sherman Alexie's "Dear John Wayne."

Basil Johnston's story "Cowboys and Indians" most directly engages with Hollywood's conventional portrayal of "the Indian" in film. Its Native characters are endowed with enough slyness to not only subvert but even profit from stereotypical expectations. A Hollywood producer and director, in an attempt at authenticity and in order to save money, decide to shoot part of their Western film project with real, "honest-to-good Indians" on the reservation:

> Their natural pigmentation would reduce expenses in cosmetics and make-up artistics; their natural horsemanship would save time and expenses usually incurred in training greenhorns to ride; their possession of herds of ponies would save time and outlay in the rental and feeding of horses; and their natural talent for art would obviate the need for anthropologists to act as consultants in authenticating Indian art and design. The only expense to be incurred was the fee of $ 2.00 per day for movie extras. (1996, 19)

The latter costs are considered negligible, since the shooting of a wagon-train attack (*the* stereotypical Indian scene) is supposed to take no longer than two days. The fatal flaw in this calculation turns out to be that the studio expects Native people to *be* nineteenth-century "Indians," that is, the simulacrum or "Indian imago" (Nischik 1996, 131) that Hollywood itself has been instrumental in creating and spreading. Ironically, even the alleged experts and historians at the Bureau of Indian Affairs, whom the filmmakers consult, subscribe to this cliché: They recommend the Crow Indians of Montana as a suitable nation, assuring the studio that they have "retained their tradition and still [own] large herds of horses" (20). The comic revelation that things are otherwise subverts both stereotypical Hollywood ideas and the BIA's and historians' expertise and authority. As readers come to realize in retrospect, the Crow chief's sole but regularly repeated interjection "How!" (mocking the taciturn Indian) during his negotiations with the producer does not signify the supposedly Indian greeting. It quite literally signals that the Crow do not know *how* they could possibly meet the director's clichéd expectations. Instead of the 500 horses the producer wants, they own "Maybe 10 . . . 20 . . . an' not very good dem" (22). They "don't know how to ride" (23) and do not have any of the bows and arrows, buckskin outfits and feather headdresses, or teepees the producer envisaged. Johnston's story thus fictionalizes what Price observes about Native acting in Hollywood: "Part of the problem is that real Indians do not behave according to the film stereotypes that have been developed about Indian behavior, so they must learn to 'act Indian'" (J. Price 1978, 211). "Cowboys and Indians" documents this process, which costs the studio several weeks of time and large amounts of money for renting horses, bringing in "artifacts" to dress the Crow up as "Indians," and paying BIA consultants to offer their advice on "war-paint designs and instruct the Crow in war-whooping" (27). Cunning tricksters, the Crow sabotage the shooting wherever they can to prolong their daily income: Either none fall off their horses dead (impossible since contradicting "history") or all do (too obvious). When the scene is shot in its supposedly final version, the director discovers that his nineteenth-century warriors are wearing sunglasses and wristwatches. While in the end the audience gets exactly what it expects, namely, the familiar perfect simulation of "the Indian," this comes at quite a price (although in a final devastating irony, the film is acclaimed for the Crows' excellent horsemanship and the producer's foresight).

Contrary to the Hollywood version of Indian-White encounters, in Johnston's wittily rewritten game of "Cowboys and Indians" the readers' sympathies lie entirely with the Indians. From the start, the studio's and experts' notion of authenticity is revealed as blatant ignorance. Yet by showing how these clichés confine contemporary Native people to a particular temporal and perceptual frame, the story demonstrates Hollywood's power in constructing the idea of Nativeness. By satirically laying open the very processes by which the simulation is created — rather than presenting their result — Johnston makes his readers look not *at* but *through* the screen, at the space beyond the polished Technicolor surface. The incongruities between the fierce warriors of the final version and the intentionally inept Crow actors and their witty chief, crowned with the exploitative producer's frustration, thus make for transformational humor that liberates Nativeness from its static and stoic simulation.

Thomas King's *Green Grass, Running Water* also comically addresses the topic of Indians in film on various levels. On the one hand, White characters are shown to constantly interpret Nativeness according to Hollywood standards. Both Eli's wife Karen and Latisha's husband George, for instance, enthusiastically comment that the traditional Blackfoot Sun Dance is "just like the movies" (203, 336). On the other hand, the novel depicts the dream factory's impact on the lives of Native characters (especially Lionel and Portland), and ridicules Hollywood in a revision of *The Mysterious Warrior*, a John Wayne and Richard Widmark movie based on the Western romance that Eli is reading. This may at first be taken to insinuate that Hollywood films are but a continuation of the literary tradition of Indian stereotyping. Since the book has "a banner stamped across the front that said, 'Based on the award-winning movie' " (160), however, instead it ironically implies that Hollywood by now is far more influential than literature in creating "the Indian." Lionel's (and other Native characters') comments on the film parallel Eli's prediction of the novel's plot: "Every one was the same as the others. Predictable. Cowboys looked like cowboys. Indians looked like Indians" (318). Humorously twisting these habitual notions, however, King rewrites the Hollywood version of the winning of the West, or rather, he has the four old Indian tricksters "fix" it. In the film *The Mysterious Warrior* — which, with its opening shot across the Monument valley, according to Flick (1999, 158) clearly alludes to John Ford's *Stagecoach* — John Wayne and Richard Widmark, along with a few dozen soldiers, get trapped between a river and a rock wall and entrench themselves behind logs and boulders to face an impending Indian attack. In the original version (which various Native characters watch at different points in the novel), the soldiers manage to kill an Indian with every bullet, while the Indians can't harm the White heroes. Eventually the cavalry comes to their rescue, attacking the Indians from behind. In the "fixed" trickster version, by contrast, the Indians do not fall off the horses dead, and in a comic inversion of the Vanishing Indian myth the cavalry, "hundreds of soldiers in bright blue uniforms with gold buttons and sashes and stripes, blue-eyed and rosy-cheeked, came over the last rise. And disappeared. Just like that" (321). The text iconoclastically dismantles the White heroes, with Widmark wetting his pants in fear before both he and Wayne, to their infinite astonishment and disbelief, get killed by Indian arrows and bullets. A switch from the original black and white to color accompanies these drastic changes in plot, implying that black and white Hollywood representations of the winning of the West spread a simplistic version of history that is in dire need of colorful revision.

Whereas the simple reversal in this case may not necessarily add complexity to the depiction of Native people, through its comic aspects it makes readers critically aware of how arbitrarily chosen, prejudiced, and limited their accustomed perspectives are. Its humor hinges very much on surprise: Readers are so conditioned by countless repetitions of the "good Cowboys versus evil Indians" plot that any deviation, let alone this playful reversal, humorously jolts them from their familiar patterns of interpretation. Triggering laughter gets readers to reconsider their customary acceptance of *the* American master narrative, the Frontier myth, and the ensuing biased portrayals of the Indians' role in westward expansion. King intentionally engages with film, the medium most forcefully instrumental in creating images of "the Indian," to reimagine "alterNatives." By revising this Western, he comically turns Hollywood's power in shaping popular images of Nativeness back on itself.

The shocked question of a sales assistant at Bill Bursum's Home Entertainment Barn, where the revised film runs, reveals both Hollywood's almost boundless control over "the Indian" and King's humorous devastation thereof: "Is it just the one movie? . . . We have lots of other Westerns. What if they all have the same problem? . . . It's still weird, though . . . Who would want to kill John Wayne?" (359). Consequently, the divided audience reaction to this reversal speaks volumes: Bill Bursum, the White owner of the home entertainment center and Lionel's patronizing boss, frantically "stab[s] at the remote" (321, 322) and replays the movie over and over, whereas the four old Indians thoroughly enjoy themselves: "Boy, that sure was a good time" (330). Johnson points out that "the oppositional current in King's work . . . is articulated in terms that expose the imperialist biases of non-indigenous media and technology, but that nonetheless escape the pitfalls of a romantic or culturally purist discourse of technophobia" (2000, 28). Rather than demonizing media representations as such, the text in a reimaginative process appropriates and transforms them. It inscribes an altered message that resists calm subordination to degrading portrayals by evoking hearty laughter at "HollyWooden" Indians.

King's novel further undercuts the filmic simulacrum of "the Indian" through the character of Portland Looking Bear, the actor who plays the Indian chief in *The Mysterious Warrior*. With Portland, the text most forcefully exposes how the Western as a genre engages in what Baudrillard referred to as the purest forms of simulation, "the generation by models of a real without origin or reality: a hyperreal" (1994, 166). During his career in Hollywood, none of Portland's "Indian actor" friends is Indian, which points to the common practice of casting non-Native actors — mostly of Italian, Mexican, or even Asian origin — for "Indian" parts; ironically, they complied more fully with the audience's expectations of what an "Indian" ought to look like (see Churchill 1992, 243; O'Connor 1998, 33; J. Price 1978, 211). Accordingly, Portland's Italian "Indian" friend C. B. Cologne ("Cristobal Colon, the famous mariner who is now running extras in Hollywood," King in Gzowski 1999, 74) explains to his son Charlie: "Just because you are an Indian doesn't mean you can act like an Indian for the movies" (185) — implicitly spelling out that the image of the Hollywood Indian exists independent of real Native people. Being Blackfoot does not sufficiently qualify Portland. He has to change his name to the more dramatic "Iron Eyes Screeching Eagle" (151), an allusion to Cherokee actor Iron Eyes Cody; he has to enact other tribal denominations, mocking the stereotype that all Indians look alike; and eventually, he even has to don a rubber nose to look the part of the menacing Indian chief to stay in business (see 152). In the end, Charlie almost fails to recognize his own father on the screen, due to the lengths Portland has gone to to turn himself into a Hollywood Indian (see 217). The text in two ways comically underlines the artificiality of Portland's transformation, which fictionalizes the experiences of actors such as Chief Thundercloud, who had to undergo similar changes for the shooting of *Geronimo* (1939; see O'Connor 1998, 33). On the one hand, it lays open the process as such through the recollections of Portland's wife about the rubber nose: "It was the silliest thing you ever saw. Portland put it on and chased me around the house. He only caught me because I was laughing so hard" (153). On the other hand, however, it shows the reactions that such masquerade elicits from a non-Native audience. Watching the movie, Joe Hovaugh assures himself that the actor playing the chief in *The Mysterious Warrior* is a real Indian: "He knew that Hollywood used Italians and Mexicans to play Indian roles, but *the man's nose* was a dead giveaway" (222; emphasis added). Ironically, it is the very part that Portland fabricates to become an Indian by Hollywood standards that is taken as the indicator of his actual Native identity — revealing the extent to which the filmic image dominates the concept of Nativeness.

In an interview, King explains that Portland's last name, Looking Bear, is "spelled B-E-A-R but in actual fact he really is sort of stripped bare by the whole experience of Hollywood" (in Andrews 1999). Indeed, when Portland tries to make a comeback after twenty years, he initially has to work at a strip joint, where, clad in a fluorescent loincloth, he chases a fake Pocahontas around the stage. The grotesqueness of rubber noses, fluorescent loin cloths, and grunting to get better tips while parking the guests' cars at an L.A. restaurant on the one hand draws attention to the phoniness and fraudulence of Hollywood's Indian portrayals. On the other hand, funny as it is, it highlights the deformation that the Native characters undergo to fit the stereotype. For Portland, the transformation is restricted to his filmic performances. Portland's nephew, the underachieving TV-salesman Lionel, however, in defiance of his Blackfoot identity, has fully internalized colonial values and (filmic) stereotypes:

> By the time Lionel was six years old, he knew what he wanted to be.
> John Wayne.
> Not the actor, but the character. Not the man, but the hero. The John Wayne who cleaned up cattle towns and made them safe for decent folk. The John Wayne who shot guns out of the hands of outlaws. The John Wayne who saved stagecoaches and wagon trains from Indian attacks.

> When Lionel told his father he wanted to be John Wayne, his father said it might be a good idea, but that he should keep his options open.
> "We got a lot of famous men and women, too. Warriors, chiefs, councillors, diplomats, spiritual leaders, healers. I ever tell you about your great-grandmother?"
> "John Wayne."
> "Maybe you want to be like her."
> "John Wayne."   (241–42)

John Wayne basically epitomizes Hollywood's Indian-hating cowboy or pioneer: "In the course of more than 150 films, with the Indian as mirroring 'other,' [John Wayne] grew into the giant figure America demanded, molding himself to match the nation's pathological craving for an archetypal hero fitted to the great, violent myth of the American West" (Owens 1998, 101). For Lionel to choose him of all people as his role model is therefore deeply ironic. It bitingly exemplifies the way in which Hollywood has restricted possible roles (and thus points of identification) for Indians to such unfavorable options that Native children, in acts of colonial mimicry, align themselves with colonial heroes rather than their own Native background.[7]

The Duke, as Wayne is called, still serves as a moral benchmark for the actions of many Americans even today. In difficult situations they ask themselves the by now proverbial question, "What would John Wayne do?" Sadly, this is exactly what Charlie asks Lionel (33, 243), who throughout the novel tries to measure up to this colonial yardstick.[8] Yet King's witty subversion of Hollywood's power over Native identity comes to optimistic closure towards the end of the novel. John Wayne's fringed leather jacket from the movie — Lionel's birthday present from the four old Indian tricksters —, which initially fit him perfectly, becomes increasingly awkward and tight, eventually "suffocating him" (382). Taking it off symbolizes Lionel's liberation from restricting colonial aspirations, precipitated by the unconventional cure administered by the four old tricksters. Also, while Lionel's sister Latisha still watches *The Mysterious Warrior* — that is, Hollywood's version of the history of the American West — her teenaged son Christian overcomes the genre's attraction. He inquires:

"How come the Indians always get killed?" When Latisha replies, "If the Indians won, it probably wouldn't be a Western," he laconically comments, "Not much point in watching it then" (192–93). King thus indicates, in a tongue-in-cheek manner, hope that Native cultural identity over time may simply "outgrow" the Hollywood stereotypes of "the Indian."

Whereas *Green Grass, Running Water* basically undercuts Wayne's glorification as an all-American hero, Sherman Alexie's short story "Dear John Wayne" comically transcodes this cultural icon. The text is a transcript of an interview conducted by Spencer Cox, a cultural anthropologist, with Etta Joseph, a supposedly famous former powwow dancer, juxtaposed with Etta's recollections of her time as an extra in the shooting of *The Searchers* (1956, directed by John Ford). Initially, the situation reeks strongly of scientific appropriation: A White anthropologist comes to a Spokane retirement home to exploit an elder as a source for his (Eurocentric) "serious and profound study on the effect of classical European ballroom dancing on the indigenous powwow" (Alexie 2001, 193). Yet soon Etta Joseph turns out to be anything but a helpless old lady: She manipulates Cox tricksterlike by presenting him with "quite an example of the oral tradition" (206), namely, the story of her affair with John Wayne.

Alexie's story preposterously upsets established conventions of the Western. Instead of the animalistic redskins lusting after and abducting innocent White women, it is John Wayne who chases and deflowers the Native virgin Etta. Instead of the imperative premature death of the Native partner in interracial love relationships (see Lutz 2002, 50; J. Price 1978, 209), it is Wayne who eventually dies, while Etta survives to tell the story. And in contrast to the man of steel, the tough keeper of law and order and manliest man imaginable, the John Wayne described by Etta is a sensitive softie. He cannot cope with his (killer) image — and thus insists on being called by his original name, Marion Morrison — is afraid of horses, often cries, and offers the most surprising liberal and emotional insights. When, during their visit on the set, he discovers his sons putting on make-up, lipstick, and mascara, for instance, his reaction defies not only the petrified boys' (who fear their father's anger) but also the readers' expectations:

John Wayne laughed.
"Oh, sons, you're just engaging in some harmless gender play. Some sexual experimentation. Every boy does this kind of thing. Every man likes to pretend he's a woman now and again. It's very healthy."
"Daddy," said the oldest. "Do you dress up like a woman?"
"Well, I don't put on a dress or anything. But often I close my eyes and try to put myself into a woman's shoes. I try to think like a woman. I try to embrace the feminine side of myself. . . . There's really not that much difference between men and women. In all things, intelligence, passion, hope, dreams, strength, men and women are pretty much equals. I mean, gender is mostly a social construction." (203)

What makes this transcoding so effective is John Wayne's status as an all-American cultural icon and idol and his continued impact on the American psyche. It is the vast discrepancy between the expectations generated by his habitual role and the unexpected opinions he expresses here that generates the humor. Along with Wayne's sons, readers are shocked into laughter:

> "Daddy!" shouted the boys. They were shocked. "That's not what you said before when you were on the radio and television."
>   "Boys, I know. I know. I have a public image to maintain. But that's not who I really am. I may act like a cowboy, I might pretend to be a cowboy, but I am not a cowboy in real life, do you understand?" (203)

The basis for Wayne's popularity in the US is precisely the close correspondence between the characters he played and his personal conviction. A strict conservative, Wayne advocated patriotic American values and ideals at all times — even during the McCarthy era, when many of his Hollywood colleagues protested or even became victims of the government's anticommunist witch hunt. By having Wayne explain that his public image vastly deviates from his personality, Alexie hollows out the myth of John Wayne and turns it into an audience projection — a reading exacerbated when Marion explains to Etta: "I'm going back to Hollywood. . . . My country needs me. They need me to be John Wayne" (204–5).

While the above-quoted passages highlight the contrast between Wayne's public conservative macho image and his privately expressed liberal views on gender, this comic discrepancy may be transferred to Marion's/Wayne's attitude towards Indians as well. The Indian hater personified by Wayne in many of his films — ironically, especially in *The Searchers* (see Stedman 1982, 111) — may be just another public image to be maintained, as in fact, the whole story plays on the impossibility of truthful representation. Etta, who as a young girl had naively assumed that Jeffrey Hunter (who played a half-breed in the movie) actually had to be a half-breed — "Otherwise, the movie would have been a lie, and John Wayne didn't lie" (197–98) — has come a long way since. Not only does she make a point of catching Spencer Cox in an insubstantial lie, which allows her to call into question his integrity with regard to his academic research (192–93), she deliberately misleads the doubting Cox by introducing little inaccuracies into her narrative, by contradicting herself, and by telling him that "an Indian has to keep her secrets or she's just not Indian. But an Indian a lot smarter than me once said: If it's fiction, it better be true" (206). The story ends with Etta introducing Cox to the alleged proof of her story, her twin sons John and Marion — their names and age indicating that they are the sons of John Wayne/Marion Morrison (see 207). Alexie's story thus constitutes an instance of what Rainwater identifies as a general tendency in contemporary Native writing, namely, that "the American Indian author-as-bricoleur subversively 'rearranges semiosis' with respect to cultural icons, converting already heavily encoded images into reservoirs of nondominant meanings and associations" (1999, 59). Like the anthropologist, who came to the interview expecting his views on Native people to be reconfirmed by what Etta could tell him about powwow dancing, readers end up with their own cultural values shaken — shaken by laughter at this ingenious transcoding of a popular culture icon.

As Paula Gunn Allen points out, "everybody in this country thinks they know what Indian is, when mostly they know what the media thinks it is" (in Coltelli 1990, 27). And as these texts by Johnston, King, and Alexie show, Native writers wittily subvert this omnipresent "knowledge" and the degrading images engrained in the audience's collective imagination. The humor Native writers direct at the clichés produced by the Californian dream factory tricks Native and non-Native readers alike into questioning Hollywood's fabrications. It exposes the dehumanizing dimensions of such depictions, effects surprising changes in perspective, and ultimately overthrows accustomed interpretations. Turning Hollywood's Indian into the object of laughter, these texts open the way for change.

New Age Stereotypes — Cosmic Harmony and its Comic Counterpart

New (and, frequently, New Age) stereotypes of the Indian as eco-saint, shaman, or sage, while more positive than the image of the bloodthirsty devil, are just as incorrect, reductive, and ultimately dehumanizing as their precedents (see Bolz 1994; Grewe-Volpp 2002, 270; Krech 1999). Steadily on the rise since the 1970s, despite their novel guise these images are but reincarnations of Rousseau's projection of the noble savage. Native writers choose various routes to demystify the Indian sage. Louis Owens's novel *Bone Game*, for instance, comically defies romanticizing or essentializing tendencies in the character of Emil Redbull, a traditional healer called in to help protagonist Cole McCurtain overcome his troubling nightmares with a sweat lodge ceremony. Redbull appears at the ceremony in a ludicrous outfit about as far from what is traditionally associated with a medicine man or shaman as it gets: Instead of being adorned with fur robe, sacred masks, or any other "ceremonial" paraphernalia, Emil shows up "wearing a pair of red gym shorts and a blue tee shirt that said, 'Don't Worry, Be Hopi'" (1994, 162) — alluding to the fact that the Arizona Hopi are the preferred target of New Age fantasies (see Sanner 1993, 149). Similar demystification strategies are at work in Sherman Alexie's short story "This Is What It Means To Say Phoenix, Arizona." Through Thomas Builds-the-Fire, a quirky storyteller, the text parades the popular idea that Indians possess supernatural powers and spiritual connections to mother nature that miraculously provide them with secret knowledge. At the reservation Trading Post, Thomas meets Victor and offers his condolences upon the death of Victor's father:

> "Victor, I'm so sorry about your father," Thomas said.
> "How did you know about it?" Victor asked.
> "I heard it on the wind. I heard it from the birds. I felt it in the sunlight. Also, your mother was just in here, crying." (61)

Within this short exchange — and even more pronouncedly in the scene from the film adaptation *Smoke Signals*, in which Thomas recites the first lines of dialog in a dreamlike voice while gazing off into the distance — Alexie builds the image of the Indian seer, just to anticlimactically collapse it in laughter.

Like other stereotypes, fabrications of the wise Indian shaman or seer serve particular purposes, for instance, to argue for environmentalist causes. The speech allegedly delivered by Chief Seattle is upheld as a prophetic document attesting to Indians' connection to "mother earth," yet it "no more represents universal native attitudes toward the earth than the Confucius of fortune cookies does the ambiguities of Chinese civilization" (Bordewich 1996, 159).[9] And as Bolz (1994, 48) points out, it has as little relevance for Native *Realpolitik* as our traffic laws would have for visitors from outer space. Yet turning the tables on White clichés, Native people may now use these preconceptions for their own purposes. This is what Corliss, the young protagonist of Sherman Alexie's story "The Search Engine," describes:

> White people, no matter how smart, were too romantic about Indians. White people looked at the Grand Canyon, Niagara Falls, the full moon, newborn babies, and Indians with the same goofy sentimentalism. Being a smart Indian, Corliss had always taken advantage of this romanticism . . . If white folks assumed she was serene and spiritual and wise simply because she was an Indian, and thought she was special based on those mistaken assumptions, then Corliss saw no reason to contradict them. The world is a competitive place, and a poor Indian girl needs all the advantages she can get. So if George W. Bush, a man who possessed no remarkable distinctions other than being the son of a former U.S. president, could also become president, then Corliss figured she could certainly benefit from positive ethnic stereotypes and not feel guilty about it. (2003, 11)

Alexie's sarcastic humor walks a thin line, possibly offending readers who fail to see the reductionism in positive stereotyping. All the same, in addition to mocking the clichés as such, the text implicitly raises the question of what motivates such stereotypes. With the narrator of another of Alexie's stories, "The Life and Times of Estelle Walks Above," readers may end up wondering: "What is it about Indians that turns otherwise intelligent, interesting, and capable people into blithering idiots? I don't think every white person I meet has the spiritual talents and service commitment of a Jesuit priest, but white folks often think we Indians are shamanic geniuses" (2003, 139).

Part of the explanation certainly lies in the convenience of such clichés for castigating the depravity of one's own society — that is, the same reasons that made Enlightenment philosophers glorify the noble savage. On the other hand, turning to "Indian" philosophies also provides escapist avoidance of confronting the problems within one's own life and society (see Bolz 1994, 53). Through their use of humor, Native writers do not answer the question raised by Alexie. But they create awareness that these stereotypes are as reductive and demeaning as their negative counterparts, denying Native people a contemporary cultural identity. Humor in this context thus humanizes Native characters by liberating them from the myth of the Indian — however positive its respective embodiment may be.

Tourist Stereotypes

Tourist stereotypes, which, strictly speaking, are more a mélange or consequence of the previously discussed aspects than a separate "category," are an assortment of distorting ideas that visitors bring to Native reservations or other sites allegedly or actually related to Native cultures, such as museums, memorials, or arts and crafts markets. Tourism, on the one hand, is a welcome and indispensable source of income to many Native nations. On the other hand, it frequently reifies Native people and Native cultures as the exotic Other to be consumed.[10] Especially this latter aspect is met with humor in contemporary Native texts. Since tourist stereotypes cannot be avoided, why not manipulate them for amusement and/or financial gain? Like Basil Johnston's Crow Indians or Sherman Alexie's Corliss, characters in fiction by Richard Wagamese, Jim Northrup, Louis Owens, and Thomas King respond to tourists' expectations by turning themselves into mocking imitations of "the Indian," while simultaneously subverting and liberating themselves from preconceived notions. "When a tourist is in the heart of Indian country and clearly a fish out of water, he becomes an easy target for trickery," writes Evans-Pritchard (1989, 98). This is literally true in Wagamese's *Keeper 'n Me*, in which Native characters play the " 'bait the tourist' game" during fishing season, intentionally misinforming the curious customers they guide about Native language and traditions (see 1994, 84–87). In Louis Owens's novel *Dark River* the young Black Mountain Apache Jessie operates a business called "Vision Quests Enterprises," charging White people huge amounts of money for temporarily leaving them to starve in the reservation wilderness in emulation of an initiation rite involving fasting and isolation.

The most pointed and at the same time most comical subversions of tourist stereotypes are provided by Thomas King in his novels *Green Grass, Running Water* and *Truth and Bright Water*. In the first, Lionel's sister Latisha's restaurant "Dead Dog Café" basically adds another layer to the simulacrum of "the Indian." Like Jessie in *Dark River*, who buys his beef jerky at the Quick Stop but then "put[s] it in a nice simulated deerskin bag bought at the casino shop and [tells his customers] it was made by an ancient medicine women specially for vision quests" (Owens 1999, 24–25), Latisha purports to serve dog meat in order to fulfill her customers' desire for the exotic Indian Other. She substantiates the alleged Indianness of the products she sells by complying with the simulations the tourists consider authentic Indian culture — a maneuver that also occurs in actual Native artist-tourist interactions (see Evans-Pritchard 1989, 95). While the Siouxs's reputation as dog-eaters — to keep from starving after the buffalo were gone — is still subject to much joking and teasing among Native people (see V. Deloria 1977, 163; Lincoln 1993, 63–64), the Blackfoot, as Lionel points out, never ate dog. Yet Latisha's capitalist instrumentalization of the dog-eater stereotype proves to be a highly successful business. Unflinchingly, she assures her patrons that she serves "Black Labrador . . . You get more meat of black Labs. . . . It's a treaty right. . . . One of our traditional foods. . . . We raise them right on the reserve . . . Feed them only horse meat and whole grain. No hormones or preservatives" (King 1994, 131–32).

A colorful fabrication, Latisha's restaurant is "the antithesis of Remmington's steak house" (Dvorak 1998, 132), the place Portland and Charlie worked at in L.A., where all the waiters dress up as cowboys and the employees who park the cars wear some indiscriminate pseudo-Indian costume. At the Dead Dog Café, the waiters wear "Plains, Southwest, or Combination" (108) style outfits, and thus demonstrate that Native people can also play the invention-game and sell generic hodge-podge ("combination") successfully. Latisha's restaurant even far outdoes its Hollywood counterpart with regard to artificiality: The menus "featured such things as Dog du Jour, Houndburgers, Puppy Potpourri, Hot Dogs, Saint Bernard Swiss Melts, with Doggie Doos and Deep-Fried Puppy Whatnots for appetizers" (109). Completing the illusion, the walls of the café are decorated with hunting pictures, specially fabricated photo montages resembling "those you see in the hunting and fishing magazines where a couple of white guys are standing over an elephant or holding up a lion's head . . . Only in these photographs it was Indians and dogs. Latisha's favorite was a photograph of four Indians on their buffalo runners, chasing down a herd of Great Danes" (109).

In addition to mocking the reification of Native cultures and goods, Latisha's ploy subversively alludes to the photographs of Edward S. Curtis, the famous "Indian photographer," who in the nineteenth century "documented" Indians with his camera throughout North America. By imposing specific poses and antiquated outfits on his Indian objects — he even took along such paraphernalia in case the Indians did not look "Indian" enough — rather than depicting people coping with the changes around them, Curtis helped to cement the cliché of the stoic Vanishing Indian. Latisha subverts both the aesthetic and the economic dimensions of what Christie has fittingly termed "photocolonialism" (1999, 53): Not only does she attract customers with these hunting pictures, she sells them as postcards, along with the menus and recipes for dog, exploiting the tourists' combination of ignorant gullibility and exotic fascination with the indigenous Other, literally, for all it is worth.

Analogous to Hollywood practices, Latisha answers market demands with what she knows will sell best — literally, two-dimensional black and white images of the Indian. King's use of humor, as well as the fact that a Native person, tricksterlike, instrumentalizes the distorting imagery, most amusingly breaks conventional patterns, though. While taking advantage of Indian clichés, Latisha herself clearly defies the stereotype of the tragic victim unable to adjust to modern times. Instead, she "demonstrates a mastery of the domains of business and commerce traditionally associated with white civilization: technology, commercialization, marketing, and packaging" (Dvorak 1998, 132–33). Humor, once again, becomes clearly mediational in King's text. While the idea of duping White tourists through blatant lies might be offensive by itself — as Dvorak points out, "among her photo montage of trophies, Latisha could have had one featuring herself holding up the head of a tourist" (1998, 133–34) — Latisha's (and King's) strategy of taking existing stereotypes *ad absurdum* (and thus exposing them for what they are) instead succeeds. Readers realize the ridiculous dimensions of such stereotyping and empathize with Latisha as a witty trickster, who moves beyond lamenting the fabrications and instead manipulates them for her own purposes. Her comic hyperbole could thus be read within the framework of Goodman's model of "humor as aikido," an Eastern martial art that uses and transforms the attacker's energy to defeat him through his own force of motion, without direct offence: "Aikido is a metaphor for how we can use humor to defuse confrontations, disarm attacks, and turn situations from abusing to amusing" (Goodman 1983, 5). In analogy, King's reimaginative text plays with the colonizers' representational power, beating it with humor and its own imaginative weapons.

King's third novel, *Truth and Bright Water*, humorously takes up the issue of tourist stereotypes once again. When once a year during the "Indian Days" festival tourists flood the small Bright Water reservation, the local Natives sell everything from "drawings of old-time Indians on horseback" to dream catchers and T-shirts. Of course, "all of it, according to the signs that everyone puts up, is 'authentic' and 'traditional' " (1999a, 209). For instance, Edna, who operates the frybread stand, repeatedly sells her recipe to customers, among them eager Germans who "want to know the secret of authentic frybread" (211). The humor of this scene hinges on the incongruity between Edna's behavior towards the German customers and her comments to Tecumseh, the adolescent protagonist/narrator: For the Germans, she puts on "her Indian face," emulates "Hollywood Injun" gestures, and even does a small round dance — generating an illusion that meets the Germans' desire for authenticity. The pseudotraditional persona is replaced by a sly business woman, however, when she turns to

Tecumseh, announces that "it's time to do some fur trading," and explains why she turned down the German's first offer of twenty-five dollars: "The Deutschmark is strong right now . . . So I'm holding out for fifty" (211). Like *Green Grass, Running Water*'s Latisha, on the surface Edna over-conforms to the cliché, while underneath she defies it. The grotesqueness of emulating "the Indian that never was" is even amplified when readers are aware that frybread (consisting of flour, salt, and lard) is hardly traditional, authentic food, but was what Native people resorted to when — deprived of their traditional possibilities to sustain themselves — they had to subsist on staples. The Germans' desire for (insider knowledge about) traditional food is therefore answered, from beginning to end, with a fabrication.

Many of the novel's Native characters cash in on White stereotypes accordingly, successfully catering to one-dimensional and essentializing notions of Indianness. Others, however, expose some of the fault lines of the tourists' fictitious and antiquating "Indian" image (like Tecumseh's father Elvin) or shatter it completely (like Native artist Monroe Swimmer). Elvin, who sells his "traditional" coyote carvings to tourists, tells his customers invented stories about the mythic coyote to increase his sales, exemplifying that "Indian craftsmen and traders sometimes respond to tourists' needs for cultural significance by telling them just what they want to hear" (Evans-Pritchard 1989, 95). Yet despite complying with customer expectations to some extent, he comically defies the masquerade of "the Indian": Instead of donning the Indian chief costume of leather, feathers, and beads, he dresses up as Elvi*s*, complete with painted sideburns and coveralls. Assisted by Lucy Rabbit, who tries hard to look like her biggest idol Marilyn Monroe, the couple points to the artificiality characteristic of *all* processes of mythmaking in American popular culture, be it show stars or Hollywood Indians.

The text blurs cultural boundaries and levels hierarchies when these Natives-dressed-as-Western-cultural-icons encounter the Germans who bought Edna's recipe. In contrast to the Native Elvin/Elvis and Lucy/Marilyn, the Germans are "all dressed in buckskin shirts and fringed leather pants. One of them is wearing a good-looking bone breastplate. Their faces are painted" (210). The subsequent exchange between Tecumseh and his father tricksterlike shows up "the Indian" as simulacrum: " 'Holy,' says my father. 'Those boys sure know how to dress.' . . . 'They're Germans,' I tell him. 'No shit,' says my father. 'Boy, these days Indians are everywhere' " (231). Elvin clearly sees "Indian" as a role to be taken on. Indeed, the Euro-American/European fascination with "playing Indian" (which Phil Deloria described in his study of the same name, 1998), while denying Native people a contemporary existence, must strike Native people as deeply ironic. King's reaction to this phenomenon is marked by sly humor rather than bitterness, though, as the character of trickster artist Monroe Swimmer exemplifies:

One time . . . [Monroe] borrowed a tuba from the Mormon church over in Cardston and got his auntie to make him a pair of short pants out of elk hide with elk hide suspenders. And when Indian Days came around and the crowds of tourists were everywhere, he marched through the booths and the tipis, puffing on the tuba, pretending to be the Bright Water German Club. "He said it was the least he could do," said Lucille, "seeing as how Germans were so keen on dressing up like Indians." (1999a, 25)

Readers cannot help but laugh at the absurdity of Monroe's behavior. The trickster perspective draws to attention that what appears ridiculous in this case is considered perfectly normal when it occurs in reverse, that is, when non-Natives, be it boy scouts or Indian clubs, pose as Indians. By reimagining Monroe as an ersatz Bavarian musician, King makes Western readers reconsider both reductive "Indian" stereotyping and the practice of mistaking Native symbols or traditions (often in decontextualized fragments, clichéd imitations, and bizarre combinations) for communal cultural property.

Stereotyping discounts Native presence today. Kept "safely in the stasis box of the 19th century" (Weaver 1997, 18), Indians are perceived to be extinct after approximately 1890. In a proliferation of stereotypes and essentializing tendencies, they have been "frozen, cryogenized, sterilized, . . . [they have] become referential simulacra" (Baudrillard 1983, 15). In defiance of this petrification, humor is first of all instrumental in exposing the processes of stereotyping by showing that "real" Indians, as Louis Owens writes, "inhabit a never-never land in the world's imagination." Furthermore, it discloses the devastating impact of such "artifactualization of Indian identity" (Owens 1998, 128), illustrating the consequences of internalization. By presenting complex, witty characters who mimic and exploit, subvert, or disrupt the clichés, and finally, by offering readers a look beyond the masquerade, Native writers comically shatter the dehumanizing illusion built up by the vast body of popular "Indian knowledge." The laughter arising from the incongruity between the two-dimensional stage props and the complex Native characters depicted in contemporary Native texts in its final consequence therefore demonstrates that, as Emma LaRoque defiantly writes, "Native people are human beings — no more and no less. The ultimate ugliness of stereotyping is that it bypasses humanity. Neither the noble red man nor the savage Indian myth says much about Indians as human beings, people who are capable of 'the good, the bad, and the ugly'" (1975, 43–44). Contemporary Native writers' deconstruction of stereotypes and representation of a more complex Nativeness thus exceeds purely aesthetic or entertaining intentions. It humanizes contemporary nonvanishing Indians and makes readers reimagine Nativeness in terms that allow for growth and development.

Debunking Eurocentric Epistemologies, Aesthetics, and Historiography

There are only truths in the plural, and never one Truth; and there is rarely falseness per se, just others' truths.
— Linda Hutcheon, "Historiographic Metafiction," 76

"There are no truths, Coyote," I says. "Only stories."
— Thomas King, *Green Grass, Running Water*, 393

In the wake of the postmodern/poststructuralist crisis of representation, scholars have explored the links between particular modes of discourse and hegemonic power structures. They have shown that allegedly objective Western scientific, historiographic, and aesthetic discourses constitute a particular body of knowledge, and that by defining both what counts as knowledge, history, and art *and* the interpretive frames within which to analyze them, these discourses self-confirmingly perpetuate and reinforce particular ideologies. "Truth," as Michel Foucault argues,

> isn't outside power. . . . Truth is a thing of this world; it is produced only by the virtue of multiple forms of constraint. And it induces regular effects of power. Each society has its own regime of truth, its "general politics" of truth; that is, the types of discourse which it accepts and makes function as true, the mechanisms and instances which enable one to distinguish true and false statements, the means by which each is sanctioned, the techniques and procedures accorded value in the acquisition of truth, the status of those who are charged with saying what is true. (1980, 131)

In *Orientalism*, Edward Said puts Foucault's ideas on discourse to work by exploring these "regular effects of power" within the framework of colonial domination. Eurocentric standards set by science or disciplines such as historiography that, deemed universal, "record" and explain the world according to Western principles are exposed as instrumental in constructing and substantiating normative dichotomies — such as savagism versus civilization, primitive and developing versus refined and intellectual. Consequently, "hegemony over truth and knowledge replaces troops and guns finally as the relevant tool of colonization" (Churchill 1992, 36). Western "knowledge" is put to use in manipulating the "unknowing" subjects of colonial oppression and cementing hegemonic power structures:

> In a very real sense, indigenous people from all over the world feel trapped in the logic and discourse of Western civilization, which seems to only examine and comprehend the intellectual origins and conceptual constructs of empire. Western academics in anthropology, history, and related social sciences seem to have created a theoretical place that exists as a "rational" explanation for the "other." (Grinde 1995, 203–4)

This Western intellectual stance serves as the benchmark according to which anything operating outside the dominant discourse is declared invalid, so that "when Jesus Christ walks on water this is treated as 'religion,' but, when Coyote steals fire in the Navajo Indian spiritual tradition, it is invariably characterized by the dominant society's discourse as 'legend,' or, worst yet, 'folklore' " (204).[11]

Faced with these practices, which effectively relegate Native people to the position of the inferior marginal other, much contemporary Native writing shows an acute awareness of the way in which Western discourses are inherently entwined with imperial agendas. As Louis Owens observes, "the authoritative discourse of European America [which] comes with its authority already fused to it and simply demands allegiance, can inspire both trauma and a tricksterish subversion" (1998, 6). How does humor figure in this subversion of allegedly objective Western epistemological, aesthetic, and historiographic frames of reference? While Native writing is to some extent concerned with correcting misrepresentations or reinscribing the previously excluded, it does not seek to replace one set of fixed values with another. Rather, it partially engages in the dominant discourses themselves in order to undermine them from within, making transparent the practices by which dominant values, standards, and Truths are presented as self-evident. Humorous subversion here becomes truly "genealogical" in Bové's sense:[12] It not only discloses the (ideologically motivated) selectivity of Western forms of discourse; by subverting the rhetoric of universality that continues to produce such self-legitimizing Western history and knowledge, it also serves to expose the concealed processes by which these discourses are imbued with coherence and authority within a context of colonial domination. For instance, when New Crows, a Native character in Gerald Vizenor's screenplay *Harold of Orange*, casually inverts the Bering Strait theory — according to which prehistorically Native North Americans must have traveled from Asia via Alaska into America (see chapter three) — and instead claims that the migration had taken place the other way around, he not only establishes Native primacy in America. By implication, he also questions the manner in which scientific reasoning is used to bolster Euro-American hegemony. The clash between New Crows's unshakable belief in his culture's origin story, according to which his people "emerged from the flood here, the first people" (1993a, 65), and the "scientific" position held by his White interlocutor turns accustomed frames of reference upside down. As a result, the clash comically sparks the realization that what is unquestioningly accepted as scientific finding may be inherently biased towards Euro-American positions.

In analogy, Simon Ortiz's story "Men On the Moon" contrasts the Western spirit of scientific exploration with Pueblo epistemologies. Faustin is an old Pueblo Indian who has never lived in the White world and hardly speaks English. When his daughter and grandson present him with a TV set for Father's Day, one of the first things he watches is the Apollo space expedition to the moon. Astonished, Faustin inquires of his grandson what the "Mericanos" are looking for up there, and Amarosho patiently explains: "The men are looking for knowledge. . . . They have some already. They've gone before and come back. . . . They brought back some rocks" (1999, 5). Part of Ortiz's trickster design is that Faustin, through his questions and observations, is portrayed as ignorant in terms of Western civilization, science, and culture. He does not even know that the "thing" he has been given is called a TV, and when one of the programs shows wrestling — in itself an ironic metacommentary on Euro-American cultural values — "the old man . . . wondered why they were fighting" (4). His nocturnal dreams about mythic characters and the way in which he interprets the world around him instead show him to be rooted in indigenous ways of knowing. Consequently, Faustin's reaction to his grandson's explanations about rocks and knowledge provides readers with a thoroughly Native and comically decentering perspective:

> Rocks. Faustin laughed quietly. The American scientist men went to search for knowledge on the moon and they brought back rocks. He kind of thought Amarosho was joking with him. His grandson had gone to Indian School for a number of years, and sometimes he would tell his grandfather strange and funny things. (5)

Amarosho has been taught by a Western system of education to accept ideas that to Faustin must appear as implausible as, in turn, the stories by which his own culture explains the world are to Western minds. As even Faustin realizes, however, Native accounts are dismissed as primitive tales that are " 'tainted' with a normative and spiritual component" (Whitt 1995, 236), whereas Western scientific findings are infused with the nimbus of Truth.

Faustin's conviction that knowledge is tied to life and is to be found inside oneself rather than on the moon undermines this authority. Presented from *his* perspective, it is the Western approach that, for a change, appears nonsensical:

> Amarosho had told him that men on earth — scientists — believed there was no life on the moon. Yet those men were trying to find knowledge on the moon. Faustin wondered if perhaps they had special tools with which they could find knowledge even if they believed there was no life on the moon. (11)

Faustin's lack of understanding of this quest for knowledge for knowledge's sake, his culturally determined failure to see the point in the "Mericanos' " exploration of space, comically triggers a reconsideration of alleged motivations and explanations. The old man's mock-confusion — and

with it the satiric destabilizing of established paradigms and rationalizations — peaks when Amarosho explains to him that the scientists will use
the knowledge they gain from collecting rocks and dirt from the surface of
the moon

> to better mankind, Nana. I've heard that. And to learn more about the
> universe in which we live. Also, some of the scientists say the knowledge
> will be useful in finding out where everything began a long time ago and
> how everything was made in the beginning.
>
>   Faustin looked with a smile at his grandson. He said, You are telling me
> the true facts, aren't you?
>
>   Why, yes, Nana. That's what they say. I'm not just making it up,
> Amarosho said.
>
>   Well, then, do they say why they need to know where and how every-
> thing began? Hasn't anyone ever told them?   (11–12)

The old man's apparently innocent questions amusingly mark the Euro-
American quest for origins in outer space as paradoxical. They refer to both
the importance in Native oral traditions of origin and creation stories that
explain the beginnings of the world and the American trauma of lacking
(Old World) tradition — aspects that make Western culture and civilization
appear deficient. The text thus humorously transforms Euro-America's
postulated science-based superiority into a display of ignorance and disorientation by Faustin's standards.[13]

The incongruity between Western epistemologies and Faustin's perspective is shown most obviously in Faustin's nightly dreams, where he
interprets the daytime information within his own frames of reference.
Within this mythological dream world, the space shuttle reappears as a terrible metal "mahkina," which not even the mythical Flintwing Boy and
Coyote are able to stop in its course of destruction. Read with the knowledge that the exploration of space has frequently been termed America's
"new" or "last frontier," conspicuous parallels between Europe's exploration and colonization of the North American continent and Euro-
America's exploration of space suggest themselves. The rationalization that
space has to be explored "to better mankind" all of a sudden tragicomically resonates with the hypocrisy of Europe's earlier civilizing mission of
North America (a parallel also insinuated in Thomas King's short story
"Traplines," 1993, 39). Again, the implication is that a particular discourse
legitimates colonial endeavors through its characteristic governing of perception within a specific framework. In Ortiz's story, Amarosho tells his
grandfather "the true facts" (11) from a Euro-American point of view. In
return, Faustin tells his grandson about his dream: "It's a dream, but it's
the truth, Faustin said. I believe you, Nana, his grandson said" (13).

While the story's humor arises mainly from the incompatibility of the
presented views, the text does not argue for a replacement of one set of truths with another. Rather, it can be read as exemplifying the poststructuralist

postulation that "all 'truths' are relative to the frame of reference which contains them; more radically, 'truths' are a function of these frames; and even more radically, these discourses 'constitute' the truths which they claim to discover and transmit" (Bové 1990, 56). Accordingly, Ortiz's story humorously undercuts the hierarchies between Western and Native paradigms and epistemologies by pointing to the absurdity of one allegedly holding the absolute authority over Truth while the other is devalued as "primitive myth."

Discursive practices by which ideologically weighted representations serve to reinforce hegemonic structures also permeate the area of aesthetics and cultural production. "Instead of recognizing that non-Europeans had a different culture, the assumption was made by the Europeans that they had no culture and thus were living no better than an animal existence" (M. Green 1995, 6). Fortunately, such rigorously exclusive Eurocentrism has given way to more encompassing notions of culture. Nevertheless, Native art and literature even today are frequently seen within a particular frame of reference — one that operates outside the Euro-American discourse, as epitomized in Kim Blaeser's sarcastic comment: "No, I'm not a poet, I just write Indian stuff" (in Young-Ing 1993, 185). Marilyn Dumont's poem "The Devil's Language" uses humor as a subversive weapon for challenging Eurocentric aesthetic criteria for "serious" or "legitimate" literature (especially poetry), which in combination with clichéd expectations still serve to exclude Native writing from the canon of American literature:

> I have since reconsidered Eliot
> and the Great White way of writing English
> standard that is
> the great white way
> has measured, judged and assessed me   all my life
> by its
> lily white words
> its picket fence sentences
> and manicured paragraphs
> one wrong sound and you're shelved in the
> Native Literature section   (1996, 54)

Despite its scathingly sarcastic tone, Dumont's poem does not rail against Western poetry or Eliot. Eliot (arguably *the* great modernist poet and himself one of the most revolutionary and innovative voices of his time) has just come to stand for powerfully normative/dogmatic ideas of what constitutes poetry — and these ideas now serve to disqualify writing that does not conform to such standards. The poem's ironic undercurrent is therefore fed by the manner in which Dumont phrases her criticism. The text points to Eurocentric hegemonic practices by appropriating the very poetic discourse that authoritatively comprises the norm. Dumont, as the poem (and her oeuvre in general) shows, is perfectly capable of producing and cherishing "manicured paragraphs." Well-versed in the "Great White way," she is prepared to subvert it from within by blurring artificial boundaries and hierarchical differentiations between Western and Native writing.

That the text does not scorn difference but rather the power imbalance inherent in an — ostensibly impartial — aesthetic paradigm that ranks one mode of writing and one language over all others also shows in the remainder of the poem. Readjusting the readers' anglocentric perspective, Dumont's text undercuts the naturalized authority of English over indigenous languages that, among other factors, contributes to a silencing of indigenous voices:

> My father doesn't read or write
> the King's English says he's
> dumb but he speaks Cree
> how many of you speak Cree? . . .
> is there a Received Pronunciation of Cree, is there
> a Modern Cree Usage?
> the Chief's Cree, not the King's English   (54–55)

Like Ortiz's story, Dumont's poem satirically points to the way in which dichotomies such as ignorance versus sophistication depend on who holds the power to set standards. Western colonial discourse relies on the naturalization of its own premises, on presenting its own standards as self-evident to corroborate its dominance and exclude all deviations. Within this process, the colonizer's language — tellingly referred to as *Standard English* — in the Derridaen sense of logocentrism, emerges as one of the strongholds of hegemonic structures, an instrument of exclusion and domination that is complicit in downplaying historical and ongoing injustices. Language itself, as Hutcheon (1995a, 78) has pointed out with regard to historical and fictional narratives, enters into the constitution of its objects of representation. And indeed, the terminology employed within colonial discourse is governed by ideological motivations, bolstering revisionist representations of Native-White history. "One sided skirmishes," for instance, "have been called massacres when the Indians won and battles when they lost" (Berner 1992, 378), so that Wounded Knee, the site of the massacre in which most of the Native people killed were unarmed women and children, appears in the *American Heritage Dictionary* as the "site of the last major battle of the Indian Wars" (quoted in Vizenor 1994b, 50).

Contemporary Native writers use humor to expose and undermine such biased terminology, laying open the processes by which language enters into the very construction and preservation of dichotomies such as civilization/savagery, educated/childlike, and sophisticated/primitive. In its final consequence, language is shown to be an instrument in the justification of colonization. Thus the Coyote in Thomas King's "Coyote Went to See the Prime Minister" exposes the phrase "Indian problem" as inherently weighed by answering the prime minister's invitation to help the government solve the Indian problem with: "Sure, . . . what's the problem?" (1999c, 252). Lenore Keeshig-Tobias's poem "The White Man's Burden" subverts this very phrase and its implication that civilizing the "primitive" people is a burdensome task, with a simple demand: "PUT DOWN THE LOAD, STUPID" (1998, 263). And the paradoxical aspects inherent in the use of the term "discovery" to refer to the European exploration and forceful conquest of settled areas (see M. L. Pratt 1988, 23–24) are highlighted by Wilf Pelletier's persona of the "Dumb Indian": With an allegedly naïve comment — "The discovery of America came as a surprise to my people. They weren't expecting anyone to discover America right then" (1972, 5) — he creates an awareness of the term's misuse, stresses Native presence on the continent, and defies linguistic constructions of absence and purity inherent in phrases like "virgin land" or "pristine wilderness."

The Native author engaging most unequivocally with the controversial qualities of colonial linguistic representation is Carter Revard. In stories such as "Report to the Nation: Claiming Europe," and poems such as "Discovery of the New World" and "The Secret Verbs" he satirically subjects the rhetoric of manifest destiny to close scrutiny. The latter's eponymous "secret verbs" are, as the text explains,

> hidden right in plain sight.
> Take UNASSIGNED LANDS for instance: what's the verb?
> TO UNASSIGN.
> a powerful verb, in 1889 it grabbed
> almost two million acres of Indian lands
> where Oklahoma City squats, and all
> those other towns, wheat farms and ranches,
> oil wells and politicians.   (1992, 44)

Revard's "grammatical analysis" dissects the colonizers' language to bring to light its complicity in pulling a smoke screen over the forceful expropriation of Creek and Seminole lands. With wry humor, the text discloses the performativity inherent in "unassigned." It thus defies euphemistic representations of the opening of the West. Such revisionist accounts, the poem makes clear, both naturalize and trivialize what by rights should be referred to as expulsion and genocide, making it seem "as if the Indians' disappearance were the result of some force completely beyond the human power to stay, like a tidal wave or a change of season" (Bordewich 1996, 49). Nevertheless, "The Secret Verbs" does not engage in a blatant pointing of fingers — which would run the risk of merely reinscribing hegemonic modes of representation. It does refer to the colonizers' actions; yet it is ultimately more concerned with the apologetic linguistic façade that intends to conceal them:

> That's all the grammar lesson for today,
> But for tomorrow why not look around,
>   at other participles and adjectives
> which have deleted agents and unspoken objects
>   and which are negative?
>   You see how powerful they are,
>   and how they hide their power? And how
>   like red-striped sheets they cover both
> the SUBJECT and the OBJECTS of their actions?
>   Just for instance,
>   the words DIScover and COVERt,
>   or DISinform, or UNAmerican,
>   or UNused Land.   (44)

Pointing to the intricacies of colonial discourse, Revard's text in itself constitutes a powerfully tragicomic reminder that "How we UNuse our language is maybe worth a thought" (44). It both illuminates and defies the practices by which Native people have been rhetorically deleted from America's discursive map, ultimately reinscribing Native presence.

"Discovery of the New World," an earlier Revard poem, also addresses the rhetoric of manifest destiny. Here, however, the emphasis shifts away from the level of the single word to the structure and enchainment of events in historiographic narrative in general. "Historical discourse," as Engler remarks, "seems to be concerned with extra-textual referents, with the indisputable and quasi self-evident 'reality' of historical facts" (1994, 16). Clearly, though, as Hayden White has demonstrated, the division of narrative into fiction, which reconstructs the past in imaginative scenarios, and history, which in its alleged closeness to science purports to objectively report the actual Truth about the past, is no longer tenable (1978; 1984). Every account of the past inherently constitutes an interpretation, be it in the value-ruled selection of the events to be represented (or left out) as "historical facts," or in the way in which these events are combined into narrative to form a meaningful coherence. The Western discourse of history, Foucault's power/knowledge paradigm implies, disempowers and excludes the repressed alterity through hegemonic structures. Tellingly,

> the emergence of history in European thought is coterminous with the rise of modern colonialism, which in its radical othering and violent annexation of the non-European world, found in history a prominent, if not *the* prominent instrument for the control of subject peoples. At base, the myth of a value free, "scientific" view of the past, the myth of the beauty of order, the myth of the story of history as a simple representation of the continuity of events, authorised nothing less than the construction of world reality. (Ashcroft, Griffiths, and Tiffin 1995, 355)

"History," as White paraphrases Lévi-Strauss, is therefore "never simply history, but always 'history-for,' history written in the interest of some infrascientific aim or vision" (1978, 55). Within the North American fourth world context, in a self-authorizing cycle, it is the present-day power-distribution that guides the kind of questions asked about the past.

Revard's "Discovery of the New World" lays bare these processes of legitimization by engaging in the colonizers' own discourse and subverting it from within. In "Report to the Nation: Claiming Europe" Revard appropriates the discourse of exploration accounts and travelogues, and parodically infuses it with a literally reversed orientation in the Osage conquest of Europe (see chapter three). In "Discovery of the New World," he also exposes the rhetoric that masks the brutally colonizing aspects of the ideology of manifest destiny — by satirizing the European colonization of North America as an alien invasion from outer space. Just like a cartoon described by V. Deloria that "showed a flying saucer landing while an Indian watched. The caption was 'Oh, no, not again'" (1977, 148), Revard's text insinuates that to the indigenous population the European invaders appeared to come from an utterly "alien" sphere. The poem is basically a report given by one of the alien intruders about their encounters with the American population:

> The creatures that we met this morning
> marveled at our green skins
> and scarlet eyes.
> They lack antennae
> and can't be made to grasp
> your proclamation that they are
> our lawful food and prey slaves   (1980, 43)

While the comic defamiliarization is obviously more radical than in "Report to the Nation," the analogies to North American history remain sufficiently clear to spark not only laughter but also some potentially uncomfortable insights:

> there was, however,
> a curious visual echo in their history
> of our coming to their earth;
> a certain General Sherman said
> about one group of them precisely what
> we have been telling you about these creatures
> it is our destiny to asterize this planet
> and they WILL not be asterized,
> so they must be wiped out.
> WE NEED their space and nitrogen
> which they do not know how to *use*   (43)

Revard's biting satire amusingly expounds Baudrillard's observation that history is "perhaps . . . the last great myth" (1994, 47). The way that the aliens' account of and rationalizations for the invasion of earth are pre-sented — "it is our destiny to asterize this planet . . . which they do not know how to *use*" — clearly alludes to the Western civilizing (rather than the blatantly similar "asterizing") mission and the Puritan idea of manifest destiny. In more general ways, however, it also parodically reveals history's alleged objectivity to be but an illusion perpetuated by those who profit from it, as it retroactively bolsters their position of dominance. In reference to the inversely proportional processes by which the history of the colo-nized is devalued, the poem continues:

> Their history bled from one this morning,
>   while we were tasting his brain,
>   in holographic rainbows,
>   which we assembled into quite an interesting
>   set of legends —
>   that's all it came to, though
>   the colors were quite lovely before we
>   poured them into our time;
>   the blue shift bleached away
> meaningless circumstances, and they would not fit
>   any of our truth matrices —   (43)

"Events," as Hutcheon points out in her influential essay on "Historio-graphic Metafiction," "are configured into facts by being related to 'con-ceptual matrices within which they have to be imbedded if they are to count as facts.' Historiography and fiction . . . constitute their objects of atten-tion; in other words, they decide which events will become facts" (1995a, 90). That the accounts of history provided by the earthly humans, when poured into the aliens' time, do not "fit any of [their] truth matrices" there-fore comically plays on our current Western practice of dismissing tradi-tional Native oral narrative as incompatible with contemporary Western standards of written historiographic documentation.[14] As a discipline, "his-tory feeds on what finds its way into a limited textual record" (Clifford 1988, 341). Therefore, a hierarchical order that ranks written over oral material simultaneously sanctions Western revisionist accounts and excludes Native viewpoints (see Clifford 1988, 339–41; Isernhagen 2001, 169). It is thus highly ironic that in Revard's poem *American* history, for a change, is relegated to the realm of "legend," the effect being that readers have to relativize their Eurocentric perspective on the validity of Western historio-graphic discourse.

The obvious parodic parallels between the poem's report about the "deplorable" effects of the alien invasion on humans and the actual devas-tating effects of European colonization on North America's indigenous population further highlight the apologetic aspects of historiography. Emulating the rationalizations of the Euro-American civilizing mission, the speaker hypocritically declares: "if we didn't have this mission it might be sad / to see such helpless creatures die / chanting their sacred psalms and bills of rights" (44). This both bitingly mocks the sentimentalizing nineteenth-century American laments about the Vanishing Indian and reveals the victims to be WASP Americans this time, which turns the poem's final lines into a sarcastic send-up: The speaker assures his fellow "aliens": "but never fear/ . . . we will be safe, and rich, and happy here, forever" (44) — ironically mirroring previous WASP assurances about *their* status in North America. A sly imaginative cautioning to White Euro-Americans not to feel too safe in their current position, this also reveals with acerbic clarity the Puritan ideology of manifest destiny to be a self-serving myth. Nevertheless, it is not so much that Revard's ploy of making the former conquerors fall prey to even more vicious colonial domination aims at (fictional) revenge. Rather, it comprises an imaginative vehicle for prominently displaying the hypocrisy inherent in Euro-America's historical self-conceptualization. Hutcheon's observation that "the lesson here is that the past once existed, but that our historical knowledge of it is semiotically transmitted" (1995a, 90) thus describes well the quintessence of these stories and poems by Revard. At base, they can be said to address not (only) the issue of stolen land but of stolen (hi)stories and ultimately also stolen identities.

The line between the discourses of the real (historiography) and of the imaginary (fiction), which Barthes and White among others have shown to be far from firm, is turned into a humorous frontier in contemporary Native texts. Through their use of humor, Native writers undercut both the distinction between history and story and the practices by which Native people are barred from the former. As Blaeser comments with respect to Vizenor's work, humorous representations of history "work to unmask and disarm history, to expose the hidden agendas of historiography and thereby remove it from the grasp of the political panderers and *return it to the realm of story*" (1996, 85; emphasis added). Novels such as Sherman Alexie's *Reservation Blues* (see chapter three) and Thomas King's *Green Grass, Running Water* (with its myriad historical references, for example, to the detention of Indian rebels at Fort Marion, the Sand Creek Massacre, and the occupation of Wounded Knee) mix Native mythology, realistic fictional narrative, and actual historical persons and events, blurring the boundaries between history and story. The humor that arises from bringing into dialog these allegedly incompatible frames highlights that what a respective culture considers its authentic history is, in fact, but a discursive construction, one particular representation.

Marilyn Dumont's poem "On the Surface" is an example of such a humorous "restorification" of history. It literally returns history to the realm of story by comically highlighting the gaps and distortions in Euro-Canadian historiographic representation:

> Moniyaw[15] are natural
> storytellers, you know?
> There's a story of
> Canada, a good story,
> but a story, nevertheless,
> that Samuel de
> Champlain was one of
> the first humans to set
> foot in this country,
> apparently the Six
> Nations were merely
> extras. You have to give
> them credit, these
> moniyaw, are pretty good storytellers (2001, 192)

In contrast to historiography or literature, "storytelling" is usually associated with children — or non-Western cultures. From a Western perspective, it is romanticized but also belittled and denied any of the validity or accuracy that Western historiography claims for itself. By turning the tables and transforming Canada's history into story, Dumont's text both debunks history's "natural" authority and defies the Eurocentric assumption that North American history began with the arrival of Europeans. Even when the historic existence of Native people is acknowledged, the poem moves on to show, the mode of representation conveys an impression of their utter unimportance and confinement to the past:

> I watch a four part history of a famous Canadian
> fortification   and knowing where beginnings usually
> begin   I am relieved and somewhat surprised, that this
> time, history begins with Indians; however, this portion
> of the film seems a bit tacked on upon viewing the
> introduction of settlement
> as an Academy Awards premiere grand music and
> fireworks herald the arrival of settlement *to appear:*
> *to star, play the lead, get top billing, have one's name in*
> *lights* "the Indian" portion of the film, however, looks
> like it's been directed by Franz Boas   who
> chiselled his own camera
> Stone age and non-threatening   half-chewed
> femurs and flint knives   matted hair (dreadlocks
> before their time)   disappointment on the
> faces of the natives that say, *Ah heck, I wanted to be a star*
> *this time.*   (192)

The exquisite irony inherent in sentences like "knowing where beginnings usually begin" amusingly exposes the paradoxical aspects of the alleged logic with which a hegemonic historiographic system customarily presents a particular course of events as self-evident. If bits of Native history are "tacked on" to the self-glorifying Canadian past, the poem implies, they are shown from a safely "non-threatening" ethnographic angle — which effectively forecloses any contemporary relevance of Native existence. The mirth evoked by the image of a stone-age-equipped Franz Boas therefore also implicitly poses the irritating question as to why Native people are customarily restricted to such a frame of reference. The remainder of the text provides some possible explanations. It sets forth its satiric attack on Canada's revisionism in rather unusual metaphors and similes, observing that

> there is a layered belief covering this idea of "Canada," no "North America"
> and this layer, thinking topsoil so to speak, appears to be known as the history
> of this continent just as Columbus thought, erroneously,
> that this country was India
> however, my colonial experience has been
> that it's as if we lived in a nation that was eternally snow covered
> that we never saw what lay beneath the fluffy stuff
> that we didn't have enough shovels
> that we were snowed-in,
> a snow-blower wasn't a luxury
> that we lived in a constant *whiteout*
> a snow job
> where snow-blindness was endemic   (193)

Playing both on Whiteness as the self-set norm with regard to skin color and on Canada's self-conceptualization as the national anthem's "True North strong and free," the snow imagery wittily conveys how Native presence in Canada is "covered up." Conventional historiography is insinuated to induce an endemic "blindness" or at least to cloud the vision towards facets of history other than those represented in Eurocentric accounts. Accordingly, the text refers to the few instances in which Native people successfully claimed their rights (Quebec's dam building projects at James Bay, full consideration in the new constitution) as "clear spots" that emerge from underneath this cover, "risky . . . icy patches, black ice / to be plowed and sanded" (193). Dumont's text itself brushes away — to remain within the metaphor — some of the "thinking topsoil" that is Canadian history. It clears some of the snow and lures readers onto the "risky patches" of playful and imaginative revisions. Again, such humorous seduction "incite[s] the reader to an imaginative re-evaluation of both the accounts and the processes of history" (Blaeser 1998, 167).

Such an imaginative reevaluation or, indeed, reimagining is most fully achieved in the final example discussed here, Thomas King's short story "Joe the Painter and the Deer Island Massacre." The story features Joe Ghoty, an apparently simple-minded retired house painter and convinced patriot, who is known first and foremost for his uncompromising honesty. In order to participate in a contest for staging the best pageant to commemorate the 100th anniversary of his hometown's founding, he writes a play about lumber magnate Matthew Larson, the town's founding father, and about what he refers to as the "Deer Island Massacre." Joe's description of Larson's first sighting of the area resounds with the idea of the "virgin land" and the hardships encountered by the pioneers — including conflicts with the Native population:

> Nothing there then but the salt flats and the bay and the trees and some Indians . . . within four months Larson had brought up about fifty families. . . . And in the middle of the night on March 31, 1863, just a bit after midnight, the massacre took place. . . . Larson's two brothers were killed. But Larson survived and built the town. (1993, 105–6)

To make the play as authentic as possible, Joe needs "Indians" (102), as he tells his friend the "Chief" (100), the only Native person he knows. As expected, the Chief does not share Joe's enthusiasm, since (like the readers) he assumes that Joe will use the "Indians" as bloodthirsty villains in yet another heroic account of how the West was won. The jury, in contrast, enthusiastically welcomes Joe's seemingly patriotic idea into the contest without even having read the script. Since Joe is White and known to be a proud American, who takes his civic duties very seriously, the jury members simply assume that he shares their positivistic concept of American history.

Up to the actual performance of the play, the story builds on familiar conceptualizations. Joe's eagerness to "make it look real" (111) — he even dresses the participating Natives as "Indians" in costumes and wigs — appears to corroborate his fervor for (Western-style) authenticity. And his announcement that the pageant is "about our founder, Matthew Larson, and how he came to Sequoia County in 1863 and *sculptured a town out of barren wilderness*" (112; emphasis added) encourages both the other characters within the story and the readers to interpret the narrative of the massacre within their accustomed frames of reference. These patterns of interpretation, with regard to the history of White settlement, are comically shattered, however, by King's subsequent thorough defamiliarization of the "historical facts" previously presented. On the day of the performance, the play starts out well enough to the White audience's tastes, evolving towards the conflict over Deer Island, the only place that the Indians had asked Larson to refrain from settling. The tension peaks on the night of the massacre: "The Indians were dancing and singing and you could hear the drum and the bloodcurdling shouts all the way up the island where Matthew Larson and his family huddled in their houses" (114). Just when everyone (including the readers), expects the "savages" to attack, the story anticlimactically turns. The Indians, tired from singing and dancing, go to sleep, and are murdered by a group of Whites led by Matthew Larson (played by Joe), who gravely explains: "I abhor the taking of human life but civilization needs a strong arm to open the frontier. Farewell, Redman. Know that from your bones will spring a new and stronger community forever" (116). Only then does it become apparent that Joe simply never mentioned who was massacred and who was doing the killing. His allegiance turns out to be to the barren facts of the historical record rather than to the spirit of revisionism that frequently governs the narrative America constructs about its past. Larson's pride in bringing "the light of civilization to this dark land" (115) suddenly appears stale, while the disqualification of Joe's play from the contest on the grounds of not being "apppprooooopriate" (117) raises the disconcerting question of being "not appropriate" according to whose standards.

Just as Joe tricks his fellow citizens, King, tricksterlike, lures the readers into applying their familiar interpretive patterns, but eventually discloses how historiography participates in constructing ideologically biased rationalizations. "Joe the Painter" achieves this goal, as Margaret Atwood observes, "not by whacking you over the head with [its] own moral righteousness, but by being funny" (1990, 244). When the Chief in the beginning of the story tells Joe that his relatives may not like the story, Joe replies: "What's to like? It's all history. You can't muck around with history. It ain't always the way we'd like it to be but there it is. Can't change it" (106). What then seemed to confirm the Chief's worst qualms and expectations, in retrospect serves as an ironic comment on the whole story and its project of destabilizing our reading of Native-White history.

In conclusion, contemporary Native writing offers a comic reassessment of epistemologies and aesthetic and historical paradigms in which White superiority appears as a given, while Native perspectives are repressed or relegated to the margin. "Because historical stories, imaginative stories, cultural stories work to form our identity, the disarming of history through satiric humour liberates and empowers us in the imagination of our destinies," writes Blaeser (1998, 172). By engaging with and humorously subverting a colonial discourse that, as Dumont's poetry suggests, "covers up" Native history, Native presence, and Native cultural production, these texts defy the stance of the Vanishing Indian. Instead, by pulling the presumably stable epistemological ground from underneath their readers' feet, they expose the workings of the "medium," that is, Western discursive practices, and thereby manage to change the message. Odo Marquard writes: "What is comic and makes us laugh is what makes the non-valid visible in what is officially valid and the valid visible in what is officially non-valid" (quoted in Hoffmann 1985, 149). Evoking laughter, these texts scrutinize officially valid Western discourses to make visible their revisionist agendas, while simultaneously validating and reinscribing historical and continued Native presence.

"Othering" Christian Religion and Patriarchal Gender Norms

"He's bigger than me
and a whole lot smarter,"
Coyote remarked
Speaking of God
"Only thing is
He isn't around much
and it's gotta be someone
lookin' out for the chickens . . ."
— Bruce Bennett, "Coyote's Metaphysics," 193

That humor plays a substantial role in Native religious traditions has already been outlined in chapter one. As the following discussion shows, it also characterizes the reactions directed at the religious and social paradigms and practices introduced by Euro-Americans. Drew Hayden Taylor claims that "Christ did more to change the lives of Canada's Indigenous people than all the explorers put together" (1999, 48–49). Accordingly, Christianity, conversion, and the churches' role in the postulated civilizing mission and the introduction of patriarchy are frequently dealt with in contemporary Native writing. The imposition of a patriarchal order on Native cultures is, historically, closely intertwined with the mission of converting the "heathen" Indians to the Christian faith. Before colonization, a substantial proportion of Native cultures in North America bore matriarchal, matrilineal, and/or matrilocal features — Allen (1992, 212) speaks of up to 70% and Jaimes and Halsey claim that "most precontact North American civilizations functioned on the basis of matrilineage and matrilocality" (1992, 318). Women were the principal decision and policy makers, and clan affiliation, as well as questions of residence and ownership, were determined through female lineage in many societies. Quite in contrast to popular depictions of "Indians," which generally focus on male braves and warriors while Native women are confined to ornamental roles, women in Native cultures occupied central positions. This changed dramatically in the aftermath of conquest. Both the economic changes arising from colonization and the missionary work undertaken to convert Native people undercut the traditional role of Native women (see Allen 1992, 37; Jaimes and Halsey 1992, 320). Women were also excluded from the official dealings with the US government, that is, there were no female voices involved in treaty making. Some scholars consider this a deliberate colonial strategy: "The reduction of status held by women within indigenous nations was a first priority for European colonizers eager to weaken and destabilize target societies" (Jaimes and Halsey 1992, 319, 323). The resulting "shifts in power from an Indigenous woman-centered way to a white-eurocanadian-christian patriarchy . . . inevitably erased Indigenous women's meaningful social, economic, political, and spiritual participation in the leadership of their communities, as well as the exercise of and control over their bodies and relations with others" (Acoose 1995, 45–46). Louis Halfe's poem "In Da Name of Da Fadder" tragicomically illustrates these drastic changes. A Native woman in a confession to the pope apologizes for showing resistance to her abusive husband:

> In da name of da fadder, poop
> my husband slap, fist and kick me
> I hit him back. I 'pologize poop
> da priest said I must of done someding
> wrong and I deserve it cuz woman is
> 'uppose to listen to man. (1996, 100)

In mimicking the role assigned to her within a Christian patriarchal frame — that of the unquestioningly submissive wife — the poem's speaker subversively discloses the hypocrisy inherent in these paradigms. Her seeming naivety and her use of "flawed" English ("poop" instead of "pope," and so on) comically disarm readers, so that they unwittingly acknowledge the implicit criticism of the church's tacit sanctioning of oppressive or misogynist behavior.

Yet this is but one aspect of the immense disruption caused by the Christian civilizing mission. Not only did the churches partially bolster land theft, it was missionaries who brought with them — if unintentionally — the pathogens that wiped out whole communities, who destroyed Native cultural systems of knowledge by denouncing them as pagan, and who alienated Native children from their communities and exposed them to abuse and suffering in residential and mission schools. In light of these devastating consequences of Christian missionary work, humor engaging with this topic in contemporary Native texts is rarely diplomatic. Angered frustration speaks, for instance, from Marilyn Dumont's poem "Still Unsaved Soul":

> If I hear one more word
> About your Christian God
> I'm gonna howl
> I'm gonna crawl outta my "heathen"
> skin and trick you into believing
> I am the Virgin
> Mary and take you to bed.
> If I hear one more line
> about your white church
> I'm gonna start singing and dancing
> with all my "false gods"
> in a giveaway dance and honour
> you with all the "unclean" sheets from my bed.

> If I hear one more blessed thought
> or witness one more holy act
> I'm gonna throw-up
> 35 years of communion hosts
> from this *still unsaved soul.*   (1996, 53)

The text in sarcastic defiance combines "heathen" practices like singing, dancing to "false gods," and giveaway ceremonies with scatological imagery. It confronts readers with literally "savage" humor in order to emulate yet subvert Western/Christian conceptualizations of "the Indian" as inferior, primitive Other. This highlights both the impact of colonial impositions and the processes by which colonial hierarchies are created, while comically denying Christian authorities the respect they demand.

The churches' role in providing rationalizations for conquest and colonization is repeatedly subject to humorous scrutiny in contemporary Native texts. Wherefrom, as Vine Deloria asks, "did Western man get his ideas of divine right to conquest, of manifest destiny, of himself as the vanguard of true civilization, if not from Christianity?" (1973, 128). Richard Wagamese's novel *Keeper 'n Me* mocks such religious bolstering when elder Keeper relates how the missionaries, upon encountering the Native population, immediately

> brought out the Great Book of Truth. Told us all we hadta do was believe in the Great Book and all the problems of the world would disappear. Get on your knees an' pray, they said. So those Indyuns back then they got on their knees . . . an' prayed. Wanted all their problems to disappear. When they looked up from all that prayin' they discovered all their land was gone. Up to then us Indyuns never figured the land was a problem but accordin' to the Great Book it musta been on accounta it was the first thing to disappear. Salvation and real estate been workin' hand in hand ever since that time. (1994, 75)

Readers may laugh at Keeper's curious explanations and the "nonsensical" causal connections they establish. Yet when they "look up from all that reading," they may just realize that the churches actually provided the ideological basis for colonization and land theft. Keeper impersonates the pseudonaïve, unknowing subject to point to the arbitrariness and self-serving aspects of Euro-American/Christian claims to authority (and ultimately power). Thus he comments on the missionaries' practice of calling the Bible "The Great Book of Truth" while denouncing Native traditions:

> Us we never knew truth to be somethin' had to be spelled out. Always figured was somethin' we each carried around inside . . . Anyways, they come here with their Great Book, lookin' strange at our ways, not takin' time to learn about it, not askin' for a guide, judgin.' Guess when your truth's all spelled out for you you got no need to learn no more. (75)

And in analogy, Wilf Pelletier's persona of the "Dumb Indian" admits that his people

> didn't even have a word for [religion]. They didn't know about all that hierarchy of saints and intermediaries and bishops and priests. They were so dumb they believed mostly in themselves. That was a real bad hangup our people had. . . . We didn't know what religion was all about. We actually thought it was a joyous celebration of life. And all the time it was really a solemn commemoration of death. (1972, 15–17)

Both texts partly mirror but simultaneously refract dogmatic Christian postulations. They present them from a point of view that purports to accept the role of the primitive subaltern, yet simultaneously sabotages the very processes by which Western/Christian superiority and authority are constructed and sustained. Through humor, they expose how Western/Christian paradigms were used to manipulate Native subjects, how the missionary apparatus reinforced its own authority with threats of hell, justified postulated hierarchies as god-given, and in effect demolished Native beliefs. Characters such as Wagamese's Keeper and Pelletier's "Dumb Indian" thus emerge as ingenious tricksters: They cunningly "shape-shift" into the colonial Other in order to expose the hypocrisies that mar the colonizers' agenda. "Ignorance" in these texts therefore does not, as the colonizers would have themselves and us believe, reside with Native people for "not knowing"; instead, it characterizes the colonizers for not wanting to know about the religious and cultural practices of the people they encounter, and for deceiving themselves about the rightfulness of their creeds, missions, and motivations.

Stuart Hall counts religious and biblical writings as one of the sources of common knowledge that the discourse of "the West" drew on in its construction of Self and Other (see 1992). Rather than the contents of the Christian faith, humor in contemporary Native texts mocks its claims to authority and universality — which necessitate a devaluation of Native belief systems as "pagan" or "savage" rituals. As, for instance, Sherman Alexie's *Reservation Blues* and Thomas King's *Green Grass, Running Water* show, humor destabilizes such claims and the ensuing hierarchies by subverting the very discourse by which the church sustains its ideological superiority as God-given and self-evident. King's text hilariously reimagines four biblical episodes from a decidedly Native perspective, thwarting the original versions by introducing four mythical Native women: First Woman (Diné/Abenaki), Changing Woman (Diné), Thought Woman (Laguna Pueblo), and Old Woman (Blackfoot/Dunne-za). Each of these female deities is initially at the center of a Native creation story, and thus part of the four attempts at "getting the story right" that form the novel's basic cyclical structure. The creation stories are told "according to" the Lone Ranger, Ishmael, Robinson Crusoe, and Hawkeye — mocking the biblical gospels of the four evangelists — and consist of fragments of the earth diver and emergence myths from the oral traditions of Native cultures (which King had analyzed in his doctoral dissertation). Thus rewriting the Bible and its authoritative claim to truth by hybridizing it with Native material already in itself constitutes an act of contestation or resistance. In addition, however, these creation stories are all based on female figures as the first beings (as indeed are most Native creation stories, see Jaimes and Halsey 1992, 319) — in contrast to the Judeo-Christian version, in which Adam's primacy serves to construct hierarchical gender relations. And they all depict creation as a collaborative act between the first human and the animals — exemplifying P. Allen's observation that "the Indian participates in destiny on all levels, including that of creation" (1979, 224) and undermining a male God's sole power.

The biblical Genesis provides the template for the novel's first encounter, when First Woman meets GOD in the garden. Yet in contrast to the biblical account, neither First Woman nor Ahdamn — King's simple-minded comical version of Adam and, as Horne points out, a classical "mimic man" (1999, 34) — are created by God, but are already in existence. Furthermore, it is First Woman who creates the garden, despite the protests of "that GOD" (King, 41), who is both audience and participant in the story. In the biblical Genesis God creates the world out of chaos and void. In King's version, First Woman is in charge of the world, while GOD causes chaos in the peaceful existence of First Woman and Ahdamn "and the animals and the plants, and all their relations" (41) by claiming everything for himself: According to GOD's "Christian rules" (69), the beings in the garden are told that they will be "very sorry" if they eat any of the food, as GOD (hilariously) threatens "with his hands on his hips, so everybody can see he's angry" (69). This selfish and impulsive character is contrasted with a serene and considerate First Woman: When GOD declines First Woman's offer to share the abundance of food, the latter simply leaves the garden in order to avoid "having a grouchy GOD for a neighbor," unperturbedly asserting that there are "lots of nice places to live" (69). With comic understatement, the text upsets the biblical account of the expulsion from paradise and caricatures GOD's reaction to this loss of control by showing him desperately clinging to the hierarchical power relations familiar from Genesis: "You can't leave my garden, that GOD says to First Woman. You can't leave, because I'm kicking you out" (69). Rather than replacing the Christian protology with a Native creation story — which would likely not generate any humor — the text enters into the familiar narrative of Genesis and reimagines the biblical account of creation with a decidedly Native slant. Despite its obvious humor, however, this revision alludes to serious issues: GOD's possessive behavior — "And just so we can keep things straight, says that GOD, this is my world and this is my garden" (68) — represents European concepts of private property that oppose an indigenous communal use of land

and resources (as suggested by First Woman). Consequently, GOD's claiming of First Woman's garden is strongly reminiscent of the European conquest of America, insinuating a connection between the Christian mission of conversion and material conquest. Moreover, by presenting readers with a female first being who is intelligent and responsible, while Ahdamn is a weak adjunct, rapidly engulfed and corrupted by the material temptations of the garden, King's story lures readers into realizing the arbitrariness of the postulated male primacy and ensuing supremacy of the original biblical account. Original sin, finally, the most imperative reason for "saving" the "poor heathens" within the civilizing mission, is tellingly missing from King's version: After initial harmony and sharing, it is GOD who annexes First Woman's garden and then accuses her of "eating his stuff." There is no snake, no temptation. Actually, First Woman's only "fault" is being there and being Native, exemplifying what a character in Drew Hayden Taylor's play *alterNatives* (2000a) sarcastically explains as "the difference between original sin and aboriginal sin. Ab-original sin meaning that being born Native was a horrible affront to God and the Church, paganism and all that" (2000a, 61–62).

The second biblical encounter revolves around Changing Woman, who as part of the creation tale falls from the Sky World, and the biblical Noah. In King's version, Changing Woman lands in the middle of the biblical account of the Flood, more specifically, in a big white canoe full of animals and full of poop (104–5, 144). Not only is this comically indigenized version of the ark filled with rather unusual animals (such as buffaloes, alligators, frogs, mosquitoes, hawks, spiders, and snakes), its captain, Noah, also differs from his biblical counterpart. The biblical Noah was the sole human of moral integrity whom God had selected to champion his new people on earth. King's Noah, in contrast, is "a little man with a filthy beard" (145), who first tries to leave the animals behind, later attempts to throw them overboard, and when his family urges him not to, throws them overboard instead. From the start, the text undercuts any pretensions at moral virtue. This lack of morality collides with Noah's outward insistence on decency, though, the former constantly subverting the latter. Noah is a firm believer in original sin — which King had so amusingly deleted from the previous part of the narrative — so that his first question to Changing Woman is: "Any relation to Eve? . . . She sinned, you know" (145). And just as GOD in the Garden story could not stand talking trees, Noah's "Christian rules" permit no talking (to) animals, something he considers "almost bestiality" (146). As Gerald Vizenor explains, in Native epistemologies "animals are not lower in evolutionary status. In all the woodland stories animals are significant beings. A language is shared, some humans remember the language, especially shamans, and there are many stories about intermarriage or relationships between humans and animals" (in Bruchac 1987a, 296). Accordingly, the Coyote in *Green Grass,*

Running Water asks the narrator: " 'What's bestiality?' . . . 'Sleeping with animals,' I says. 'What's wrong with that?' says Coyote" (146).

Even more so than in the previous episode, in this reimagined version of the flood an anthropocentric, male-dominated hierarchical worldview humorously clashes with a more encompassing Native approach, not least because Noah blatantly embodies the same narrow-mindedness with which European missionaries and explorers interpreted everything within their own predetermined frames of reference (see Fitz 2001, 146). For instance, he believes Changing Woman has been sent to him by God to be his new wife. In a side-splitting scene, the heroic savior of mankind thus mutates into an old lecher who chases Changing Woman around the canoe, shouting "time for procreating" (146) and who modifies the Ten Commandments to his own liking, remaking the first rule: "Thou Shalt Have Big Breasts" (147). The full extent of his hypocrisy is revealed when he subsequently leaves Changing Woman on an island and explains this with his strict adherence to Christian values: "This is a Christian ship . . . I am a Christian man. This is a Christian journey. And if you can't follow our Christian rules, then you're not wanted on the voyage" (148). This announcement, on the one hand, sets the stage for Changing Woman's later encounter with *Moby Dick*'s Captain Ahab, who nonchalantly explains, "This is a Christian world, you know. We only kill things that are useful or things we don't like" (196). On the other hand, it alludes to Timothy Findley's *Not Wanted on the Voyage* (1984), whose protagonist "Doctor Noyes" is modeled on the biblical Noah but shares many features with King's reimagined version:

> In both books, the Noah myth is interpreted as being emblematic of what, from a postcolonial point of view, is offensive about the Judeo-Christian tradition: its obsession with rules, transgression, and punishment, its denial of pleasure, in particular sexuality, its concomitant hypocrisy, and, most important, its insistence on the clear separation of categories which leads to "othering" and discrimination on the grounds of race, gender, and sexual preference. (Petzold 2000, 250)

Just as GOD's behavior in claiming the garden for himself was reminiscent of the European conquest of the American continent, Noah's demand that Changing Woman either comply with "Christian rules" or be left behind recalls the paradigm of forced assimilation that for the longest time dominated American and Canadian Indian policies. Legislations and practices such as the American Allotment Act of 1887, the residential and boarding school system of the nineteenth and twentieth centuries, and the forced relocation and termination policies of the 1950s and 1960s were fundamentally designed to eliminate Native cultures by reforging Native people as "productive mainstream citizens." Eliciting laughter at the biblical character's obsession with rules, the text thus also implicitly denounces the imposition of Euro-American standards on indigenous people.

The third biblical incident, an encounter between the mythical Thought Woman and A. A. (Archangel) Gabriel, scrutinizes yet another facet of Native-White relations, and shows even more clearly that King's humor carries multiple implications. Gabriel is described as a windy "little short guy with a big briefcase" (269) and a two-sided business card, Canadian Security and Intelligence Service printed on one side, Heavenly Host printed in gold letters on the other. His attempts to make Thought Woman sign an obscure agreement quite transparently allude to land theft through fraudulent White treaty-making practices. Accordingly, the narrator comments in reaction to the business card, singing "Hosanna da": "This song goes 'Hosanna da, our home on Natives' land' " (270) — playing on the national anthem's first line "O Canada, our home and native land." Furthermore, the paper Gabriel mistakenly pulls out of his suitcase first is a "White Paper," announcing "in a nice, deep voice": "As long as the grass is green and the waters run" (271). While the phrase itself refers to Native-White treaty making in general, the designation "White Paper" constitutes a sideswipe at the Trudeau government, which in its 1969 "White Paper" suggested a radical termination policy to abolish the special status of Native people in Canada.

A. A. Gabriel's routinely businesslike demeanor and his boredom with the job of getting Thought Woman to sign the "virgin verification form" (270) and fulfill her task of bearing the savior create, of course, a highly comical contrast to the biblical annunciation. By undermining the air of uniqueness and solemnity that surrounds the biblical annunciation, the text, on the one hand, challenges the Puritan creed of exceptionality by which the settlers conceptualized themselves as a chosen people. On the other hand, the scene refers to more recent chapters in Canadian Indian policy, for instance, when Gabriel casually renames Thought Woman: "Name? Thought Woman, says Thought Woman. Mary, says A. A. Gabriel" (270). Exemplifying more than just male colonial arrogance, ignoring Thought Woman's indigenous female voice alludes to the common practice of renaming and reeducating Native children along Western lines at the residential schools that existed in Canada until the 1950s. In these institutions, countless Native girls were indeed transformed into indiscriminate "Maries," as they were robbed not only of their original names but also of their family background, cultural heritage, and Native appearance. (The title of Robert Alexie's first novel, *Porcupines and China Dolls*, refers to what the Native boys and girls looked like after they received the standard haircuts.) In yet another implication, Gabriel's matter-of-fact instructions to Thought Woman to "sign here . . ., lie down here, and we'll get on with the procreating" (271), while hilarious by itself, recalls an especially vicious practice sanctioned by official Indian policies: the uncountable instances of sterilization conducted on Native women without their assent or knowledge by the US Indian Health Services during the late 1960s and 1970s (see Jaimes and Halsey 1992, 326). The laughter triggered by King's text thus walks a thin line between joking and choking: The text amuses its readers yet confronts them with dark aspects of Native-White history, wittily yet unwittingly demanding an allegiance with Native perspectives.

All of the rewritten Native/biblical episodes are characterized by the male characters' lack of respect for the Native women — as exemplified in A. A. Gabriel's reaction to Thought Woman's refusal of the annunciation: "No, says Thought Woman. Absolutely not. . . . So, says A. A. Gabriel, you really mean yes, right?" (271) — and by the contrast between Western individualism and what Jace Weaver termed Native "communitism" (1997, 43). These features are most pronounced, however, in the final biblical encounter between Old Woman and Jesus, uproariously renamed as pseudo-Indian "Young Man Walking on Water" (349). The renaming and the ensuing flat joke by which Old Woman greets "Young Man Walking on Water" — "Hello, says Old Woman. Nice day for a walk" (349) — from the start comically defamiliarize and debunk the biblical narrative. It is resituated in a Native cultural framework, which deprives it of its authoritative and miraculous status and "return[s] it to the realm of story" (Blaeser 1996, 85). The original biblical episode of Jesus on the Sea of Galilee remains clearly identifiable: Young Man Walking on Water also tries to save his disciples, who are caught in a boat in rough water. Readers are comically dislodged from their accustomed interpretive patterns, however, by several playful distortions. Not only does Young Man Walking on Water constantly forget the correct designation of those he is trying to save, so that Old Woman suggests: "Factotums? . . . Civil servants? Stockholders? . . . Deputies? . . . Subalterns? Proofreaders?" (349–50); his inflated authoritarian demeanor also proves of little use in calming the waves that threaten to kill his disciples. He declines Old Woman's offer to help (according to Flick, Old Woman is "an archetypical helper to a culture hero," in this instance, "the 'Christian culture hero,'" 1999, 161), expanding the by now familiar set of "Christian rules": "the first rule is that no one can help me. The second rule is that no one can tell me anything. Third, no one is allowed to be in two places at once. Except me" (350). Within the Judeo-Christian master narrative, the figure of Christ most clearly embodies values like charity, empathy, and caring. Laughing at the childish and egocentric character of Young Man Walking on Water, Western readers are thus brought to realize that the actions of a society that relies on colonial repression for its very existence bear little resemblance to the Judeo-Christian values it is allegedly built on. They are enticed to imaginatively identify with Old Woman, who eventually calms the waves and the rocking boat by singing a song. It is Young Man Walking on Water who takes the credit for saving the apostles, though:

Hooray, says Young Man Walking on Water. *I* have saved you.

Actually, says those men, that other person saved us.

Nonsense, says Young Man Walking on Water. That other person is a woman. That other person sings songs to waves. . . .

A woman? Says those men. *Sings songs to waves?* They says that too.

That's me, says Old Woman. That's me.

By golly, says those men. Young Man Walking on Water must have saved us after all. We better follow him around. (351; emphasis added)

King's text here hilariously demonstrates the processes of devaluing at work in the discursive construction of the (Native, female) Other within a Western, Judeo-Christian framework. An egocentric, incompetent savior indulges in stereotypical reactions to hurt male pride — but he nevertheless retains his power, because the men's actual experience is incompatible with their prefabricated frames of reference. King thus discloses the extent to which (Eurocentric) interpretations are conditioned by (colonial) representations; and he inscribes Native moral superiority to undermine actual Euro-American supremacy.

King's comic alterations endow the characters of his new versions with motivations not present in the source text. The hypocrisy of a Judeo-Christian society and the unfavorable role played by the church in the process of colonization are projected onto some of the very pillars of the Judeo-Christian faith: God, Noah, Archangel Gabriel, and Jesus Christ. At the same time, the biblical *grand récits* are infiltrated by caring, witty Native women who offer alternative paradigms. In all of these episodes, humor arises from the playful incongruity readers perceive between the familiar biblical versions and these reimagined narratives. Yet this incongruity also suggests a deeper contrast between two conflicting worldviews: an anthropocentric, male-dominated, individualistic and hierarchical Western view, epitomized in the constant invocation of the arbitrary and self-serving "Christian rules" (69, 145–47, 349–51) and a female holistic, egalitarian Native view, determined by mutual respect among all parts of creation and expressed in the concept of "minding your relations" (39, 41, 68, 351). Starting with the reconceptualization of God as a Coyote Dream and crowned by the immaculate conception as one of Coyote's pranks (see chapter three), King's reimagined narratives follow a strategy of humorous decentering and rely on humor's capacity to transgress or dissolve clean-cut boundaries. Sparking imaginative reconsideration of the biblical master narrative, they shed a new light on various historical and contemporary aspects of colonization. Like Coyote (whom King uses as a stand-in for the implied reader to make his decentering scheme transparent), most readers will not only know the biblical "stories," they will have accepted — however unconsciously —the discursively constructed hierarchy that ranks biblical tales above Native mythology. The text upsets familiar categories — the established, written, dominant Christian protology versus the "quaint but merely mythical" Native oral creation stories — and through its amalgamations compels readers to reimagine *both* texts. Humor manages to render previous evaluations invalid almost as unwittingly as they had previously been inscribed, which shows King to be the fifth of the "Indian tricksters" who try to "fix the world" by getting the story right.

Despite its humor, Dumont's previously quoted "Still Unsaved Soul" is clearly confrontational, and even King's hybrid juxtaposition of Native and biblical mythology can be read that way (see Petzold 2000, 251). Other contemporary Native texts more visibly reflect the transcultural approach that many Native people today use to integrate elements from Christian creeds into their own belief systems (see Fitz 2002). Native people thus oppose the exclusiveness preached by the missionaries with an inclusive approach of their own, as described in Sherman Alexie's "Sasquatch Poems":

> Do you take the bread and wine
> because you believe them to be the body and blood?
> I take them, as other Indians do, too
> because that colonial superstition is as beautiful
> as any of our indigenous superstitions   (1996c, 108)

While comically relegating Native and Christian beliefs to a shared level of "superstition" and thus undercutting accustomed hierarchies, the text, rather than dismissing Christianity as an instrument of subjectification, shows transcultural integration at work. Alexie "maintains an admirable equilibrium, neither wholly contemptuous nor wholly valorizing of white religion," Vickers (1998, 145) claims, in an assessment of the all-Indian reservation rock band in Alexie's novel *Reservation Blues*. And indeed, some of the novel's characters (the sisters Checkers and Chess) draw stability, inner grounding, and hope from their Catholic faith, while the text also shows the darker aspects of Christian missionary work — for instance, through Victor's history of sexual abuse at the hands of a Catholic priest or through the consequences of forced conversion for Native cultures, related in the lyrics of the song "My God Has Dark Skin" (1996a, 131–32). When it was observed in an interview that "as a writer, your attitude towards Jesus is ambivalent, to say the least," Alexie offered this distinction:

> Not towards Jesus himself. I'd say I'm ambivalent towards Christians. [Laughter] Mostly I'm ambivalent toward churches, who haven't been very good to Native Americans and reservations in this country. They've participated fully in the genocide of Native Americans culturally. The priest and nuns at boarding school beat kids for speaking their native language. There *have* been public apologies made in the Pacific Northwest, and different areas, for the Church's actions. But that doesn't make me any less suspicious of churches. (in Bellante and Bellante 1994, 14)

Accordingly, there is a bitter streak in some of the humor directed at the topic within the novel. Thomas Builds-the-Fire, the novel's protagonist, presents a darkly sarcastic version of the Decalogue, "The Reservation's

Ten Commandments as Given by the United States of America to the Spokane Indians" (154–55, see chapter three). In memory of a book burning, at which a hypocritical priest claims to destroy "*the devil's tools*" (146), he further puns that he is "a recovering Catholic" (155). And Father Arnold, the faltering Catholic reservation priest, is consoled by a hypocritical and patronizing bishop: "I know it's never easy ministering to such a people as the Indians. They are lost people, God knows" (267).

Still, with both subtle irony and roaring humor, Alexie also shows that Christianity and Native spirituality "upon close examination . . . do not exclude each other" (Fitz 2002, 10–11). These transcultural aspects mostly hinge on the characters of Father Arnold and Big Mom, the traditional Spokane healer and teacher. Neither of these characters embodies the prototypical priest or sage. Rather, both characters blur boundaries, avoid binary oppositions, and engage the readers' imagination in an exercise of deconstruction. Father Arnold assures Checkers that Jesus, due to his Jewish origins, "probably had dark skin and hair" (141), and he believes in the mythical powers of a dream catcher given to him by the oldest Spokane Indian Catholic — tellingly decorated with rosary beads (see 250). He is "impressed by the Spokanes' ability to laugh. He'd never thought of Indians being funny. . . . Father Arnold learned to laugh at most everything, which strangely made him feel closer to God" (36). Father Arnold's Catholic faith therefore does not exclude but is enriched by Native elements, which is also what characterizes his Native counterpart, Big Mom. While she clearly embodies traditional Spokane beliefs, she walks across Benjamin Pond (27, 199) and multiplies fry bread in clear emulations of Christ's doings at the Sea of Galilee and his feeding of the masses at the Sermon on the Mount (see chapter three). Combining "buckskin and beads" with CNN (9), she caters as little to stereotypical expectations towards "Indian wisdom" as Father Arnold stands for the institutional conceit of the Catholic church. The text stresses their shared humanity regardless of skin color, gender, or confession. Instead of being mutually exclusive, these characters — and, by implication, the beliefs they stand for — make up part of an organic whole, as an entry from Checkers's diary suggests:

> Big Mom felt like she came from a whole different part of God than Father Arnold did. Is that possible? Can God be broken into pieces like a jigsaw puzzle? What if it's like one of those puzzles that Indian kids buy at secondhand stores? You put it together and find out one or two pieces are missing. I looked at Big Mom and thought that God must be made mostly of Indian and woman pieces. Then I looked at Father Arnold and thought that God must be made up of white and man pieces. I don't know what's true. (205)

Humor in *Reservation Blues* not only pinpoints the church's role in colonization and undercuts its hypocritical tendencies, it also breaks down categorizations and essentializing ideas in general by demonstrating that Christianity and traditional Native beliefs, like Big Mom and Father Arnold, actually make "a great team" (280; see Fitz 2002, 12). However cynical Alexie's humor may be with regard to other issues, as it pertains to religion in this novel, it reimagines a reconciliatory picture of choice rather than force. This is reflected in the comment Chess makes when she is confronted with the wrongdoings of the church: "one of the mysteries of faith" is that "we all get to make the choice. But that don't mean we all choose good" (167–68).

The humor contemporary Native texts direct at imposed religions and social systems is as heterogeneous and complex as these issues themselves. While, as the last example showed, it may be reconciliatory, it mostly engages with and exposes the processes and paradigms by which a patriarchal White European Christian society constructed Native North American cultures as savage/heathen Other. Holding up Western Judeo-Christian values and norms for inspection from a Native point of view, it for once "others" and dislocates *these* beliefs from their complacent centrality, while at the same time reinforcing the validity of Native religious traditions.

Confronting Cultural Imperialism, Appropriation, and Reification

> To discover your Inner Indian, just pick up your phone and dial 1-900-WANNABE. Make your reservation today.
> — Anna M. Sewell and Crystal Lee Clark,
> "Discovering the Inner Indian," 57

In addition to the blatant misrepresentations discussed above, Native people today are also confronted with a vast misdirected enthusiasm for "Indian" spirituality and (New Age) philosophies of living in harmony with mother earth. Non-Natives emulate, appropriate, even market elements from Native cultures and traditions — or what they take to be Native cultures and traditions. Be it ceremonial practices like vision quests, sweats, or Sun Dances (see Aldred 2000), Native stories, artistic practices, or material objects (see Lutz 2002, 83–97): non-Natives frequently help themselves without hesitation to anything Native, in the end even to Native identity. The phenomenon of "playing Indian" — discussed by Phil Deloria in his study of the same title and in Rayna Green's "The Tribe Called Wannabee" — which mostly only imitates simulacra in the first place, is closely intertwined with the appropriation of Native cultural practices, traditions, and texts, so that one cannot clearly distinguish between the two. What all forms of cultural imperialism and appropriation have in common, though (in addition to a total lack of respect for the sovereignty of Native cultures), is that they take away interest and economic income from Native people.

Sherman Alexie directs biting sarcasm against such practices, which in his novel *Reservation Blues* are embodied by the White "New Age princesses" (1996a, 41) Betty and Veronica. Ironically, these two get the contract that the record company originally promised the all-Indian reservation rock band Coyote Springs because they seem "a more reliable kind of Indian" (272) than "any goddamn just-off-the-reservation Indians" (269). As the company executive explains about the White duo: "We dress them up a little. Get them into the tanning booth. Darken them up a bit. Maybe a little plastic surgery on those cheekbones. Get them a little higher, you know? Dye their hair black. Then we'd have Indians. People want to hear Indians" (269) — and so Cavalry Records is going to sell Indians. Just as Betty and Veronica's "Indian" appearance is a fabrication, their first recorded song is a satiric "Indian spirituality" mesh. It refers to mother earth, father sky, eagles, the four directions, and tobacco and sweetgrass offerings, culminating in the telling chorus:

> And my hair is blonde
> But I'm Indian in my bones
> And my skin is white
> But I'm Indian in my bones
> And it don't matter who you are
> You can be Indian in your bones   (296)

The attitude towards Nativeness satirized in these lines — which is also a highly ironic reference to "The Little Black Boy" from William Blake's *Songs of Innocence and Experience:* "And I am black, but O! my soul is white" — testifies to Aldred's observation that the New Age movement is basically "part of the larger context of consumer culture": It treats Native culture, spirituality, and identity as "commodities for purchase" (2000, 337), which are easily acquirable to compensate for the spiritual emptiness perceived in one's own life. Sadly, Alexie's fictional text but slightly exaggerates extratextual reality: Wendy Rose reports that she was replaced by more compliant (non-Native) poets for readings when she refused to do the little "Indian-dance," that is, wear buckskin, beads, and turquoise, and focus on pastoral and natural images (see 1992, 413). And "while American Indians struggle to regain power to determine their cultural identities and futures through economic, governmental, social, educational, and kinship refigurations, the 'Indian' voices most popular in mainstream America are often those of would-be Indians, who re-inscribe nineteenth-century, romantic images of 'noble savages'" (Shanley 2001, 28).

These circumstances could be expected to elicit scorn rather than mirth. Yet cultural appropriation, impostors, and so-called wannabes (that is, people who "want to be" Indian) are a recurring focus of humor among Native people, be it in Sewell and Clark's above-quoted satire "Discovering Your Inner Indian," in Jim Northrup's response to the popular claim of being "part Indian" by sardonically musing "which part? The right hand or the whole arm? The liver or spleen?" (1997, 111), or in the many jokes about every other White person allegedly having a Cherokee princess for a grandmother. Humor in contemporary Native texts serves to highlight the phenomenon as such, either through the use of comic reversal — as in King's *Truth and Bright Water*, in which trickster Monroe Swimmer dresses up as "Bright Water German Club" with tuba and elk hide pants and suspenders (1999a, 25) — or through satirical depictions of wannabe behavior. Thus Drew Hayden Taylor mocks "wannabes, groupies, and do-gooders" by paraphrasing their attitude as "I-really-respect-and-honour-your-culture-and-want-to-be-a-part-of-it-so-please-let-me-participate-and-learn-from-your-sacred-and-ancient-ceremonies-so-I-can-understand-your-ways-this-isn't-just-a-phase-I'm-going-through-I-really-mean-it-so-can-I-huh?" (1998, 108). With biting irony, authors like Sherman Alexie and Louis Owens implicitly explore the question: "Why would anyone *want* to be an Indian in contemporary America, given the degraded survival and racism that most modern Indians are heir to?" (Vickers 1998, 148). In Alexie's *Reservation Blues*, Chess answers Betty and Veronica's romantic declaration that "White people want to be Indians. You have all the things we don't have. You live in peace with the earth. You are so wise" with a reference to the biggest reservation alcoholic: "You've never met Lester FallsApart, have you? . . . You never spent a few hours in the Powwow Tavern. I'll show you wise and peaceful" (168).[16] And Native professor Cole McCurtain, the protagonist of Louis Owens's novel *Bone Game*, reacts to his White teaching assistant Robert's wish to participate in an Indian ceremony with open sarcasm:

> "Why would you want to participate in an Indian religious service?"
> "I want to learn. Native Americans have a lot to teach all of us."
> "Like what?"
> "How to live in harmony with the world, the environment."
> "You ever see a reservation, Robert? Go to a reservation sometime, and you'll see junked cars, arroyos full of wrecked refrigerators, broken bottles, cans — all the same squalor you'll see anywhere, maybe worse. Not very harmonious." (1994, 119)

To counter appropriative tendencies by pointing to the undesirability of the object may seem a rather surprising strategy at first. Yet it simultaneously exposes the romantic cliché of the spiritual Indian and denounces the blatant need felt by those who commit such acts of appropriation; Drew Hayden Taylor thus mockingly defines wannabes as "elements of mainstream society suffering from culture-envy" (1998, 125).

The ersatz religions dealt out by so-called "plastic medicine men" that answer the New Agers' demand for spiritual guidance (see Whitt 1995, 227–28) are a source of both irritation and humor among Native people. Richard Wagamese's novel *Keeper 'n Me* and Simon Ortiz's short story "The San Francisco Indians" clearly illustrate the latter response. Because Ortiz's story has a rather detached narrative tone and sparse, paratactic style, the humor initially appears subtle. In the end, it is all the sharper, however, since it does not really allow for shared laughter. The story centers on an encounter between a group of White (hippie) wannabes, led by the self-proclaimed "Chief Black Bear,"[17] and an old Indian man looking for his grandchild in San Francisco. The members of the "Black Bear Tribe" meet the old man in front of the Indian Center, where they had been "looking for an Indian." By telling him that he might find his granddaughter at the Haight, they manipulate him into accompanying them there. The text refrains from explicit commentary. Still, its juxtaposition of the Native man's reality and the fake Indians' ideas of Nativeness serves to create a sharp ironic contrast: Whereas the old Indian is dressed in an — albeit wrinkled — gray suit, the "Chief" is described as "a young White man with a blanket around his shoulders and beads around his neck" (1999, 118), obviously trying to "look Indian." A tribe member's commentary upon finding the Indian Center closed — "Maybe it's a day off or something" (117) — is comically mirrored by the old Indian's observations of Haight Street: "The Indian saw mostly young people just sitting or just walking. Like the young men with whom he walked, some were dressed in Indian fashion. Since no one seemed to be doing anything but sitting or walking, the Indian wondered if it was a day off" (119). The very idea of "taking a day" off from being Indian shows that Nativeness is seen from a White point of view as being a matter of choice rather than descent, something to be acquired in accordance with one's personal preferences. Ortiz' story thus confirms Whitt's observation about a " 'no-fault' assumption that has a tenacious grip on the assorted practitioners and consumers of AIS [American Indian Spiritualism]; the belief that the literary, artistic, scholarly, and commercial products of AIS are neither epistemologically nor ethically suspect or at fault" (1995, 228). This impression is exacerbated when the old Indian finds out that he has been invited along because he is supposed to conduct a "ceremony" to initiate a new "member" into the "Tribe," a young girl with blond hair and "very white" skin (120). That the Indian is considered but a generic commodity to enhance the authenticity of their bogus ritual becomes blatantly obvious in the girl's comment: "I asked Chief Black Bear to find an Indian to guide us in the ceremony. So it can be real when I join the Tribe" (120). Ironically, her careful scrutiny of the old man indicates that he might not meet her expectations about "real" Indians; but as Chief Black Bear can find no other Indians, he will have to do. To readers, the girl's desperate desire for the procedure "to be real" constitutes a comical contrast to the fact that the whole "Tribe," including its "Chief," are but fabrications. Moreover, the old man's reflection that he "did not know how a person could *join* a Tribe" (121) bitingly exposes their inconsiderate appropriation of Native identity. Leaving, the last thing the old man hears is "the girl's anguished cry, 'I want it to be real'" (121). As this is also the story's deeply ironic but simultaneously disconcerting final sentence, readers are left pondering possible motivations for and practices of appropriation. Humor in Ortiz' account of the White characters' pathetic attempts to emulate Indianness forms the counterweight to the pain inflicted on Native people by cultural ignorance, exploitation, and commodification. It exposes the irony inherent in the fact that the members of the dominant society desperately seek spiritual guidance from the very people they continue to marginalize. In addition to targeting widespread misconceptualizations about Native spirituality and denouncing appropriation, the story thus also delights in the implication that White America's pride and self-confidence is but a part of a glamorous façade that hides disorientation and emptiness.

Ortiz's story achieves no synthesis, but remains bound up with an antagonistic viewpoint. In contrast, the humor Richard Wagamese's *Keeper 'n Me* directs at non-Native appropriative tendencies, though decidedly less subtle, in the end proves to be more reconciliatory. In one of the novel's most hilarious scenes, Garnet's uncle Gilbert, a fishing guide, plays the "bait the tourist" game (1994, 83) with one of his American customers. When approached by the American about conducting a special "Indian ceremony . . . to ensure good fishing" (84), Gilbert immediately puts on his "stoic Indian" expression and pretends to hesitantly comply with the American's wish in exchange for money. To enhance the effect, he desperately urges the American to keep the sacred blessing to himself, and not to make any mistake with it — lest it turn into a curse. He explains:

> first you say . . . an' say it slow an' serious now . . . you say . . . O-wah. Got it? O-wah. . . . Second part's like this . . . you go . . . Tah-goo. Get that? Tah-goo. . . . 'Kay. Listen close. Most sacred parta all. . . . The word is . . . real sacred, "member . . . gotta get it right! Word is . . . Fye-am. Fye-am, got it? . . . You keep practicin' that while we go across the lake to the spot. An' when you get there you gotta lean out over the boat, spread your hands out, palms down over the water where you're gonna fish, make big wide circles over the water an' you say them words over an' over real slow, real serious an' loud. (85)

Of course, the American is flattered by the unexpected trust placed in him: "Boy, those other guys are sure gonna be surprised when I bless the water with a real sacred traditional Indian thing!" (86). Out on the lake, he does exactly what Gilbert told him:

"O-WAH! TAH-GOO! FYE-AM! O-WAH! TAH-GOO! FYE-AM!"
By about the fifth time through, everyone was laughing so hard the
boat was rocking and water was sloshing up into it. The guy suddenly
realized what he was really saying and looked at his hands still stretched
out in front of him palms down over the water, and stared and stared and
stared while the rest of them, including Gilbert, just bust up laughing.
After a while his shoulders starting to shake and tears started rolling down
his face as he busted up laughing, too. (86)

Together with the American fishermen, readers not only experience a
humorous demystification of the Indian sage but also are shown that Native
culture is not up for grabs for anyone willing to pay. Instead of the tragically poor Indian willing to sell his soul, whom the American expects,
Gilbert turns out to be a witty trickster who puts the White fascination with
the Indian Other to his own use and teaches a lesson. The text amalgamates
comedy with commentary in the character of Gilbert, who defies appropriative tendencies and dissolves the intra- and extratextual audience's preconceptions about ancient "Indian" wisdom into joint fits of laughter.
Using humor as a tool for mediation that effortlessly overcomes binary
oppositions or one-sided allocations of blame, it creates a *communitas* of
laughers who are brought to reevaluate their assessment of Euro-American
practices and Native spirituality. The scene thus in exemplary manner transcends a laughing *at* in favor of a laughing *with*, literally "luring" readers
into reconsideration, just as Gilbert baits the American fisherman.

Next to the commodification of Native spirituality (which is also the
target of humorous deconstruction in E. Donald Two-Rivers's short story
"Spirit Sticks," 1998), it is especially literary appropriation that invites contemporary Native writers' mockery. Not least for their own financial gain
and increase in reputation, White writers enthusiastically embrace and
instrumentalize selected elements of Native cultures or claim to have been
initiated by Natives and to write "from a Native perspective" — some
prominent examples being Carlos Castaneda and his "Yaqui Spirituality"
books (see Churchill 1992, 43–64), Ruth Bebe Hill and *Hanta Yo* (see
Churchill 1992, 67–75), and Lynn Andrews and her fictionalized feminist
"Indian ideologies" (see Aldred 2000, 331). This phenomenon was
termed "whiteshamanism" by Hobson in the US in the 1970s (see 1979)
and twenty years later precipitated the "appropriation of voice" debate in
Canada, in which First Nations writers demanded: "stop stealing our stories" (see Lutz 2002). As Leslie Silko sarcastically comments, "white poets
delight in saying 'Indians believe in sharing,' and so they go on 'sharing,'
collecting book royalties on plagiarized materials" (1979, 212).

Literary appropriation of this kind is the subject of Lenore Keeshig-
Tobias's "How To Catch a White Man (Oops) I Mean Trickster," which
is part of her longer cycle "Trickster Beyond 1992: Our Relationship."
The story combines the format of an orally told trickster tale with a satiric

attack on the contemporary issues of appropriation of land and stories. It advises an implied Native reader to stand in a forest and tell stories, predicting with sharp irony:

> Soon the white man! (I mean Trickster) will come by, carrying a big pack on his back. In that pack, he carries the voices of his women and the voices of other people he has walked over with his long legs. "I'm going to tell those stories for you," he'll say. "You're far too primitive to tell them yourself. I'm going to let the world know what you think. I am going to tell the world how you think when you think. And I'm going to build a golf course here, too. These trees are so old, and besides, you're not using them trees." (1998, 263)

The text first of all caricatures the combination of colonial condescension and literary appropriation that has resulted in countless Euro-American tellings of Native people's stories. But it also alludes to the Oka crisis of 1990, when plans for the expansion of a golf course onto Mohawk sacred sites in Kanesatake and Kahnawake precipitated an extended and at times violent confrontation between Mohawk protestors and provincial police and Canadian military. And finally, it calls upon the justification for land theft used throughout American history — that Indians allegedly "do not make use of the land anyway." Cultural appropriation, as thus becomes clear, for many Native people constitutes but a continuation of the earlier Euro-American annexation of Native lands. Accordingly, Hobson comments that "it is still the same old ballgame: Indians are still being exploited, both materially and culturally, but the forms now employed are much more subtle than the forms used a century ago by the mountain men and the Seventh Cavalry" (1979, 100). Keeshig-Tobias's story parodies the rationales underlying both forms of appropriation, for once casting the White man as a (blundering) trickster. Like his traditional predecessor, Keeshig-Tobias's trickster/white man is driven by greed. The text therefore recommends that once his attention is captured, he can be trapped by offers of

> better stories and a better place for a golf course, perhaps even a h-y-d-r-o-e-l-e-c-t-r-i-c dam or two. . . . Anyhow, tell him he could make the stories into TV movies, docudramas, feature films. He could write novels using the stories. He could receive all kinds of literary awards for his great imagination, with these stories. He could even achieve world acclaim for telling others how it is with the "Native Indian." (263)

Because he is "clever. But not smart" (263), the white man's egotism will make him fall into the trap, just as the traditional trickster's schemes often backfire due to his or her greediness. When both golf course and stories are denied to him, the text predicts in another allusion to Oka, the trickster/white man will rush on with "guns and tanks" to force the land and stories off the Native informants, yet in his anger will end up "shooting himself in the foot, . . . and tumbling into the hole" previously dug for him, ironically, with "his foot in his mouth" (264).

As chapter three points out, traditional trickster tales often work by setting a negative example. They show where the trickster's selfishness takes him or her, so that as "trickster errs, we learn" (Blaeser 1993, 56). Keeshig-Tobias's story follows this traditional didactic pattern: Listing all the tempting opportunities for appropriation, it shows the trickster/white man's seduction, but also his undoing by giving in to them. Whereas in the real world White authors usually succeed in their appropriative schemes, in Keeshig-Tobias's reimagined version the white man's aggressive appropriative tendencies with regard to Native stories turn on him. The (female and minority) voices that the white man appropriated and carried around in his pack for 500 years are finally freed in this satiric utopia, and the text ends with advice to "tell the children. Teach them. Teach them the history of this land, the real history, before 1492 and since. Those stories will guide them into the next 500 years. Tell them not to do as the trickster (I mean white man) has done" (264). Imagining a humorous "alterNative" to a reality in which Native people all too often lose the struggle over the control of stories and rituals ultimately proves to be a more effective means of raising consciousness than any lament or angry polemic. Embedded in the framework of the trickster tale, readers are presented with an original Native perspective that both tackles contemporary cultural politics and shows the ongoing vitality of traditional storytelling, not least in its educating function.

Appropriation is not restricted to spiritually interested New Agers, wannabes, and sporadic non-Native writers. Academics also see themselves faced with allegations of exploiting Native cultures in the name of science. Unreflected wholesale condemnations of research conducted on Native issues by non-Native researchers — which often come from essentialist Native camps — are certainly of little value either to academics or Native people. Yet one has to acknowledge that Western academic conduct in some cases seems to lack the necessary respect and willingness to incorporate Native perspectives and wishes. It is such cases that Hobson refers to when he claims:

> The assumption seems to be that one's "interest" in an Indian culture makes it okay for the invader to collect "data" from Indian people, when, in effect, this taking of the essentials of cultural lifeways, even in the name of Truth or Scholarship or whatever, is as imperialistic as those simpler forms of theft, such as the theft of homeland by treaty. (1979, 101)

Leslie Silko puts it in even clearer terms when she calls it a "racist assumption . . . that the prayers, chants, and stories weaseled out by the early white ethnographers, which are now collected in ethnological journals, are public property" (1979, 212). Among Native people, instances of being treated as interesting objects of study have led to a widespread aversion to academic research in Native cultures in general, and to the discipline of anthropology in particular. Vine Deloria carries it to extremes when commenting: "Into each life, it is said, some rain must fall. Some people have bad horoscopes, others take tips on the stock market. . . . But Indians have been cursed above all other people in history. Indians have anthropologists" (1977, 78).

On a more serious note, Deloria claims that anthropological research has even "contributed substantially to the invisibility of Indian people today" (1977, 81). While some work in anthropology has contributed to an archaic depiction of Native people, brought forth in such an encompassing fashion, this claim has to be taken with a grain of salt. To bar non-Natives from research on Native cultures on essentialist grounds would in effect foreclose most research in the field and diminish serious interest in Native cultures — certainly not a desirable alternative. Nevertheless, institutionalized Western academic discourse constitutes a particular perceptual frame and thus determines a particular — often historicizing — reading of Native people. This becomes problematic especially when, along the lines of Foucault's power/knowledge paradigm, Western academic discourse on Native people is granted absolute authority while Native voices themselves are devalued or silenced. "Native culture" then becomes what non-Native experts proclaim it to be, not what Native people practice and live (see Deloria in W. Rose 1992, 404). It is such constellations (not academic research in general) in which humor may figure as a kind of counter-discourse to scientific anthropological discourse, "establishing a kind of binary; it's anthropologists and then play, humor and imagination" (Vizenor in Coltelli 1990, 169).

A basic humorous reaction to scientific reification is to shatter an inflexible perceptual frame, as in Carroll Arnett's poem "Powwow":

> Hair the color of
> Tobacco ash, the fair lady
> anthro asked, Excuse
> me please, . . . sir
> (guess it beats Chief),
> Does that red patch
> On your blanket symbolize
> Something?
>   Yes mam,
> it surely does, it
> symbolizes that once
> upon a time there
> was a hole
> in the blanket   (1979, 127)

The poem humorously collapses the anthropologist's attempt to interpret everything within her academic epistemology, revealing its narrow (minded) limits.

Transcending this first step of breaking the frame, however, humor may also arise from tricksterlike inversion, or from duping non-Native anthropologists by meeting them on their own ground. Louis Owens's trickster character Alex Yazzie dissects the contested issue of material appropriation at the hands of unscrupulous archaeologists — "bone robber barons," as Vizenor dubs them (1990, 67) — who sometimes unquestioningly confiscated Native "artifacts" and remains for research and exhibition purposes.[18] In Louis Owens's novel *Bone Game*, Alex exposes the Western rationalizations for such conduct by entering into its very discourse and subverting it from within. His "study project" on Puritan remains emulates similar projects by Western academics in

> an NSF proposal for a team of Indian anthropologists to do a dig in the cemetery at the Old North Church in Boston. That's where they buried all those Puritans. The Winthrops are buried there. My basic argument is that it's imperative we Indians learn more about Puritan culture. Puritans had a significant impact on us. . . . In the proposal I said we would document everything from the health and disease patterns of colonial settlers to burial customs, diet, nutrition, and social status. We'll do cranial measurements to figure out how intelligent the Puritans were, compared to us, and test teeth and bone samples for dietary information. Puritans were a primitive but fascinating people. (1994, 180)

Adopting the rhetoric and line of argument employed in Western research proposals for studying "primitive" cultures' habits and ways of life, but combining them with the unexpected context of WASP history, the text parades Euro-American vindications that present Western academic practices as self-evident and logical. The text not only shows how allegedly neutral scientific paradigms and epistemologies can, in fact, be arbitrary and self-serving, it also renders the hierarchies inherent in such binary notions as "primitive" versus "refined" and "science" versus "superstition" invalid. Thus, the doubleness inherent in irony "can also act to contest the singleness of authority and the ahistorical claim to eternal and universal value that frequently underlies it" (Hutcheon 1992, 16), challenging an alleged Euro-American monopoly on Truth. The very fact that readers laugh at the absurdity of Alex's suggestion initiates a critical reassessment of the grounds on which such conduct is considered justified when Euro-American scientists study Native cultures — but not the other way round. In accordance with Paul Radin's observation about the Winnebago trickster — "If we laugh at him, he grins at us. Whatever happens to him happens to us" (1972, 159) — by laughing at this trickster's elaborate inversion, Euro-American readers basically laugh at themselves, as they are put in Native people's shoes and brought to see their ancestors described as "a primitive but fascinating people." The point is driven home by Alex's tongue-in-cheek explanation: "Some of those Boston people may be a little squeamish about digging up their ancestors, and that's understandable, but, hey, it's science, Cole. We can't allow their primitive superstitions to stand in the way of science" (180). The text thus on the one hand levels hierarchies by reducing Christianity to as much of a primitive superstition as tribal beliefs allegedly are. On the other hand, it reveals the hypocrisy inherent in appropriating tribal remains in the name of science and education. Alex suggests donating the dug-up skeletons to tribal museums that would "like to have a Puritan skeleton on display, for educational purposes" (180). Owens's amusing shift of perspectives and habitual patterns of interpretation is truly both educating and entertaining.

Obviously, much of the humor directed at dubious academic practices hinges on an apparently willing compliance with their demands, just to subsequently subvert them from within. A scene from Drew Hayden Taylor's play *alterNatives* vividly exemplifies this in the context of the collection of Native cultures' oral traditions. Native protagonist Angel and his friend Bobby made up bogus "authentic Ojibway stories" as little boys to make money off the anthropologists visiting their reserve. As a grown-up, he discovers these stories in a book that his non-Native partner teaches in her Native literature class at university. To Angel's comment, "Not an ounce of truth in those stories, were there?" Bobby replies, "Of course not. Our legends were none of their business" (2000a, 128–29), a widespread attitude among Native people.

Thomas King's "One Good Story, That One" also subscribes to this attitude, yet its trickster-defense is more subtle: Not only are the Native stories protected, the anthropologists are served their own *grand récits* in Native guise. The protagonist and first-person narrator of King's story, an old Native storyteller, relates how he was visited by three White anthropologists whom his friend, Napiao, brought along because they want to hear a story. Napiao's introductory comment — "Maybe not too long, he says. Those ones pretty young, go to sleep pretty quick. Anthropologists, you know" (1993, 4) — from the start subverts the researchers' authority by conceptualizing them as children, thereby reversing the way in which Native informants were sometimes described as childlike. Still they know what they want: Not the contemporary stories the old man considers interesting, but "old stories . . . maybe how the world was put together. Good Indian story like that . . . Those ones have tape recorders, he says" (5). So the old man proceeds to tell them a creation myth, and while this is what they came for, the particular story he dishes up becomes irritatingly familiar as he goes along, basically revealing itself to be an indigenized version of Genesis. As in King' novel *Green Grass, Running Water*, the original outline is clearly recognizable. The storyteller gives his rendering a decidedly comic twist, however, by changing some details: The first beings, Ah-damn

and Evening live in "Evening's Garden" (6), implying that creation is first
and foremost a female accomplishment. The tree that curious Evening
encounters not only bears apples ("mee-so") but also potatoes, pumpkin,
corn, and all kinds of berries — the original diet of many Native cultures.
Moreover, the narrator in a hilarious aside compares god's selfish crankiness
to the behavior of an acquaintance of his who abuses his wife: "That one,
god . . . Maybe like Harley James. Bad temper, that one. Always shouting. . . . That one goes to town, get drunk, come home, that one, beat his
wife" (7). Finally, he simply forgets about the snake and the whole issue of
original sin, adding this detail after he already finished the story: "There is
also a Ju-poo-pea, whiteman call him snake. . . . I forgot this part. He lives
in tree with mee-so. That one try to get friendly with Evening, so she stick
a mee-so in his mouth, that one. Crawl back into tree. Have trouble talking,
hissss, hissss, hissss, hissss. Maybe he is still there" (9).

As Holden's work on Native peoples on the West Coast and especially
the Northwest Salish shows, the ploys fictionalized by Taylor and King
were indeed a frequent occurrence (see Holden 1976, 260), as Native
informants played jokes upon unsuspecting anthropologists. They made
up stories, adjusted their own stories to accommodate new circumstances,
and mirrored the White researchers' own stories back to them, "reshaped
to comment ironically on the White presence" (Holden 1976, 272). An
especially interesting case reported by Holden, a "neo-Adam and Eve
myth told to missionary Myron Eels in the late 1900s" (285), shows astonishing parallels to King's story:

> In that tale, there is a kind of Garden of Eden, but with a difference.
> There are two people in the paradise of this tale, the first man and first
> woman representing, respectively, the ancestries of the European and the
> native American. As in our own biblical version of this tale, there is a fall
> from grace here, but only on the part of one of those peoples. The
> woman, who ignores the rules of god's paradise and gathers berries —
> one presumes, in her traditional cultural mode, to feed her people —
> mothers the native American. As a consequence of the activity of their
> ancestress, the latter are doomed to be "ignorant, foolish, and dark-
> skinned. But the man did not eat of the berries and to his children were
> given letters, the knowledge of letters, and a white skin." (285)

Accordingly, in King's story, both god and Ah-damn are clearly identified
as "whitemen," whereas "Evening, she be Indian woman, I guess" (9).
Moreover, the storyteller not only spoils the "authenticity" of the "old
story" with remarks like Evening's admonishment to the upset god to
"calm down, watch some television" (9), by making god appear selfish and
rude, and "Ah-damn not so smart" (9), like Eels's informants, he also
implicitly reveals his view on White presence. He even weaves in criticism
of colonization when he relates that god "says that Evening and Ah-damn
better leave that good place, garden, Evening's garden, go somewhere

else. Just like Indian today" (9). But while the story collected by Eels basically mirrors the White interpretation of Native-White relations and leaves its absurdity to speak for itself, the story told by King's narrator — as a consequence of the forgotten "minor details" such as male primacy and original sin — turns out to be a lot less tragic than the biblical account. While god still expels Evening and the cowardly Ah-damn from paradise for having eaten his apples, Evening counters that there are "many good places around here" (9), and the story ends anticlimactically: "Evening and Ah-damn leave. Everybody else leave, too. That tree leave, too. Just god and Ju-poo-pea together. Ah-damn and Evening come out here. Have a bunch of kids" (10).

Pretending to abide by the conventions of anthropological discourse and to deliver the sought-after "myth," the narrator shows the White anthropologists one of their most fundamental narratives through the lens of a Western ethnographic mode. He thus tricks them into experiencing what Native people are confronted with when White researchers, due to lack of cultural knowledge, simplify, misinterpret, and distort Native material (see also Atwood 1990, 250). The informant undermines the alleged authority of the biblical Genesis by opening his story with "Once upon a time" (5), the conventional fairy tale formula — inherently leveling established hierarchies between biblical accounts and Native "myths." In an inconspicuous little side-plot, he moreover introduces Coyote, the archetypical Native trickster: When Ah-damn writes down the names of all the animals, he gets tricked by Coyote who comes by "maybe four, maybe eight times. Gets dressed up, fool around" (8) to receive different names and to confuse Ah-damn. Tellingly, Coyote manages to fool Ah-damn, who concentrates hard on cataloguing things in writing, while the perceptive Evening sees right through the trick. This has important implications for the story's ending, as the narrator recounts: "We watch [the anthropologists] go. My friend, Napiao, put the pot on for some tea. *I clean up all the coyote tracks on the floor*" (10; emphasis added). This not only shows that the trickster Coyote transcends story boundaries, wandering between the embedded story of Ahdamn and Evening and the frame narrative of the old man and the anthropologists, it also implies that, like Coyote coming around several times in different guises to fool Ah-damn, who meticulously wants to record creation, the old storyteller brings around the story of Genesis in different versions to fool the anthropologists, who want to record traditional indigenous folktales. The old storyteller thus frustrates both the anthropologists' desire to record Native oral traditions and their stereotypical expectations as to what an "old Indian story" ought to be like. Eventually, while Napiao compliments his friend — "One good story, that one, my friend" (10) — the anthropologists have to politely hide their disappointment. As Margaret Atwood summarizes: "If the narrator has a 'good Indian story' to tell, he's kept it to himself. He certainly isn't going to tell it to white anthropologists . . . Instead he's fed them one of their own stories back, but he's changed the moral . . . to convey to the whites more or less what he thinks of white behaviour in general" (1990, 249). Holden's conclusion to consider the stories she analyzed as "a repayment in kind, if little enough, for that which the members of our own culture worked upon the culture of the native Coast Salish" (1976, 290) thus holds equally true for King's story. Indeed, her observation that "part of what [the anthropologists] brought away with them and published in their own written record was in fact an image of themselves — hardly flattering, but surely accurate" (290) almost reads like an interpretation of "One Good Story, That One." Both anthropologists and readers find themselves at the mercy of King's ingenious narrator, as he humorously reimagines an approach that tends to reduce Nativeness to but an interesting (and ancient) phenomenon to study.

Contemporary Native writing brings to attention how appropriation and scientific reification affect Native cultures. Linking laughter to learning, these texts show how Western philosophical, artistic, and scientific paradigms serve to justify claims to Native cultural production or even identity. Beyond that, however, Native writing uses (sometimes very weighted) trickster humor as a subversive weapon in direct defense against appropriation and cultural or scientific imperialism. Instead of accepting conceptualizations of Native cultures as open to everyone in search of alternative philosophies, literary ideas, or anthropological data, Native writers comically reimagine plots in which such appropriation fails and Native characters end up victors rather than victims.

Laughter as Good Medicine:
Humor in Native Communities

When Indians make lots of money from corporations . . . we can all hear our ancestors laughing in the trees. But we never can tell whether they're laughing at the Indians or the whites. I think they're laughing pretty much at everybody.
— Sherman Alexie, *The Lone Ranger and Tonto*, 13

Native realities today cannot be viewed in isolation from the experience of colonization. Still, to write about Native humor exclusively in terms of its engagement with Euro-American presence, that is, without discussing its role in intragroup Native relations and situations, would comprise an unduly limited and Eurocentric perspective. Non-Native researcher Roger Spielman reports about his time living in an Anishinaabe community: "I never laughed so hard as I did living at Pikogan. Sometimes the jokes, stories, and teasing revolved around White people; but just as often it was grounded in Aboriginal experience, laughing at themselves as much as they did about people and perspectives from non-Native traditions" (1998, 111–12). Humor in this context constitutes a means of forging social cohesiveness and strengthening group identity in several related ways. It helps Native people confront and deal with a sometimes painful reality by contributing to individual and collective healing. In the form of teasing and self-deprecating humor, it functions as an instrument of social control that sanctions particular codes of conduct by ridiculing deviant behavior. Engaging in and accepting mutual ribbing, members of a group assure each other that they share a particular humor and assessment of things (see Fine 1983, 173), since laughter always relies on a common set of references. And last but not least, through its mediational and differentiating qualities, humor allows Native writers to point to problems prevalent in Native communities (poverty, unemployment, alcoholism, violence) in a way that transcends the binary choice of either trivializing these issues or resorting to the tragic mode Vizenor so fervently cautions against (see 1989; 1994b). Humor serves as a cohesive power in terms of identification, and it constitutes an instrument for revising or asserting group values, a function that ultimately helps communities adapt to social and cultural changes. Although one has to be careful not to idealize such humor by ignoring its potential to generate or exacerbate conflict, it may even be called "communitist" — a neologism Jace Weaver coined from "community" and "activist" in reference to contemporary Native writing in general — "to the extent that it has a proactive commitment to Native community, including the wider community" (Weaver 1997, 43). That sharing laughter unites people is a truism, and it will hardly be questioned that "ethnic humor plays an important role in group identity formation and solidarity" (Lowe 1986, 440). But where exactly does this integrative capacity of humor show, and how do the cohesive effects of laughter come about?

Quite obviously, joint laughter at the expense of an out-group, especially a dominant out-group, may help a group close its ranks (see Fine 1983, 173; Boskin and Dorinson 1985, 83). Making White people (see J. Price 1978, 217; Sanner 1994, 31; Lincoln 1993, 62–63) or historical events (see Deloria 1977, 148–50) the butts of Native jokes can be instrumental in creating a pan-Indian "us" through drawing a collective boundary "versus them." Such humor constitutes a form of defiance against colonial oppression and asserts continued presence. In addition, laughter in contemporary Native writing may also figure as a way for Native people to keep their dignity. John, the Indian protagonist in Alexie's novel *Indian Killer*, has been "adopted out" by White foster parents at an early age and grows up in an all-White surrounding. Watching an all-Indian basketball tournament as a young man, what strikes him most is the laughter:

Many Indians barely paid attention to the game. They were talking, telling jokes, and laughing loudly. So much laughter. John wanted to own their laughter, never realizing that their laughter was a ceremony used to drive away personal and collective demons. The Indians who were watching the game reacted mightily to each basket or defensive stop. They moaned and groaned as if each mistake were fatal, as if each field goal meant the second coming of Christ. But always, they were laughing. John had never seen so many happy people. (1996b, 21)

When John encounters homeless Indians in Seattle he "watched those Indians, in dirty clothes and thirdhand shoes, miles and years from their reservations, estranged from their families and tribes, yet still able to laugh, to sing" (144). John's observations underline the survival qualities of Native humor and embody Native people's defiance against emotionally surrendering to colonization by giving in to self-pity. Instead, through self-determined and irrepressible laughter, Native people defy the colonially assigned role of the tragic victim.

In part, it is humor's capacity to distance adverse circumstances that speaks from those scenes. Yet humor, especially the communal kind described here, also gives Native people the strength to directly confront the reality around them more immediately by enabling them to share distressing experiences. When Father Arnold, the White priest in Sherman Alexie's novel *Reservation Blues* asks himself: "What did [Indians] have to laugh about? Poverty, suicide, alcoholism?" (36), he therefore poses the wrong question: It is exactly this communal humor that *keeps* Native people from despairing, that offers "a way of recalling and going beyond tragedy, of working through the hurt of personal history, of healing old wounds and hearing the truth of what's happening among Native Americans" (Lincoln 1993, 116).

Consequently, humor is the instrument of choice in many contemporary Native texts addressing essentially tragic situations within Native communities. Poverty is comically deflated in countless jokes on commodity food, broken down cars, and substandard housing and health care. That Marie and Reggie, two Native college students in Alexie's novel *Indian Killer*, can only afford cereal for dinner, for instance, is just another "small tragedy" to be overcome with humor: " 'Quite the feast, huh?' asked Marie and laughed. 'Well, at least it's traditional,' said Reggie, fighting back a smile. 'Yeah, don't mind us, we're indigenous.' They laughed together" (95). Excessive drinking and alcoholism, despite their horrible consequences, are comically dealt with in Alexie's *Reservation Blues*, where Thomas's alcoholic father is nicknamed "Drunk and Disorderly" (95) since this is what he is most frequently charged with and arrested for. Jimi Hendrix, Janis Joplin, and Elvis are even made "honorary members of the Spokane Tribe" — because they "all drank so much and self-destructed so successfully" (201). In mockery of American patriotism, the Native patients at a treatment center in Jim Northrup's "The Jail Trail" "solemnly placed their hands over their livers when they raised the flag" (2003, 88). And drinking and its effects on Native communities provide most of the subject matter of plays as vastly dissimilar as Hanay Geiogamah's darkly humorous *Body Indian* (1980) and Drew Hayden Taylor's lighthearted comedy *The Bootlegger Blues* (1991). Basil Johnston's *Indian School Days* (1998) and Richard Wagamese's *Keeper 'n Me* (1994) even manage to shed a humorous light on the boarding and residential school experience, one of the darkest chapters in North American history. Keeper, for instance, relates that at residential school he was told that "our way of livin' and prayin' was wrong and evil. Got beat up for speakin' Indyun. If we did that, we'd all burn in hell they told us. Me I figured I was already brown why not burn the rest of the way, so I ran away" (36). Wagamese thus fictionalizes what Tim Giago reports about his time at mission school. He recounts that even today, "when a group of us gets together and the conversation turns back to our mission days, we share one humorous story after another about those good, bad, and ugly times. The laughter reminds us that it was our own sense of humor that carried us through. Today, we realize that our approach to hard times in boarding school paralleled the broader Native American experience throughout history" (1990, 53–54). Apparently, no facet of Native life, not even sickness or death, is exempt from humor, so that the therapy that an Anishinaabe Vietnam war veteran has to undergo to overcome posttraumatic stress disorder is rendered most comically in Jim Northrup's "Shrinking Away" (1993, 8–9) — pun intended. The eulogy that Frank Snake Church plans to deliver at his father's funeral in Alexie's story "Whatever Happened to Frank Snake Church" (2003, 198–200) is even comprised entirely of more or less flat jokes.

Native humor constitutes first and foremost a response to Native life, that is, *all* aspects of it, including the downsides. Self-deprecating humor and teasing, which are especially prominent in this context, are frequently even considered the most characteristic forms of Native humor in general.[19] Within a colonial framework, self-disparaging humor is sometimes conceptualized as a "pre-emptive strike to minimize the agony suffered in the event of the joke being told by the white outsider" (Jannetta 2001, 122–23), or as a way of claiming a share of the power of the dominant joke tellers (see Purdie 1993, 65). In the context of Native intragroup relations, however, self-deprecating humor rather constitutes a way of responding to or even anticipating teasing (see V. Deloria 1977, 147; Spielman 1998, 123–24). This way, the self-deprecating aspects of humor may be considered as "just the other side of the teasing coin — teasing turned inwards" (Kelly 2005, 62) to demonstrate humility and solidarity. Strengthening cultural identity and belonging, it serves as a testing device for someone's perception of what is funny, their culturally determined definition of humor (see Theisz 1989, 23). As Drew Hayden Taylor points out: "Oftentimes you don't know you've been accepted into a community until you've been teased" (2005, 75), just as looking at one's own weaknesses and imperfections with a grain of trickster salt may forge mutual trust and solidarity by eliciting shared laughter. Such humor "is a sign of a community of awareness even as it reinforces that same community. Recognizing their own specific cultural traits and even foibles, and commenting on them in jokes also helps the group to maintain a sense of community and identity" (Cohen 1985, 207).

There are many examples of such literally self-conscious humor dealing with Native characteristics. Joking remarks on being on "Indian time" mock the more "flexible" Native handling of time (see Shutiva 1994, 117–18), as in Curtis Jonnie's song "Indian Time," in which an Indian girl whose fiancé wanted to check just briefly on his trapline before they get married has "been waiting for a year / He's on Indian time" (1999, 36). Humor is directed at the "moccasin telegraph," that is, the way information and gossip travels mouth-to-mouth among Native people (see Alexie 1996b, 230). The Native predilection for gambling, especially bingo, is mocked in Alexie's *Reservation Blues*, when Victor comments on the huge crowd showing up for a concert: "They must think it's bingo night" (52); in Jim Northrup's story "Goose, Goose," when a cold spell "kept everyone inside. Only essential trips were made: groceries, medical appointments, court, and bingo" (106); and in Tomson Highway's much-acclaimed play *The Rez Sisters*, in which the world's biggest bingo game rules the protagonists' lives. Finally, the "insufficient" Native command of English is subject to such laughter, for instance, when elder Keeper in Wagamese's *Keeper and Me* watches Sunday mass on TV and wonders about there being "Smoke ev'rywhere. Garnet said this partic'lar church was into the incense. Hmmpfh. Me I thought incense was somthin' bad you done with your own fam'ly. Glad the boy straightened me out there" (4). Here and elsewhere, what would be considered an extreme insult coming from an outsider can thus become a form of humorous bonding, an assurance of shared cultural membership, and a backhanded compliment to another person's sense of humor. Accordingly, Sherman Alexie's frequent use of the term "skins," or the fact that the all-Native reservation rock band Coyote Springs in *Reservation Blues* initially considers naming themselves "Bloodthirsty Savages" (44) is not meant to denigrate Native characters or Native people. It simply spells out Spielman's observation that in many Native communities "such terms are commonly used for joking, teasing, and, perhaps most importantly, for expressing group solidarity" (1998, 9).

Self-deprecating humor, then — even of the kind that uses distorting stereotypes in self-description — is not to be mistaken for masochism or a symptom of self-hatred. Yet it sometimes walks a thin line, as a passage from Sherman Alexie's "Spokane Tribal Celebration, September 1987" demonstrates: "We all laugh, especially me, because I/know the only time Indian men/get close to the earth anymore is when Indian men/pass out and hit the ground" (1992, 74). Similarly, in Thomas King's *Truth and Bright Water* Lucy Rabbit finds evidence for her claim that Marilyn Monroe was actually Indian in the fact that "she died young, of drugs. Sounds like an Indian to me" (200). King reports: "When I read that in public it's funny what the laughter will do. It'll come out and then just cut off when the audience realizes that, whoa, wait a minute, am I supposed to be laughing at that?" (King in Andrews 1999). Sometimes, the point of such self-disparaging humor is even missed altogether. In these cases, "the outside observer takes the veneer for the core because he does not understand the construction, and so mistakes the thin, reflective surface for deep ridicule of the in-group" (Cohen 1985, 207). While one can easily see how a lack of familiarity with Native cultures may cause a White audience to react to such humor with uneasiness rather than laughter, it is interesting to note that such reactions also come from Native readers and Native critics. Native texts working with such humor (most prominently those by Sherman Alexie and Adrian Louis) have been accused of being "self-destructive and self-deprecatory" (Owens 1998, 76), of "catalogu[ing] the deficit model of Indian reservation life" (Cook-Lynn 1996, 68), or of "perpetuat[ing] many of the stereotypes of native peoples" (Bird 1995, 47) and the image of the "doomed savage" (Owens 1998, 93). Quite in contrast to the claim that it "deflects any 'lesson in morality' from the non-Native reader" (Owens 1998, 76) and "maintains an aggressive posture regarding an essential 'authentic' Indianness" (76), however, such humor actually frees Native fiction form the prescriptive, backwards-oriented (and illusory) idea of an exclusive authentic Indianness. Would it not, after all, be a form of positive stereotyping and romantic idealizing to disregard or gloss over the thornier or controversial aspects of contemporary Native existence? To address them in a humorous rather than a tragic mode does not primarily present Native issues in a way that is "nonthreatening to a white readership" (76). Rather, through the humorous depiction of the strengths *and* weaknesses of Native characters and communities, the writers discussed here acknowledge the complexity and very humanity of Native people. In addition to defying romanticizing clichés of the noble savage, they offer a *Native* audience a viable way to confront the dark spots on the Native map.

Kimberley Blaeser's text "Twelve Steps to Ward Off Homesickness" satirically recommends a cure of recreating on-reserve living conditions to serve as a tragicomic reminder of its shortcomings: spreading lighted cigarettes around the house; living exclusively off commodity foods and taking one's vitamins with warm, flat beer; parking wrecked cars on the lawn; and assembling stray dogs in the garden. Furthermore:

IV.   Look in the mirror and say "Damn Indian" until you get it right. Stop only when you remember the voice of every law officer that ever chanted those words. . . .

VI.   Enter your car through the passenger door. Drive it without using reverse. Continue for one week or until you remember a rez car is not a picturesque metaphor.

VII.   Read the police report in your hometown paper. Read the letters to the editor in your tribal paper. Read the minutes from the last RBC meeting. Read the propaganda from each candidate in the tribal election. List every area of disagreement and try to decide who is telling the truth.

VIII.   In summer, turn off the AC and open the windows to let in the flies and mosquitoes. . . .

XI.   Recite the names of all the suicided Indians. (1997, 64–65)

Blaeser's poem achieves several things at once: Through its acknowledgement of bleak reservation realities, it cautions against idealizing life on the reserve, which (also in Native writing) is often romanticized as the last resort of tradition and wholeness. Still, by portraying these realities as a shared experience, as a struggle Native people have to go through together, the text also creates a bond. It directs unifying humor at a state of existence that is admittedly far from ideal, but still gives the impression of a caring community, the only home many Native people experience. Accordingly, the poem eventually recommends "XII. If all fails, move back" (65) — an ending that underlines the deep-rootedness of many Native people in their community.

Not the least important aspect of humor in Native cultures and Native writing is its capacity to act as a coping strategy and to promote healing from all kinds of emotional trauma, including some of the destructive effects of colonization.[20] Humor enables Native people to not only confront but also overcome hurtful situations and issues, as it can "take the bruises and scars of depression, oppression and suppression and act as a salve or tonic to take the pain away. It often works as an antidote, even" (Taylor 2005, 69). With regard to contemporary Native writing, healing humor may work on different levels. Coping and healing may happen *within* the text, that is, on the level of plot, as in Sherman Alexie's short story "The Approximate Size of My Favorite Tumor." This tragicomic and beautifully bizarre homage to the strength of Native humor in the face of horror relates the story of Jimmy Many Horses, who calls humor "an antiseptic that cleaned the deepest of personal wounds" (1994, 164) and can't stop cracking jokes even as he is dying of cancer. While humor here does not heal in a medical sense, since it cannot alleviate the symptoms themselves, it offers a way of keeping one's sanity and dignity. The text implies that by adopting the attitude of the trickster — who is, after all, the ultimate survivor — that is, by taking nothing too seriously, one can cope with everything. *The Heirs of Columbus* even more explicitly spells out Gerald Vizenor's belief in the healing powers of humor (see Vizenor in D. Miller 1995, 80): Not only is Point Assinika termed "the first nation in the histories of the modern world dedicated to protean humor and the genes that would heal" (Vizenor 1991, 119), the heirs are reported to have found a way to treat deformed tribal children with humor: "scientists are only part of the healing, as you know. The heirs, and a collection of people too incredible to describe . . . [heal] with stories and humor, and what they say becomes, in some way, the energy that heals" (164).

Yet rather than being but part of the plot, healing humor in this and many other instances of Native writing extends *beyond* the text itself. As Blaeser writes: "Through Vizenor's new Columbus story, his other trickster tales and his narrative histories, readers in general and perhaps tribal people in particular are, like the deformed children of the *Heirs* novel, 'mended in one way or another'" (1998, 172). That is, humor affects healing on the metalevel between text and reader. It counters the sense of alienation, disorientation, and betrayal that, although not to be mistaken as "the Native condition" in general, may afflict Native people as a consequence of their present situation. Taking the problems that arise from being rather powerless with a grain of trickster salt can enable Native people to transform traumatic experiences into subjects of communal laughter. Inevitably, Native people in the vein of DuBoisian "double consciousness" will be aware of the "Indian" stereotypes held by mainstream society. To apply these stereotypes to themselves in parody and mocking laughter not only exposes the distorting and erroneous outside views to ridicule; it draws the group together.

According to Vizenor, people experience a "kind of liberation [of] the mind" (172) from humor, indicating that trickster can be a healer also or especially from the "sickness" of strict categorization and the rigidity of conventionalized views. Loosening restrictive classifications, humor is instrumental in upsetting established values and images, allowing for flexibility and openness. In addition to its capacities as a coping strategy, it therefore opens up a space for the renegotiation of Native cultural values. In expressing approval or disapproval with regard to issues especially important to the group or an individual's behavior within the group, humor may either reinforce existing views and shared values, or try to revise them (see Fine 1983, 174; Fagan 2005, 35; Lewis 1989, ix, 36; Martineau 1972). Through this "control function" (see Stephenson 1951; Martineau 1972) it can affirm common sentiments or reinforce traditions by ridiculing deviant views or violations of the norm. But it can also do the opposite by subversively questioning or dislocating accepted paradigms, undermining moral standards and established rules. In Native cultures, such community humor has a long tradition. Group coherence in tribal cultures generally held far greater importance than in Western societies, as is expressed in the concept of "minding your relations" common to most Native cultures.[21] A violation of the norms in institutionalized clowning, simple teasing, or trickster stories could be of literally vital importance, as it tested group resilience through permitted disrespect (see Lincoln 1993, 312). A disguised code of conduct, it inoffensively held up a mirror to transgressors:[22]

> For centuries before the white invasion, teasing was a method of control of social situations by Indian people. Rather than embarrass members of the tribe publicly, people used to tease individuals they considered out of step with the consensus of tribal opinion. In this way egos were preserved and disputes within the tribe of a personal nature were held to a minimum. (V. Deloria 1977, 147)

Teasing as a means of intragroup control is still omnipresent in Native cultures, leading Drew Hayden Taylor to quip: "You ain't Indian if you can't tease or be teased — it's mentioned somewhere in the Royal Commission on Aboriginal People, Section 4.3.6: 'The Federal Government will acknowledge the right of all Aboriginal people in this country to tease, be teased, as well as hunt and fish and all the rest of it' " (2002, 48).

Richard Wagamese's novel *Keeper 'n Me* is packed with such humor in the form of harmless banter. The novel's young Ojibway protagonist Garnet Raven has grown up in White foster care in an urban environment. While Ojibway by blood, the young man has next to no knowledge of Ojibway culture at the time of his return to his family on the reserve. Consequently, his presence there is not uncontroversial, giving rise to some questions that are emblematic of the present discussion of Nativeness, first and foremost, whether he is Indian due to his descent or, to the contrary, can never be Indian due to his lack of cultural education (that is, whether Nativeness is determined by nature or nurture). Wagamese's novel here illustrates how teasing in effect conveys Native attitudes and ideas by integration rather than confrontation. At the time of his first visit to the reserve, Garnet goes through an Afro-phase (initiated by the closest he ever came to a surrogate family, his Black Toronto friends) and in addition to an afro hairstyle and a cloud of perfume wears "mirrored shades, a balloon-sleeved yellow silk shirt with the long tapered collar, lime green baggy pants with the little cuffs and my hippest pair of platform shoes, all brown with silver spangles, and three gold chains around my neck" (31). This look by itself makes Garnet visibly different from his Ojibway relatives, as evidenced in the reaction of the cab driver hired by Garnet to take him out to the reserve: "you're not quite what we're used to seein' from our Indians, y-you know" (32). Upon his arrival, Garnet's community does not take long to recover from its initial awed silence and express its incredulous amazement by teasing: " 'Sure he's a Raven?' someone asked. 'Looks like a walkin' fishin' lure or somethin'!' 'Yeah, that hair's a good reminder to the kids 'bout foolin' round with the electrical!' 'An' what's that smell? Smell like that should have fruit flies all around his head!'" (35). Humorously, they signal to him that he does not conform to regular Ojibway appearance, both because of what he wears and because of his undue attention to his exterior in general.

As a result of his status as a cultural outsider, Garnet at first does not understand this kind of humor. In retrospect, he can give a name to it, though: "Teasing's big around here. . . . You get lotta teasing from people on accounta teasing's really a way of showing affection for someone" (40–41). Accordingly, his family greets him with comments such as "Not Halloween yet, is it?" "Thought he was coming from T'rana, not Disneyland!" and "Ahh, he's just dressed fer huntin' . . . Wanna make sure he don't get mistook fer no deer" (41). Playing on his last name, Garnet's sister Jane even tells him that he is a "funny-lookin' Indyun right now, kinda look more like a parakeet than a raven"; yet she continues: "but this is your home, these are your people and your family" (43). All the teasing Garnet is subjected to is, after all, a way of establishing and affirming his Native identity. Testing his capabilities of cultural belonging, the humorous challenges serve both integration and instruction. On the one hand, they try to convey cultural competence by pointing out how he deviates from Ojibway standards and what he will have to learn to fit into the community and survive on the reserve — a strategy that runs throughout the novel. On the other hand, they signal acceptance by addressing Garnet in Native communicative patterns, including him in a community that is tightly knit together by such familiar teasing.

The latter aspect is borne out especially at the end of the novel. Wagamese's text comes to a humorous full circle when Garnet, after several years of apprenticeship with elder Keeper, is given back the outfit he wore when he arrived on the reserve — transformed into Ojibway attire that signals his hybrid identity: His lime green pants now line a buckskin jacket, and his yellow balloon-sleeved shirt has been converted into a ribbon-shirt. In a final instance of teasing-as-bonding, Keeper amiably ribs Garnet: "'Do you know what kinda underwear you were wearin' that day? ' . . . they just might surface in that beaver hat'" (210). Communal and healing humor and teasing in Wagamese's partly autobiographical novel turn out to be of prime importance in helping Garnet overcome his traumatic past, his lifelong sense of alienation and disorientation. These practices instruct him about his Ojibway heritage, integrate him, and solve conflicts that might arise within the community due to his presence, while simultaneously avoiding a sentimental idealization of Ojibway life that such a happy-ending, homing-in plot would otherwise be prone to.

Amidst dominant Western societies that (however covertly) for the longest time advocated an ideal of assimilation, searching for and adhering to tradition constitute important issues for Native cultures. People of Native descent have had to face enormous changes in their encounters with Euro-America. Today, they follow lifestyles so diverse that a common denominator is sometimes hard to find, leading to heated discussions of the very concept of Nativeness as such. Conflicts can and do arise among Native people, depending, for instance, on whether they hold a traditional or more progressive outlook, on whether they are urban or reservation-based, fullbloods or mixedbloods, educated in the Western academic system and/or in traditional Native ways. Humor enters into these renegotiations by both feeding on and acting as "social lubricant" for (Lewis 1989, 36) the intragroup controversy about contemporary Native identity. As English explains:

> The inescapable heterogeneity of society, the ceaseless conflict of social life, the multiple and irreconcilable patterns of identification within which relationships of solidarity and hierarchy must be negotiated — these are what our laughter is "about. " . . . While humor seeks to shore up identifications and solidarities, it does so by working on those very contradictions of "society" which assure that all such identifications and solidarities will be provisional, negotiable, unsettled. (1994, 9–10)

Through humorous discourse, contemporary Native writers may indeed seek to "shore up identifications and solidarities" in the controversial negotiation of Nativeness, exposing certain characteristics or opinions to ridicule and thus implicitly promoting others. At the same time, a humorous debate of Nativeness is based on the very recognition of the diversity and instability inherent in contemporary concepts of Native identity, and thus defies homogenizing tendencies. In contrast to dogmatic essentialism, any discussion in the playfully destabilizing register of humor is by definition aware of its own provisionality, that is, of the fact that it can only offer *possible* points of identification. In this manner, contemporary Native writing comically broaches anxieties and divisive subjects such as exaggerated essentialism, the internalization of imposed stereotypes or legal definitions, and the assimilation of Native people to Euro-American values and ambitions.

Through humor, tradition itself may be presented as flexible and alive rather than a rigid ethnostalgic principle, as in Keeper's tricksterlike concept of "Tra-dish-unn" (2), his panacea for fooling White people, getting help, and teaching; or in the ideas of Onatima and Luther, the Choctaw elders in Louis Owens's novel *Bone Game* (1994). The two come all the way from Mississippi to California to help Cole, the novel's protagonist, overcome his recurring nightmares. On the one hand, they look at Cole's afflictions from within a framework of Native spirituality and mythology and want to "exorcize" the spirits that haunt him by traditional means. On the other hand, they are also very much in touch with contemporary realities and endowed with an unshakeable sense of humor. Onatima, for instance, is well aware that more than just spiritual factors contribute to Cole's crisis and admonishes him: "It's time you got some perspective on this midlife crisis and stopped feeling sorry for yourself. . . . Indian male menopause is a terrible thing" (144–45). In addition to defying romanticizing clichés about Native spirituality, this observation also suggests that traditional concepts by themselves no longer suffice to explain contemporary conditions, and that more flexible and hybrid approaches are needed to deal with a complex and hybrid contemporary Native existence. Accordingly, the traditional path to a cure that Luther prescribes to Cole — and that eventually contributes to his survival and victory over the evil gambler — is comically put into perspective. Luther ceremoniously tells Cole: "You have prepared yourself well, Grandson. For many months now you have put away the appetites of men. You have fasted and gone into the sweat lodge, and you have prayed and been given a vision" (208); Cole's response, however, dislodges these facts from Luther's traditional frame of interpretation and thus gives the scene a decidedly funny twist:

> Cole shook his head. "I think we may be dealing with semantics here, Uncle Luther. The truth is that I haven't been with a woman for all these months not because I was being pure, but because I was afraid." He glanced at Onatima. "I've done what you call fasting only because until Abby came I was too sick to eat. Alex dragged me into the sweat lodge and into another ceremony in which I ate a hallucinogenic drug that nearly killed me. To call all of that purification is wish fulfillment, I'm afraid." (208)

It is the incongruous clash between the paradigms of traditional healing and contemporary realities that generates the humor, intensified by the fact that Cole's response almost constitutes a form of (semantic) discourse analysis of these incongruities. Yet, importantly, it is not tradition as such that is undercut through comic demystification. Rather, Cole's remark challenges romanticizing clichés or essentialist ideas about Native practices, implying that tradition has to face contemporary realities, and that humor is its best option to do so.

Marie Annharte Baker observes: "We are in the age (hangover of the new age) when it is fashionable to be orthodox even about one's Aboriginal identity. We must appreciate the many traditional Indians who want to follow custom in an authoritative, authoritarian, and are-so-sore-and-bitter-about-it manner" (1991, 48); she adds, however: "With a tendency to take ourselves too seriously, we have always needed trickster insurance" (48). Especially through the character of Luther, Owens demonstrates just what forms such trickster insurance may take. Luther is a traditional seer and healer, but unceremoniously enjoys such pranks as creating his own bogus traditions. Told by Cole that his braid is in his coffee,

Luther glanced at the cup, where the end of one braid soaked. "That's a
old Indian trick, Grandson, and I'm a old Indian. Us Choctaws always
did that for the warpath, you see, when we might not get coffee for a long
time. We'd go along sucking on braids. That's why we all got that black
hair, too. We used to all be blond-headed Indians, but good coffee wicks
right to the roots." He laid the toast down and lifted the braid from the
cup, carefully drying it with a napkin. "It's wonderful hearing the traditional stories of my ancestors," Cole added. (226)

Luther's humor here, on the one hand, amusingly defies the idea that "tradition" is only respected and respectable if approached with grave seriousness — an attitude more typical of Western religions than Native
ceremonies. On the other hand, it implicitly rejects the notion that Native
traditions have to be consistently safeguarded against "contamination" by
external influences and miscegenation. Quite on the contrary, throughout
the novel Owens subversively demonstrates that a nostalgic romanticizing
of tradition and a fundamentalist condemnation of Euro-American influences are ultimately detrimental to the survival of Native cultures. *Bone
Game* thus illustrates how, on a deeper level, lighthearted humor can break
down boundaries (past versus present, Native versus White) and facilitate
a constant negotiation of the complex situations Native cultures find themselves in today.

In addition to promoting flexibility, such a negotiation also entails criticism of an all-too-ready assimilation or a sellout of Native (cultural) values, however. Significant, in this context, are cases of Native politicians
who have been corrupted by the small share of decision-making power
they possess in the framework of tribal self-governance.[23] As Bruchac
points out, "humor can be used to remind people — who because of their
achievements might be feeling a little too proud or important — that they
are no more important than anyone else in the circle of life. Teasing someone who gets a little too 'tall' may help them shrink back to the right
height" (1987b, 26). Consequently, contemporary Native texts mock self-
possessed tribal authorities who put their power to their own, rather than
the community's, use. When, for instance, in Thomas King's novel *Truth
and Bright Water*, Franklin, the tribal chairman, complacently announces
his (conspicuously Puritan) credo that "the only people in this world who
eat are the ones who work for it," he is teased by his brother: "Unless they
can steal it. . . . Or get elected chief" (99). And the corruption of tribal
officials and their willing participation in the colonization of their own
people are parodied in Thom E. Hawke's chief "Ton O Bucks," who is on
"the same payroll as John [Wayne]" (Hawke 1998, 419); or in Sherman
Alexie's tribal chairman David Walks Along, who, as the name implies,
"walked along with BIA [Bureau of Indian Affairs] policy so willingly that
he took to calling his wife *a savage in Polyester pants*" (1994, 94). Walks
Along, in both *Reservation Blues* and *The Lone Ranger and Tonto Fistfight*

in Heaven, is satirically shown to be complicit in the oppression and exploitation of his community in return for personal power and privileges. As Alexie observes in an interview: "If there's only one thing we've assimilated fully as Native Americans, it's political corruption. For the most part, the tribal council people I've known have been self-serving, manipulative capitalists. And certainly tribal councils themselves are no different. After being powerless all their lives, they acquire a little power on the rez, and it corrupts them" (in Bellante and Bellante 1994, 14). In the depiction of such corrupt characters (and implicitly, their real life models), ridicule proves even more bitingly acerbic than overt indictment: Shared laughter at the expense of the transgressors unites the laughers in their judgment of the subject, and thus constitutes a univocal condemnation.

This union is exemplified in Paul Seesequasis's satirical story "The Republic of Tricksterism," in which greed for power, sex, and money drive the tribal chairman and his officials. Comprised of autobiographical, realistic/actual, and fictional/imaginative components, the story combines the author's family history with historical and political facts in the form of a trickster tale. At its center are the consequences of the internalization of colonial standards by tribal administrators, especially for people of mixed descent. Tobe, the Grand Chief portrayed in the text, went into politics in order to "attend conferences and get laid in hotels" (Seesequasis 1998, 412), and he distributes government money at his own discretion — for blonde assistants, luxurious offices, and shiny cars. Drunk on their power, he and his tribal council proclaim: "We are the Chiefs! . . . The big white men in Ottawa said so." Accordingly, they consider any criticism of their work "blasphemy and [a challenge to] our noble and sacred institutions" (415). Tobe exemplifies the "mimic man" (Bhabha 1994) who has adopted colonial paradigms in order to partake in colonial power (as underlined by his hyperbolic and pompous register), yet is but a puppet on the Canadian government's strings. The official announcement of Tobe's promotion to Grand Chief hence rationalizes: "Who better to speak the politicians' garble? Who better to hide the truth between platitudes of self-government and economic development than Tobe?" (416). In the character of Tobe, the text exposes the corruption of tribal politics with slanted satire. Moreover, it caustically points to the devastating effects of the unquestioning adoption of colonial legal standards by Native people. Tobe is shown to have embraced and vigorously reinforced the discriminating practices of the Indian Act designed by the Canadian government: "He denounced Indian women who had married white men," and "chased mixedbloods from the reserve and has created a world of urban orphans" (411, 414).[24] The mixedblood narrator suffers from this policy, as he is one of the "prisoners of bureaucratic apartheid, of red tape and parliamentary decrees" (411). His family, as a result of the marriage between his Cree mother and White father, is in effect banished from their community on the reserve, and he grows up in the city in a world that never fully accepts him. In contrast, Tobe, despite being the mixedblood son of a Cree father and White mother himself, can even become Grand Chief — and hypocritically orthodox about his Indian identity at that: "He would grow up as a mixed-race pure-blood, purer than thou and given to exaggerating the quantity of his half cup of tribal blood. Tobe lived in denial of his white parentage . . . The Indian Act enabled Tobe to imagine himself as pure-blood" (411).

Seesequasis's story fictionalizes a sad reality: As Lawrence points out, "it has been the Indian Act which has played the largest role . . . in excluding mixed-race people from Native communities, thereby externalizing them from 'Indianness' " (2000, 81). To address this dark chapter of internal discrimination in Native Canadian history with satiric humor conveys at once biting criticism and the possibility of healing laughter. In its blurring of boundaries between history and story, the text humorously opens up a space for both instructive commentary and coping. On the one hand, the text is interspersed with facts from recent Canadian (Indian) politics: Tobe is the "Grand Chief of the Fermentation of Saskatchewan Indian Nations (FSIN)" (411), a comically distorted version of the Federation of Saskatchewan Indian Nations (FSIN), which has its own history of corruption scandals; he shakes hands with then Saskatchewan Premier Allan Blakeney; and he is described as having enthusiastically "joined Wild Jean's Indian Affairs Bandwagon and Wild West Show" (412), a sarcastic renaming of the Ministry of Indian Affairs and Northern Development, which between 1968 and 1974 was headed by later Prime Minister Jean Chrétien. On the other hand, the story is very much a traditional trickster tale and fulfills this genre's traditional didactic tasks. The narrator's uncle Morris, who is identifiable through various clues as Métis activist Malcolm Norris (1900–1967), is a "rigoureau; a mixed-blood shape-shifter." He assails the corrupt tribal administrators or "cannibal spirits with the hairy hearts" (413), as he calls them in the register of traditional mythology. And he wants to establish a "Republic of Tricksterism," the revolution and proclamation of this "Republic of Tricksterism" fictionalizing the events during Norris's time as the director of the Prince Albert Indian Métis Friendship Centre in the 1960s. Miscegenation thus not only determines the text's subject matter in describing the Native discrimination against mixed marriage and mixedblood offspring, it is also the very principle of the text itself, which in humorous hybridity mixes fact and fiction, Western history or a realistic narrative mode and Native storytelling.

Healing and criticism, two major aspects of the text's humor, figure both within the text itself and between text and reader. Within the framework of the trickster tale, the "cannibal spirits" feed on people's souls — a sickness to be cured only with humor, so that the healing humor the story administers to its readers reappears within the story itself in the form of

Morris's healing laughter: At the clinic where the mother's narrator works as a nurse, Morris offers "humour to those who were forgetting how to laugh. He played the compassionate trickster, upsetting the plans of the cannibal spirits, and frustrating the violent emotions of the hairy hearts. Many a body was purged of poison" (413). The text's humorous criticism of corruption and internal colonization is exemplified within the story when Tobe and his "Indiancrats" (416) are "'trick[ed] with humour. . . . We will create a story. A myth. That is something that cannot be destroyed by violence. It will annoy him immensely, because we will create a world he cannot shatter with hate for it exists here,' Morris said, pointing to his head" (414). With his tale about a "Republic of Tricksterism, a place where humour rules and hatred is banished . . . [and a]ll skins are equal" (414), Seesequasis spins just such a story and puts it to work on readers' minds to dislodge internalized colonial stratifications. The text frustrates colonial paradigms and overthrows the strict categorizations that had been established by the Canadian government along the lines of *divide et impera*. (Indeed, many Native people today "behave as if the different categories of Nativeness, such as status Indian, nonstatus, and Métis, have always existed — instead of recognizing that these categories were created by the settler government to divide us"; Lawrence 2000, 76). It creates a healthy amount of chaos, transgresses established boundaries, and breaks down hard and fast norms in flaunting both racial categorizations and the conventions of fiction. Seesequasis himself explains:

> I want my writing to deal with transformation and crossing boundaries. I hope my writing contains a "trickster spirit" in that it challenges the readers as much as it entertains them. . . . I think we are entering a new nomadic age where especially in the urban wilderness, there are cross-breeding, cross-gender, and cross-culture things happening. Nothing is pure and the only constants are love and change. In these new meetings I think the trickster can thrive. (Seesequasis in Moses and Goldie 1998, 519)

"The Republic of Tricksterism" thus imaginatively fulfils Seesequasis's and the trickster's common agenda of shaking things up in its renegotiation of established values and concepts of Nativeness. Despite Morris's death, Seesequasis's story ends on an upbeat note: Bill C-31 ends the legal discrimination of people of mixed Native-White ancestry, and Morris — just like tricksters in traditional story cycles, who can reassemble themselves from parts and take on animal shape — somehow sneaks into the next story: "Rumour has it that even today he has led an army of termites into a certain national chief's organization where he is currently munching away at the legs of that chief's chair" (416).

In contrast, Jack Forbes's darkly humorous story "Only Approved Indians" denies readers such comic escape. Its humor hinges entirely on irony and sarcasm, building up throughout the story to deliver the final blow with disquieting force. The brief, carefully designed text offers a snapshot of the finals of an all-Indian basketball tournament to illustrate the devastating consequences of Native submission to colonial rules. Before the game has even started, the two finalist teams begin to question each others' Nativeness: Rumors start that the team from Tucson really consists of Chicanos, which would in effect disqualify them, since "the Indian Sports League had a rule that all players had to be of one-quarter or more Indian blood and that they had to have their BIA roll numbers available if challenged" (Forbes 1995, 3). Their opponents from the Great Lakes region can all produce the required proof of status, "their BIA iden- tification cards, encased in plastic," and thus qualify as "land-based, feder- ally-recognized Indians" (3). In addition to its ironic tone, the text comically undercuts the validity of official enrollment as a criterion for Nativeness by insinuating that the card-carrying Indians live off the reserve, do not speak their Native language, and that some of them are only 1/16th Indian. The Tucson team members, who lack BIA identifica- tion cards, in contrast, are shown to be very much rooted in their tribal traditions, land, and language. Still, in the ensuing discussion, the Great Lakes players and tournament officials argue increasingly along the lines of United States Indian policy. One of the Tucson players who doesn't have a status card is even told by the Great Lakes players: "You're not an offi- cial Indian. All official Indians are under the white man's rule now. We all have a number given to us to show that we are recognized" (4). Eventually, the Tucson team is disqualified, and the Great Lakes team, amidst huge applause, is declared winner by default.

Forbes's humor may evoke uneasiness rather than delightful laughter from (especially Native) readers, due to the increasingly obvious internal colonization of the majority of the Native characters. This "unsettling" strategy peaks in the story's ambiguous final sentence: Commenting on the disqualification, a "white BIA official wiped the tears from his eyes and said to a companion, 'God bless America. I think we've won'" (5). The tragicomic parable thus demonstrates that when Native communities adopt discriminating Euro-American legal definitions, they also "by default" (that is, by lack of Native resistance against or even reflection upon such policies) declare the colonizer the ultimate winner. It questions colonial criteria for Native identity and introduces culturally based alter- natives (James Clifford's "Identity in Mashpee" argues along similar lines). The text once again demonstrates how contemporary Native writ- ers employ humor to sustain rather than foreclose dialog (which might be the effect of overt criticism): Through humor, they get readers to imagi- natively and emotionally experience the consequences of colonization, and they spark a reconsideration that serious analysis may not be able to effect.

Both of these stories by Seesequasis and Forbes shed an ironic light on the politics of Native identity and critically engage in the constant renegotiation of Nativeness. They caution Native readers against the danger of conceptualizing themselves in colonial frames of reference. This, as Forbes's story so acerbically shows, would comprise the colonizers' most triumphant victory, after all. Using humor as an instrument to loosen the fronts in an emotionally charged discussion, they illustrate the dire need for a decolonizing of the mind. Morris's summons to "Burn your status cards . . . and throw away your colonial pedigree papers. Don't let the white man define us" is directed not only at his mixedblood urban audience within the text, it extends beyond the text to (especially Native) readers holding orthodox beliefs about blood quanta or colonial legislation. By calling attention to the counterproductive consequences of internalized hierarchies and the hostile climate in which these controversies take place,[25] both texts demonstrate how desperately Baker's "trickster insurance" is really needed.

In his (non-fictional) tongue-in-cheek analysis "How Native is Native if You're Native?" Drew Hayden Taylor attempts to answer this need by becoming "Drew Hayden Taylor-Aboriginal Attitude and Attributes Assessor (DHT-AAAA)" (2000b, 58). He comically traces essentialist rejections of miscegenation, urban life, Western education, and economic success to their advocates' insecurities about their own Nativeness, ridiculing the idea that "the only true 'Native' people are uneducated, poor people with poor vocabularies who live on reserves" (58). Throughout, the text uses humor as a negotiation strategy for determining Nativeness in a minefield of clichés, essentialism, and assimilation, and thus presents Taylor's own survival strategy in a nutshell. According to Taylor, nowadays "the darker you are, the more acceptable you are," an attitude that "reeks of potential internal racism within our community" (2001, 106). The son of a White father and Ojibway mother, who grew up on the Curve Lake reserve in Ontario, Taylor himself is often assailed because of his light-skinned, blue-eyed appearance (which gave origin to his four volumes of humorous *Observations from a Blue-Eyed Ojibway*). Tired of explaining about his mixed heritage, he formulates a

> declaration of independence. My declaration of independence.
> I've spent too many years explaining who and what I am repeatedly, so, as of this moment, I officially secede from both races. I plan to start my own separate nation. Because I am half Ojibway and half Caucasian, we will be called the Occasions. And of course, since I'm founding the new nation, I will be a special occasion. (1998, 8)

Instead of accepting the role of the deplorable deracinated mixedblood, Taylor comically transforms his mixed ancestry into something positive.

With trickster humor, he transcends established categories and defies dichotomies that are considered insurmountable by people on both sides of the racial boundary. Refusing to trod along the "predetermined and well-worn path between signifier and signified" for "the sign 'Indian'" (Owens 1992, 231), Taylor comically emancipates himself, his declaration of independence liberating him, first and foremost, from restrictive notions of Indianness. For Taylor — as for Seesequasis, who declares himself "fascinated with the creative potential of miscegenation" (in Moses and Goldie 1998, 518) — hybridity as epitomized in the merger of Ojibway and Caucasian into Occasion is not burden but chance, an enrichment and a source of creativity.

The fictional character who most clearly embodies such an attitude is Vivian Twostar, in Louise Erdrich and Michael Dorris's collaborative novel *The Crown of Columbus* (discussed at the beginning of this chapter). Vivian defies the seriousness of the subject of Native identity by discussing her own heritage in a register vastly incongruous with a supposedly solemn subject. She refers to her baby daughter Violet, who is of mixed Native-WASP parentage, in terms of "beaded herringbone, the look for the nineties" (Erdrich and Dorris 1991, 64), and her self-description forcefully testifies to what Baker has called "one of the greatest gifts of an Aboriginal heritage": "To be able to laugh at oneself . . . . For even the one who is the teensy bit Indian, the gift of this self-clowning is humungous" (48):

> I belong to the lost tribe of mixed bloods, that hodgepodge amalgam of hue and cry that defies easy placement. When the DNA of my various ancestors — Irish and Coeur d'Alene and French and Navajo and God knows what else — combined to form me, the result was not some genteel, undecipherable puree that comes from a Cuisinart. You know what they say on the side of the Bisquick box, under instruction for pancakes? Mix with fork. Leave lumps. That was me. (166)

Not only does Vivian's identity have "lumps," unresolved aspects that arise from originating from more than one culture, she also illustrates that identity has little to do with "identical" in the sense of constant sameness, that it is no fixed, unalterable core but always in flux, adapting to changing contexts and expectations. Vivian knows that she constantly has to reinvent herself, depending on the circumstances. Rather than decrying a missing sense of belonging, however, she stresses the positive aspects of such flexibility and considers herself enriched by "a million stories":

> There are advantages to not being this or that. You have a million stories, one for every occasion, and in a way they're all lies and in another way they're all true. When Indians say to me, "What are you?" I know exactly what they mean, and answer Coeur d'Alene. I don't add "Between a

quarter and a half" because that's information they don't ask for, first off (though it may come later if I screw up and they're looking for reasons why). If one of my Dartmouth colleagues asks me, "Where did you study," I pick the best place, the hardest one to get into, in order to establish that I belong. If a stranger on the street asks me where Violet gets her light brown hair and dark skin, I say the Olde Sodde and let them figure it out. There are times when I control who I'll be, and times when other people decide. I'm not all anything, but I'm a little bit of a lot. My roots spread in every direction and if I water one set of them more often than others, it's because they need it more. To the College I am a painless affirmative action, to Roger I'm presentably exotic, to Nash I'm too white, to Grandma I'm too Anglo, to Hilda and Racine I'm the romantic American friend. (166–67)

Vivian plays this game of repositioning herself like the traditional shape-shifting trickster: with humor and creativity. Rather than ponder its jeopardies, she enjoys the opportunities offered by her mixed origins, despite the precariousness of her self-conceptualization. The problem Vivian sees herself confronted with is not her mixed origin, but keeping her job and getting tenure despite the fact that her CV is "top-heavy with teaching experience at four different schools but light on . . . scholarly production" (17). In this dilemma, Vivian tricksterlike even puts her mixedblood origin to use for tipping the scales in her favor, and assures herself that in these politically correct times no one at Dartmouth would really "fire the only aboriginal assistant professor" (17). She thus refuses the role of the victim, and her defiance explodes the very categories of center and margin. To identify with representations that show Native or mixedblood people as tragic (but inevitable) casualties in the process of colonization would, in effect, perpetuate White hegemony. Vivian demonstrates how this cycle can be broken through a humorous and reimaginative shift in perspective:

> I've read learned anthropological papers written about people like me. We're called marginal, as if we exist anywhere but on the center of the page. Our territory is the place for asides, for explanatory notes, for editorial notation. We're parked on the bleachers looking into the arena, never the main players, but there are advantages to peripheral vision. Out beyond the normal bounds you at least know where you're not. You escape the claustrophobia of belonging, and what you lack in security you gain by realizing — as those insiders never do — that security is an illusion. We're jealous of innocence, I'll admit that, but as the hooks and eyes that connect one smug core to the other we have our roles to play. "Caught between two worlds," is the way it's often put in clichéd prose, but I'd phrase if differently. We are the *catch*. (167)

This play on words counts on the multiple connotations and denotations evoked by "catch" (see also Rayson 1991, 28), the most obvious being that of a prize, a valuable trophy to be gained. Read in confluence with Vivian's observation on "the hooks and eyes that connect one smug core to the other," it implies that both Native and White communities should consider themselves enriched by such human links, who — as "catch" in the sense of clasp or latch entails — fasten these societies together by enhancing mutual understanding. On the other hand a "catch" is also something to get caught on or tripped up by; like the "lumps" in the batter, it is something not smooth enough to be easily passed over. Accordingly, Vivian's unwillingness to conform to stereotypical expectations humorously "catches" the readers' attention and effects an imaginative liberation from fixed notions by directing healing laughter at something usually considered too serious to joke about. Most importantly, by conceptualizing herself as "the catch," Vivian confidently reclaims representational power for herself. In light of the existing depictions of the tragic character of the halfbreed, Vivian cannot identify with the images she is presented with. She therefore humorously reimagines mixedblood heritage anew, creating different images and thus new representational options (for) herself.

Clearly, the question of Nativeness entails far more than blood quanta. Surrounded by an overwhelming Euro-American society and culture, Native people in general continuously struggle with retaining and negotiating a distinct cultural identity for themselves. In the face of enormous cultural destruction, humor often constitutes the only possible option to address the loss of cultural origins and the ensuing disorientation. One of the most self-ironic accounts of a Native identity crisis comes from the Spokane narrator of Sherman Alexie's story "The Life and Times of Estelle Walks Above":

> To this day I rarely look in the mirror and think, I am an Indian. I don't necessarily know what an Indian is supposed to be. After all, I don't speak my tribal language, and I'm allergic to the earth. If it grows, it makes me sneeze. In Salish, "Spokane" means "Children of the Sun," but I'm slightly allergic to the sun. If I spend too much time outside, I get a nasty rash. I doubt Crazy Horse needed talcum powder to get through a hot summer day. Can you imagine Sacajawea sniffling her way across the Continental Divide? I'm hardly the poster boy for aboriginal pride. (Alexie 2003, 134)

Asking not only "am I Indian?" but "what is Indian?" the text tragicomically illustrates how extended colonization, how being imagined and defined by an overpowering society, calls into question the very tenets of one's identity. Crazy Horse (1840–77), the famous Lakota leader who resisted the US government's efforts to confine all Native Americans to reservations and defeated Custer at Little Big Horn, is a pan-Indian hero; Sacajawea (1786–1884), in contrast, together with Pocahontas and Squanto ranks among the most well-known and cherished "Indians" in the eyes of mainstream America, and is sometimes considered a traitor to indigenous people for leading Lewis and Clark across the "unexplored" continent. In this jumble of representations, where to select one's own constituents of Native identity? The incongruity between the narrator's self-description and the typically "Indian" characteristics and icons of Native American history is more than just funny. On the one hand, humor humanizes the narrator for the reader, frees him from the grasp of popular clichés of "Indianness," and defies discursive patterns that refer to Nativeness exclusively in terms of moral indignation and/or (self-)pity. On the other hand, the passage raises disconcerting questions about authenticity, identity, and representation. In his search for reliable criteria for Nativeness, the narrator ends up partly complying with popular ideas that in general confine Native people to the past. He cannot find Nativeness in external markers, announcing that "maybe I am proud to be an Indian. But I don't want to wear a T-shirt with my tribal enrollment number printed on the front and a photograph of Sitting Bull ironed on the back" (Alexie 2003, 135); yet by shunning external markers, Native people risk "vanishing" as Indians altogether, since they are no longer recognizable to a society that holds fixed images of Nativeness. Consequently, "in order to be recognized, to claim authenticity in the world—*in order to be seen at all*—the Indian must conform to an identity imposed from the outside" (Owens 1998, 12–13).

The resulting distortion of Native self-conceptualization is among the most devastating consequences of colonization: In an attempt to be as "Indian" as possible, Native people partly resort to stereotypical images of Indianness that were only simulacra to begin with. In addition to the sarcastic dismantling of the adoption of Euro-American legal standards and essentialist notions of purity, a further aspect of the project of humorously liberating Native people from restrictive ideas is therefore to draw attention to the danger of complying with externally imposed clichés. A literary (and filmic) renegotiation of contemporary Native identity not only subverts stereotypes themselves; it cautions against tendencies of actually *becoming* the "HollyWooden Indian." This is most comically exemplified in a scene from Sherman Alexie's screenplay *Smoke Signals* (1998), based on several of the stories from his collection *The Lone Ranger and Tonto Fistfight in Heaven*. Thomas Builds-the-Fire, a notorious storyteller, and Victor Joseph (characters also appearing in Alexie's novel *Reservation Blues*) are on a bus trip from Spokane, Washington, to Phoenix, Arizona, to retrieve the remains of Victor's deceased father. Victor, unnerved by Thomas's constant stories, rebukes him for allegedly emulating the Hollywood cliché of the "Indian sage":

> VICTOR: You're always trying to sound like some damn medicine man or something. I mean, how many times have you seen *Dances With Wolves*? A hundred, two hundred times?
> *Embarrassed, Thomas ducks his head.*

VICTOR: (*cont'd*) Oh, jeez, you have seen it that many times, haven't you? Man. Do you think that shit is real? God. Don't you even know how to be a real Indian?

THOMAS: (*whispering*) I guess not.

Victor is disgusted.

VICTOR: Well, shit, no wonder. Jeez, I guess I'll have to teach you then, enit?

Thomas nods eagerly. (61)

Thomas's grinning eagerness and appearance seem to underline Victor's accusation: His slender figure is clad in an old-fashioned suit, he wears thick glasses and braids, and he carries his money in a penny jar. Especially in contrast to Victor, whose jeans and cowboy boots, broad shoulders, and mane of black hair give off the air of a contemporary version of the "Indian brave," Thomas appears both un-Indian and decidedly uncool. The audience is thus effectively lured into unconsciously subscribing to Victor's criticism — although prior to this scene, there are indications that Thomas, the storyteller, is among the more traditional people on the Spokane reservation, whereas Victor cares little about Spokane cultural traditions, drinks too much, and would leave if only he could muster up the courage and energy to do so. The full satiric force of the scene is therefore unleashed only when Victor makes good on his offer and starts to lecture Thomas on how to be a "real Indian":

VICTOR: First of all, quit grinning like an idiot. Indians ain't supposed to smile like that. Get stoic.

Thomas tries to look serious. He fails.

VICTOR: No, like this.

Victor gets a very cool look on his face, serious, determined, warriorlike.

VICTOR: You got to look mean or people won't respect you. White people will run all over you if you don't look mean. You got to look like you just got back from killing a buffalo.

THOMAS: But our tribe never hunted buffalo. We were fishermen.

VICTOR: What? You want to look like you just came back from catching a fish? It ain't Dances With Salmon, you know? Man, you think a fisherman is tough? Thomas, you got to look like a warrior. (61–62)

As this emulation of the stoic warrior type reveals, Victor's own unreflected version of the "real Indian" is determined by Hollywood to a far greater degree than Thomas's initial self-conceptualization. The audience therefore starts out laughing at Thomas, but ends up laughing at itself: Caught within their formulaic expectations, they have mistaken Victor's warrior appearance and pseudocompetent demeanor for cultural expertise, and have accepted his assessment of Thomas as being un-Indian. As a result, they find themselves trapped in the recognition that they themselves, along with Victor, had unconsciously bought into the Hollywood stereotype. The joke, initially on Thomas for his awkwardness and lack of

"Indianness," through Victor's instruction forcefully turns back on Victor himself and, in its last consequence, on the audience. Humor here functions as an eye-opener in intercultural communication, most amusingly triggering a reconsideration of previously unquestioned images and ideas as well as a recognition of the intricacies inherent in the processes of representation and identity formation for Native people.

With its emphasis on community, humor in contemporary Native texts assures the continuity of Native cultures. Even more so than in the preceding sections, humor in this context has emerged as a strategy for coping or even healing, but also for critically scrutinizing Native cultural identity in an intracultural framework. Native writers put humor to use to help Native people free themselves from colonial paradigms — not only by achieving legal and political sovereignty, but also in their cultural self-conceptualizations. In the epigraph to this section, Alexie's Indians are "laughing pretty much at everybody," that is, also at themselves. It is this ability of Native people to direct humor at themselves and at the very concept of Nativeness that, furthering humor's traditional role, allows contemporary Native writers to renegotiate just what Nativeness is. By offering diverse, complex, and comically self-critical depictions of Native characters and communities, the texts provide Native people with manifold opportunities to reimagine themselves in a literally wholesome way.

Notes

[1] Sifton is ironically named after an "aggressive promoter of settlement in the West through the Prairie West movement, . . . a champion of the settlers who displaced the Native population and later superintendent of Indian Affairs in Laurier's government in the late 1890s" (Flick 1999, 150).

[2] The term stereotype itself — derived from the Greek words stereos, "solid," and typos, "to make an impression or model" — originated in printing, where it referred to a fixed plate cast or mold from which a large number of copies can be printed uniformly and efficiently (see Franke 1999, 19). "The word has since been generalized to mean any narrow and fixed idea about someone or something that distorts reality. A Stereotype is a preconceived and routinized belief, the cognitive part of a prejudice" (J. Price 1978, 218). Hanson and Rouse (1987) provide an encompassing overview in "Dimensions of Native American Stereotyping."

[3] In accordance with Hayden White's view of history as (a type of) narrative (see, e.g, 1978, 89, 98), the following discussion does not always distinguish between "factual" accounts or "fictional" texts as they pertain to the construction of "the Indian." This approach is also taken by Churchill in his (rather polemic) essay "Literature as a Weapon in the Colonization of the American Indian" (1992), which, like Gordon Johnston's more differentiated and semiotically oriented "An Intolerable Burden of Meaning: Native Peoples in White Fiction" (1987), provides a concise overview of the representation of Indians in American literary history.

4   For the influences of the Enlightenment and Puritanism and their underlying ideologies on the image of "the Indian" see Bordewich (1996, 34–35); P. Deloria (1998, 4); and Vickers (1998, 26–36, 40–44).

5   For analyses of the binary conceptualizations of Native women as "princesses" or "squaws" see Stedman (1982, 17–41); Acoose (1995, 43–45, 55); Brant (1998, 167); and in most detail R. Green (1990).

6   For detailed analyses of the stereotyping of Indians in the movies see Bataille and Silet (1980); Kilpatrick (1999); and Rollins and O'Connor (1998). Concise overviews are provided by Churchill, Hill, and Hill (1978); Lutz (2002, 48–61); and Stedman (1982, 155–72).

7   Garnet, the protagonist of Richard Wagamese's semiautobiographical novel *Keeper 'n Me* exemplifies this. Taken from his Ojibway family at age three and placed in White foster care, he recollects: "The most popular way of learning about Indians was television. Man, I remember Saturday mornings watching them Westerns and cheering like crazy for the cowboys like everyone else and getting all squirmy inside when the savages were threatening and feelin' the dread we were all supposed to feel when their drums would sound late at night. Injuns. Scary devils. Heathens" (1994, 12).

8   See Johnson (2000, 39), who demonstrates that Lionel's mimicry is closely intertwined with the very media he sells at the home entertainment center. For a discussion of Lionel as a mimic man see Horne (1999, 44–45).

9   See Bordewich (1996, 132–33) for the dubious origin and development of the speech now ascribed to Seattle, which in its most popular version was put together by Texan scriptwriter Ted Perry in 1972.

10   As Evans-Pritchard points out, reification and the wish for consumption often extend beyond the goods themselves to the people who sell them (see 1989, 97–98). This is the case in Eden Robinson's short story "Queen of the North," in which a tourist buys fry bread from Adelaine, a young Haisla, and eyes her as if she were up for sale as well. While she remains outwardly polite, her thoughts humorously reveal how she judges his behavior: "'How should I eat these?' he interrupted me. With your mouth, asshole. 'Put some syrup on them, or jam, or honey. Anything you want.' 'Anything?' he said, staring deep into my eyes. Oh, barf. 'Whatever'" (1999, 208; see Hoy 2001, 3–5, for a discussion of this scene).

11   With disarming mock-simplicity, Ottawa comedian Wilf Pelletier, in his "Dumb Indian" routine, lays open the very processes of devaluing Native cultures and draws attention to the ways in which colonized people are brought to see themselves according to the colonizers' standards: "Anyway, we thought knowing was inherent . . . just there, in your brains . . . like blood in veins or sight in eyes or hearing in ears. We didn't realize that knowing is all in books and that if you don't know how to read and have no books your brain will just remain vacant and you will never know anything. We were really in a bad way. All we knew how to read was smoke, and animal footprints, and clouds . . . things like that" (1972, 9).

12   As Bové describes it, "genealogy lets us confront how power constructs truth-producing systems in which propositions, concepts, and representations generally assign value and meaning to the objects of the various disciplines that treat them. . . . [It tries] to unmask discourses' association with power and materialities" (1990, 57, 60).

13 In "What Indians Do" (Ortiz 1999, 129–39), which reveals the source for "Men on the Moon" to be a Laguna Pueblo friend's narrative about his grandfather, Ortiz makes the trickster nature of the old man on whom Faustin is modeled very explicit.

14 Thomas King, in his tongue-in-cheek manner, elaborates on the difference between Euro-American and indigenous notions of history vs. story in "How I Spent My Summer Vacation: History, Story, and the Cant of Authenticity" (1998). He observes that Western historiography very much hinges on authenticity, on the distinction between "fact" and "fiction," whereas this distinction seems to be of little importance in Native cultural narrative. Rather, Native "storifications" of the past tend to be concerned with timeless characteristics and recurring constellations of (human) existence.

15 The Cree expression for White people.

16 Betty and Veronica are literally enamored with anything Native, their New Age consumer desire also extending to Native men as an exotic/erotic treat (see 43).

17 The name likely alludes to " 'Sun Bear' (Vincent LaDuke, a Chippewa) who . . . has been able to make himself rather wealthy over the past few years by forming (on the basis of suitable 'membership fees') what he calls 'the Bear Tribe,' and selling ersatz sweat lodge and medicine wheel ceremonies to anyone who wants to play Indian for a day and can afford the price of admission" (Churchill 1992, 190).

18 For the current policy on handling Native remains see Bordewich (1996, 162–203).

19 See Baker (1991, 48); Edmunds (1976, 149–50); Hirch (2005, 107); Kelly (2005, 62); and Taylor (2002, 48–49 and 2005, 75).

20 Healing humor was analyzed by Michelle A. Poirier in her MA Thesis "Humour is Good Medicine: The Algonquin Perspective on Humour in Their Culture and of Outsider Constructions of Aboriginal Humour" (Carleton University, 2000); by Kirby for "Zuni, Ojibway, and Canadian Dakota cultures, where clowning (especially caricature) was deemed therapeutic" (qtd. in Lowe 1994, 104); and by Toelken (1987, 390–91), who postulates a medicinal level of Coyote tales.

21 Thomas King explains about "All My Relations," a phrase used at the beginning or end of a speech, prayer, or story, that it is "first a reminder of who we are and of our relationship with both our family and our relatives. It also reminds us of the extended relationship we share with all human beings . . ., all the animate and inanimate forms that can be seen or imagined. More than that, 'all my relations' is an encouragement for us to accept the responsibilities we have within this universal family by living our lives in a harmonious and moral manner (a common admonishment is to say of someone that they act as if they have no relations)" (1992, ix).

22 Such teasing has been described for the Nez Perce by Skeels (1954, 58); for the Navajo by Toelken (1969, 1987, 389); for the Lakota by Theisz (1989, 15); and for the Pueblo by Whitaker (1947) and Babcock (1982). For teasing in a contemporary context see Basso (1979 on the Apache); Sanner (1993 on the Hopi); Shutiva (1994); and S. Pratt (1998).

23   For the problematic aspects of tribal self-governance (often no separation of executive, legislative, and judiciary powers) see Bordewich (1996, 72, 85–91). See also Jim Northrup's tongue-in-cheek essay on "Politics" (1997, 125–55) and his story "Jabbing and Jabbering" (1993, 137–47), which centers on the financial aspects of treaty rights and a corrupt tribal committee.

24   Canada's Indian policy aimed for over a century at complete assimilation. Between 1876 and 1985, under Canada's Indian Act, Native people not only lost their status if they were enfranchised (while "halfbreeds" were not recognized as "Indian" in the first place), in outrageous gender discrimination, Native women lost their status if they married non-Native or nonstatus Native men, while in the reverse case Native men kept status and their non-Native or nonstatus wives were even granted status. Especially after 1951, Native women who had lost status due to mixed marriage were forced to leave the reserve and were denied their treaty rights (see Lawrence 2000, 76–80). This only changed with Bill C-31, passed in 1985 in accordance with the Canadian Charter of Rights and Freedoms.

25   This charged controversy extends to the Native literary scene, with essentialist critics like Elizabeth Cook-Lynn openly denouncing urban mixedblood writers, Gloria Bird lamenting the assimilative tendencies of Native writers, and Leslie Silko accusing Louise Erdrich's work of not faithfully representing her community. Cook-Lynn lashes out against "the major self-described mixed-blood voices of the decade," among them Gerald Vizenor, Louis Owens, Michael Dorris, Thomas King, and Paula Gunn Allen: "While there is in the writing of these intellectuals much lip service given to the condemnation of America's treatment of the First Nations there are few useful expressions of resistance and opposition to the colonial history at the core of Indian/White relations" (1996, 67). Gloria Bird calls Sherman Alexie's characters "cultural anomalies" (1995, 49) and compares his writing to Spike Lee films for imitating mainstream ideas of Indians. Silko, finally, writes: "Although I read [Erdrich's novel *The Beet Queen*] three times, I am still not sure which characters are of Indian ancestry" (1986, 181), and she basically denounces the novel's reconciliatory mood and the unrealistic absence of suffering and pain in the Native realities depicted.

Conclusion

Words are powerful beyond our knowledge, certainly. And they are beautiful. Words are intrinsically powerful, I believe. And there is magic in that. Words come from nothing into being. They are created in the imagination and given life in the human voice.

— N. Scott Momaday, "The Magic of Words," 183

To study the word as such, ignoring the impulse that reaches out beyond it, is just as senseless as to study psychological experience outside the context of that real life toward which it was directed and by which it is determined.

— Mikhail Bakhtin, *The Dialogic Imagination*, 292

AS THESE EPIGRAPHS INDICATE, this study took into consideration not only the delight and magic that humor in contemporary Native writing sparks, but also its powerfully performative potential. Rather than only providing light-hearted entertainment or diversion (which of course it also does), humor in contemporary Native writing constitutes a strategic textual device: It promotes intercultural understanding — if often through humorous criticism — and participates in the positioning of the Native subject and Native communities in an intra- and intercultural context. Humor thus deals with serious issues, performs serious work, and should therefore be taken seriously. It is not irreconcilable with the traumatic aspects of Native history and the lasting consequences of colonization for Native existence. On the contrary, as this study has shown, humor serves simultaneously as an instrument for criticism, a cultural mediator, and a coping strategy, by providing an approach for addressing these issues in a manner that elicits both reconsideration and healing. Because humor relies on incongruity, on a surprising shift of perspective, it enables readers to transcend their accustomed ideas and culturally determined frames of reference. Moreover, because laughter relies on shared assessment, humor unwittingly generates a bond of understanding and consensus across contested terrain — be it within Native communities or across Native-White cultural boundaries.

This literally creative function of humor is what allows readers to reimagine Nativeness anew. Distorting representations that depict Native people as Other and reinvigorate the simulacrum of "the Indian" leave Native people bereft of valid points of identification, severely affecting Native cultural identity. It is within these dynamics that contemporary Native writing intervenes, as the wide and heterogeneous range of contemporary Native texts discussed here shows. It engages with, yet deconstructs and/or transforms previous representations. It makes the processes of Other-construction and naturalization of difference transparent and reencodes the images such processes generate, ultimately subverting dominant representations from within. Elder Luther in Louis Owens's novel *Bone Game* comically describes this latter process in rather confrontational terms: "They got too many stories about us. We need to write books about them now. Get even" (1994, 226). In this study, however, humorous writing has emerged as a form of inter- and intra-cultural mediation. Trickster tales in many Native cultures have served and continue to serve as tools for examining the state of society and for playfully imagining alternatives to existing paradigms and rules. Native writers today continue this tradition by putting humor and imagination to use in exploring and renegotiating concepts of Nativeness, both in Native-White relations and in the context of Native communities.

As postulated in the model of reimagining, it is through humor and imagination (the very terrain in which the idea of "the Indian" is so firmly lodged) that the texts discussed here create a liminal space where the readers' previous patterns of interpretation and frames of reference are rendered invalid. Humor here is both unsettling and liberating: It defamiliarizes or even shatters habitual depictions and assessments; yet by laughing, readers are free to reorient themselves, to imaginatively cross boundaries otherwise considered insurmountable, and to identify with unfamiliar characters and (Native) perspectives. By exposing degrading images and readings to such liberating laughter, the texts set off processes of reconsideration. In the process of establishing a framework for analyzing humor in Native writing, theories from Western cultural studies on the constitutive nature of representation, on the one hand, and traditional Native paradigms on the generative powers of language and imagination, on the other, complement one another, both implying a reciprocal connection between word and world. Thus both Stuart Hall and N. Scott Momaday basically conceptualize identities as stories we tell to ourselves and about ourselves. The texts discussed here accordingly offer *new* stories, putting humor and imagination to work in ultimately creating new realities and new identities. They spell out change by making readers reimagine previous representations and by enabling them to conceive of themselves and the world in different terms. Such reimagined images and interpretations — which, importantly, work *with* the powerful existing depictions and readings, yet endow them with different meanings — offer Native readers new points of identification, that is, new ways to imagine themselves. Conversely, they increase non-Native readers' sensitivity to and understanding of Native cultures and offer them a fresh view of their own culture, subversively enticing them to question and reconsider their own premises and epistemologies.

The linguistic, literary, and cultural forms and techniques Native writers enlist for these humorous *re*-presentations have been shown to originate in both Western and Native cultural traditions — which seems fitting in view of both the authors' backgrounds and envisaged readership and the strongly transcultural aspects of a reimagining through humor. Using techniques like parody, satire, caricature, and intertextuality (especially with regard to Western master narratives), contemporary Native writers most clearly re-present previous representations. Narrative devices such as irony and wordplay, through their playful double encoding and destabilizing effects, inherently disrupt linear readings, undermining one-dimensional authoritative depictions and interpretations *per se*. Like the mocking and/or indigenized use of English, they contest colonial paradigms on the level of linguistic representation itself. In addition, humor allows for multiple transgressions: It blurs the boundary between reality and fiction through the humorous use of metafiction, naming, and historical allusion; between the rational and the fantastic through trickster characters and the grotesque; but also between text and reader through the integration of elements and techniques from oral storytelling and the concept of trickster discourse. It consequently turns readers into participants by drawing them into the text and engaging them in imaginative activity to an extent that may change their practices of interpretation beyond the given text, that is, in subsequent encounters with similar ideas and images. The exploration of these and other techniques shows the writers themselves to be witty tricksters who — often through strategies of raising and defying audience expectations — humorously "lure" readers into reimagining stereotypical representations and predetermined interpretations.

Humor in texts by contemporary Native writers is directed at a wide array of topics. The history of colonization and its continued impact on contemporary Native existence leave their imprint on contemporary Native writing in general and on Native humor in particular. This is not to say, however, that humor in the texts discussed here hinges entirely on Native-White relations; clearly, much traditional humor that originates within and is directed at Native communities lives on in contemporary writing. The texts' humorous (re)negotiation of Nativeness accordingly engages with both externally assigned representations of Nativeness and notions of Native cultural identity coming from Native voices themselves.[1] The functional scope of such humor has been mapped as ranging all the way from criticism and the deconstruction of biased and clichéd images of Nativeness to reconstruction and healing, be it by ex*or*cising pain through laughter at the oppressor, or by ex*er*cising traditional Native humor in order to create the flexibility needed for contemporary conceptualizations of Nativeness. As the text analyses have demonstrated, in either case such humor shifts the readers' perspectives. It provides an instrument for inoffensively addressing controversial issues in Native-White history and relations, which, especially for Euro-American readers, can trigger reassessments: of the injustices perpetrated against America's indigenous populations, and of Euro-America's self-conceptualization.

Humor also constitutes one of the most promising means of shattering and imaginatively displacing stereotypical representations of Native people, with all their negative implications for Native cultural identity. Drew Hayden Taylor comments on audience reactions to his comedies in recent years: "It's amazing what can happen in a little over half a decade. The public looks at us now as being almost three-dimensional! It's astonishing what a good laugh will get you" (2002, 96). Moreover, humor serves a strategy for exposing how Western epistemologies and scientific, aesthetic, and historiographic discourses may inherently condition one-dimensionally Eurocentric responses and interpretations. Engaging with, yet sabotaging, such self-legitimizing processes of Other-construction from within, the texts discussed here most amusingly undercut Euro-American authoritative claims to "Truth" and (representational) power. They disrupt the very practices by which Euro-America retroactively bolsters its present position and represents its dominance as self-evident. Shifting accustomed patterns of interpretation, they unwittingly forge new allegiances and identifications, thereby defying Native people's relegation to the margin and their depiction in stereotypical terms.

Some of the most profound changes for Native cultures resulted from the imposition of Christianity and its concomitant anthropocentric and patriarchal structures. As illustrated in this analysis, contemporary Native texts address this subject with disruptive or hybrid humor, undercutting not so much the Judeo-Christian paradigm as such, but its notions of superiority and exclusivity as well as its missionary impetus. By the same token, ridiculing processes of appropriation and reification of Native cultures comprises a gesture of defiance that not only targets appropriative practices. Instead, it humorously exposes and subverts the unreflected self-assurance and matter-of-factness with which various Euro-American groups proceed to help themselves to Native cultural material.

Last but not least, humor plays an important constructive role in the constant and contested renegotiation of Nativeness within Native communities. Issues such as nature versus nurture-based concepts of Nativeness, the internalization of legal definitions and stereotypes, and essentialist tendencies in Native communities are addressed with — sometimes bitingly acerbic — humor. Similar to the humor directed at aspects of Native-White relations, intracultural Native humor serves as a mediator in a sometimes heated controversy, allowing for criticism without foreclosing further dialog. Simultaneously, as a strategy for healing and coping, such community-based humor proves survival humor in the best sense, ensuring the continuity of Native cultures. In 1969, Vine Deloria wrote: "Humor, all Indians will agree, is the cement by which the coming Indian movement is held together. When a people can laugh at themselves and laugh at others and hold all aspects of life together without letting anybody drive them to extremes, then it seems to me that that people can survive" (1977, 167).

As this study has shown, contemporary Native writing has since borne out Deloria's hopes. Through its use of humor, it not only helps Native people to survive but to thrive, celebrating Native cultural identity.

Considering the continued fourth world status of Native people and the mass of blatant misrepresentations Native cultures are still faced with, contemporary Native writing in itself already constitutes an act of decolonization, since it reclaims the representational sovereignty from the colonizer.[2] Instead of accepting the role of "the Indian" as a passive object of White fiction, Native writers now intervene in the processes of image-making, creating new representations and thus ultimately "alterNative" points of identification. As Paula Gunn Allen points out: "When an individual's sense of self is . . . distorted by the impact of contradictory points of view, colonization and its terrible effects will not be assuaged by mere retention of land rights or economic self-sufficiency" (1985, 110). It is, therefore, all the more important for contemporary Native writing to contribute to a *decolonization of the mind*, that is, an emancipation from externally imposed definitions and ideas. It is no coincidence that humor is its instrument of choice: "By exploiting the potential for change inherent in social conflict, humour is capable of realigning the bases for individual and collective identifications" (Mackin 2002, 201). To elicit laughter may therefore, on the one hand, reverse patterns such as Native children cheering for the cowboys in Hollywood movies and instead trick Western readers into identifying with witty Native characters and viewpoints. On the other hand, the liminal space generated by humor and imagination constitutes a site of contestation, liberation, and regeneration for Native readers, contributing to a constant flexible renewal of Native cultural identity. Muskogee poet Joy Harjo writes: "Stories and songs are like humans who when they laugh are / Indestructible" (1994, 18). Residing within a tradition that not only believes strongly in the generative powers of language and imagination but also awards humor a central position, ultimately, the "stories" examined here do nothing short of helping Native people to reimagine themselves — laughing, indestructible.

Notes

[1] While simplifying here for the sake of the argument, I am of course aware that such a distinction in cultural insiders and outsiders is highly precarious. Moreover, Native ideas on Nativeness are frequently inseparably intertwined with external depictions through processes of internalization or overcompensation.

[2] Bell Hooks writes: "Moving from silence into speech is for the oppressed, the colonized, the exploited, and those who stand and struggle side by side, a gesture of defiance that heals, that makes new life, and new growth possible. It is that act of speech, of 'talking back' that is no mere gesture of empty words, that is the expression of moving from object to subject, that is the liberated voice" (1990, 340).

Appendix: The State of Research on Humor in Native Writing

IN MOST LIBRARY CATALOGUES, a keyword search on "Native American humor" ironically turns up Walter Blair's *Native American Humor* (1937) — which does not concern itself with the humor of the indigenous population in the least, but rather contrasts US American with European humor. Native humor seems as absent from the academic mind as from the public consciousness in general, a deficit acknowledged on a regular basis by studies on ethnic humor (see Lowe 1986, 454; Theisz 1989, 12–13). Whereas there has been much attention paid to Black or Jewish humor, and at least some to the humor of hyphenated Americans (for example, Polish-Americans and Italian-Americans), interest in Native humor has mostly been restricted to anthropological and ethnographic studies of ritual humor. On the one hand, humor studies in general are an area rather neglected by literary criticism; on the other hand, those academic fields in which humor research is conducted tend to ignore literary production: "Much of the best recent work in humor research has been done by psychologists, sociologists, and anthropologists, not by literary critics. Ironically, few of these social scientists appear to be familiar with ethnic literature; thus, the texts for their analyses are almost always jokes" (Lowe 1986, 449).

Dating from the beginning of the Native American Renaissance, "Indian Humor," a chapter in Vine Deloria's *Custer Died for Your Sins: An Indian Manifesto* (1969), comprises the first comment that exceeds a narrowly anthropological focus and discusses contemporary Native humor at large — albeit not in literature but in everyday interaction and jokes. In 1993, the thus far only monograph on the topic appeared, Lincoln's *Indi'n Humor: Bicultural Play in Native America*. In Lincoln's own words, the text covers "ethnic literary humor, from jokes in bars and at meetings and in kitchens; to the quieter wit of old wise people; to historical ironies still salting intercultural politics; to the outrageous license of holy fools in mythic times and at contemporary Indian ceremonies; to the written literature of the Native American renaissance that began in the late 1960s" (1993, 5). Spanning such a wide range of subjects without a clearly stated systematic methodology — as Lincoln seems to acknowledge himself, anticipating that his critics "will badger the lack of systematic tidiness" (8) — runs the risk of not illuminating but eclipsing a topic from public and scientific view. This indeed is the case, as Lincoln's book appears to lose focus on the subject instead of becoming clearer on what exactly characterizes "Indi'n Humor." After an introductory chapter establishing the terminology and introducing some aspects of "Red" humor and the White view thereof, the study moves on to discuss humor in as-told-to autobiographies by Native Americans, the "Whiteman's" obsession with playing Indian, the character of Coyote and trickster's presence in the lives of contemporary Natives as well as the role of Indian women and Native feminists' work. Lincoln's study concludes with what mainly constitutes an application of Northrop Frye's ideas on comedy to specific contemporary Native texts: Louise Erdrich's *Love Medicine*, James Welch's *Winter in the Blood*, N. Scott Momaday's *House Made of Dawn*, and Howard Norman's *The Northern Lights*. Lincoln proclaims that the paradigms of Indian humor ought to be approached "interculturally and intertextually in an interdisciplinary field of serious Western play — Acoma to Austria; psychology to biology; Koestler, Babcock, and Kristeva to Welch, Hogan, and Whiteman" (311). Yet one cannot help but agree with the criticism expressed by Vasudeva in her review of *Indi'n Humor*, identifying the weaknesses of Lincoln's study in his readings of Erdrich, Welch, Momaday, and Norman from a decidedly *Western* perspective: "Here, Lincoln brings the work of Northrop Frye to bear on the novels discussed. I had hoped for something that did not so blatantly bring together West and not-West. In fact, I would have liked to see something new: perhaps a critical apparatus that Lincoln developed from his work on 'Indi'n' humor that was distinctly not-West" (1997, 192). Especially Lincoln's application of Frye's prescriptive category of comedy and Huizinga's notion of play to Native American humor seem not only imposed, but not especially helpful either.

In recent years, in addition to Lincoln's monograph, there have been a number of articles on humor in Native American literature, most recently in Drew Hayden Taylor's collection on the topic, entitled *Me Funny* (2005). By and large, these contributions focus either on humor in the works of specific authors or genres, or on particular aspects of Native humor, such as the trickster. The most comprehensive overview is probably Lowe's entry on Native humor in the *Dictionary of Native American Literature* (1994), which discusses humor in Native oral traditions and contemporary Native American literature. Lowe's article shows how contemporary Native humor draws on the traditional humor of ceremonies and trickster stories, and suggests various functions of such humor: coping with traumatic events, releasing social pressure, intratribal corrective or intertribal teasing, and dealing with problematic issues in Indian-White relations. Lowe's discussion focuses mostly on canonical early Native Renaissance writers such as N. Scott Momaday, Leslie Silko, and James Welch, as well as the later Louise Erdrich and Gerald Vizenor. But he also makes reference to Alexander Posey, Joy Harjo, Diane Burns, Simon Ortiz, and Hanay Geiogamah. By and large, Lowe's article offers a valuable, wide-

ranging first survey of Native humor, although the format necessarily forecloses a more thorough discussion of the literary works he points to.

Vangen (1987) provides more specific and detailed analyses in her discussion of humor as a means of defiance in Maria Campbell's *Halfbreed*
and James Welch's *Winter in the Blood*. While her hypothesis that Native
writers must overcome stereotypes by creating new images (see 189) is
promising, her argument that Campbell and Welch confront and subvert
clichéd expectations by (all too willingly) fulfilling them is not entirely conclusive (though more so for *Halfbreed*, which makes its subversive strategy
rather explicit, than for *Winter in the Blood*): This use of humor may be
subversive, yet how it creates "new faces" (see 197) does not really become
clear. Ward's more recent article "Prayers Shrieked to Heaven: Humor and
Folklore in Contemporary American Indian Literature" (1997) examines
works by Louise Erdrich and, again, James Welch. Ward discusses Welch's
and Erdrich's writing in the light of Huizinga's, Henri Bergson's, and
Sigmund Freud's work on play and humor, relying strongly on Lincoln's
Indi'n Humor. He points in the right direction when he writes that
"humor can be generative, causing the audience to reach new understanding" (272), and that Erdrich and Welch use humor to "mediate the reality of their culture" (278). Yet, overall, Ward's comprehension of Native
humor appears lacking at times, and his close readings of Erdrich's and
Welch's novels do not sufficiently expound how such a reassessment is
achieved. Especially when compared to previous critical assessments,
Ward's readings thus hardly offer new insights. A more rewarding study of
(part of) Erdrich's work had already been provided, after all, by Gleason's
"'Her Laugh an Ace': The Function of Humor in Louise Erdrich's *Love
Medicine*" (1987). Gleason unearths the initially frequently overlooked
sophisticated use of humor and wordplay, slapstick and sarcasm in
Erdrich's novel, and emphasizes Native humor's important empowering
qualities. His analysis establishes valid links between Erdrich's novel and
the traditional Native humor of Plains Indian clowns and the trickster; yet
once again, his use of Johan Huizinga's theory of play as established in
Homo Ludens — like Lincoln's and Ward's — is not fully convincing.

Mirjam Hirch's insightful article "Subversive Humor: Canadian
Native Playwrights' Winning Weapon of Resistance" discusses humor in
the works of Canada's most renowned Native playwrights, Tomson
Highway and Drew Hayden Taylor. Hirch, on the one hand, traces the origins of Native drama in the oral storytelling tradition and, on the other
hand, sees the origins of contemporary Native humor in religious ceremonies, ritual clowning, and teasing. She identifies humor in contemporary Native Canadian drama as a means of subversion, even a weapon, but
also as "an artistic strategy both to heal from and to understand historical
and personal trauma," as well as a "cross-cultural language" (2005, 104,
116). Focusing on a less canonical author, LaLonde (1997) points to

humor as survival and coping strategies in Jim Northrup's *Walking the Rez Road*, and in this context stresses humor's potential to transform pain into laughter and to disrupt stereotypes. Coulombe (2002), in his excellent discussion of humor in Sherman Alexie's *The Lone Ranger and Tonto Fistfight in Heaven*, also highlights these qualities, and defends Alexie's fiction against allegations of showing no ethical responsibility in his representations of Native people (as brought forth by Bird 1995 or Cook-Lynn 1996). In contrast, according to Coulombe, Alexie's humor heals and strengthens Native cultural identity and community, while additionally acting as an intercultural mediator, triggering a reconsideration of fixed ideas in both Native and non-Native readers. His argument is thus in line with the argument made in this study, as is Mackin's rather specific article on "Trickster-Outlaws and the Comedy of Survival" (2002). Mackin offers an examination of the way in which Erdrich and Vizenor use humor to address Anishinaabe-White sociopolitical and legal dealings. The analysis compellingly demonstrates that the characters in Erdrich's and Vizenor's fiction display a tricksterlike ability to subversively reposition themselves within the Euro-American discourse, and highlights the "peculiar efficacy" (195) of humor in accomplishing social and political ends. Mackin emphasizes that "for both Erdrich and Vizenor, jokes provide a way of repositioning the subject. By exploiting the potential for change inherent in social conflict, humour is capable of realigning the bases for individual and collective identifications" (201). Blaeser's article on the humorous subversion of Western historiography in works by Carter Revard, Gerald Vizenor, and Gordon Henry points, to some extent, in a similar direction: Blaeser claims that the authors "through their play and bantering . . . force a reconsideration of the processes and powers of historical reckoning and thus, essentially, liberate the reader from preconceived notions and incite an imaginative reevaluation of history" (1998, 163).

The social functions of humor in Native communities, as depicted in texts by contemporary Native authors from Canada, are at the center of a recent analysis by Fagan. Placing the emphasis on humor in the interactions between Native characters and communities rather than in Native-White relations, Fagan ventures into little explored territory, at least in the literary sphere. In her lucid discussion, she highlights humor's potential to both build and challenge community in an ongoing process by allowing for tolerance and also by teaching and affirming social norms (see 2005, 25). The most thorough analyses of humor in contemporary Native literature are offered by Jennifer Andrews in her articles on humor in the poetry of Joy Harjo (Andrews 2000) and Thomas King's *Green Grass, Running Water* (Andrews 2002). Andrews stresses humor's potential to negotiate Native identity and to subvert dominant paradigms, identifying humor as "a compelling strategy for documenting a long history of oppression, debunking stereotypes, and celebrating the cultural vitality and sophistication of Native peoples" (2002, 92). Andrews concentrates on the border-crossing aspects of King's work. She describes how both linguistic and scatological humor in *Green Grass, Running Water* level Native and non-Native readers in a pattern of inclusion and rejection on the basis of shared humanity and cultural specificity. Most importantly, however, Andrews, like Coulombe, underlines humor's mediational characteristics by which Native authors may address controversial issues playfully. In her discussion of humor in Joy Harjo's poetry, she applies Linda Hutcheon's observations on irony and Arthur Koestler's concept of "bisociation" to highlight humor's potential for contesting stereotypes and negotiating identity, emphasizing that humor both subverts colonial authority and strengthens Native community.

In summary, the subject of humor in Native literature has attracted increasing interest in recent years, though studies still remain very limited both in focus and number. Whereas initial discussions seem to offer little insight into the topic, more recent articles by Andrews (2000, 2002), Blaeser (1998), Coulombe (2002), and Mackin (2002) point in the direction also followed in this study, conceiving of humor as a strategy not only of defiance but of negotiation.

Works Cited

Primary Texts

Alexie, Sherman. *The Business of Fancydancing*. Brooklyn, NY: Hanging Loose, 1992.

———. *First Indian on the Moon*. Brooklyn, NY: Hanging Loose, 1993a.

———. *Indian Killer*. New York, NY: Atlantic Monthly, 1996b.

———. *The Lone Ranger and Tonto Fistfight in Heaven*. New York, NY: HarperPerennial, 1994 [1993].

———. *Old Shirts, New Skins*. Native American Series 9. Los Angeles, CA: American Indian Studies Center, University of California, 1993b.

———. *Reservation Blues*. New York, NY: Warner, 1996a [1995].

———. *Smoke Signals: A Screenplay*. New York, NY: Hyperion, 1998.

———. *The Summer of Black Widows*. Brooklyn, NY: Hanging Loose, 1996c.

———. *Ten Little Indians*. New York, NY: Grove, 2003.

———. *The Toughest Indian in the World*. London: Vintage, 2001 [2000].

Allen, Paula Gunn, and Carolyn Dunn Anderson, eds. *Hozho: Walking in Beauty: Native American Stories of Inspiration, Humor, and Life*. Chicago, IL: Contemporary, 2001.

Armstrong, Jeannette C. "Indian Woman." In Moses and Goldie, 229–30.

Arnett, Carroll (Gogisgi). "Powwow." In *The Remembered Earth: An Anthology of Contemporary Native American Literature*, edited by Geary Hobson, 127. Albuquerque, NM: Red Earth, 1979.

Baker, Marie Annharte. "Coyote Columbus Café." In Moses and Goldie, 191–95.

———. "Squaw Guide." *Gatherings: The En'owkin Journal of First North American Peoples* VIII (1997): 29–31.

Bennett, Bruce. "Coyote's Metaphysics." In *A Coyote Reader*, edited by William Bright, 129. Berkeley, CA: U of California P, 1993.

Blaeser, Kimberley. "Twelve Steps to Ward Off Homesickness." *Gatherings: The En'owkin Journal of First North American Peoples* VIII (1997): 64–65.

Brant, Beth. *Mohawk Trail*. Toronto, ON: Women's, 1985.

Burns, Diane. "Sure You Can Ask Me a Personal Question." In *Songs from This Earth on Turtle's Back: Contemporary American Indian Poetry*, edited by Joseph Bruchac, 40. Greenfield Center, NY: The Greenfield Review Press, 1983.

Dumont, Marilyn. "On the Surface." *Prairie Fire* 22.3 (Autumn 2001): 192–93.

———. *A Really Good Brown Girl*. London, ON: Brick, 1996.

Erdoes, Richard, and John Fire. *Lame Deer: Seeker of Visions*. New York, NY: Simon and Schuster, 1972.

Erdrich, Louise. *Love Medicine*. New York, NY: Harper Perennial, 2001 [1984].

Erdrich, Louise, and Michael Dorris. *The Crown of Columbus*. New York, NY: HarperPaperbacks, 1991.

Forbes, Jack. *Only Approved Indians: Stories*. Norman, OK and London: U of Oklahoma P, 1995 [1983].

Geiogamah, Hanay. *New Native American Drama: Three Plays*. Norman, OK: U of Oklahoma P, 1980.

Halfe, Louise. *Bear Bones and Feathers*. Regina, SK: Coteau, 1994.

Harjo, Joy. *The Woman Who Fell from the Sky*. New York, NY: Norton, 1994.

Hawke, Thom E. "The Death of John Wayne." In Moses and Goldie, 418–19.

Howe, LeAnne. "An American in New York." In *New York Fiction*, edited by Reingard M. Nischik, 92–108. Stuttgart: Reclam, 2000.

Joe, Joyce B., and Susan M. Beaver, eds. *Shaking the Belly, Releasing the Sacred Clown. Gatherings: The En'owkin Journal of First North American Peoples* VIII (1997).

Johnston, Basil. "Cowboys and Indians." In *American Film Stories*, edited by Reingard M. Nischik, 18–32. Stuttgart: Reclam, 1996.

———. *Indian Schooldays*. Toronto, ON: Porter, 1998.

Jonnie, Curtis (Shingoose). "Indian Time." Quoted in Allan J. Ryan, *The Trickster Shift: Humour and Irony in Contemporary Native Art*, 36. Vancouver, BC: UBC P, 1999.

Keeshig-Tobias, Lenore. "Trickster Beyond 1992: Our Relationship." In Moses and Goldie, 258–67.

King, Thomas. "Coyote Sees the Prime Minister." *Canadian Literature* 161/162 (Summer/Autumn 1999c): 252.

———. *Green Grass, Running Water*. Toronto, ON: HarperPerennial, 1994 [1993].

———. *Medicine River*. Toronto, ON: Penguin, 1995 [1989].

———. *One Good Story, That One*. Toronto, ON: HarperCollins, 1993.

———. "A Short History of Indians in Canada." *Canadian Literature* 161/162 (Summer/Autumn 1999b): 62–64 [originally published in *Toronto Life*, 1997].

———. *Truth & Bright Water*. New York, NY: Grove, 1999a.

Mojica, Monique. "Post-Colonial Traumatic Stress Disorder: A Theatrical Monologue." *Prairie Fire: A Canadian Magazine of New Writing* 22.3 (2001): 88–90.

———. *Princess Pocahontas and the Blue Spots: Two Plays*. Toronto, ON: Women's, 1991.

Momaday, N. Scott. *The Way to Rainy Mountain*. Albuquerque, NM: U of New Mexico P, 1976 [1969].

Moses, Daniel David, and Terry Goldie, eds. *An Anthology of Canadian Native Literature in English*, 2nd ed. Toronto, ON and Oxford: Oxford UP, 1998.

Northrup, Jim. *The Rez Road Follies: Canoes, Casinos, Computers, and Birch Bark Baskets*. New York, NY: Kodansha International, 1997.

———. "Shinnob Jep." In *Humor Me: An Anthology of Humor by Writers of Color*, edited by John McNally, 187–202. Iowa City, IA: U of Iowa P, 2002.

———. *Walking the Rez Road*. Stillwater, MN: Voyageur, 1993.

Ortiz, Simon. *Men On the Moon: Collected Short Stories*. Tucson, AZ: U of Arizona P, 1999.

Owens, Louis. *Bone Game*. American Indian Literature and Critical Studies Series 10. Norman, OK: U of Oklahoma P, 1994.

———. *Dark River*. American Indian Literature and Critical Studies Series 30. Norman, OK: U of Oklahoma P, 1999.

Pelletier, Wilf. "Dumb Indian." In *Who is the Chairman of This Meeting? A Collection of Essays*, edited by Ralph Osborne, 1–20. Toronto, ON: Neewin, 1972.

Poirier, Mickie. "Quail Trail." *Gatherings: The En'owkin Journal of First North American Peoples* VIII (1997): 50.

Posey, Alexander. *The Fus Fixico Letters*. Edited by Daniel F. Littlefield Jr., and Carol Petty Hunter. Lincoln, NE: U of Nebraska P, 1993.

Quintasket, Christine (Mourning Dove). *Coyote Stories by Mourning Dove (Humishuma)*. Edited by Heister D. Guie. Lincoln, NE: U of Nebraska P, 1990 [1933].

Revard, Carter. *Cowboys and Indians, Christmas Shopping: Poems by Carter Revard*. Norman, OK: Point Riders, 1992.

———. "Never Quite a Hollywood Star." In Allen and Anderson, 53–62.

———. *Ponca War Dancers*. Norman, OK: Point Riders, 1980.

———. "Report To The Nation: Claiming Europe." In *Earth Power Coming: Short Fiction in Native American Literature*, edited by Simon J. Ortiz, 166–81. Tsaile, AZ: Navajo Community CP, 1983.

Robinson, Eden. *Traplines*. London: Abacus, 1999 [1996].

Russell, Suleiman. "How Old Man Coyote Lost His Manhood." In Allen and Anderson, 69–74.

Seesequasis, Paul. "The Republic of Tricksterism." In Moses and Goldie, 411–16.

Sewell, Anna M., and Crystal Lee Clark. "Discovering the Inner Indian." *Gatherings: The En'owkin Journal of First North American Peoples* VIII (1997): 56–57.

Silko, Leslie Marmon. *Ceremony*. New York, NY: Penguin, 1977.

Slipperjack, Ruby. "Snuff Chewing Charlie at University." *Prairie Fire* 22.3 (Autumn 2001): 165–86.

Taylor, Drew Hayden. *alterNatives*. Burnaby, BC: Talonbooks, 2000a.

———. *The Bootlegger Blues*. Saskatoon, SK: Fifth House, 1991.

———. *Funny You Don't Look Like One: Observations from a Blue-Eyed Ojibway*. Revised edition. Penticton, BC: Theytus, 1998.

———. *Furious Observations of a Blue-Eyed Ojibway: Funny, You Don't Look Like One, ~~Two~~ Three*. Penticton, BC: Theytus, 2002.

———. *Further Adventures of a Blue-Eyed Ojibway: Funny, You Don't Look Like One, ~~Too~~ Two*. Penticton, BC: Theytus, 1999.

———. *Futile Observations of a Blue-Eyed Ojibway: Funny, You Don't Look Like One ~~Two Three~~ Four*. Penticton, BC: Theytus, 2004.

———. "Half Empty or Half Full." *Prairie Fire* 22.3 (2001): 105–7.

———. "How Native is Native if You're Native?" In *Expressions in Canadian Native Studies*, edited by Ron F. Laliberte, 57–59. Saskatoon, SK: Extension, 2000b.

Two-Rivers, E. Donald. *Survivor's Medicine: Short Stories*. American Indian Literature and Critical Studies Series 29. Norman, OK: U of Oklahoma P, 1998.

Vizenor, Gerald. *Harold of Orange: A Screenplay. Studies in American Indians Literatures* 5.3 (1993a): 53–88.

———. *The Heirs of Columbus*. Hanover, NH: Wesleyan UP, 1991.

———. "Reservation Café: The Origins of American Indian Instant Coffee." In *Earth Power Coming: Short Fiction in Native American Literature*, edited by Simon J. Ortiz, 31–36. Tsaile, AZ: Navajo Community CP, 1983.

———. *Shadow Distance: A Gerald Vizenor Reader*. Hanover, NH: Wesleyan UP, 1994a.

Wagamese, Richard. *Keeper 'n Me*. Toronto, ON: Doubleday Canada, 1994.

———. *A Quality of Light*. Toronto, ON: Doubleday Canada, 1997.

Warrior, Emma Lee. "Compatriots." In *All My Relations: An Anthology of Contemporary Canadian Native Fiction*, edited by Thomas King, 48–59. Norman, OK: U of Oklahoma P, 1992.

Works Consulted

Abrams, M. H. *A Glossary of Literary Terms*, 7th ed. Fort Worth, TX: Harcourt Brace, 1999.

Acoose, Janice, and Misko-Kìsikàwihkwè (Red Sky Woman). *Iskwewak — Kah' Ki Yaw Ni Wahkomakanak: Neither Indian Princesses Nor Easy Squaws*. Toronto, ON: Women's, 1995.

Aldred, Lisa. "Plastic Shamans and Astroturf Sundances." *American Indian Quarterly* 24.3 (Summer 2000): 329–52.

Alexie, Sherman. "I Hated Tonto (Still Do)." *Los Angeles Times*, 28 June 1998. http://www.fallsapart.com/tonto.html (accessed November 1, 2007).

Allen, Graham. *Intertextuality*. London and New York, NY: Routledge, 2000.

Allen, Paula Gunn. "Introduction." In *Hozho: Walking in Beauty: Native American Stories of Inspiration, Humor, and Life*, edited by Paula Gunn Allen and Carolyn Dunn Anderson, xi–xxiv. Chicago, IL: Contemporary, 2001.

"The Sacred Hoop: A Contemporary Indian Perspective on American Indian Literature." In *The Remembered Earth: An Anthology of Contemporary Native American Literature*, edited by Geary Hobson, 222–39. Albuquerque, NM: Red Earth, 1979.

———. *The Sacred Hoop: Recovering the Feminine in American Indian Traditions*. Boston, MA: Beacon, 1992.

———. "'Whose Dream Is This Anyway?' Remythologizing and Self-Redefinitions of Contemporary American Indian Fiction." In *Literature and the Visual Arts in Contemporary Society*, edited by Suzanne Ferguson and Barbara Groseclose, 95–122. Columbus, OH: Ohio State UP, 1985.

Amossy, Ruth. "Stereotypes and Representation in Fiction." *Poetics Today* 5.4 (1984): 689–770.

Anderson, Benedict. *Imagined Communities: Reflections on the Origins and Spread of Nationalism*. London: Verso, 1983.

Andrews, Jennifer. "Border Trickery and Dog Bones: A Conversation with Thomas King." *Studies in Canadian Literature* 24.2 (1999): 161–85.

———. "In the Belly of a Laughing God: Reading Humor and Irony in the Poetry of Joy Harjo." *American Indian Quarterly* 24.2 (Spring 2000): 200–218.

———. "Reading Thomas King's *Green Grass, Running Water*: Border-Crossing Humour." *English Studies in Canada* 28.1 (March 2002): 91–116.

Apte, Mahadev L. *Humor and Laughter: An Anthropological Approach*. Ithaca, NY: Cornell UP, 1985.

———. "Humor Research, Methodology, and Theory in Anthropology." In *Handbook of Humor Research*, edited by Paul E. McGhee and Jeffrey H. Goldstein, 1:183–212. New York, NY: Springer, 1983.

Armstrong, Jeannette. "The Disempowerment of First North American Native Peoples and Empowerment Through Their Writing." Paper prepared for Saskatchewan Writers Guild 1990 Annual Conference. In Moses and Goldie, 239–42.

Ashcroft, Bill, Gareth Griffiths, and Helen Tiffin, eds. *The Postcolonial Studies Reader*. London/New York, NY: Routledge, 1995.

Assmann, Jan. *Das kulturelle Gedächtnis: Schrift, Erinnerung, und politische Identität in frühen Hochkulturen*, 2nd ed. Munich: Beck, 1997.

Atwood, Margaret. "A Double-Bladed Knife: Subversive Laughter in Two Stories by Thomas King." *Canadian Literature* 124/125 (Spring/Summer 1990): 243–53.

Babcock, Barbara, and Jay Cox. "The Native American Trickster." In *Dictionary of Native American Literature*, edited by Andrew Wiget, 99–105. New York, NY: Garland, 1994.

Babcock-Abrahams, Barbara. "Ritual Undress and the Comedy of Self and Other." In *A Crack in the Mirror: Reflexive Perspectives in Anthropology*, edited by Jay Ruby, 187–203. Philadelphia, PA: U of Pennsylvania P, 1982.

———. " 'A Tolerated Margin of Mess': The Trickster and His Tales Reconsidered." *Journal of the Folklore Institute* 11 (1974): 147–86.

Baker, Marie Annharte. "An Old Indian Trick Is to Laugh." *Canadian Theatre Review* 68 (Fall 1991): 48–49.

Bakhtin, Mikhail. *The Dialogic Imagination: Four Essays by M. M. Bakhtin.* Ed. Michael Holquist. Trans. Caryl Emersin and Michael Holquist. Austin, TX: U of Texas P, 1981.

Baldick, Chris. *A Concise Dictionary of Literary Terms.* Oxford and New York, NY: Oxford UP, 1996.

Ballinger, Franchot. "Coyote He/She Was Going There: Sex and Gender in Native American Trickster Stories." *Studies in American Indian Literatures* 12.4 (Winter 2000): 15–42.

Barbe, Katharina. *Irony in Context.* Pragmatics & Beyond New Series 34. Amsterdam/Philadelphia, PA: John Benjamins, 1995.

Basso, Keith. *Portraits of "The Whiteman": Linguistic Play and Cultural Symbols among the Western Apache.* Foreword by Dell Hymes. Cambridge, MA: Cambridge UP, 1979.

Bataille, Gretchen. "Introduction." In *Native American Representations: First Encounters, Distorted Images, and Literary Appropriations*, edited by Gretchen Bataille, 1–7. Lincoln, NE: U of Nebraska P, 2001.

Bataille, Gretchen M., and Charles L. P. Silet, eds. *The Pretend Indians: Images of Native Americans in the Movies.* Ames, IA: Iowa State UP, 1980.

Baudrillard, Jean. *Simulacra and Simulations.* Trans. Sheila Faria Glaser. Ann Arbor, MI: U of Michigan P, 1994.

———. *Simulations.* Trans. Paul Foss, Paul Patton, and Phillip Beichman. New York, NY: Semiotext(e), 1983.

Beck, Peggy V., and Anna Lee Walters. *The Sacred: Ways of Knowledge, Sources of Life.* Tsaile, AZ: Navajo Community CP, 1977.

Beidler, Peter G. "Review of Louise Erdrich, Michael Dorris, *The Crown of Columbus.*" *Studies in American Indian Literatures* 3.4 (Winter 1991): 47–50.

Bell, Betty Louise. "Pocahontas: 'Little Mischief' and the 'Dirty Men.' " *Studies in American Indian Literatures* 6.1 (Spring 1994): 63–70.

Bellante, John, and Carl Bellante. "Sherman Alexie: Literary Rebel." *Bloomsbury Review* 14 (May/June 1994): 14–15, 26.

Bergson, Henri. *Laughter: An Essay on the Meaning of the Comic.* Trans. Cloudesley Brereton and Fred Rothwell. London: Macmillan, 1991 [1900].

Berkhofer, Robert F., Jr. *The White Man's Indian: Images of the American Indian from Columbus to the Present.* New York, NY: Vintage, 1978.

Berner, Robert L. "American Myth: Old, New, Yet Untold." *Genre: Forms of Discourse and Culture* 25.4 (Winter 1992): 377–89.

———. *Defining American Indian Literature: One Nation Divisible.* Native American Studies 6. Lewiston, ME and Queenston, ON: Mellen, 1999.

Bhabha, Homi K. "Culture's In-Between." In *Questions of Cultural Identity,* edited by Stuart Hall and Paul du Gay, 53–60. London and Thousand Oaks, CA: Sage, 1996.

———. *The Location of Culture.* London and New York, NY: Routledge, 1994.

———. "The Other Question: Difference, Discrimination, and the Discourse of Colonialism." In *Out There: Marginalization and Contemporary Cultures,* edited by Russell Ferguson, Martha Gever, Trinh T. Minh-ha, and Cornel West, 71–87. Cambridge and London: MIT P, 1990.

Bird, Gloria. "The Exaggeration of Despair in Sherman Alexie's *Reservation Blues.*" *Wicazo Sa Review* 11.2 (Fall 1995): 47–52.

Blaeser, Kimberly M. *Gerald Vizenor: Writing in the Oral Tradition.* Norman, OK: U of Oklahoma P, 1996.

———. "The New 'Frontier' of Native American Literature: Dis-Arming History with Tribal Humor." In *Native-American Writers,* edited by Harold Bloom, 161–73. Philadelphia, PA: Chelsea House, 1998.

———. "Trickster: A Compendium." In *Buried Roots and Indestructible Seeds: The Survival of American Indian Life in Story, History, and Spirit,* edited by Mark Linquist and Martin Zanger, 47–66. Madison, WI: U of Wisconsin P, 1993.

Bolz, Peter. "Indianer als Öko-Heilige? Gedanken zur Entlarvung eines neuen Klischees." In *Indianische Realität: Nordamerikanische Indianer in der Gegenwart,* edited by Wolfgang Lindig, 47–55. Munich: dtv, 1994 [1983].

Booth, Wayne C. *A Rhetoric of Irony.* Chicago, IL: U of Chicago P, 1974.

Bordewich, Fergus M. *Killing the White Man's Indian: Reinventing Native Americans at the End of the Twentieth Century.* New York, NY: Doubleday, 1996.

Boskin, Joseph, and Joseph Dorrinson. "Ethnic Humor: Subversion and Survival." *American Quarterly* 37.1 (1985): 81–97.

Bové, Paul A. "Discourse." In *Critical Terms for Literary Study,* edited by Frank Lentricchia and Thomas McLaughlin, 2nd ed., 50–65. Chicago, IL and London: U of Chicago P, 1990.

Bowers, Neal, and Charles P. Silet. "An Interview with Gerald Vizenor." *MELUS* 8.1 (1981): 45–47.

Brant, Beth. "Grandmothers of a New World." In Moses and Goldie, 163–74.

Breinig, Helmbrecht. "(Hi)storytelling as Deconstruction and Seduction: The Columbus Novels of Stephen Marlowe and Michael Dorris/Louise Erdrich." In *Historiographic Metafiction in Modern American and Canadian Literature,* edited by Bernd Engler and Kurt Müller, 325–46. Paderborn: Schöningh, 1994.

Bright, William. "The Natural History of Old Man Coyote." In *Recovering the Word: Essays on Native American Literature*, edited by Brian Swann and Arnold Krupat, 339–87. Berkeley, CA: U of California P, 1987.

Bruchac, Joseph. "Striking the Pole: American Indian Humor." *Parabola* 12.4 (Winter 1987b): 22–29.

———. *Survival This Way: Interviews with American Indian Poets.* Tucson, AZ: U of Arizona P, 1987a.

Bruyere, Florence. "Never Indian Enough?" In *Issues in the North*, edited by Jill Oaks and Rick Riewe, 2:195–99. Canadian Circumpolar Institute/ Department of Native Studies, U of Manitoba, 1997.

Burton, Henrietta K. "Their Fun and Humor." *Indians at Work* 3.9 (1935): 24.

Canton, Jeffrey. "Coyote Lives: Thomas King." In *The Power to Bend Spoons: Interviews With Canadian Novelists*, edited by Beverley Daurio, 90–97. Toronto, ON: Mercury 1998.

Chadwick, Allen. "Hero With Two Faces: The Lone Ranger as Treaty Discourse." *American Literature* 68.3 (September 1996): 609–38.

Chamberlain, Alexander. "Humor." In *Handbook of American Indians of North Mexico*, edited by Frederick Webb Hodge, 578. Bureau of American Ethnology. Bulletin 30, Part 1. Washington, DC: Government Printing Office, 1907.

Christie, Stuart. "Time-Out: (Slam)Dunking Photographic Realism in Thomas King's *Medicine River*." *Studies in American Indian Literatures* 11.2 (Summer 1999): 51–65.

Churchill, Ward. "Literature as a Weapon in the Colonization of the American Indian." In *Fantasies of the Master Race: Literature, Cinema and the Colonization of American Indians*, edited by M. Annette Jaimes, 17–41. Monroe, ME: Common Courage Press, 1992.

Churchill, Ward, Norbert Hill, and Mary Ann Hill. "Media Stereotyping and Native Response: An Historical Overview." *The Indian Historian* 11.4 (1978): 45–56.

Clifford, James. "Identity in Mashpee." *The Predicament of Culture: Twentieth Century Ethnography, Literature, and Art*, 288–346. Cambridge, MA and London: Harvard UP, 1988.

Cohen, Sandy. "Racial and Ethnic Humor in the United States." *Amerikastudien/American Studies* 30.2 (1985): 203–12.

Coltelli, Laura. *Winged Words: American Indian Writers Speak*. Lincoln, NE and London: U of Nebraska P, 1990.

Cook-Lynn, Elizabeth. "American Indian Intellectualism and the New Indian Story." *American Indian Quarterly* 20.1 (1996): 57–76.

Coulombe, Joseph L. "The Approximate Size of His Favorite Tumor: Alexie's Comic Connections and Disconnections in *The Lone Ranger and Tonto Fistfight in Heaven*." *American Indian Quarterly* 26.1 (2002): 94–115.

Cox, Jay. "Dangerous Definitions: Female Tricksters in Contemporary Native American Literature." *Wicazo Sa Review* 5.2 (1989): 17–21.

Damm, Kateri. "Says Who: Colonialism, Identity and Defining Indigenous Literature." In *Looking at the Words of Our People: First Nations Analysis of Literature*, edited by Jeanette C. Armstrong, 9–25. Penticton, BC: Theytus, 1993.

de Certeau, Michel. *The Writing of History*. Trans. Tom Conley. New York, NY: Columbia, 1988.

Deloria, Phil. *Playing Indian: American Identities from the Boston Tea Party to the New Age*. New Haven, CT: Yale UP, 1998.

Deloria, Vine. *Custer Died For Your Sins: An Indian Manifesto*. New York, NY: Macmillan, 1977 [1969].

———. *God Is Red*. New York, NY: Grosset and Dunlap, 1973.

Dentith, Simon. *Parody*. The New Critical Idiom. London and New York, NY: Routledge, 2000.

Doty, William G. "Native American Tricksters: Literary Figures of Community Transformers." In *Trickster Lives: Culture and Myth in American Fiction*, edited by Jeanne Campbell Reesman, 1–15. Athens, GA and London: U of Georgia P, 2001.

Doueihi, Anne. "Inhabiting the Space Between Discourse and Story in Trickster Narratives." In *Mythical Trickster Figures: Contours, Contexts, and Criticism*, edited by William J. Hynes and William G. Doty, 193–201. Tuscaloosa, AL and London: U of Alabama P, 1993.

Draxlbauer, Michael. "America's Dearest Daughter: Misrepresentations of Pocahontas from Smith to Disney." In *Multiculturalism and the American Self*, edited by William Boelhower and Alfred Hornung, 19–49. American Studies 75. Heidelberg: Winter, 2003.

Dumont, Marilyn. "Popular Images of Nativeness." In *Looking at the Words of Our People: First Nations Analysis of Literature*, edited by Jeannette Armstrong, 46–50. Penticton, BC: Theytus, 1993.

Dvorak, Marta. "Thomas King's Christopher Cartier and Jaques Columbus." *Arachne* 5.1 (1998): 120–39.

———. "The World According to Thomas King." *Anglophonia* 1 (1997): 67–76.

Eckardt, A. Roy. *Sitting in the Earth and Laughing: A Handbook of Humor*. New Brunswick, NB and London: Transaction, 1992.

Edmunds, R. David. "Indian Humor: Can the Red Man Laugh?" In *Red Men and Hat-Wearers: Viewpoints in Indian History*, edited by D. Tyler, 141–54. Colorado State University Conference on Indian History. Boulder, CO: Pruett, 1976.

Eigenbrod, Renate. "Can 'The Subaltern' Be Read? The Role of the Critic in Post-Colonial Studies. An Epilogue to a Workshop." In *Can "The Subaltern" Be Read?*, edited by Tobias Döring, Uwe Schäfer, and Mark Stein, 97–101. *ACOLIT* Special Issue no. 2. Frankfurt a.M.: Institut für England- und Amerikastudien, 1996.

———. " 'Don't Fence Me In': Insider-Outsider Boundaries in and around Indigenous Literatures." In *Connections: Non-Native Responses to Native*

Canadian Literatures, edited by Hartmut Lutz and Coomi S. Vevaina, 34–59. New Delhi: Creative Books, 2003.

———. "Not Just a Text: 'Indigenizing' the Study of Indigenous Literatures." In *Creating Community: A Roundtable on Canadian Aboriginal Literature*, edited by Renate Eigenbrod and Jo-Ann Episkenew, 68–87. Penticton, BC: Theytus, 2002.

Engler, Bernd. "The Dismemberment of Clio: Fictionality, Narrativity, and the Construction of Historical Reality in Historiographic Metafiction." In *Historiographic Metafiction in Modern American and Canadian Literature*, edited by Bernd Engler and Kurt Müller, 13–33. Beiträge zur englischen und amerikanischen Literatur 13. Paderborn: Schöningh, 1994.

English, James F. *Comic Transactions: Literature, Humor, and the Politics of Community in Twentieth-Century Britain*. Ithaca, NY and London: Cornell UP, 1994.

Evans-Pritchard, Deidre. "How 'They' See 'Us': Native American Images of Tourists." *Annals of Tourism Research* 16 (1989): 89–105.

Fagan, Kristina. "Teasing, Tolerating, Teaching: Laughter and Community in Native Literature." In *Me Funny*, edited by Drew Hayden Taylor, 23–46. Vancouver, BC and Berkeley, CA: Douglas & McIntyre, 2005.

Fanon, Franz. *The Wretched of the Earth*. New York, NY: Grove, 1988 [1963].

Farrell, Susan. "Colonizing Columbus: Dorris and Erdrich's Postmodern Novel." *Critique* 40.2 (Winter 1999): 121–35.

Fast, Robin Riley. "Babo's Great-Great-Granddaughter: The Presence of *Benito Cereno* in *Green Grass, Running Water*." *American Indian Culture and Research Journal* 25.3 (2001): 27–46.

Feinberg, Leonard. *Introduction to Satire*. Ames, IA: Iowa State UP, 1967.

Fine, Gary Alan. "Sociological Approaches to the Study of Humor." In *Handbook of Humor Research*, edited by Paul E. McGhee and Jeffrey H. Goldstein, 1:159–81. New York, NY: Springer, 1983.

Fitz, Karsten. "Native and Christian: Religion and Spirituality as Transcultural Negotiation in American Indian Novels of the 1990s." *American Indian Culture and Research Journal* 26.2 (2002): 1–15.

———. *Negotiating History and Culture: Transculturation in Native American Fiction*. Regensburger Arbeiten zur Anglistik und Amerikanistik 43. Frankfurt: Lang, 2001.

Flick, Jane. "Reading Notes for Thomas King's *Green Grass, Running Water*." *Canadian Literature* 161/162 (Summer/Autumn 1999): 140–70.

Forbes, Jack. "Colonialism and Native American Literature: Analysis." *Wicazo Sa Review* 3.2 (Fall 1987): 17–23.

Foucault, Michel. *Power/Knowledge*. Brighton: Harvester, 1980.

Franke, Astrid. *Keys to Controversies: Stereotypes in Modern American Novels*. New York, NY: Campus/St. Martin's, 1999.

Frye, Northrop. "The Nature of Satire." In *Satura: Ein Kompendium moderner Studien zur Satire*, edited by Bernhard Fabian, 108–22. Hildesheim: Olms, 1975.

Gelo, Daniel J. "Powwow Patter: Indian Emcee Discourse on Power and Identity." *Journal of American Folklore* 112.443 (Winter 1999): 40–57.

Genette, Gérard. *Palimpsests: Literature in the Second Degree*. Trans. Channa Newman and Claude Doubinsky. Lincoln, NE and London: U of Nebraska P, 1997.

Georgi-Findlay, Brigitte. "Indianische Literatur." In *Amerikanische Literaturgeschichte*, edited by Hubert Zapf, 376–402. Stuttgart/Weimar: Metzler, 1997.

Giago, Tim. "My Laughter." Illustrations by Marty G. Two Bulls. *Native Peoples Magazine* 3.3 (1990): 52–56.

Gleason, William. " 'Her Laugh an Ace': The Function of Humor in Louise Erdrich's *Love Medicine*." *American Indian Culture and Research Journal* 11.3 (1987): 51–74.

Goetsch, Paul. "Funktionen von 'Hybridität' in der postkolonialen Theorie." *Literatur in Wissenschaft und Unterricht* 30.2 (1997): 135–45.

Goldman, Marlene. "Mapping and Dreaming: Native Resistance in *Green Grass, Running Water*." *Canadian Literature* 161/162 (Summer/Autumn 1999): 18–41.

Goodman, Joel. "How to Get More Smileage Out of Your Life: Making Sense of Humor, Then Serving It." In *Handbook of Humor Research*, edited by Paul E. McGhee and Jeffrey H. Goldstein, 2:1–21. New York, NY: Springer 1983.

Green, Michael. "Cultural Identities: Challenges for the Twenty-First Century." In *Issues in Native American Cultural Identity*, edited by Michael Green, 1–38. Critic of Institutions 2. New York, NY: Lang, 1995.

Green, Rayna. "The Pocahontas Perplex: The Image of Indian Women in American Culture." In *Unequal Sisters: A Multicultural Reader in U.S. Women's History*, edited by Ellen C. DuBois and Vicki L. Ruiz, 15–21. New York, NY: Routledge, 1990.

———. "The Tribe Called Wannabee: Playing Indian in America and Europe." *Folklore* 99.1 (1988): 30–55.

Greenblatt, Stephen. "Culture." In *Critical Terms for Literary Study*, edited by Frank Lentricchia and Thomas McLaughlin, 225–32. Chicago, IL and London: U of Chicago P, 1990.

Grewe-Volpp, Christa. "The Ecological Indian vs. the Spiritually Corrupt White Man: The Function of Ethnocentric Notions in Linda Hogan's *Solar Storms*." *Amerikastudien/American Studies* 47.2 (2002): 269–82.

Grinde, Donald A., Jr. "Historical Narratives of Nationhood and the Semiotic Construction of Social Identity: A Native American Perspective." In *Issues in Native American Cultural Identity*, edited by Michael Green, 201–22. Critic of Institutions 2. New York, NY: Lang, 1995.

Gruber, Eva. "Identity/Politics: Literary Negotiations of Canadian Indian Policy and Concepts of Nativeness." In *What is Your Place?" Indigeneity and Immigration in Canada*, edited by Hartmut Lutz, 61–73. Beiträge zur Kanadistik 14. Augsburg: Wißner, 2007.

Gzowski, Peter. "Peter Gzowski Interviews: Thomas King on *Green Grass, Running Water.*" *Canadian Literature* 161/162 (Summer/Autumn 1999): 65–76.

Hall, Stuart. "Cultural Identity and Cinematic Representation." *Framework* 36 (1989): 68–81.

———. "Fantasy, Identity, Politics." In *Cultural Remix: Theories of Politics and the Popular*, edited by Erica Carter, James Donald, and Judith Squires, 63–69. London: Lawrence & Wishart, 1995.

———. "Introduction." In *Representation: Cultural Representations and Signifying Practices*, edited by Stuart Hall, 1–11. London and Thousand Oaks, CA: Sage, in association with the Open University, 1997a.

———. "Introduction: Who Needs Identity?" In *Questions of Cultural Identity*, edited by Stuart Hall and Paul du Gay, 1–17. London and Thousand Oaks, CA: Sage, 1996.

———. "New Ethnicities." In *The Postcolonial Studies Reader*, edited by Bill Ashcroft, Gareth Griffiths, and Helen Tiffen, 223–27. London and New York, NY: Routledge, 1995.

———. "The Spectacle of the Other." In *Representation: Cultural Representations and Signifying Practices*, edited by Stuart Hall, 223–90. London and Thousand Oaks, CA: Sage, in association with the Open University, 1997b.

———. "The West and the Rest: Discourse and Power." In *Formations of Modernity*, edited by Stuart Hall and Bram Gieben, 275–331. Oxford and Cambridge: Polity/Open University, 1992.

Hanson, Jeffrey R., and Linda P. Rouse. "Dimensions of Native American Stereotyping." *American Indian Culture and Research Journal* 11.4 (1987): 33–58.

Hardin, Michael. "The Trickster of History: *The Heirs of Columbus* and the Dehistorization of Narrative." *MELUS* 23.4 (Winter 1998): 25–45.

Harjo, Suzan Shown. "Without Reservation." *Native Peoples* 11.3 (May–July 1998): 50–55.

Hellenthal, Michael. *Schwarzer Humor: Theorie und Definition*. Literaturwissenschaft in der Blauen Eule 1. Essen: Die Blaue Eule, 1989.

Hill, W. W. *Navajo Humor*. General Series in Anthropology 9. Menasha, WI: George Banta, 1943.

Hirch, Mirjam. "Subversive Humor: Canadian Native Playwrights' Winning Weapon of Resistance." In *Me Funny*, edited by Drew Hayden Taylor, 99–119. Vancouver, BC and Berkeley, CA: Douglas & McIntyre, 2005.

Hobson, Geary. "The Rise of the White Shaman as a New Version of Cultural Imperialism." In *The Remembered Earth: An Anthology of Contemporary*

Native American Literature, edited by Geary Hobson, 100–109. Albuquerque, NM: Red Earth, 1979.

Hoffmann, Gerhard. "Definitions of Humor, Comedy and Parody and their Relevance to American Fiction." *Amerikastudien/American Studies* 30.2 (1985): 140–59.

Holden, Madronna. "Making All the Crooked Ways Straight: The Satirical Portrait of Whites in Coast Salish Folklore." *Journal of American Folklore* 89.353 (1976): 271–93.

Hooks, Bell. "Narratives of Struggle." In *Critical Fictions: The Politics of Imaginative Writing*, edited by Philomena Mariani, 53–61. Dia Center for the Arts Discussions in Contemporary Culture 7. Seattle, WA: Bay, 1991.

————. "Talking Back." In *Out There: Marginalization and Contemporary Culture*, edited by Russell Ferguson, Martha Gever, Trinh T. Minh-ha, and Cornel West, 337–40. Cambridge, MA and London: MIT Press, 1990.

Horne, Dee. *Contemporary American Indian Writing: Unsettling Literature.* American Indian Studies 6. New York, NY: Lang, 1999.

————. "To Know the Difference: Mimicry, Satire, and Thomas King's *Green Grass, Running Water*." *Essays on Canadian Writing* 56 (1995): 255–73.

Hoy, Helen. *How Should I Read These? Native Women Writers in Canada.* Toronto, ON and Buffalo, NY: U of Toronto P, 2001.

————. "Review of Louise Erdrich/Michael Dorris, *The Crown of Columbus*." *Studies in American Indian Literatures* 3.4 (Winter 1991): 50–55.

Hughes, Langston. *Simple Stakes a Claim.* New York, NY: Rinehart, 1957.

Huntsman, Jeffrey. "Introduction" to *New Native American Drama: Three Plays*, by Hanay Geiogamah, ix–xxiv. Norman, OK: U of Oklahoma P, 1980.

Hutcheon, Linda. "Historiographic Metafiction." In *Metafiction*, edited by Mark Currie, 71–91. London and New York, NY: Longman, 1995a.

————. "Introduction." In *Double-Talking: Essays on Verbal and Visual Ironies in Contemporary Canadian Art and Literature*, edited by Linda Hutcheon, 11–38. Toronto, ON: ECW, 1992.

————. *Irony's Edge: The Theory and Politics of Irony.* London and New York, NY: Routledge, 1995b.

————. *Narcissistic Narrative: The Metafictional Paradox.* New York, NY and London: Methuen, 1984.

————. *A Theory of Parody: The Teachings of Twentieth-Century Art Forms.* New York, NY and London: Methuen, 1985.

Hynes, William J. "Mapping the Characteristics of Mythic Tricksters: A Heuristic Guide." In *Mythical Trickster Figures: Contours, Contexts, and Criticism*, edited by William J. Hynes and William G. Doty, 33–45. Tuscaloosa, AL and London: U of Alabama P, 1993.

Isernhagen, Hartwig. "Identity and Exchange: The Representation of 'The Indian' in the Federal Writers Project and in Contemporary Native

American Literature." In *Native American Representations: First Encounters, Distorted Images, and Literary Appropriations*, edited by Gretchen Bataille, 168–95. Lincoln, NE: U of Nebraska P, 2001.

———. "Multiculturalism, Ethnicity, and Contemporary Anglophone Canadian Indian Literature." In *Probing Canadian Culture*, edited by Peter Easingwood et al., 188–202. Augsburg: AV, 1991.

Jaimes, M. Annette. "Native American Identity and Survival: Indigenism and Environmental Ethics." In *Issues in Native American Cultural Identity*, edited by Michael Green, 273–96. Critic of Institutions 2. New York, NY: Lang, 1995.

Jaimes, M. Annette, and Theresa Halsey. "American Indian Women: At the Center of Indigenous Resistance in Contemporary America." In *The State of Native America: Genocide, Colonization, and Resistance*, edited by M. Annette Jaimes, 311–44. Boston, MA: South End, 1992.

Jannetta, Armando E. *Ethnopoetics of the Minority Voice: An Introduction to the Politics of Dialogism and Difference in Métis Literature*. Beiträge zur Kanadistik 10. Augsburg: Wißner, 2001.

Johnson, Brian. "Plastic Shaman in the Global Village: Understanding Media in Thomas King's *Green Grass, Running Water*." *Studies in Canadian Literature* 25.2 (September 2000): 24–49.

Johnston, Gordon. "An Intolerable Burden of Meaning: Native Peoples in White Fiction." In *The Native in Literature*, edited by Thomas King, Cheryl Calver, and Helen Hoy, 50–66. Oakville, ON: ECW Press, 1987.

Kant, Immanuel. *Kritik of Judgment*. Trans. J. H. Bernard. London: Macmillan, 1982 [1790].

Kelly, Don. "And Now, Ladies and Gentlemen: Get Ready for Some (Ab)Original Stand-up Comedy." In *Me Funny*, edited by Drew Hayden Taylor, 51–65. Vancouver, BC and Berkeley, CA: Douglas & McIntyre, 2005.

Kilpatrick, Jacquelyn. *Celluloid Indians: Native Americans and Film*. Lincoln, NE and London: U of Nebraska P, 1999.

King, Thomas. "Godzilla vs. Post-Colonial." *World Literature Written in English* 30.2 (1990): 10–16.

———. "How I Spent My Summer Vacation: History, Story, and the Cant of Authenticity." In *Landmarks: A Process Reader*, edited by Roberta Birks, Tomi Eng, and Julie Walchli, 248–55. Scarborough, ON: Prentice Hall Allyn and Bacon Canada, 1998.

———. "Introduction." *Canadian Fiction Magazine* 20 (1987): 4–10.

———. "Introduction." In *All My Relations: An Anthology of Contemporary Canadian Native Fiction*, edited by Thomas King, ix–xvi. Norman, OK: U of Oklahoma P, 1992.

———. "Performing Native Humour: The Dead Dog Café Comedy Hour." In *Me Funny*, edited by Drew Hayden Taylor, 169–83. Vancouver, BC and Berkeley, CA: Douglas & McIntyre, 2005.

Krech, Shepard, III. *The Ecological Indian: Myth and History.* New York, NY: Norton, 1999.

Krupat, Arnold. *The Turn to the Native: Studies in Criticism and Culture.* Lincoln, NE and London: U of Nebraska P, 1996.

LaLonde, Christopher A. "Stories, Humor, and Survival in Jim Northrup's *Walking the Rez Road.*" *Studies in American Indian Literatures* 9.2 (Summer 1997): 23–40.

LaRoque, Emma. *Defeathering the Indian.* Agincourt, ON: The Book Society of Canada, 1975.

Lawrence, Bonita. "Mixed-Race Urban Native People: Surviving a Legacy of Policies of Genocide." In *Expressions in Canadian Native Studies,* edited by Ron F. Laliberte et al., 69–94. Saskatoon, SK: U of Saskatchewan Extension P, 2000.

Lee, A. Robert. *Multicultural American Literature: Comparative Black, Native, Latino/a and Asian American Fictions.* Edinburgh: Edinburgh UP, 2003.

Levin, Harry, ed. *Veins of Humor.* Harvard English Studies 3. Cambridge, MA: Harvard UP, 1972.

Lewis, Paul. *Comic Effects: Interdisciplinary Approaches to Humor in Literature.* Albany, NY: State U of New York P, 1989.

Lincoln, Kenneth. *Indi'n Humor: Bicultural Play in Native America.* New York, NY and Oxford: Oxford UP, 1993.

Linton, Patricia. "'And Here's How It Happened': Trickster Discourse in Thomas King's *Green Grass, Running Water.*" *Modern Fiction Studies* 45.1 (Spring 1999): 212–34.

Littlefield, Daniel F. Introduction to *The Fus Fixico Letters,* by Alexander Posey. Eds. Daniel F. Littlefield and Carol Petty Hunter, 1–48. Lincoln, NE: U of Nebraska P, 1993.

Louis, Adrian C. Foreword to *Old Shirts & New Skins,* by Sherman Alexie, vii–x. Native American Series 9. Los Angeles, CA: American Indian Studies Center, U of California, 1993.

Lowe, John. "Coyote's Jokebook: Humor in Native American Literature and Culture." In *Dictionary of Native American Literature,* edited by Andrew Wiget, 193–205. New York, NY: Garland, 1994.

———. "Theories of Ethnic Humor: How to Enter, Laughing." *American Quarterly* 38 (1986): 439–60.

Lutz, Hartmut. *Approaches: Essays in Native North American Studies and Literatures.* Beiträge zur Kanadistik 11. Augsburg: Wißner, 2002.

———. *Contemporary Challenges: Conversations with Canadian Native Authors.* Saskatoon, SK: Fifth House, 1991.

———. *"Indianer" und "Native Americans": Zur sozial- und literarhistorischen Vermittlung eines Stereotyps.* Hildesheim, Zurich, and New York, NY: Olms, 1985.

Mackin, Joanna. "Trickster-Outlaws and the Comedy of Survival." In *Comedy, Fantasy, and Colonialism*, edited by Graeme Harper, 189–204. London and New York, NY: Continuum, 2002.

Martineau, William H. "A Model of the Social Functions of Humor." In *The Psychology of Humor*, edited by Jeffrey H. Goldstein and Paul E. McGhee, 101–25. New York, NY and London: Academic Press, 1972.

Mattina, Anthony. *The Golden Woman: The Colville Narrative of Peter J. Seymour.* Trans. Anthony Mattina and Madeline de Sautel. Tucson: U of Arizona P, 1985.

McMaster, Gerald. "Border Zones: The 'Injun-uity' of Aesthetic Tricks." *Cultural Studies* 9.1 (1995): 74–90.

Mieder, Wolfgang. "The Only Good Indian is a Dead Indian: History and Meaning of a Proverbial Stereotype." *DeProverbio.com* 1.1 (1995). http://www.deproverbio.com/DPjournal/DP,1,1,95/INDIAN.html (28.06.2003).

Miller, Dallas. "Mythic Rage and Laughter: An Interview with Gerald Vizenor." *Studies in American Indian Literatures* 7.1 (Spring 1995): 77–96.

Miller, Frank C. "Humor in a Chippewa Tribal Council." *Ethnology* 6 (1967): 263–71.

Momaday, N. Scott. "The Magic of Words: An Interview with N. Scott Momaday," conducted by Joseph Bruchac. In *Survival This Way: Interviews with American Indian Poets*, edited by Joseph Bruchac, 173–91. Tucson, AZ: U of Arizona P, 1987.

———. "The Man Made of Words." In *The Remembered Earth: An Anthology of Contemporary Native American Literature*, edited by Geary Hobson, 162–73. Albuquerque, NM: Red Earth, 1979.

Morreall, John. *Taking Laughter Seriously.* Albany, NY: State U of New York P, 1983.

Moses, Daniel David, and Terry Goldie. "Notes on the Authors." In Moses and Goldie, 492–526.

Muecke, Douglas C. *Irony.* The Critical Idiom 13. London: Methuen, 1970.

Nischik, Reingard M. "Zu den Autoren und Stories: Basil Johnston, 'Cowboys and Indians.'" In *American Film Stories*, edited by Reingard Nischik, 129–31. Stuttgart: Reclam, 1996.

O'Connor, John. "The White Man's Indian: An Institutional Approach." In *Hollywood's Indian: The Portrayal of the Native American in Film*, edited by Peter C. Rollins and John O'Connor, 27–38. Lexington, KY: UP of Kentucky, 1998.

Owens, Louis. "As if an Indian Were Really an Indian: Native American Voices and Postcolonial Theory." In *Native American Representations: First Encounters, Distorted Images, and Literary Appropriations*, edited by Gretchen Bataille, 11–24. Lincoln, NE: U of Nebraska P, 2001.

Owens, Louis. *Mixedblood Messages: Literature, Film, Family, Place*. Norman, OK: Oklahoma UP, 1998.

———. *Other Destinies: Understanding the American Indian Novel*. Norman, OK and London: U of Oklahoma P, 1992.

Palmer, Jerry. *Taking Humour Seriously*. London and New York, NY: Routledge, 1994.

Perry, Dennis R. "Hybrid History: The Pequot War and American Indian Humor." *Studies in American Humor* 7 (2000): 25–33.

Petrone, Penny. *Native Literature in Canada: From the Oral Tradition to the Present*. Toronto, ON: Oxford UP, 1990.

Petzold, Dieter. "Thomas King's *Green Grass, Running Water*: A Postmodern Postcolonial Puzzle; or, Coyote Conquers the Campus." In *Lineages of the Novel*, edited by Bernhard Reitz and Eckart Voigts-Virchow, 243–54. Trier: Wissenschaftlicher Verlag, 2000.

Pfister, Manfred. "Introduction: A History of English Laughter." In *A History of English Laughter: Laughter from Beowulf to Beckett and Beyond*, edited by Manfred Pfister, v–x. Amsterdam and New York, NY: Rodopi, 2002.

Plant, John. *Heyoka: Die Contraries und Clowns der Plainsindianer*. Wyk auf Foehr: Verlag für Amerikanistik, 1994.

Poirier, Michelle A. "Humour is Good Medicine: The Algonquin Perspective on Humour in Their Culture and of Outsider Constructions of Aboriginal Humour." MA Thesis, Carleton University, 2000.

Pratt, Mary Louise. "Arts of the Contact Zone." *Profession* 13.9 (1991): 33–40.

———. "Conventions of Representation: Where Discourse and Ideology Meet." In *The Taming of the Text: Explorations in Language, Literature and Culture*, edited by Willie van Peer, 15–34. London and New York, NY: Routledge, 1988.

———. "Transculturation and Autoethnography." In *Colonial Discourse/Postcolonial Theory*, edited by Francis Barker, Peter Hulme, and Margaret Iversen, 24–46. Manchester and New York, NY: Manchester UP, 1994.

Pratt, Steven B. "Razzing: Ritualized Uses of Humor as a Form of Identification among American Indians." In *Communication and Identity Across Cultures*, edited by Dolores V. Tanno and Alberto González, 56–79. Thousand Oaks, CA: Sage Publications, 1998.

Price, Darby Li Po. "Laughing Without Reservation: Indian Standup Comedians." *American Indian Culture and Research Journal* 22.4 (1998): 255–71.

Price, John A. *Native Studies: American and Canadian Indians*. Toronto, ON: McGraw-Hill Ryerson, 1978.

Purdie, Susan. *Comedy: The Mastery of Discourse*. Toronto, ON: U of Toronto P, 1993.

Purdy, John. "Clear Waters: A Conversation with Louis Owens." *Studies in American Indian Literatures* 10.2 (Summer 1998): 6–22.

———. "Crossroads: A Conversation with Sherman Alexie." *Studies in American Indian Literatures* 9.4 (Winter 1997): 1–18.

———. "Tricksters of the Trade: 'Remagining' the Filmic Images of Native Americans." In *Native American Representations: First Encounters, Distorted Images, and Literary Appropriations*, edited by Gretchen Bataille, 100–118. Lincoln, NE: U of Nebraska P, 2001.

Radin, Paul. *The Trickster: A Study in American Indian Mythology*. New York, NY: Schocken, 1972. First published in 1955.

Rainwater, Catherine. *Dreams of Fiery Stars: The Transformations of Native American Literature*. Philadelphia, PA: U of Pennsylvania P, 1999.

Rayson, Ann. "Shifting Identity in the Work of Louise Erdrich and Michael Dorris." *Studies in American Indian Literatures* 3.4 (Winter 1991): 27–36.

Redfern, Walter. *Puns: More Senses Than One*. London: Penguin, 2000 [1984].

Ridington, Robin. "Theorizing Coyote's Canon: Sharing Stories with Thomas King." In *Theorizing the Americanist Tradition*, edited by Lisa Philips Valentine and Regna Darnell, 19–37. Toronto, ON and Buffalo, NY: U of Toronto P, 1999.

Rishel, Mary Ann. *Writing Humor: Creativity and the Comic Mind*. Humor in Life and Letters Series. Detroit, MI: Wayne State UP, 2002.

Rollins, Peter C., and John O'Connor, eds. *Hollywood's Indian: The Portrayal of the Native American in Film*. Lexington, KY: UP of Kentucky, 1998.

Rooke, Constance. "Interview With Tom King." *World Literature Written in English* 30.2 (1990): 62–76.

Rose, Margaret A. *Parody: Ancient, Modern, and Post-Modern*. Literature, Culture, Theory 5. New York, NY: Cambridge UP, 1993.

———. *Parody/Meta-Fiction: An Analysis of Parody as a Critical Mirror to the Writing and Reception of Fiction*. London: Croom Helm, 1979.

Rose, Wendy. "The Great Pretenders: Further Reflections on White Shamanism." In *The State of Native America: Genocide, Colonization and Resistance*, edited by M. Annette Jaimes. Boston, MA: South End Press, 1992.

Ruffo, Armand Garnet. "From Myth to Metafiction: A Narratological Analysis of Thomas King's 'The One About Coyote Going West.'" *International Journal of Canadian Studies* 12 (Fall 1995): 135–54.

Ruppert, James. *Mediation in Contemporary Native American Fiction*. American Indian Literature and Critical Studies Series 15. Norman, OK: U of Oklahoma P, 1995.

Ryan, Allan J. *The Trickster Shift: Humour and Irony in Contemporary Native Art*. Vancouver, BC and Toronto, ON: UBC P, 1999.

Said, Edward. *Orientalism: Western Conceptions of the Orient*. London: Penguin, 1991.

Sanner, Hans Ulrich. "'Another Home Run for the Black Sox': Humor and Creativity in Hopi Ritual Clown Songs." In *New Voices in Native American Literature Criticism*, edited by Arnold Krupat, 149–73. Washington, DC and London: Smithsonian Institution Press, 1993.

Sarkowsky, Katja. "Writing (and) Art — Native American/First Nations Art and Literature Beyond Resistance and Reconciliation." In *Resistance and Reconciliation: Writing in the Commonwealth*, edited by Bruce Bennett, 90–101. Canberra: Association for Commonwealth Literature and Language Studies, 2003.

Schorcht, Blanca. *Storied Voices in Native American Texts: Harry Robinson, Thomas King, James Welch, and Leslie Marmon Silko*. New York, NY and London: Routledge, 2003.

Shanley, Kathryn. "The Indians America Loves to Love and Read: American Identity and Cultural Appropriation." In *Native American Representations: First Encounters, Distorted Images, and Literary Appropriations*, edited by Gretchen Bataille, 26–49. Lincoln, NE: U of Nebraska P, 2001.

Shutiva, C. "Native American Culture and Communication Through Humor." In *Our Voices: Essays in Culture, Ethnicity, and Communication*, edited by M. Houston Gonzáles and V. Chen, 117–21. Los Angeles, CA: Roxbury, 1994.

Silberman, Robert. "Gerald Vizenor and *Harold of Orange:* From Word Cinemas to Real Cinema." *American Indian Quarterly* 9 (Winter 1985): 5–21.

Silko, Leslie Marmon. "Here's an Odd Artifact for the Fairy-Tale Shelf." *Studies in American Indian Literatures* 10.4 (1986): 178–84.

———. "An Old Time Indian Attack Conducted in Two Parts." In *The Remembered Earth: An Anthology of Contemporary Native American Literature*, edited by Geary Hobson, 211–16. Albuquerque, NM: Red Earth, 1979.

Skeels, Dell. "A Classification of Humor in Nez Percé Mythology." *Journal of American Folklore* 67 (1954): 57–63.

Smith, Jeanne Rosier. *Writing Tricksters: Mythic Gambols in American Ethnic Literatures*. Berkeley, CA and New York, NY: U of California P, 1997.

Spielman, Roger. *You're So Fat: Exploring Ojibway Discourse*. Toronto, ON: U of Toronto P, 1998.

Stedman, Raymond W. *Shadows of the Indian: Stereotypes in American Culture*. Norman, OK: U of Oklahoma P, 1982.

Stephenson, R. M. "Conflict and Control Functions of Humor." *American Journal of Sociology* 56 (1951): 569–74.

Steward, Julian Haynes. *The Clown in Native North America*. New York, NY: Garland, 1991 [1929].

Stierstorfer, Klaus. "Liminalität." In *Metzler-Lexikon Literatur- und Kulturtheorie: Ansätze — Personen — Grundbegriffe*, edited by Ansgar Nünning, 2nd ed., 370–71. Stuttgart and Weimar: Metzler, 2001.

Stratton, Florence. "Cartographic Lessons: Susanna Moodie's *Roughing It in the Bush* and Thomas King's *Green Grass, Running Water.*" *Canadian Literature* 161/162 (Summer/Autumn 1999): 82–102.

Tama, Jose Torres. "Healing With Humor: New American Perspectives from James Luna and Dan Kwong." *Art Papers* 25.5 (September/October 2001): 17.

Taylor, Drew Hayden. "Introduction." In *Me Funny*, edited by Drew Hayden Taylor, 1–3. Vancouver, BC and Berkeley, CA: Douglas & McIntyre, 2005.

———, dir. *Trickster, Redskins, and Puppy Stew: The Healing Powers of Native Humour.* Documentary produced by Louise Lore, Nancy C. Johnston, and Silva Basmajian. National Film Board (NFB), 2000c.

———. "Whacking the Indigenous Funny Bone." In *Me Funny*, edited by Drew Hayden Taylor, 67–80. Vancouver, BC and Berkeley, CA: Douglas & McIntyre, 2005.

Theisz, R. D. "Social Control and Identity in American Indian Humor." *Studies in Contemporary Satire* 16 (1989): 12–32.

Thompson, William R. "The American Indians' Attempt to get the Last Laugh." *Studies in Contemporary Satire* 16 (1989): 1–10.

Toelken, Barre. "Life and Death in Navajo Coyote Tales." In *Recovering the Word: Essays on Native American Literature*, edited by Brian Swann and Arnold Krupat, 388–401. Berkeley, CA and Los Angeles, CA: U of California P, 1987.

———. "The 'Pretty Language' of Yellowman: Genre, Mode, and Texture in Navaho Coyote Narratives." *Genre* 2.3 (1969): 212–35.

Turcotte, Gerry. "Re/marking on History, or, Playing Basketball With Godzilla: Thomas King's Monstrous Post-colonial Gesture." In *Connections: Non-Native Responses to Native Canadian Literature*, edited by Hartmut Lutz and Vevaina S. Coomi, 205–35. Creative New Literatures Series 62. New Delhi: Creative Books, 2003.

Turner, Victor. *The Ritual Process.* Ithaca, NY: Cornell UP, 1969.

———. "Variations on a Theme of Liminality." In *Secular Ritual*, edited by S. F. Moore and B. G. Myerhoff, 36–52. Amsterdam: Rodopi, 1977.

Vangen, Kate. "Making Faces: Defiance and Humour in Campbell's *Halfbreed* and Welch's *Winter in the Blood.*" In *The Native in Literature*, edited by Thomas King, Cheryl Calver, and Helen Hoy, 188–205. Oakville, ON: ECW Press, 1987.

van Keuren, Luise. "The American Indian as Humorist in Colonial Literature." In *A Mixed Race: Ethnicity in Early America*, edited by Frank Shuffelton, 77–91. New York, NY and Oxford: Oxford UP, 1993.

Vasudeva, Mary. "Re-creating Native American Literary History: The Past Looks Towards the Future." *College Literature* 24 (1997): 183–94.

Velie, Alan. "Indians in Indian Fiction: The Shadow of the Trickster." *American Indian Quarterly* 8.4 (Fall 1984): 315–29.

Velie, Alan. "The Trickster Novel." In *Narrative Chance: Postmodern Discourse on Native American Indian Literatures*, edited by Gerald Vizenor, 121–39. Albuquerque, NM: U of New Mexico P, 1989.

Vickers, Scott B. *Native American Identities: From Stereotype to Archetype in Art and Literature*. Albuquerque, NM: U of New Mexico P, 1998.

Vivan, Itala. "Hybridity and Aesthetics in the Era of Postcolonial Literatures." In *Crossover: Hybridity in Ethnicity, Gender, and Ethics*, edited by Therese Steffen, 3–12. Tübingen: Stauffenburg, 2000.

Vizenor, Gerald. "Gerald Vizenor: The Trickster Heir of Columbus: An Interview," conducted by Laura Coltelli. *Native American Literatures Forum* 2–3 (1990–91): 101–15.

———. *Manifest Manners: Postindian Warriors of Survivance*. Hanover, NH and London: Wesleyan UP, 1994b.

———. "Trickster Discourse: Comic and Tragic Themes in Native American Literature." In *Buried Roots and Indestructible Seeds: The Survival of American Indian Life in Story, History and Spirit*, edited by Mark A. Lindquist and Martin Zanger, 67–83. Madison, WI: U of Wisconsin P, 1993b.

———. "Trickster Discourse: Comic Holotropes and Language Games." In *Narrative Chance: Postmodern Discourse on Native American Indian Literatures*, edited by Gerald Vizenor, 187–211. Albuquerque, NM: U of New Mexico P, 1989.

Voeglin, E. W. "Humor (North American Indian)." In *Funk and Wagnall's Standard Dictionary of Folklore, Mythology, and Legend*, edited by Maria Leach, 510–11. New York, NY: Harper and Row, 1949.

Wallace, William. "The Role of Humor in the Hupa Indian Tribe." *Journal of American Folklore* 66 (1953): 135–41.

Ward, A. Joseph. "Prayers Shrieked to Heaven: Humor and Folklore in Contemporary American Indian Literature." *Western Folklore* 56.3–4 (Summer/Fall 1997): 267–80.

Weaver, Jace. *That the People Might Live: Native American Literatures and Native American Community*. Oxford and New York, NY: Oxford UP, 1997.

Whitaker, V. K. "The Humorless Indian." *Pacific Spectator* 1 (Autumn 1947): 458.

White, E. B. *The Second Tree From the Corner*. New York, NY: Harper & Row Perennial Library, 1989.

White, Hayden. *Metahistory. Tropics of Discourse: Essays in Cultural Criticism*. Baltimore, MD and London: Johns Hopkins UP, 1978.

———. "The Question of Narrative in Contemporary Historical Theory." *History and Theory* 23.1 (1984): 1–33.

Whitt, Laurie Anne. "Indigenous Peoples and the Cultural Politics of Knowledge." In *Issues in Native American Cultural Identity*, edited by

Michael Green, 223–71. Critic of Institutions 2. New York, NY: Lang, 1995.

Wiget, Andrew. "His Life in His Tail: The Native American Trickster and the Literature of Possibility." In *Redefining American Literary History*, edited by A. LaVonne Brown Ruoff and Jerry W. Ward Jr., 83–96. New York, NY: Modern Language Association, 1990.

Witherspoon, Gary. *Language and Art in the Navajo Universe*. Ann Arbor, MI: U of Michigan P, 1977.

Womack, Craig. *Red on Red: Native American Literary Separatism*. Minneapolis, MN: U of Minnesota P, 1999.

Woodward, Kathryn. "Concepts of Identity and Difference." In *Identity and Difference*, edited by Kathryn Woodward, 7–63. London and Thousand Oaks, CA: Sage, in association with the Open University, 1997.

Young-Ing, Greg. "Aboriginal People's Estrangement: Marginalization in the Publishing Industry." In *Looking at the Words of Our People: First Nations Analysis of Literature*, edited by Jeannette Armstrong, 178–87. Penticton, BC: Theytus, 1993.

Zenner, Walter P. "Joking and Ethnic Stereotyping." *Anthropological Quarterly* 43 (1970): 93–113.

Index

Abrams, M. H., 56, 112 n. 4,
113 n. 10
Acoose, Janice, 137, 173, 221 n. 5
Adams, Henry, 137
Aldred, Lisa, 184, 185, 189
Alexie, Robert, works by: *Porcupines
and China Dolls*, 14, 179
Alexie, Sherman, 14, 17, 27, 28, 46,
58, 59–60, 68, 88, 91, 126, 133,
152, 182, 186, 202, 210, 220,
223 n. 25, 232
Alexie, Sherman, works by: "The
Approximate Size of My Favorite
Tumor," 57, 203; "Dear John
Wayne," 114 n. 16, 142, 148–50;
First Indian on the Moon, 16; *Flight*,
14; "Giving Blood," 115 n. 21;
"How to Write the Great American
Indian Novel," 112 n. 7, 139–40;
Indian Killer, 14, 91, 114 n. 16,
133, 198–99; "The Life and Times
of Estelle Walks Above," 151,
217–18; *The Lone Ranger and Tonto
Fistfight in Heaven*, 12, 15, 197,
209–10, 218, 232; *Old Shirts, New
Skins*, 16; "Postcards to Columbus,"
119; *Reservation Blues*, 14, 43, 59,
66, 68, 92–94, 114 n. 16, 167, 175,
182–84, 185, 186, 199, 201,
209–10, 218; "Saint Junior," 69;
"Sasquatch Poems," 182; "The
Search Engine," 151; *Smoke Signals*,
12, 151, 218–20; "Song of
Ourself," 80; "South by
Southwest," 107; "Spokane Tribal
Celebration, September 1987," 202;
The Summer of Black Widows, 16;
Ten Little Indians, 15; "This Is
What It Means To Say Phoenix,
Arizona," 150–51; *The Toughest
Indian in the World*, 15; "Translated
from the American," 73–74;
"Whatever Happened to Frank
Snake Church?," 69–70, 200
Allen, Graham, 81, 83–84
Allen, Paula Gunn, 7, 9–10, 20, 25,
28, 42, 43–44, 81, 96, 113 n. 11,
113 n. 14, 130, 150, 172, 176,
223 n. 23, 228
Allen, Paula Gunn, works by: *Hozho:
Walking in Beauty*, 17
allusion, 14, 63, 66, 69, 81, 88,
91–95, 109, 110, 114 n. 15, 126,
127, 130, 133, 136, 139, 146, 190,
226
American Allotment Act of 1887, 178
American Indian Movement (AIM),
69, 88, 112 n. 2, 113 n. 8
Amossy, Ruth, 29
Anderson, Benedict, 34
Anderson, Carolyn Dunn, 10, 113 n. 14
Andrews, Jennifer, 106, 113 n. 13,
115 n. 25, 146, 202, 232–33
Andrews, Lynn, 189
anthologies of Native humorous texts:
Me Funny, 17, 230; *Shaking the
Belly, Releasing the Sacred Clown*, 17
anthropologists, 8, 12, 28, 99, 108,
113 n. 11, 148–50, 191–97, 229
anticlimax, 110–11
appropriation, 99, 100, 148, 152,
154–56, 184–97, 227; academic,
148, 191–97; literary/"white-
shamanism," 189–91; New Age,
184–89
Apte, Mahadev L., 18 n. 1, 95, 115 n. 25
Aristotle, 36
Armstrong, Jeannette C., 17, 47
Armstrong, Jeannette C., works by:
"Indian Woman," 58
Arnett, Carroll, 15
Arnett, Carroll, works by: "Powwow,"
192–93
Ashcroft, Bill, 26, 89, 164
Assmann, Jan, 21, 50 n. 1, 51 n. 6
Atwood, Margaret, 1, 47, 171, 196
authenticity, 21, 99, 131–32, 134,
137–38, 142–43, 154, 169–70,
187, 195, 217–18, 222 n. 14
autoethnography, 29–31, 33

Babcock-Abrahams, Barbara, 96, 106, 115 n. 22, 115 n. 23, 115 n. 24, 222 n. 22, 230

Baca, Lorenzo, 15

Baca, Lorenzo, works by: "San Lorenzo Day in Laguna," 113 n. 14

Baker, Marie Annharte, 17, 95, 115 n. 25, 208, 214, 215, 222 n. 19

Baker, Marie Annharte, works by: "An Old Indian Trick is to Laugh," 44; *Being on the Moon*, 16; *Coyote Columbus Café*, 16, 76; "Squaw Guide," 75

Baldick, Chris, 66, 113 n. 10

Ballinger, Franchot, 115 n. 23

Bakhtin, Mikhail, 49, 105, 224

Barbe, Katharina, 55, 56, 58

Barker, James Nelson, works by: *The Indian Princess*, 133

Barthes, Roland, 113 n. 15, 167

Basso, Keith, 54 n. 23, 222 n. 22

Bataille, Gretchen, 51 n. 4, 221 n. 6

Baudrillard, Jean, 145, 156, 165

Beck, Peggy V., 8, 9, 18 n. 1, 113 n. 11

Beidler, Peter G., 121

Bell, Betty Louise, 133, 134, 137

Bellante, Carl, 92, 182, 210

Bellante, John, 92, 182, 210

Bennett, Bruce, works by: "Coyote's Metaphysics," 172

Bergson, Henri, 36, 37, 231

Berkhofer, Robert F., 19, 48, 50 n. 3, 51 n. 4, 63, 104, 138, 141, 142

Berner, Robert L., 5 n. 3, 114 n. 19, 162

Bhabha, Homi K., 23, 31, 32, 52 n. 11, 52 n. 12, 210

biblical intertexts, 9, 60, 66, 70–72, 81, 105, 109, 111 n. 1, 114 n. 17, 173–74, 175–82, 194

Bird, Gloria, 202, 223 n. 25, 232

Blaeser, Kimberley, 17, 64, 96, 98, 101, 102, 115 n. 22, 115 n. 24, 161, 167, 169, 171, 180, 191, 204, 232, 233

Blaeser, Kimberley, works by: "Twelve Steps to Ward Off Homesickness," 202–3

Blake, William, works by: *Songs of Innocence and Experience*, 185

Blue Cloud, Peter, works by: *Elderberry Flute Song*, 15; *I Am Turtle*, 15; *The Other Side of Nowhere*, 15

Boas, Franz, 12, 169

Bolz, Peter, 150, 151, 152

Booth, Wayne C., 55

Bordewich, Fergus M., 51 n. 5, 151, 163, 221 n. 4, 221 n. 9, 222 n. 18, 223 n. 23

Boskin, Joseph, 198

Bové, Paul A., 158, 161, 221 n. 12

Bowers, Neal, 96, 99

Brant, Beth, 15, 133, 221 n. 5

Brant, Beth, works by: "Coyote Learns a New Trick," 97, 104, 115 n. 23; *Food and Spirits*, 15; *Mohawk Trail*, 15

Breinig, Helmbrecht, 121, 122

Bright, William, 95, 96, 115 n. 22

Bruchac, Joseph, 7, 10, 46, 53 n. 18, 98, 102, 113 n. 11, 125, 177, 209

Bruyere, Florence, 22, 113 n. 9

Bureau of Indian Affairs (BIA), 126, 143, 209, 213

burlesque, 60, 65–67, 113 n. 10

Burns, Diane, 114 n. 16, 230

Burns, Diane, works by: *Riding the One-Eyed Ford*, 16; "Sure You Can Ask Me a Personal Question," 61

Burton, Henrietta K., 8

Canadian national anthem, 68, 169, 179

Canton, Jeffrey, 48

caricature, 12, 37, 60, 67, 119, 222 n. 20, 226

Castaneda, Carlos, 189

Campbell, Maria, 76, 231

Campbell, Maria, works by: *Halfbreed*, 13, 231

Chadwick, Allen, 74

Chamberlain, Alexander, 8, 113 n. 11

Christie, Stuart, 153

Chrystos, 114 n. 16

Chrystos, works by: *Not Vanishing*, 16

Churchill, Ward, 51 n. 4, 132, 138, 146, 157, 189, 220 n. 3, 221 n. 6, 222 n. 17

Clark, Crystal Lee, works by: "Discovering the Inner Indian," 184, 186

Clifford, James, 166

Clifford, James, works by: "Identity in Mashpee," 213

code-switching, 77–78, 113 n. 13

Cohen, Sandy, 210, 202
colonization, 117, 128–30, 157, 163–66, 168, 172–75, 178, 181, 226
Coltelli, Laura, 9, 20, 28, 44, 113 n. 11, 118, 150, 192
Columbus, 14, 19, 63, 70, 81, 101–2, 119–26, 204
comic reversal, 80, 88–89, 186
communitas, 49, 96, 188–89
contraries, 71
conversion, 77, 97, 109, 117, 129, 136, 171–75, 182
Cook-Lynn, Elizabeth, 5 n. 2, 202, 223 n. 25, 232
Cooper, James Fenimore, 132
Cooper, James Fenimore, works by: *Deerslayer*, 138; *Leatherstocking Tales*, 81, 90, 113 n. 7, 114 n. 17, 133, 137–38, 139
Coulombe, Joseph L., 232, 233
Coyote, 1, 2, 44, 70–72, 79, 86, 89, 95, 97–98, 104, 105, 106, 107, 109, 111, 115, 119, 126, 139, 155, 158, 160, 163, 177–78, 181, 196
Cox, Jay, 96, 106, 115 n. 22, 115 n. 23
Crazy Horse, 115 n. 21, 217
creation myth/s. *See* creation story/ies
creation story/ies, 27, 30, 70–72, 82–84, 105, 111 n. 1, 114 n. 18, 160, 175–81, 194–96
creative hybridity, 31
cultural identity, 19, 23–24. *See also* Native cultural identity
Curtis, Edward S., 89, 153
Custer, George Armstrong, 93, 115 n. 21, 217

Da, Popovi, 69
Damm, Kateri, 22
de Certeau, Michel, 65
decolonization, 228
Defoe, Daniel, works by: *Robinson Crusoe*, 81, 83, 137
Deloria, Phil, 51 n. 4, 89, 155, 184, 221 n. 4
Deloria, Vine, 7, 20, 22, 40, 43, 53 n. 18, 54 n. 23, 69, 74, 115 n. 21, 126, 153, 165, 174, 192, 198, 200, 205, 227, 228
Deloria, Vine, works by: *Custer Died For Your Sins*, 17, 117, 229

Dentith, Simon, 63
discourse, 24, 58, 102, 157–58, 160–62, 164, 171, 192, 227; colonial discourse, 23, 31, 32, 128, 162, 164, 165, 171; historical/historiographic discourse, 21, 65, 164, 166, 227. *See also* trickster discourse
Dorinson, Joseph, 198
Dorris, Michael, 14, 223 n. 25
Dorris, Michael, works by: *The Crown of Columbus*, 14, 119–22, 124, 125, 126, 215–17
Doty, William G., 115 n. 23, 115 n. 25
Doueihi, Anne, 85, 104
dramatic irony, 55, 103, 109–11
Draxlbauer, Michael, 137
Dumont, Marilyn, 5 n. 2, 22–23, 80, 171
Dumont, Marilyn, works by: "The Devil's Language," 161–62; "On the Surface," 167–69; *A Really Good Brown Girl*, 16; "Still Unsaved Soul," 173–74, 182
Dvorak, Marta, 139, 153, 154

Eastman, Alexander, 13
Eckardt, A. Roy. 37, 40, 42, 50, 53 n. 16, 108
Edmunds, R. David, 8, 9, 53 n. 16, 126, 222 n. 19
Eigenbrod, Renate, 3, 77
Eliot, T. S., 80, 161
Elvis, 155, 199
Engler, Bernd, 164
English, James F., 117, 207
Enlightenment philosophy, 132, 152, 221 n. 4
Erdoes, Richard, 10
Erdrich, Louise, 14, 44, 104, 114 n. 16, 223 n. 25, 230, 231, 232
Erdrich, Louise, works by: *The Beet Queen*, 14, 223 n. 25; *The Crown of Columbus*, 14, 119–22, 124, 125, 126, 215–17; *Love Medicine*, 14, 45, 68, 230, 231
essentialism, 207, 213–14, 222, 227
Evans-Pritchard, Deidre, 152, 153, 155, 221 n. 10

Fagan, Kristina, 204, 232
Fanon, Franz, 21
Farrell, Susan, 121, 122

Farmer, Gary, 117
Fast, Robin Riley, 114 n. 17
Feinberg, Leonard, 58, 60, 61, 62, 109, 137
Ferguson, Ian, 17
Findley, Timothy, works by: *Not Wanted on the Voyage*, 178
Fine, Gary Alan, 36, 37, 53 n. 16, 198, 204
Fire, John, 10
Fitz, Karsten, 31, 114 n. 18, 178, 182, 183, 184
Flick, Jane, 70, 113 n. 13, 115 n. 20, 127, 144, 180, 220 n. 1
Fonseca, Harry, 1, 2, 11
Forbes, Jack D., 17, 51 n. 8
Forbes, Jack D., works by: "The Caged," 138; "An Incident on a Tour Among the Natives," 56; "Only Approved Indians," 212–13, 214; *Only Approved Indians*, 15
Ford, John, 148
Ford, John, works by: *The Searchers* (film), 148, 149; *Stagecoach* (film), 144
Foucault, Michel, 58, 131, 157, 164, 192
Franke, Astrid, 131, 220 n. 2
Freud, Sigmund, 37, 231
Frontier myth, 119, 138, 143, 160, 167
Frost, Robert, works by: "Stopping By Woods on a Snowy Evening," 80
Frye, Northrop, 45, 57, 60, 112 n. 4, 114 n. 17, 230

Gatherings: The En'owkin Journal of First North American Peoples, 17
Geiogamah, Hanay, 41, 75, 114 n. 16, 230
Geiogamah, Hanay, works by: *Body Indian*, 16, 75, 110, 200; *Foghorn*, 16, 54 n. 24, 58–59, 62, 75–76, 110, 112 n. 4, 113 n. 8, 126, 133; *New Native American Drama*, 16
Gelo, Daniel J., 11
Genette, Gérard, 84, 113 n. 15
Georgi-Findlay, Brigitte, 18
Giago, Tim, 10, 18 n. 1, 117, 200
Glancy, Diane, works by: *Firesticks*, 15; *Monkey Secret*, 15; *Trigger Dance*, 15; *The Voice That Was in Travel*, 15

Gleason, William, 44
Gleason, William, works by: "'Her Laugh an Ace,'" 231
Goetsch, Paul, 52 n. 11
Goldie, Terry, 212, 215
Goldman, Marlene, 83
Goodman, Joel, 88, 154
Green, Michael, 20, 138, 161
Green, Rayna, 133, 135, 221 n. 5
Green, Rayna, works by: "The Tribe Called Wannabee," 184
Greenblatt, Stephen, 27
Grewe-Volpp, Christa, 150
Griffiths, Gareth, 26, 89, 164
Grinde, Donald A., 157
grotesque, 95, 103, 107–9, 226
Gruber, Eva, 22
Gzowski, Peter, 82, 146

Halfe, Louise, works by: *Bear Bones and Feathers*, 16; "Body Politics," 115 n. 25; "Der Poop," 76–77; "In Da Name of Da Fadder," 76, 173; "My Ledders," 76; "Stones," 76; Valentine Dialogue," 76
Hall, Stuart, 23–24, 25, 27, 29, 95, 131, 138–39, 175, 225
Halsey, Theresa, 172, 176, 180
Hanson, Jeffrey R., 220 n. 2
Hardin, Michael, 124
Harjo, Joy, 228, 230, 232, 233
Harjo, Joy, works by: *She Had Some Horses*, 16; *The Woman Who Fell From the Sky*, 16
Harjo, Suzan Shown, 11
Hawke, Thom E., 209
Hellenthal, Michael, 60, 107
Hendrix, Jimi, 93, 199
Henry, Gordon, 15, 232
Highway, Tomson, 231
Highway, Tomson, works by: *Dry Lips Oughta Move to Kapuskasing*, 16; *The Rez Sisters*, 16, 201
Hill, Charlie, 18 n. 2
Hill, Mary Ann, 221 n. 4
Hill, Norbert, 221 n. 4
Hill, Ruth Bebe, 189
Hill, W. W., 8, 113 n. 11
Hirch, Mirjam, 41, 222 n. 19, 231
historiography, 37, 51 n. 4, 65, 80, 85, 87, 92–94, 100–102, 157, 164–71, 222 n. 14, 227

Hobbes, Thomas, 36
Hobson, Geary, 20, 189, 190, 191; "whiteshamanism," 189
Hoffmann, Gerhard, 41, 52 n. 15, 53 n. 17, 171
Hogan, Linda, 230
Holden, Madronna, 195, 197
Hooks, Bell, 34, 228 n. 2
Horne, Dee, 31–32, 33, 52 n. 12, 96, 114 n. 18, 139, 176, 221 n. 8; "creative hybridity," 31; "subversive mimicry," 31, 32, 90, 98, 135
Howe, LeAnne, 15
Howe, LeAnne, works by: "An American in New York," 126
Hoy, Helen, vii, 3, 121, 122, 221 n. 10
Hughes, Langston, 45
Huizinga, Johan, 230, 231
humor: cultural specificity/relativity of, 39–40, 45; definition of, 38; scatological, 96, 115 n. 25, 174; theories of, 36
Huntsman, Jeffrey, 62
Hutcheon, Linda, 56, 58, 65, 80, 85, 87, 112 n. 3, 112 n. 6, 162, 167, 193, 233
Hutcheon, Linda, works by: "Historiographic Metafiction," 157, 166
Hynes, William J., 115 n. 22

identification, 24, 50
imagination, 20, 25, 27, 29, 32–35, 48–49, 88, 95, 104, 225, 228
"Indian," as cliché or simulacrum, 19–20, 22, 25, 26, 33, 34, 35, 56–58, 61, 73, 75, 76, 91, 99, 108, 131–33, 137–40, 142–43, 145, 148, 150–56, 172, 174, 186, 218, 220 n. 3, 221 n. 4, 224–25, 228. See also Native people: stereotypes; wannabes/playing Indian
Indian Act, 210, 211, 223 n. 24
"Indianlect," 72–76, 113
intertextuality, 14, 41, 55, 80–84, 91, 104, 105, 113–14 n. 15, 137, 226
irony, 14, 37, 41, 42, 55–58, 60, 61, 77, 81, 111–12 nn. 2–3, 168, 183, 186, 188, 190, 193, 213, 226, 233
Irving, Washington, 8
Isernhagen, Hartwig, 51 n. 8, 166

Jaimes, Annette, 117, 172, 176, 180
James Bay Great Whale Project, 127, 169
Jannetta, Armando E., 200
Johnson, Ben, 53 n. 15
Johnson, Brian, 145, 221 n. 8
Johnson, E. Pauline, 13
Johnston, Basil H., 150, 152
Johnston, Basil H., works by: "Cowboys and Indians," 142–44; Indian School Days, 15, 200; Moose Meat and Wild Rice, 15
Johnston, Gordon, 72, 220 n. 3
Jonnie, Curtis, works by: "Indian Time," 201
Joplin, Janis, 93, 199

Kant, Immanuel, 37, 70, 110
Kelly, Don, 2, 17, 41, 54 n. 22, 200, 222 n. 19
Keeshig-Tobias, Lenore, 16
Keeshig-Tobias, Lenore, works by: "How To Catch a White Man (Oops) I Mean Trickster," 189–91 "Trickster Beyond 1992," 69, 189; "The White Man's Burden," 69, 163
Kilpatrick, Jacquelyn, 51 n. 4, 221 n. 6
King, Thomas, 4, 5 n. 3, 11, 12, 17, 26, 28, 32, 39, 41, 47–48, 53 n. 20, 67, 70–72, 74, 76, 77–78, 79, 81, 82, 83, 84, 88, 89–90, 91, 96, 97, 104, 106–7, 113 n. 7, 114 n. 16, 114 n. 17, 127, 133, 144–48, 150, 152, 157, 160, 171, 182, 202, 222 n. 21, 223 n. 25
King, Thomas, works by: "A Coyote Columbus Story," 97, 115 n. 23, 119; "Coyote Went to See the Prime Minister," 163; "Dead Dog Café Comedy Hour" (CBC radio show), 11; "Godzilla vs. Post-Colonial," 52 n. 13; Green Grass, Running Water, 14, 67, 68, 69, 70–72, 74, 77–78, 79, 81–84, 85–87, 89–90, 101, 105–7, 109–10, 111 n. 1, 112 n. 2, 113 n. 7, 113 n. 13, 114 n. 16, 114 n. 20, 115 n. 25, 126–27, 133, 137–39, 141, 142, 144–48, 152–54, 155, 157, 167, 175–82, 194, 232–33; "How Corporal Colin Sterling Saved

King, Thomas, works by (continued):
Blossom, Alberta, and Most of the
Rest of the World as Well," 107;
"How I Spent My Summer
Vacation," 222 n. 14; "Inventing the
Indian," 139; "Joe the Painter and
the Deer Island Massacre," 169–71;
Medicine River, 12, 14, 91; "The
One About Coyote Going West,"
85, 97, 115 n. 23, 115 n. 25; "One
Good Story, That One," 78–79, 85,
194–97; *One Good Story, That One*,
15; "A Seat in the Garden," 113 n.
7; "A Short History of Indians in
Canada," 107–8; *A Short History of
Indians in Canada*, 15; "Traplines,"
160; *Truth & Bright Water*, 14, 74,
115 n. 25, 152, 154–56, 186, 202,
209
Kinsella, W. P., works by: *Shoeless Joe*,
113 n. 7
Koestler, Arthur, 37, 230, 233
Krech, Shepard, III., 150
Kristeva, Julia, 113 n. 15, 230
Krupat, Arnold, 3, 52 n. 13, 114 n. 16

LaLonde, Christopher A., 231
Lame Deer, 10
language: creative/formative dimen-
sions of, 27; linguistic signification,
98, 103, 106–7, 129, 162–64
LaRoque, Emma, 72–73, 156
Lawrence, Bonita, 22, 51 n. 5, 211,
212, 223 n. 24
Lazarus, Emma, works by: "The New
Colossus," 124
Lee, A. Robert, 138
Lévi-Strauss, Claude, 165
Levin, Harry, 36, 52–53 n. 15
Lewis, Paul, 36, 38, 42, 53 n. 16, 53 n.
17, 204, 207
Lewis and Clark expedition, 218
liminality/liminal space, 2, 48–49,
54 n. 25, 96, 100, 111, 122, 130,
225, 228
Lincoln, Kenneth, 4, 38, 41, 44, 47,
53 n. 17, 53 n. 18, 54 n. 21, 76,
115 n. 22, 115 n. 26, 126, 153,
198, 199, 205, 231
Lincoln, Kenneth, works by: *Indi'n
Humor*, 229–30
Linton, Patricia, 127
Littlefield, Daniel F., 12

logocentrism, 162
Longfellow, H. W., works by: *The Song
of Hiawatha*, 133
Louis, Adrian C., 27, 202
Lowe, John, vii, 18, 18 n. 1, 38–39,
53 n. 18, 76, 95, 96, 198, 222 n.
20, 229, 230
Luna, James, 118
Lutz, Hartmut, 50 n. 3, 51 n. 4, 72,
76, 91, 114 n. 19, 148, 184, 189,
221 n. 6

Mackin, Joanna, 228, 232, 233
manifest destiny, 19, 58, 65, 100, 122,
163, 164, 165, 166, 167, 174; "lit-
erary Manifest Destiny," 132
Marquard, Odo, 171
Martineau, William H., 36, 204
Masayesva, Arthur, 32
master narrative/s, 49, 60, 65, 70, 72,
80, 85, 119, 145, 180, 181,
226
Mather, Cotton, 91, 132
Mather, Cotton, works by: *Magnalia
Christi Americana*, 133
Mathews, John Joseph, 13
matrilineage/matrilocality, 172
Mattina, Anthony, 76
McMaster, Gerald, 11, 51 n. 5
McNally, John, works by: *Humor Me*,
17
McNickle, D'Arcy, 13
mediation, 9, 10, 36, 45–47, 96, 118,
130, 154, 188, 197, 224–25, 227
Melville, Herman, works by: *Benito
Cereno*, 114 n. 17; *Moby Dick*, 81,
90, 137, 178
metafiction, 41, 80, 84–88, 104, 105,
226
Mieder, Wolfgang, 20
Miller, Dallas, 204
Miller, Frank C., 11, 130
mimicry, 8, 32, 52 n. 12, 63, 147,
221 n. 8
Mojica, Monique, works by: "Post-
Colonial Traumatic Stress Disorder,"
16, 128–30; *Princess Pocahontas and
the Blue Spots*, 16, 77, 114 n. 16,
133, 134–37
Momaday, N. Scott, 13, 27, 114 n. 16,
225, 230
Momaday, N. Scott, works by: *House
Made of Dawn*, 13, 114 n. 16, 230;

"The Magic of Words," 224; "The Man Made of Words," 27, 35; *The Way to Rainy Mountain*, 27
Monroe, Marilyn, 155, 202
Morreall, John, 37, 40, 53 n. 16, 53 n. 17, 127
Moses, Daniel David, 212, 215
Mourning Dove, 12
Mourning Dove, works by: *Coyote Stories by Mourning Dove (Humishuma)*, 12
Muecke, Douglas C., 58, 111–12 n. 2

naming, 89–92, 94–95, 97, 99, 114 n. 18, 146, 226
Native American Renaissance, 13, 14, 54 n. 21, 229, 230
Native cultural identity, 19, 22–23, 25, 97, 103, 205–19, 226; discussion of among Native people, 206–19, 227–28; impact of representation on, 25
Native humor: in art, 11; centrality to Native cultures, 1, 7, 8; characteristics of, 41–43; cohesive function of, 197–98, 200–201, 204, 224; definition of, 2, 39–40; didactic function of, 10, 189–91, 197, 211; early accounts of, 8–9; as gallows humor, 3–44; healing aspects of, 16, 125, 197, 203–4, 206, 211, 222 n. 20, 226, 227; intercultural vs. intracultural, 3, 9, 41, 116, 224–25; in media and in stand-up comedy, 11–12; within Native communities, 197–223; in Native-White relations, 45–48; in oral traditions, 2; pan-tribal characteristics of, 38–39; ritual dimension of, 8–9, 10; role in contemporary Native writing, 35, 47–50; self-deprecating aspects of, 200–203; as social instrument, 197–98; state of research on, 14–18, 229–33; survey, 7–18; as survival strategy, 44–45, 198, 227
Native people: in American mythology, 7, 19; contemporary existence of, 19, 21; historical discourse on, 21; legal definition of, 21–22, 207, 209–12, 222; legal definition of, Bill C-31, 222; legal definition of, Indian Act, 210, 222; self-governance and corruption, 209–15; stereotypes, 7, 20–21, 50, 73–74, 88, 100, 130–56,

204; stereotypes, historical and literary, 131–41, 220 nn. 2–3; stereotypes, internalization of, 22, 142, 147, 156, 207, 218–19, 220, 227, 228; stereotypes, media/Hollywood, 20, 72–73, 141–50, 218–20; stereotypes, New Age, 150–52; stereotypes, tourist, 152–56; terminology/nomenclature, 1, 4
Native Renaissance. *See* Native American Renaissance
Native-White (power) relations, 2, 3, 37, 47–49, 98, 127, 179, 196, 225, 226
New Historicism, 26
Nischik, Reingard M., vii, 143
noble savage, 19, 62, 142, 150, 152, 185, 202
Norman, Howard, 230
Norman, Howard, works by: *The Northern Lights*, 230
Norris, Malcolm, 211
Northrup, Jim, 9, 17, 90, 152, 186
Northrup, Jim, works by: "Goose, Goose," 201; "Holiday Inndians," 68; "Jabbing and Jabbering," 223 n. 23; "The Jail Trail," 200; "Looking with Ben," 91; "Politics," 223 n. 23; *Shinnob Jep*, 16; "Shrinking Away," 200; *Walking the Rez Road*, 15, 232
Northsun, Nila, works by: *diet pepsi & nacho cheese*, 16; *A Snake in Her Mouth*, 16

O'Connor, John, 72, 142, 146, 221 n. 6
Oka crisis, 189–90
oral tradition/s, 1, 12, 15, 30, 35, 54 n. 22, 55, 80, 81–82, 95, 105, 114 n. 19, 115 n. 21, 115 n. 22, 121, 148, 160, 176, 193–94, 196, 230
Ortiz, Fernando, 52 n. 10
Ortiz, Simon, 16, 162, 230
Ortiz, Simon, works by: *Men On the Moon*, 15, 158–61; "The San Francisco Indians," 187–88; "What Indians Do," 78, 222 n. 13
Oskinson, John Milton, 13
Owens, Louis, 3, 14, 19, 26, 27, 35, 41, 50, 50 n. 1, 52 n. 13, 80, 104, 132, 138, 147, 152, 156, 158, 186, 202, 215, 218, 223 n. 25

Owens, Louis, works by: *Bone Game*, 14, 80, 81, 115 n. 21, 150, 186, 193–94, 207–9, 225; *Dark River*, 14, 152; *The Sharpest Sight*, 14; *Wolfsong*, 14

Palmer, Jerry, 18 n. 1, 46, 53 n. 16
parody, 37, 41, 55, 59, 60, 63–65, 66, 80, 89, 90, 91, 105, 112–13 nn. 5–8, 113 n. 10, 114 n. 15, 123, 127, 204, 226
Pelletier, Wilf, 10, 163, 175, 221 n. 11
Perry, Dennis R., 9
Perry, Ted, 221 n. 9
Petrone, Penny, 27
Petzold, Dieter, 178, 182
Pfister, Manfred, 45, 46
Plant, John, 18 n. 1
Plato, 36
Pocahontas, 110–11, 133–37, 146, 217
Poirier, Michelle A., works by: "Humour is Good Medicine," 222 n. 20
Poirier, Mickie, 16
Poirier, Mickie, works by: "Wet Dream Catcher Drive-In," 68
Posey, Alexander, 12–13, 14, 17, 230
Posey, Alexander, works by: *The Fus Fixico Letters*, 12
postcolonial theory, 52 n. 13
Pratt, Mary Louise, 29–31, 33, 52 n. 10, 163; autoethnography, 29–31, 33; transculturation, 29–31, 72
Pratt, Steven B., 11, 222 n. 22
Price, Darby Li Po, 11
Price, John A., 25, 72, 143, 146, 148, 198, 220 n. 2
Profeit-Leblanc, Louise, 17
puns/punning, 8, 41, 42, 54 n. 23, 68–72, 77, 79, 102, 113 n. 11, 129, 200
Purdie, Susan, 46, 49, 53 n. 19, 112 n. 5, 200
Purdy, John, 3, 32–33, 46, 52 n. 14, 139
Purdy, John, works by: "remaging," 32, 33, 52 n. 14; "Tricksters of the Trade," 32

Quintasket, Christine. *See* Mourning Dove

Radin, Paul, 12, 96, 193
Radin, Paul, works by: *The Trickster*, 12

Rainwater, Catherine, 82, 149
Rayson, Ann, 216
Red English/rez English, 13, 14, 41, 76–77
Redfern, Walter, 68, 72
reification, 108, 148, 152–53, 184, 192, 221 n. 10, 227
reimagining, 33–35, 48–50, 72, 81, 103, 104, 116
representation, 24–25, 217
re-presentation, 4, 28–35, 58, 84, 90, 225
Revard, Carter, 15, 41–42, 88, 112 n. 7, 167, 232
Revard, Carter, works by: "Discovery of the New World," 119, 163, 164–67; "Never Quite a Hollywood Star," 87–88; *Ponca War Dancers*, 119; "Report to the Nation," 63–65, 88, 119, 163, 165; "The Secret Verbs," 163–64
rewriting, 48, 60, 70, 78, 81, 112 n. 6, 176. *See also* re-presentation
Ridington, Robin, 74, 84
Riel, Louis, 79
Riley, Patricia, 15
Rishel, Mary Ann, 37, 38, 52 n. 15, 53 n. 16, 53 n. 17, 60, 113 n. 10
Robinson, Eden, works by: *Monkey Beach*, 14; "Queen of the North," 221 n. 10; *Traplines*, 15
Robinson, Gary, 15
Robinson, Harry, 15, 78
Robinson, Harry, works by: *Nature Power*, 15; *Write It On Your Heart*, 15. *See also* Wickwire, Wendy
Rogers, Will, 13, 18 n. 2
Rollins, Peter C., 221 n. 6
Rooke, Constance, 6 n. 3
Rose, Margaret A., 63, 112 n. 5
Rose, Wendy, 185, 192
Ross, Ian, 28
Ross, Ian, works by: *fareWel*, 16; "Joe from Winnipeg" (CBC radio show), 12
Roth, Philip, works by: *The Great American Novel*, 139
Rourke, Constance, works by: *American Humor*, 54 n. 21
Rouse, Linda P., 220 n. 2
Rousseau, Jean-Jacques, 133, 150
Rowlandson, Mary, 132, 133

Ruffo, Armand Garnet, 85
Ruppert, James, 28
Russell, Suleiman, 15
Russell, Suleiman, works by: "How Old Man Coyote Lost His Manhood," 85, 97, 113 n. 14
Ryan, Allan J., 11, 41, 53 n. 18, 113 n. 11, 117

Sacajawea, 217
Said, Edward, 23
Said, Edward, works by: *Orientalism*, 20, 157
Sainte-Marie, Buffy, works by: "Trickster Song," 97, 102
Salabiye, Vee, 126
Sanner, Hans Ulrich, 18 n. 1, 113 n. 11, 150, 198, 222 n. 22
sarcasm, 13, 14, 37, 41, 55, 58–60, 62, 112 n. 5, 185, 186, 213, 231
Sarkowsky, Katja, 11, 130
satire, 3, 13, 14, 17, 37, 41, 42, 60–63, 65, 83, 99–100, 112 nn. 4–6, 137, 165, 186, 210, 226
Schopenhauer, Arthur, 37
Schorcht, Blanca, 84, 114 n. 17
science, 100–102, 157–60, 191, 192–93, 227
Scott, Thomas, 79
Seesequasis, Paul, 15, 210–12, 214, 215
Seesequasis, Paul, works by: "The Republic of Tricksterism," 115 n. 25, 210–12
Sewell, Anna M., works by: "Discovering the Inner Indian," 184, 186
Shakespeare, William, 81
Shanley, Kathryn, 185
Sheridan, Phil, 20, 92–94
Shutiva, C., 11, 201, 222 n. 22
Silberman, Robert, 98
Silet, Charles P., 51 n. 4, 96, 99, 221 n. 6
Silko, Leslie Marmon, 9–10, 113 n. 11, 114 n. 16, 118, 189, 191–92, 223 n. 25, 230
Silko, Leslie Marmon, works by: *Ceremony*, 13, 27, 114 n. 16
Skeels, Dell, 8, 222 n. 22
Slipperjack, Ruby, works by: *Snuff Chewing Charlie at University*, 16

Smith, Jeanne Rosier, 104
Smith, John, 110, 132, 134, 136
Smith, John, works by: *Generall Historie of Virginia, New-England, and the Summer Isles*, 133
Spencer, Herbert, 37
Spielmann, Roger, 40, 197, 200, 201
Squanto, 217
Standing Bear, Luther, 13
Stedman, Raymond W., 51 n. 4, 73, 74, 113 n. 12, 133, 137, 138, 142, 149, 221 n. 5, 221 n. 6
Stephenson, R. M., 36, 204
Steward, Julian Haynes, 18 n. 1
Stierstorfer, Klaus, 54 n. 25
storytelling, 55, 77–79, 85, 87, 103–5, 107, 168, 191, 211, 226, 231. *See also* oral tradition/s
Strachey, William, 134
Stratton, Florence, 115 n. 20
subversive mimicry, 31–32, 90, 98, 135
Swift, Jonathan, 36

Tama, Jose Torres, 118
Taylor, Drew Hayden, 6 n. 3, 11, 12, 16, 17, 26, 28, 39, 41, 46, 47, 53 n. 19, 54 n. 24, 59, 66, 102, 113 n. 8, 131, 172, 186, 195, 201, 203, 205, 214–15, 222 n. 19, 227, 231
Taylor, Drew Hayden, works by: *alterNatives*, 17, 177, 194; *The Bootlegger Blues*, 17, 200; *Fearless Warriors*, 15; *Funny You Don't Look Like One*, 17, 214; "How Native is Native if You're Native?," 131, 214; *Me Funny*, 17, 230; *Redskins, Tricksters, and Puppy Stew*, 11
Tapahonso, Luci, vii, 9
Tapahonso, Luci, works by: *Blue Horses Rush In*, 15
teasing, 3, 8, 11, 41, 153, 197, 198, 200–201, 204–6, 209, 222 n. 22, 230, 231
Theisz, R. D., 11, 53 n. 18, 201, 222 n. 22, 229
Thom, Jo-Ann, 16
Thompson, William R., 9
Tiffin, Helen, 26, 89, 164
Toelken, Barre, 115 n. 24, 222 n. 20, 222 n. 22
transculturation, 29–31, 72

treaty making, 126–27, 172, 179
trickster, 8, 71, 95–103, 106, 189–91;
classical trickster figures, 86, 95–96,
97, 103, 115; contemporary trickster characters, 82–83, 96–103, 209,
211–12, 215–16; functions of trickster tales, 96, 115, 190–91, 225
trickster discourse, 42, 103–7, 226
Turner, Victor, 49, 54 n. 25, 96; "communitas," 49, 96, 188–89
Two-Rivers, Donald E., 9
Two-Rivers, Donald E., works by:
"Spirit Sticks," 189; Survivor's
Medicine, 15

van Gennep, Arnold, 25
van Keuren, Luise, 9
Vangen, Kate, 13, 231
Vanishing Indian, 59, 65, 108, 144,
153, 167, 171
Vasudeva, Mary, 230
Velie, Alan, 13, 115 n. 22
Vickers, Scott B., 20, 21, 50 n. 3, 182,
186, 221 n. 4
Vivan, Itala, 52 n. 11
Vizenor, Gerald, 14, 26, 28, 32, 42,
89, 95, 96, 97–103, 104, 105, 107,
124–25, 133, 162, 167, 177, 192,
198, 204, 223 n. 25, 230, 232
Vizenor, Gerald, works by: Darkness in
Saint Louis Bearheart, 13; Harold of
Orange (screenplay and film), 12,
16, 33, 97–103, 133, 158; The
Heirs of Columbus, 14, 81, 114 n.
16, 119, 122–24, 125–26, 204;
"Reservation Café," 133; "Trickster
Photography," 89
Voeglin, E. W., 8, 18 n. 1

wa Thiong'o, Ngugi, works by:
Decolonizing the Mind, 130
Wagamese, Richard, 90, 152
Wagamese, Richard, works by: Keeper
'n Me, 10, 14, 21, 73, 76, 113 n.
14, 118, 152, 174, 175, 187,
188–89, 200, 201, 205–6, 221 n. 7;
A Quality of Light, 131–32
Wallace, William, 8, 113 n. 11
Walters, Anna Lee, 8, 9, 18 n. 1,
113 n. 11

wannabes/playing Indian, 14, 89, 91,
100, 155, 184–87, 189, 230
Ward, A. Joseph., 231
Warrior, Emma Lee, 15
Warrior, Emma Lee, works by:
"Compatriots," 91
Wayne, John/Morrison, Marion, 76,
89, 106, 114 n. 16, 144–45,
147–49, 209
Wayne, John/Morrison, Marion,
works by: The Searchers (film), 148,
149
Weaver, Jace, 21, 22, 26, 127, 156,
180, 198
Webber, Charles, W., 132
Welch, Jim, 13, 113 n. 11, 230, 231
Welch, Jim, works by: The Death of
Jim Loney, 13, 114 n. 16; Winter in
the Blood, 13, 230, 231
Whitaker, V. K., 222 n. 22
White, E. B., vii
White, Hayden, 164, 165, 167, 220 n.
3
White Paper, 127, 179
whiteshamanism, 189–90. See also
appropriation
Whitman, Walt, 80
Whitt, Laurie Anne, 159, 187
Wickwire, Wendy, works by: Nature
Power, 15; Write It On Your Heart,
15. See also Robinson, Harry
Widmark, Richard, 89, 114 n. 16,
144
Wiget, Andrew, 103, 115 n. 23, 115 n.
24
Williams, William Carlos, works by:
"The Red Wheelbarrow," 80
Witherspoon, Gary, 51 n. 7, 114 n.
18
Womak, Craig, 27
Woodward, Kathryn, 24
wordplay, 41, 55, 68–72, 113 n. 11,
129, 216, 226, 231
Wright, George, 92–94

Young-Ing, Greg, 161

Zenner, Walter P., works by: "Joking
and Ethnic Stereotyping," 45, 46,
47